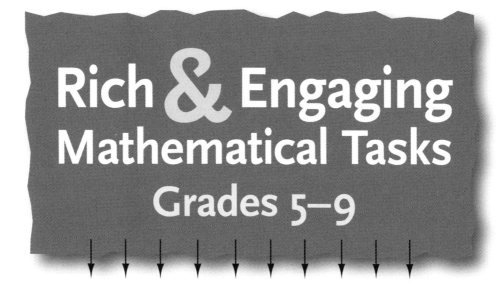

Rich & Engaging Mathematical Tasks
Grades 5–9

Articles and Activities from
Teaching Children Mathematics
Mathematics Teaching in the Middle School
Mathematics Teacher
Student Math Notes
NCTM Yearbooks

Edited by

Glenda Lappan
Michigan State University

Margaret S. Smith
University of Pittsburgh

Elizabeth Jones
Lansing Public Schools, Lansing, Michigan

NATIONAL COUNCIL OF
TEACHERS OF MATHEMATICS

Copyright © 2012 by
The National Council of Teachers of Mathematics, Inc.
1906 Association Drive, Reston, VA 20191-1502
(703) 620-9840; (800) 235-7566; www.nctm.org
All rights reserved
Second printing 2013

Library of Congress Cataloging-in-Publication Data

Rich and engaging mathematical tasks : grades 5-9 / compiled by Glenda
Lappan ... [et al.].
        p. cm. -- (Activities for junior high school and middle school
mathematics ; v. 3)
    "Articles from Teaching children mathematics; Mathematics teaching in
the middle school; Mathematics teacher; Student math notes; the 2001,
2002, and 2003 NCTM yearbooks; and Classroom activities for learning
and teaching measurement."
    ISBN 978-0-87353-633-2
    1. Mathematics--Study and teaching (Middle school)--Activity programs.
I. Lappan, Glenda. II. National Council of Teachers of Mathematics.
    QA135.6.R533 2011
    510.71'2--dc23
                                2011034850

The National Council of Teachers of Mathematics is the public voice of mathematics
education, supporting teachers to ensure equitable mathematics learning of the highest
quality for all students through vision, leadership, professional development, and research.

Printed in the United States of America

Table of Contents

3. Ratios, Rate, and Proportional Relationships   65

4. Numbers and Number Theory   109

5. Patterns and Functions   137

6. Linear Equations   163

Preface

The editors of this book have worked to select articles from past issues of the NCTM Journals that are relevant in classrooms today. Each article includes activities for teachers to use with their students to promote understanding of the mathematical content highlighted in the article. The selected articles were organized into content strands and ordered within a strand to promote the development of important areas of mathematics. These mathematical areas are all highlighted in the Common Core State Standards for Mathematics (CCSSM) as important for students' progress in mathematics.

The book's first section, "Designing and Enacting Rich Instructional Experiences," provides an important set of articles that individual teachers can use to enhance their students' engagement in rich mathematical tasks. A school or district can also use these articles in professional development settings. The section aims to help teachers examine their classroom practices with an eye toward improving students' engagement with, and success in, learning to think and reason in rich mathematical situations.

Each remaining section of the book highlights articles on an important area of mathematics promoted in the CCSSM: rational numbers, proportional reasoning, numbers, number theory, patterns and functions, linear equations, measurement, geometry, and probability and statistics. Each article in a section has a mathematical exploration on the focus topic, ready to copy and use with students.

A team of three NCTM members—two professors, Glenda Lappan at Michigan State University and Margaret "Peg" Smith at the University of Pittsburgh, and an outstanding middle school teacher in the Lansing, Mich., School District, Elizabeth "Liz" Jones—selected the articles. Our different perspectives were invaluable to the selection process. We hope these selected articles can help you enliven your classroom and push your students' mathematical creativity.

Lastly, additional articles for each content strand are available in NCTM's e-book, *More Rich and Engaging Mathematical Tasks: Grades 5–9*, which can be purchased at www.nctm.org/catalog. We hope that you will enjoy the articles as we have grouped them, and that you find them useful in challenging your students and in enlivening your students' engagement in mathematical thinking and reasoning.

Acknowledgments

The Editors of this volume would like to express our deep appreciation and thanks to Jean Beland for her considerable effort to ensure that the work on this volume was done on time and of high quality. Jean organized our work, kept us on task, edited our writing, kept track of the strand articles, organized our face-to-face and phone conferences and most of all, advocated for the teachers who would use this work with their students. Jean's patient editing of our writing through multiple iterations has made the text material in the volume clearer, more to the point, and more helpful to those who use the volume. Her joy in doing something good for students and their teachers was a gift to the editors that made our work together so much more enjoyable.

We would also like to express our appreciation to Chelsea Maxson for her assistance during the volume preparation. Chelsea worked on locating journal articles and books relevant to our work, assisted in building the reference list, and helped in organizing the work and maintaining the flow among editors.

We thank you, Jean and Chelsea.

SECTION 1

Designing and Enacting
Rich Instructional Experiences

Introduction

Mathematically rich and engaging tasks—such as those featured in the articles in this volume—provide excellent opportunities for students to learn what mathematics is and how one does it. Such tasks, however, are also the most difficult to implement well during instruction. Research makes salient that tasks that promote thinking, reasoning, and problem solving often decline during implementation as a result of various classroom factors. When this occurs, students are left to apply previously learned rules and procedures with no connection to meaning or understanding, and the opportunities for thinking and reasoning are lost.

Hence there are two pivotal factors to consider in optimizing students' learning opportunities that emerge from research on mathematical tasks: (1) the nature of the mathematical task that a teacher selects and enacts matters—not all tasks have the same learning potential; and (2) the way in which a teacher supports students' engagement in mathematical activity during a lesson based on the task matters. Reaching the full educative power of a mathematical task depends on the norms and practices for doing mathematics that are in play in the classroom and the pedagogical moves that the teacher makes that enable students to engage in high-level activity without the teacher taking over the thinking and reasoning for them.

In this section we provide a set of articles that are intended to help teachers in selecting mathematical tasks and designing instructional experiences around tasks that will facilitate students' development of the broad range of mathematical proficiencies described in the articles. The ideas that emerge from the articles in this section should be helpful both in considering how best to use the materials in this book and in planning instruction more generally.

The first article, "Selecting and Creating Mathematical Tasks: From Research to Practice" (Smith and Stein 1998), focuses on making distinctions among mathematical tasks based on the kind and level of thinking required to solve the tasks. The four levels of cognitive demand that are introduced can be used in selecting and evaluating tasks and in matching tasks with your goals for students' learning.

"Thinking through a Lesson: Successfully Implementing High-Level Tasks" (Smith, Bill, and Hughes 2008) provides a tool for designing lessons based on challenging mathematical tasks. The planning protocol is intended to help teachers anticipate what students will do and generate questions they can ask that will promote students' learning prior to teaching a lesson.

The article "A Model for Understanding Understanding in Mathematics" (Davis 2006), provides a list of moves that teachers can use to plan instruction and assess students' knowledge. The identified moves are intended to help teachers evaluate and diagnose what students understand about specific components of mathematical knowledge—concepts, generalizations, procedures, and numerical facts.

References

Davis, Edward J. "A Model for Understanding Understanding in Mathematics." *Mathematics Teaching in the Middle School* 12 (November 2006): 190–97.

Smith, Margaret Schwan, and Mary Kay Stein. "Selecting and Creating Mathematical Tasks: From Research to Practice." *Mathematics Teaching in the Middle School* 3 (February 1998): 344–50.

Smith, Margaret S., Victoria Bill, and Elizabeth K. Hughes. "Thinking through a Lesson: Successfully Implementing High-Level Tasks." *Mathematics Teaching in the Middle School* 14 (October 2008): 132–38.

Selecting and Creating Mathematical Tasks: From Research to Practice

Margaret Schwan Smith and Mary Kay Stein

What features of a mathematics classroom really make a difference in how students come to view mathematics and what they ultimately learn? Is it whether students are working in small groups? Is it whether students are using manipulatives? Is it the nature of the mathematical tasks that are given to students? Research conducted in the QUASAR project, a five-year study of mathematics education reform in urban middle schools (Silver and Stein 1996), offers some insight into these questions. From 1990 through 1995, data were collected about many aspects of reform teaching, including the use of small groups; the tools that were available for student use, for example, manipulatives and calculators; and the nature of the mathematics tasks. A major finding of this research to date, as described in the article by Stein and Smith in the January 1998 issue of *Mathematics Teaching in the Middle School,* is that the highest learning gains on a mathematics-performance assessment were related to the extent to which tasks were set up and implemented in ways that engaged students in high levels of cognitive thinking and reasoning (Stein and Lane 1996). This finding supports the position that the nature of the tasks to which students are exposed determines what students learn (NCTM 1991), and it also leads to many questions that should be considered by middle school teachers. In particular, results from Stein and Lane (1996) suggest the importance of starting with high-level, cognitively complex tasks if the ultimate goal is to have students develop the capacity to think, reason, and problem solve. As was noted in our earlier discussion of Ron Castleman (Stein and Smith 1998), selecting and setting up a high-level task well does not guarantee students' engagement at a high level. Starting with a good task does, however, appear to be a necessary condition, since low-level tasks almost never result in high-level engagement. In this article, we focus on the selection and creation of mathematical tasks, drawing on QUASAR's research on mathematical tasks and on our own experiences with teachers and teacher educators.

Knowing a Good Task When You See One

When classifying a mathematical task as "good," that is, as having the potential to engage students in high-level thinking, we first consider the students—their age, grade level, prior knowledge and experiences—and the norms and expectations for work in their classroom. Consider, for example, a task in which students are asked to add five two-digit numbers and explain the process they used. For a fifth- or sixth-grade student who has access to a calculator, the addition algorithm, or both, and for whom "explain the process" means "tell how you did it," the task could be considered routine. If, however, the task is given to a second grader who has just started work with two-digit numbers, who has base-ten pieces available, and for whom "explain the process" means "you need to explain your thinking," the task may indeed be high level. Therefore, when a teacher selects a task for use in a classroom setting, all these factors need to be considered to determine the extent to which a task is likely to afford an appropriate level of challenge for her or his students.

A second step we use in classifying tasks as good is to consider the four categories of cognitive demand described in Stein and Smith (1998):

The preparation of this paper was supported by a grant from the Ford Foundation (grant no. 890-0572) for the QUASAR Project. Any opinions expressed herein are those of the authors and do not necessarily represent the views of the Ford Foundation. This paper grew out of a research report by Mary Kay Stein, Barbara Grover, and Marjorie Henningsen (1996). The authors wish to acknowledge the helpful comments of Judith Zawojewski on an earlier draft of this article.

Reflection:
*Can you think of a task you used that was harder or easier for students than you had
anticipated? What factors do you think contributed to the level of difficulty of the task
for your students?*

- Memorization
- Procedures without connections to concepts or meaning
- Procedures with connections to concepts and meaning
- Doing mathematics

Using these categories as templates, we ask ourselves what kind of thinking a task will demand of the students. Tasks that ask students to perform a memorized procedure in a routine manner lead to one level of thinking; tasks that ask students to think conceptually lead to a very different set of thinking processes.

In our work with teachers, we have found that they do not always agree with one another—or with us—on how tasks should be categorized. For example, some have categorized task D (shown in **fig. 1**) as a high-level task because it says that students must "explain the process you used" or because it is a word problem. Similarly, some have thought that task F (shown in **fig. 1**) was high level because it used manipulatives and featured a diagram. But we have classified both tasks as low level because each required the use of a procedure as *stated* (task F) or as *implied* by the problem (task D). Neither task presented any ambiguity about what needed to be done or how to do it or had any connection to meaning. So even though the problem might look high level, an observer must move beyond its surface features to consider the kind of thinking it requires.

Reflection:
*Consider the eight tasks shown in figure 1. How would your students go about solving these tasks? Using
the four categories of cognitive demand, how would you categorize each of the tasks for your students?*

A Tool for Analyzing Cognitive Demands

On the basis of the findings regarding the importance of using cognitively demanding tasks in classroom instruction, we, along with our colleague and collaborator, Marjorie Henningsen, created a task-sort activity and a task-analysis guide for use in professional-development sessions to help teachers with the selection and creation of tasks. The task-sort activity consists of twenty carefully selected instructional tasks that represent the four categories of cognitive demand for middle school students. The eight tasks shown in **figure 1** are a subset of the tasks that are included in the sort.

Reflection:
*Can you think of other factors that might make a task appear to be high level on the surface but that
actually only require recall of memorized information or procedures?*

In addition to differing with respect to cognitive demand, the tasks in this activity also differ with respect to other features that are often associated with reform-oriented instructional tasks (NCTM 1991; Stein, Grover, and Henningsen 1996). For example, some tasks require an explanation or description (e.g., tasks A, C, D, and G); can be solved using manipulatives (e.g., tasks A, E, and F); have real-world contexts (e.g., B, C, and D); involve multiple steps, actions, or judgments (e.g., A, B, C, D, E, and G); and make use of diagrams (e.g., A, E, F, and G). Varying tasks with respect to these features across categories of cognitive demand requires an analysis of the task that goes beyond superficial features to focus on the kind of thinking in which students must engage to complete the tasks.

TASK A

Manipulatives/Tools: Counters

For homework Mark's teacher asked him to look at the pattern below and draw the figure that should come next.

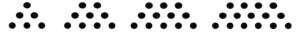

Mark does not know how to find the next figure.

A. Draw the next figure for Mark.

B. Write a description for Mark telling him how you knew which figure comes next.

(QUASAR Project—QUASAR Cognitive Assessment Instrument—Release Task)

TASK B

Manipulatives/Tools: None

Part A: After the first two games of the season, the best player on the girls' basketball team had made 12 out of 20 free throws. The best player on the boys' basketball team had made 14 out of 25 free throws. Which player had made the greater percent of free throws?

Part B: The "better" player had to sit out the third game because of an injury. How many baskets, out of an additional 10 free-throw tries, would the other player need to take the lead in terms of greatest percentage of free throws?

(Adapted from *Investigating Mathematics* [New York: Glencoe Macmillan/McGraw-Hill, 1994])

TASK C

Manipulatives/Tools: Calculator

Your school's science club has decided to do a special project on nature photography. They decided to take a few more than 300 outdoor photos in a variety of natural settings and in all different types of weather. They want to choose some of the best photographs and enter the state nature photography contest. The club was thinking of buying a 35 mm camera, but one member suggested that it might be better to buy disposable cameras instead. The regular camera with autofocus and automatic light meter would cost about $40.00, and film would cost $3.98 for 24 exposures and $5.95 for 36 exposures. The disposable cameras could be purchased in packs of three for $20.00, with two of the three taking 24 pictures and the third one taking 27 pictures. Single disposables could be purchased for $8.95. The club officers have to decide which would be the better option and justify their decisions to the club advisor. Do you think that they should purchase the regular camera or the disposable cameras? Write a justification that clearly explains your reasoning.

TASK D

Manipulatives/Tools: None

The cost of a sweater at a department store was $45. At the store's "day and night" sale it was marked 30 percent off the original price. What was the price of the sweater during the sale? Explain the process you used to find the sale price.

TASK E

Manipulatives/Tools: Pattern blocks

1/2 of 1/3 means one of two equal parts of one-third.

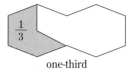 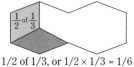

one-third   1/2 of 1/3, or 1/2 × 1/3 = 1/6

Find 1/3 of 1/4. Use pattern blocks. Draw your answer.

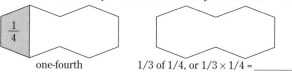

one-fourth   1/3 of 1/4, or 1/3 × 1/4 = _____.

Find 1/4 of 1/3. Use pattern blocks. Draw your answer.

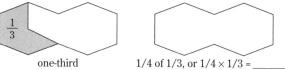

one-third   1/4 of 1/3, or 1/4 × 1/3 = _____.

TASK F

Manipulatives/Tools: Square pattern tiles

Using the side of a square pattern tile as a measure, find the perimeter of, or distance around, each train in the pattern-block figure shown.

Train 1   Train 2   Train 3

TASK G

Manipulatives/Tools: Grid paper

The pairs of numbers in (a)–(d) represent the heights of stacks of cubes to be leveled off. On grid paper, sketch the front views of the columns of cubes with these heights before and after they are leveled off. Write a statement under the sketches that explains how your method of leveling off is related to finding the average of the two numbers.

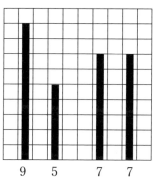

9   5   7   7

(a) 14 and 8   (b) 16 and 7   (c) 7 and 12   (d) 13 and 15

By taking two blocks off the first stack and giving them to the second stack, I've made the two stacks the same. So the total number of cubes is now distributed into two columns of equal height. And that is what average means.

(Taken from Bennett and Foreman [1989/1991])

TASK H

Manipulatives/Tools: None

Give the fraction and percent for each decimal.

0.20 = _____ = _____.
0.25 = _____ = _____.
0.33 = _____ = _____.
0.50 = _____ = _____.
0.66 = _____ = _____.
0.75 = _____ = _____.

Fig. 1. Sample tasks from the task-sort activity

Reflection:
How might you use this tool in professional development sessions to stimulate rich and lively discussions about mathematical tasks and the levels of thinking required to solve them?

The task-analysis guide (**fig. 2**) consists of a listing of the characteristics of tasks at each level of cognitive demand. It serves as a judgment template—a kind of scoring rubric—that can be applied to all kinds of mathematical tasks, permitting a rating of the tasks. Also included in the task-analysis guide is an example of a task at each level, as shown in **figure 3**. Note that each of the four tasks shown in **figure 3** involves fraction multiplication, yet the tasks vary with respect to the demands they place on students.

Using the Tool to Facilitate Discussion

To date, the task-sort activity and the task-analysis guide have been used in a range of settings with preservice and in-service teachers and with teacher educators. In one situation, thirty-three preservice teachers were asked to place each of the twenty tasks into one of the four categories of cognitive demand, without the aid of the list of characteristics in **figure 2**. Thus, the teachers were not only sorting but also engaging in discourse about students' levels of thinking as they negotiated definitions for the categories. Once each group had accomplished its assignment, the classifications were tallied in a table. The tally revealed that several tasks had complete or near consensus! Many of these tasks had the hallmarks of a particular category of cognitive demand. For example, task E was categorized by all groups as *procedures with connections*. The discussion brought out the facts that the task focused on what it means to take a fraction of a fraction, as opposed to using an algorithm, such as "multiply the numerators and multiply the denominators"; and that it could not be completed without effort, that is, students needed to think about what their actions meant as they worked on the problem. From the specifics of the example, we began to extract characteristics of the category more generally. In this example, the tasks categorized as *procedures with connections* focus on meaning, require effort, and involve a procedure. Similar discussions surrounding consensus tasks served to develop descriptors of the other categories of cognitive demand.

For other tasks, such as task A, little agreement occurred. Some teachers classified task A as *procedures without connections*; some, as *procedures with connections*; and others, as *doing mathematics*. The ensuing discussion highlighted the fact that no procedure or pathway was stated or implied for task A, yet the group had included the use of a procedure as a hallmark of tasks that were classified as *procedures without connections* and *procedures with connections*. A more focused look at the characteristics of *doing mathematics* brought out the fact that tasks in this category required students to explore and understand the nature of relationships—a necessary step in extending and describing the pattern in task A. The discussion concluded with the preservice teachers deciding to classify the task as *doing mathematics*. By using the established descriptions created by the group as a template against which to judge little-consensus tasks, the group had a principled basis for the discussions it made.

Reflection:
What do the classifications "procedures with connections" and "doing mathematics" mean to you? How are they alike? How are they different? In what ways can these classifications be helpful in selecting and creating worthwhile mathematics tasks for use in your own classroom?

Once teachers had fairly refined ideas of the characteristics of each category of cognitive demand, it was time to start digging deeper. We began to discuss tasks for which they disagreed on the category, for example, *procedures with connections* versus *doing mathematics*, but, for the most part, we agreed on the level of thinking required, for example, high level. We saw an almost even split in terms of the categorization of task G as either *procedures with connections* or *doing mathematics*. After reviewing the criteria established by the group for these two categories, the teachers determined that *procedures with connections* was a better choice, since a procedure was given—leveling off stacks of cubes—and the procedure was connected to the

Levels of Demand

Lower-level demands (memorization):

- Involve either reproducing previously learned facts, rules, formulas, or definitions or committing facts, rules, formulas or definitions to memory.
- Cannot be solved using procedures because a procedure does not exist or because the time frame in which the task is being completed is too short to use a procedure.
- Are not ambiguous. Such tasks involve the exact reproduction of previously seen material, and what is to be reproduced is clearly and directly stated.
- Have no connection to the concepts or meaning that underlie the facts, rules, formulas, or definitions being learned or reproduced.

Lower-level demands (procedures without connections):

- Are algorithmic. Use of the procedure either is specifically called for or is evident from prior instruction, experience, or placement of the task.
- Require limited cognitive demand for successful completion. Little ambiguity exists about what needs to be done and how to do it.
- Have no connection to the concepts or meaning that underlie the procedure being used.
- Are focused on producing correct answers instead of on developing mathematical understanding.
- Require no explanations or explanations that focus solely on describing the procedure that was used.

Higher-level demands (procedures with connections):

- Focus students' attention on the use of procedures for the purpose of developing deeper levels of understanding of mathematical concepts and ideas.
- Suggest explicitly or implicitly pathways to follow that are broad general procedures that have close connections to underlying conceptual ideas as opposed to narrow algorithms that are opaque with respect to underlying concepts.
- Usually are represented in multiple ways, such as visual diagrams, manipulatives, symbols, and problem situations. Making connections among multiple representations helps develop meaning.
- Require some degree of cognitive effort. Although general procedures may be followed, they cannot be followed mindlessly. Students need to engage with conceptual ideas that underlie the procedures to complete the task successfully and that develop understanding.

Higher-level demands (doing mathematics):

- Require complex and nonalgorithmic thinking—a predictable, well-rehearsed approach or pathway is not explicitly suggested by the task, task instructions, or a worked-out example.
- Require students to explore and understand the nature of mathematical concepts, processes, or relationships.
- Demand self-monitoring or self-regulation of one's own cognitive processes.
- Require students to access relevant knowledge and experiences and make appropriate use of them in working through the task.
- Require students to analyze the task and actively examine task constraints that may limit possible solution strategies and solutions.
- Require considerable cognitive effort and may involve some level of anxiety for the student because of the unpredictable nature of the solution process required.

These characteristics are derived from the work of Doyle on academic tasks (1988) and Resnick on high-level-thinking skills (1987), the *Professional Standards for Teaching Mathematics* (NCTM 1991), and the examination and categorization of hundreds of tasks used in QUASAR classrooms (Stein, Grover, and Henningsen 1996; Stein, Lane, and Silver 1996).

Fig. 2. Characteristics of mathematical instructional tasks

Lower-Level Demands

Memorization

What is the rule for multiplying fractions?

Expected student response:

You multiply the numerator times the numerator and the denominator times the denominator.

or

You multiply the two top numbers and then the two bottom numbers.

Procedures without Connections

Multiply:

$$\frac{2}{3} \times \frac{3}{4}$$

$$\frac{5}{6} \times \frac{7}{8}$$

$$\frac{4}{9} \times \frac{3}{5}$$

Expected student response:

$$\frac{2}{3} \times \frac{3}{4} = \frac{2 \times 3}{3 \times 4} = \frac{6}{12}$$

$$\frac{5}{6} \times \frac{7}{8} = \frac{5 \times 7}{6 \times 8} = \frac{35}{48}$$

$$\frac{4}{9} \times \frac{3}{5} = \frac{4 \times 3}{9 \times 5} = \frac{12}{45}$$

Higher-Level Demands

Procedures with Connections

Find 1/6 of 1/2. Use pattern blocks. Draw your answer and explain your solution.

Expected student response:

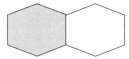 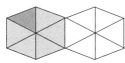

First you take half of the whole, which would be one hexagon. Then you take one-sixth of that half. So I divided the hexagon into six pieces, which would be six triangles. I only needed one-sixth, so that would be one triangle. Then I needed to figure out what part of the two hexagons one triangle was, and it was 1 out of 12. So 1/6 of 1/2 is 1/12.

Doing Mathematics

Create a real-world situation for the following problem:

$$\frac{2}{3} \times \frac{3}{4} \, .$$

Solve the problem you have created without using the rule, and explain your solution.

One possible student response:

For lunch Mom gave me three-fourths of a pizza that we ordered. I could only finish two-thirds of what she gave me. How much of the whole pizza did I eat?

I drew a rectangle to show the whole pizza. Then I cut it into fourths and shaded three of them to show the part Mom gave me. Since I only ate two-thirds of what she gave me, that would be only two of the shaded sections.

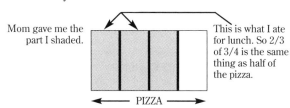

Fig. 3. Examples of tasks at each of the four levels of cognitive demand

meaning of *average.* The discussion focused attention on the various forms that procedures can take, such as algorithms and general pathways through the problem, and on an important characteristic of *doing mathematics* tasks that this particular task did not possess: the need for students to impose their own structure and procedure.

> **Reflection:**
> *What other issues might be important to raise in a discussion of tasks? What task would you add to the sort to stimulate additional discussion?*

We concluded the session by distributing the task-analysis guide and comparing the teachers' descriptors with those that appeared in the guide. By distributing the guide *after* the task-sorting activity was completed, we did not constrain the earlier discussion by the characteristics listed in the guide and participants had the opportunity to construct a listing in their own language. The long-term goal of this activity was twofold: to raise awareness of how mathematical tasks differ with respect to the levels of cognitive engagement that they demand from students and to facilitate teachers' development of a deep and sustained appreciation for the principles of task selection and design.

Sharing Your Reflections

In this article we shared our findings concerning the importance of beginning with a task that has the potential to engage students at a high level if your goal is to increase students' ability to think and reason. The point is that the task you select and evaluate should match your goals for student learning. We encourage you to (*a*) reflect on the extent to which the tasks you use match your goals for student learning, (*b*) reflect on the extent to which your students have the opportunity to engage in tasks that require thinking and reasoning, (*c*) use the eight tasks that are listed in **figure 1** in a discussion with your colleagues, and (*d*) share the results of your experiences through the "Teacher to Teacher" department in this journal.

References
Bennett, Albert B., and Linda Foreman. *Visual Mathematics Course Guide: Integrated Math Topics and Teaching Strategies for Developing Insights and Concepts,* vol. 1. Salem, Ore.: Math Learning Center, 1989/1991.

Doyle, Walter. "Work in Mathematics Classes: The Context of Students' Thinking during Instruction." *Educational Psychologist* 23 (February 1988): 167–80.

National Council of Teachers of Mathematics (NCTM). *Professional Standards for Teaching Mathematics.* Reston, Va.: NCTM, 1991.

Resnick, Lauren. *Education and Learning to Think.* Washington, D.C.: National Academy Press, 1987.

Silver, Edward A., and Mary K. Stein. "The QUASAR Project: The 'Revolution of the Possible' in Mathematics Instructional Reform in Urban Middle Schools." *Urban Education* 30 (January 1996): 476–521.

Stein, Mary Kay, Barbara W. Grover, and Marjorie Henningsen. "Building Student Capacity for Mathematical Thinking and Reasoning: An Analysis of Mathematical Tasks Used in Reform Classrooms." *American Educational Research Journal* 33 (October 1996): 455–88.

Stein, Mary Kay, and Suzanne Lane. "Instructional Tasks and the Development of Student Capacity to Think and Reason: An Analysis of the Relationship between Teaching and Learning in a Reform Mathematics Project." *Educational Research and Evaluation* 2 (October 1996): 50–80.

Stein, Mary Kay, Suzanne Lane, and Edward Silver. "Classrooms in Which Students Successfully Acquire Mathematical Proficiency: What Are the Critical Features of Teachers' Instructional Practice?" Paper presented at the annual meeting of the American Educational Research Association, New York, April 1996.

Stein, Mary Kay, and Margaret S. Smith. "Mathematical Tasks as a Framework for Reflection." *Mathematics Teaching in the Middle School* 3 (January 1998): 268–75.

Thinking through a Lesson: Successfully Implementing High-Level Tasks

Margaret Schwan Smith, Victoria Bill, and Elizabeth K. Hughes

Mathematical tasks that give students the opportunity to use reasoning skills while thinking are the most difficult for teachers to implement well. Research by Stein and colleagues (Henningsen and Stein 1997; Stein and Lane 1996; Stein, Grover, and Henningsen 1996) makes the case resoundingly that cognitively challenging tasks that promote thinking, reasoning, and problem solving often decline during implementation as a result of various classroom factors. When this occurs, students must apply previously learned rules and procedures with no connection to meaning or understanding, and the opportunities for thinking and reasoning are lost. Why are such tasks so difficult to implement in ways that maintain the rigor of the activity? Stein and Kim (2006, p. 11) contend that lessons based on high-level (i.e., cognitively challenging) tasks "are less intellectually 'controllable' from the teacher's point of view." They argue that since procedures for solving high-level tasks are often not specified in advance, students must draw on their relevant knowledge and experiences to find a solution path. Take, for example, the Bag of Marbles task shown in **figure 1**. Using their knowledge of fractions, ratios, and percents, students can solve the task in a number of different ways:

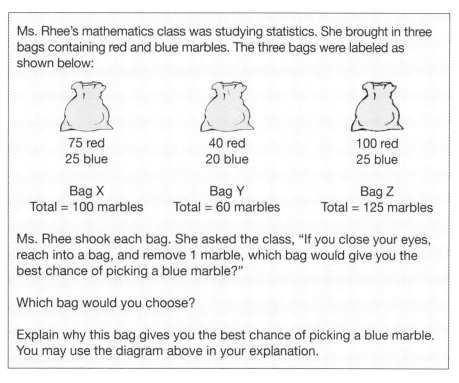

Ms. Rhee's mathematics class was studying statistics. She brought in three bags containing red and blue marbles. The three bags were labeled as shown below:

75 red 25 blue	40 red 20 blue	100 red 25 blue
Bag X Total = 100 marbles	Bag Y Total = 60 marbles	Bag Z Total = 125 marbles

Ms. Rhee shook each bag. She asked the class, "If you close your eyes, reach into a bag, and remove 1 marble, which bag would give you the best chance of picking a blue marble?"

Which bag would you choose?

Explain why this bag gives you the best chance of picking a blue marble. You may use the diagram above in your explanation.

Fig. 1. The Bag of Marbles task

- Determine the fraction of each bag that is blue marbles, decide which of the three fractions is largest, then select the bag with the largest fraction of blue marbles

- Determine the fraction of each bag that is blue marbles, change each fraction to a percent, then select the bag with the largest percent of blue marbles

- Determine the unit rate of red to blue marbles for each bag and decide which bag has the fewest red marbles for every 1 blue marble

- Scale up the ratios representing each bag so that the number of blue marbles in each bag is the same, then select the bag that has the fewest red marbles for the fixed number of blue marbles

- Compare bags that have the same number of blue marbles, eliminate the bag that has more red marbles, and compare the remaining two bags using one of the other methods

- Determine the difference between the number of red and blue marbles in each bag and select the bag that has the smallest difference between red and blue (not correct)

The lack of a specific solution path is an important component of what makes this task worthwhile. It also challenges teachers to understand the wide range of methods that a student might use to solve a task and think about how the different methods are related, as well as how to connect students' diverse ways of thinking to important disciplinary ideas.

One way to both control teaching with high-level tasks and promote success is through detailed planning prior to the lesson. The remainder of this article focuses on TTLP: the Thinking Through a Lesson Protocol. TTLP is a process that is intended to further the use of cognitively challenging tasks (Smith and Stein 1998). We begin by discussing the key features of the TTLP, suggest ways in which it can be used with collaborative lesson planning, and conclude with a discussion of the potential benefits of using it.

Exploring the Lesson Planning Protocol

The TTLP, shown in **figure 2**, provides a framework for developing lessons that use students' mathematical thinking as the critical ingredient in developing their understanding of key disciplinary ideas. As such, it is intended to promote the type of careful and detailed planning that is characteristic of Japanese lesson study (Stigler and Hiebert 1999) by helping teachers anticipate what students will do and generate questions teachers can ask that will promote student learning prior to a lesson being taught.

The TTLP is divided into three sections: Part 1: Selecting and Setting Up a Mathematical Task, Part 2: Supporting Students' Exploration of the Task, and Part 3: Sharing and Discussing the Task. Part 1 lays the groundwork for subsequent planning by asking the teacher to identify the mathematical goals for the lesson and set expectations regarding how students will work. The mathematical ideas to be learned through work on a specific task provide direction for all decision making during the lesson. The intent of the TTLP is to help teachers keep "an eye on the mathematical horizon" (Ball 1993) and never lose sight of what they are trying to accomplish mathematically. Part 2 focuses on monitoring students as they explore the task (individually or in small groups). Students are asked questions based on the solution method used to assess what they currently understand so as to move them toward the mathematical goal of the lesson. Part 3 focuses on orchestrating a whole-group discussion of the task that uses the different solution strategies produced by students to highlight the mathematical ideas that are the focus of the lesson.

Using the TTLP as a Tool for Collaborative Planning

Many teachers' first reaction to the TTLP may be this: "It is overwhelming; no one could use this to plan lessons *every day!*" It was never intended that a teacher would write out answers to all these questions every day. Rather, teachers have used the TTLP periodically (and collaboratively) to prepare lessons so that, over time, a repertoire of carefully designed lessons grows. In addition, as teachers become more familiar with the TTLP, they begin to ask themselves questions from the protocol as they plan lessons *without explicit reference to the protocol*. This sentiment is echoed in the comment made by one middle school teacher: "I follow this

PART 1: SELECTING AND SETTING UP A MATHEMATICAL TASK

What are your mathematical goals for the lesson (i.e., what do you want students to know and understand about mathematics as a result of this lesson)?

In what ways does the task build on students' previous knowledge, life experiences, and culture? What definitions, concepts, or ideas do students need to know to begin to work on the task? What questions will you ask to help students access their prior knowledge and relevant life and cultural experiences?

What are all the ways the task can be solved?

- Which of these methods do you think your students will use?
- What misconceptions might students have?
- What errors might students make?

What particular challenges might the task present to struggling students or students who are English language learners? How will you address these challenges?

What are your expectations for students as they work on and complete this task?

- What resources or tools will students have to use in their work that will give them entry into, and help them reason through, the task?
- How will the students work—independently, in small groups, or in pairs—to explore this task? How long will they work individually or in small groups or pairs? Will students be partnered in a specific way? If so, in what way?
- How will students record and report their work?

How will you introduce students to the activity so as to provide access to all students while maintaining the cognitive demands of the task? How will you ensure that students understand the context of the problem? What will you hear that lets you know students understand what the task is asking them to do?

PART 2: SUPPORTING STUDENTS' EXPLORATION OF THE TASK

As students work independently or in small groups, what questions will you ask to—

- help a group get started or make progress on the task?
- focus students' thinking on the key mathematical ideas in the task?

- assess students' understanding of key mathematical ideas, problem-solving strategies, or the representations?
- advance students' understanding of the mathematical ideas?
- encourage all students to share their thinking with others or to assess their understanding of their peers' ideas?

How will you ensure that students remain engaged in the task?

- What assistance will you give or what questions will you ask a student (or group) who becomes quickly frustrated and requests more direction and guidance in solving the task?
- What will you do if a student (or group) finishes the task almost immediately? How will you extend the task so as to provide additional challenge?
- What will you do if a student (or group) focuses on nonmathematical aspects of the activity (e.g., spends most of his or her (or their) time making a poster of their work)?

PART 3: SHARING AND DISCUSSING THE TASK

How will you orchestrate the class discussion so that you accomplish your mathematical goals?

- Which solution paths do you want to have shared during the class discussion? In what order will the solutions be presented? Why?
- In what ways will the order in which solutions are presented help develop students' understanding of the mathematical ideas that are the focus of your lesson?
- What specific questions will you ask so that students will—

1. make sense of the mathematical ideas that you want them to learn?
2. expand on, debate, and question the solutions being shared?
3. make connections among the different strategies that are presented?
4. look for patterns?
5. begin to form generalizations?

How will you ensure that, over time, each student has the opportunity to share his or her thinking and reasoning with their peers?

What will you see or hear that lets you know that all students in the class understand the mathematical ideas that you intended for them to learn?

What will you do tomorrow that will build on this lesson?

Fig. 2. Thinking Through a Lesson Protocol (TTLP)

model when planning my lessons. Certainly not to the extent of writing down this detailed lesson plan, but in my mind I go through its progression. Internalizing what it stands for really makes you a better facilitator." Hence, the main purpose of the TTLP is to change the way that teachers think about and plan lessons. In the remainder of this section, we provide some suggestions on how you, the teacher, might use the TTLP as a tool to structure conversations with colleagues about teaching.

Getting started

The Bag of Marbles task (shown in **fig. 1**) is used to ground our discussion of lesson planning. This task would be classified as high level. Since no predictable pathway is explicitly suggested or implied by the task, students must access relevant knowledge and experiences, use them appropriately while working through the task, and explain why they made a particular selection. Therefore, this task has the potential to engage students in high-level thinking and reasoning. However, it also has the greatest chance of declining during implementation in ways that limit high-level thinking and reasoning (Henningsen and Stein 1997).

You and your colleagues may want to select a high-level task from the curriculum used in your school or find a task from another source that is aligned with your instructional goals (see Task Resources at the end of the article for suggested sources of high-level tasks). It is helpful to begin your collaborative work by focusing on a subset of TTLP questions rather than attempting to respond to all the questions in one sitting. Here are some suggestions on how to begin collaborative planning.

Articulating the goal for the lesson

The first question in part 1—What are your mathematical goals for the lesson?—is a critical starting point for planning. Using a selected task, you can begin to discuss what you are trying to accomplish through the use of this particular task. The challenge is to be clear about what mathematical ideas students are to learn and understand from their work on the task, not just what they will do. For example, teachers implementing the Bag of Marbles task may want students to be able to determine that bag Y will give the best chance of picking a blue marble and to present a correct explanation why. Although this is a reasonable expectation, it presents no detail on what students understand about ratios, the different comparisons that can be made with a ratio (i.e., part to part, part to whole, two different measures), or the different ways that ratios can be compared (e.g., scaling the parts up or down to a common amount, scaling the whole up or down to a common amount, or converting a part-to-whole fraction to a percent). By being clear on exactly what students will learn, you will be better positioned to capitalize on opportunities to advance the mathematics in the lesson and make decisions about what to emphasize and de-emphasize. Discussion with colleagues will give you the opportunity to broaden your view regarding the mathematical potential of the task and the "residue" (Hiebert et al. 1997) that is likely to remain after the task.

Anticipating student responses to the task

The third question in part 1—What are all the ways the task can be solved?—invites teachers to move beyond their own way of solving a problem and consider the correct and incorrect approaches that students are likely to use. You and your colleagues can brainstorm various approaches for solving the task (including wrong answers) and identify a subset of the solution methods that would be useful in reaching the mathematical goals for the lesson. This helps make a lesson more "intellectually controllable" (Stein and Kim 2006) by encouraging you to think through the possibilities in advance of the lesson and hence requiring fewer improvisational moves during the lesson. If actual student work is available for the task being discussed, it can help you anticipate how students will proceed. For example, reviewing the student work in **figure 3** can provide insight into a range of approaches, such as comparing fractions in **figure 3d**, finding and comparing percents in **figure 3b**, or comparing part-to-part ratios in **figure 3g**. Student work will also present opportunities to discuss incorrect or incomplete solutions such as treating the ratio 1/3 as a fraction in **figure 3a**, comparing differences rather than finding a common basis for comparison in **figure 3f**, and correctly comparing x and z but failing to then compare x and y in **figure 3h**. In addition, there should

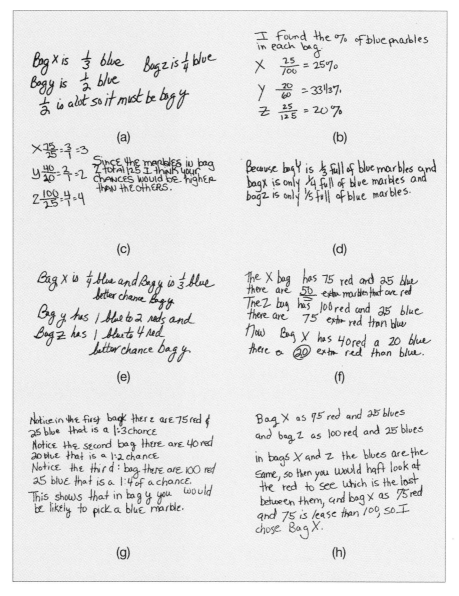

Fig. 3. Student solutions to the Bag of Marbles task

also be opportunities to discuss which strategies might be most helpful in meeting the goals for the lesson. Although it is impossible to predict everything that students might do, by working with colleagues, you can anticipate what may occur.

Creating questions that assess and advance students' thinking

The main point of part 2 of the TTLP is to create questions to ask students that will help them focus on the mathematical ideas that are at the heart of the lesson as they explore the task. The questions you ask during instruction determine what students learn and understand about mathematics. Several studies point to both the importance of asking good questions during instruction and the difficulty that teachers have in doing so (e.g., Weiss and Pasley 2004).

You and your colleagues can use the solutions you anticipated and create questions that can *assess* what students understand about the problem (e.g., clarify what the student has done and what the student understands) and help students *advance* toward the mathematical goals of the lesson. Teachers can extend students beyond their current thinking by pressing them to extend what they know to a new situation or think about something they are not currently thinking about. If student responses for the task are available, you might generate assessing and advancing questions for each anticipated student response. Consider, for example, the responses shown in **figure 3** to the Bag of Marbles problem. If you, as the teacher, approached the student who produced response (c) during the lesson, you would notice that the student compared red marbles to blue marbles, reduced these ratios to unit rates (number of red marbles to one blue marble), and then wrote the whole numbers (3, 2, and 4). However, the student did not use these calculations to determine that in bag Y the number of red marbles was only twice the number of blue marbles, whereas in bag X and Z the number of red marbles were 3 and 4 times, respectively, the number of blue marbles. You might want to ask the student who produced response (c) a series of questions that will help you *assess* what the student currently understands:

- What quantities did you compare and why?
- What did the numbers 3, 2, and 4 mean in terms of the problem?
- How could the mathematical work you are doing, making comparisons, help you answer the question?

Determining what a student understands about the comparisons that he or she makes can open a window into the student's thinking. Once you have a clear sense of how the student is thinking about the task, you are better positioned to ask questions that will *advance* his or her understanding and help the student build a sound argument based on the mathematical work.

Potential Benefits of Using the TTLP

Over the last several years, the TTLP has been used by numerous elementary and secondary teachers with varying levels of teaching experience who wanted to implement high-level tasks in their classrooms. The cumulative experiences of these teachers suggests that the TTLP can be a useful tool in planning, teaching, and reflecting on lessons and can lead to improved teaching. Several teachers have commented, in particular, on the value of solving the task in multiple ways before the lesson begins and devising questions to ask that are based on anticipated approaches. For example, one teacher indicated, "I often come up with great questions because I am exploring the task deeper and developing 'what if' questions." Another participant suggested that preparing questions in advance helps her support students without taking over the challenging aspects of the problem for them:

> Coming up with good questions before the lesson helps me keep a high-level task at a high level, instead of pushing kids toward a particular solution path and giving them an opportunity to practice procedures. When kids call me over and say they don't know how to do something (which they often do), it helps if I have a ready-made response that gives them structure to keep working on the problem without doing it for them. This way all kids have a point of entry to the problem.

The TTLP has also been a useful tool for beginning teachers. In an interview about lesson planning conducted at the end of the first semester of her yearlong internship (and nearly six months after she first encountered the TTLP), another preservice teacher offered the following explanation about how the TTLP had influenced her planning:

> I may not have it sitting on my desk, going point to point with it, but I think: What are the misconceptions? How am I going to organize work? What are my questions? Those are the three big things that I've taken from the TTLP, and those are the three big things that I think about when planning a lesson. So, no, I'm not matching it up point for point, but those three concepts are pretty much in every lesson, essentially.

Although this teacher does not follow the TTLP in its entirety each time she plans a lesson, she has taken key aspects of the TTLP and made them part of her daily lesson planning.

Conclusion

The purpose of the Thinking Through a Lesson Protocol is to prompt teachers to think deeply about a specific lesson that they will be teaching. The goal is to move beyond the structural components often associated with lesson planning to a deeper consideration of how to advance students' mathematical understanding during the lesson. By shifting the emphasis from what the teacher is doing to what students are thinking, the teacher will be better positioned to help students make sense of mathematics. One mathematics teacher summed up the potential of the TTLP in this statement:

> Sometimes it's very time-consuming, trying to write these lesson plans, but it's very helpful. It really helps the lesson go a lot smoother and even not having it front of me, I think it really helps me focus my thinking, which then [it] kind of helps me focus my students' thinking, which helps us get to an objective and leads to a better lesson.

In addition to helping you create individual lessons, the TTLP can also help you consider your teaching practice over time. As another teacher pointed out, "The usefulness of the TTLP is in accepting that [your practice] evolves over time. Growth occurs as the protocol is continually revisited and as you reflect on successes and failures."

Task Resources

Bright, George W., Dargan Frierson Jr., James E. Tarr, and Cynthia Thomas. *Navigating through Probability in Grades 6–8*. Reston, Va.: National Council of Teachers of Mathematics, 2003.

Bright, George W., Wallece Brewer, Kay McClain, and Edward S. Mooney. *Navigating through Data Analysis in Grades 6-8*. Reston, Va.: National Council of Teachers of Mathematics, 2003.

Bright, George W., Patricia Lamphere Jordan, Carol Malloy, and Tad Watanabe. *Navigating through Measurement in Grades 6-8*. Reston, Va.: National Council of Teachers of Mathematics, 2005.

Brown, Catherine A., and Lynn V. Clark, eds. *Learning from NAEP: Professional Development Materials for Teachers of Mathematics*. Reston, Va.: National Council of Teachers of Mathematics, 2006.

Friel, Susan, Sid Rachlin, and Dot Doyle. *Navigating through Algebra in Grades 6–8*. Reston, Va.: National Council of Teachers of Mathematics, 2001.

Illuminations. illuminations.nctm.org/Lessons.aspx.

Parke, Carol S., Suzanne Lane, Edward A. Silver, and Maria E. Magone. *Using Assessment to Improve Middle-Grades Mathematics Teaching and Learning: Suggested Activities Using QUASAR Tasks, Scoring Criteria, and Students' Work*. Reston, Va.: National Council of Teachers of Mathematics, 2003.

Pugalee, David K., Jeffrey Frykholm, Art Johnson, Hannah Slovin, Carol Malloy, and Ron Preston. *Navigating through Geometry in Grades 6–8*. Reston, Va.: National Council of Teachers of Mathematics, 2002.

Rachlin, Sid, Kathy Cramer, Connie Finseth, Linda Cooper Foreman, Dorothy Geary, Seth Leavitt, and Margaret Schwan Smith. *Navigating through Number and Operations in Grades 6–8*. Reston, Va.: National Council of Teachers of Mathematics, 2006.

References

Ball, Deborah L. "With an Eye on the Mathematical Horizon: Dilemmas of Teaching Elementary School Mathematics." *The Elementary School Journal* 93 (1993): 373–97.

Boaler, Jo, and Karin Brodie. "The Importance of Depth and Breadth in the Analysis of Teaching: A Framework for Analyzing Teacher Questions." In the *Proceedings of the 26th Annual Meeting of the North American Chapter of the International Group for the Psychology of Mathematics Education*, pp. 773–80. Toronto, Ontario: PME, 2004.

Henningsen, Marjorie, and Mary Kay Stein. "Mathematical Tasks and Student Cognition: Classroom-Based Factors that Support and Inhibit High-Level Mathematical Thinking and Reasoning." *Journal for Research in Mathematics Education* 29 (November 1997): 524–49.

Hiebert, James, Thomas P. Carpenter, Elizabeth Fennema, Karen C. Fuson, Diana Wearne, Hanlie Murray, Alwyn Olivier, and Piet Human. *Making Sense: Teaching and Learning Mathematics with Understanding*. Portsmouth, N.H.: Heinemann, 1997.

Smith, Margaret Schwan, and Mary Kay Stein. "Selecting and Creating Mathematical Tasks: From Research to Practice." *Mathematics Teaching in the Middle School 3* (February 1998): 344–50.

Stein, Mary Kay, and Susanne Lane. "Instructional Tasks and the Development of Student Capacity to Think and Reason: An Analysis of the Relationship between Teaching and Learning in a Reform Mathematics Project." *Educational Research and Evaluation* 2 (1996): 50–80.

Stein, Mary Kay, Barbara W. Grover, and Marjorie Henningsen. "Building Student Capacity for Mathematical Thinking and Reasoning: An Analysis of Mathematical Tasks Used in Reform Classrooms." *American Educational Research Journal* 33 (Summer 1996): 455–88.

Stein, Mary Kay, and Gooyeon Kim. "The Role of Mathematics Curriculum in Large-Scale Urban Reform: An Analysis of Demands and Opportunities for Teacher Learning." Paper presented at the annual meeting of the American Educational Research Association, San Francisco, California, April 2006.

Stigler, James W., and James Hiebert. *The Teaching Gap: Best Ideas from the World's Teachers for Improving Education in the Classroom.* New York: The Free Press, 1999.

Weiss, Iris, and Joan D. Pasley. "What Is High-Quality Instruction?" *Educational Leadership* 61 (February 2004): 24–28.

A Model for Understanding Understanding in Mathematics

Edward J. Davis

Although this article was written almost thirty years ago, its content is relevant to today's conversations about the roles of conceptual understanding and procedural fluency in the teaching of mathematics.

Teachers strive to help students understand their subject. But what does it mean to understand something? Holt (1964, pp. 136–37), in trying to help teachers come to grips with understanding, offers the following:

> It may help to have in our minds a picture of what we mean by understanding. I feel I understand something if and when I can do some, at least, of the following: (1) state it in my own words; (2) give examples of it; (3) recognize it in various guises and circumstances; (4) see connections between it and other facts or ideas; (5) make use of it in various ways; (6) foresee some of its consequences; (7) state its opposite or converse. This list is only a beginning; but it may help us in the future to find out what our students really know as opposed to what they can give the appearance of knowing, their real learning as opposed to their apparent learning.

Holt's operational definition of understanding is an attempt to guide teachers in planning instruction and in assessing learning. Holt feels his list is only a beginning.

Van Engen (1953, pp. 76–77) describes understanding as a process of organizing and integrating knowledge according to a set of criteria. But what are these criteria? Are the criteria the same for all kinds of knowledge?

Both Holt and Van Engen view understanding as a continuum. Students can have partial understandings. Surely teachers are helped when they know the status of a student's understanding and the additional knowledge students need to acquire more complete understanding.

More recently, Smith (1969), Henderson (1971), and Cooney, Davis, and Henderson (1975) call attention to the kinds of logical things (moves) teachers do in teaching mathematics. It turns out, teachers make different kinds of moves in teaching different kinds of mathematical knowledge. Teachers behave differently, in a logical sense, when teaching a mathematical concept (e.g., place value, exponent, six, triangle) than when teaching children to become skilled at carrying out a procedure (e.g., long division, adding fractions, bisecting a line segment).

This article attempts to advance and demonstrate the proposition that *moves in teaching mathematics can serve as a basis for defining understanding of mathematics.* Since the moves are specific to teaching mathematics, it is hoped teachers will view them as ways to assess students' knowledge and to plan instruction. Moves occur as a result of questions, exercises, problems, explanations, demonstrations, directions on task cards, and almost any other form of teacher-student interaction.

Moves also identify objectives that give a fairly complete picture of understanding. In addition to planning to make moves, teachers can use moves to evaluate and diagnose the degree of understanding held by a particular student for a given item of mathematical knowledge. Students can be said to have understanding *to the extent* that they can make a complete set of moves.

The work of Cooney, Davis, and Henderson has identified the following types of mathematical knowledge commonly taught in school mathematics: concepts, generalizations, procedures, and numerical facts. Understanding depends on the type of mathematical knowledge. Understanding a concept is different from understanding a procedure.

Note: Other research on issues raised by Bruner and others is being coordinated by the Teaching Strategies Project of the Georgia Center for the Study of Learning and Teaching Mathematics (Cooney 1976, p. 5). The author also wishes to express appreciation to Dwain Small of Valencia Community College in Orlando, Florida, for many insightful suggestions made during the [original] preparation of this article.

Understanding Mathematical Concepts

Concepts are frequently denoted by single terms or phrases. *Addition, three-fourths, similar figures, equation, line,* and *greater than* are examples of mathematical concepts. Concepts are probably the most basic kind of subject matter in mathematics. Word lists at the end of a chapter and the index of a mathematics textbook are largely composed of concepts. In **figure 1**, the concept *prime number* will be used to illustrate the various moves.

Understanding Mathematical Generalization

Statements of relationships between concepts are called generalizations. Most generalizations in school mathematics are statements we can show are true. Others are assumed to be true. Theorems are generalizations. The distributive law, the sum of the angles of a triangle is 180 degrees, and the sum of two odd

---

Level 1: Examples and nonexamples of the concept

Children understand a concept to the extent they can make the following moves:

Some sample questions to assess understanding of the concept *prime number*:

1. Give or identify examples of the concept

    1. Which of the following numbers are prime? 7, 9, 2, 17, 21
    Can you find two prime numbers greater than 20 but less than 30?

2. Defend choices of examples of the concept

    2. Why did you choose 17 as a prime number? Two is a prime number? I don't see how. Why do you think so?

3. Give or identify nonexamples of the concept

    3. Two of these numbers are not prime. Can you find them? 1, 2, 3, 4, 5

4. Defend choices of nonexamples of the concept

    4. You say 1 and 4 are not prime numbers. What are your reasons?

Level 2: Characteristics of the concept

5. Identify things that are necessarily true about examples of the concept

    5. Suppose I tell you that 97 is prime. What can you say for sure about 97? I have written a number on the back of this card. I promise it is a prime number. Can you tell me five things that are true about it?

6. Determine properties sufficient to make something an example of the concept

    6. How can you tell for sure a number is prime? If a number is odd does it have to be prime? Why?

7. Tell how one concept is like (or unlike) another concept

    7. What is true about both prime numbers and composite numbers? How are prime numbers different from composite numbers?

8. Define the concept

    8. Who can tell me exactly what prime numbers are?

9. Tell how we use the concept

    9. What can we do with prime numbers—how can they help us?

Fig. 1

numbers is an even number, are generalizations taught in elementary school mathematics. The last generalization is the focus of the questions in **figure 2**.

Understanding Mathematical Procedures

The elementary school mathematics curriculum includes many mathematical procedures. The algorithms for adding, subtracting, multiplying, and dividing whole numbers and rational numbers receive a great deal of instructional and learning time. The study of high school mathematics and college mathematics also

---

Level 1: Understanding *what* the generalization says

Children understand a generalization to the extent they can make the following moves:

Some sample questions to assess understanding of the generalization, that the sum of two odd numbers is an even number:

1. Show understanding of the concepts in the generalization

1. See concept moves and questions for even, odd, and sum.

2. State the generalization in their own words (paraphrase it)

2. Can you say this in your own words? I don't understand it as it is written in the book.

3. Create or recognize instances of the generalization

3. Can you show me two odd numbers whose sum is an even number?

4. Tell when the generalization can be used or state conditions under which it is true

4. When can you be sure the sum of two numbers will be an even number?

5. Apply the generalization in exercises and simple problems

5. One of these sentences can't be true. Can you find it without doing any adding?
$73 + 67 = 140$
$37 + 121 = 158$
$47 + 97 = 144$
$73 + 125 = 195$

Level 2: Understanding *why* the generalization is true

6. Give a plausible argument or proof why the generalization is true

6. An odd number is one more than an even number. How can this help us to convince someone that two odd numbers add to make an even number?

7. Use physical or numerical examples to illustrate the rule

7. Can you show me this generalization using only red Cuisenaire rods and white Cuisenaire rods? Remember, a train of all red rods will always be an even number.

8. Recognize the applicability of the generalization in unfamiliar contexts

8. There are 25 children in this room and everyone in line out in the hall except one child has a partner. If we all join the line outside, could everyone have a partner?

Fig. 2

contains many mathematical procedures. Solving equations, constructing proofs, geometric constructions, synthetic division, and differentiating are mathematical procedures. The distinction between Level 1 understandings and Level 2 understandings for procedures is a well-known issue in teaching mathematics. Many adults do not completely understand *why* some of the procedures in elementary school mathematics work.

In **figure 3**, the procedure of adding rational numbers in fractional form is used in the sample questions.

Level 1: Understanding *how* the procedure works

Children understand a procedure to the extent they can make the following moves:

1. Accurately carry out the procedure

2. Show another student how to do the procedure

3. Paraphrase the procedure step by step

4. Tell when they can use the procedure

5. Execute the procedure rapidly and accurately

6. Understand prerequisite knowledge

7. Find errors in work

Some sample questions to assess understanding of the procedure for adding fractions:

1. Can you add 2/3 and 3/4 for me?

2. Terry, you were here yesterday, will you show Al how to add these fractions?

3. Before you pick up your pencil, can you tell me everything you are going to do to add 5/3 and 4/5?

4. On which of these problems do we need to find a common denominator?

5. Can you work these two additions in only one minute?

6. See concept moves for: numerator, denominator, common denominator, fraction, adding, and equivalent fraction. The child would also need to understand the procedure for adding common fractions with the same denominator.

7. I made a mistake in my work. Can you find it?

Level 2: Understanding *why* the procedure works

8. Show answers obtained as a result of the procedure are reasonable

9. Give a plausible argument or proof justifying the procedure

10. Recognize the applicability of the procedure in new contexts

8. You have an answer of 11/12 for 2/3 + 1/4. Can you use these Cuisenaire rods or the geoboard to show that 2/3 + 1/4 = 11/12 is true?

9. Let's go over your work step by step. Can you convince me what is really happening in each step? Why do we find a common denominator?

10. Can you now add 3 2/3 and 5 1/4?

Fig. 3

Understanding Number Facts

Many numerical facts are generalizations. Hence, moves for generalizations apply to number facts. However, since basic arithmetic facts such as $4 < 5$, $6 = 6$, $3 + 2 = 5$, and $4 \times 7 = 28$ have played such a large role in school mathematics, an attempt is made to tailor moves for understanding generalizations specifically for number facts. The fact $5 + 4 = 9$ is used in **figure 4** in the sample questions.

Level 1: Understanding *what* the fact says

Children understand a number fact to the extent they can make the following moves:

Some sample questions to assess understanding of the fact $5 + 4 = 9$:

1. Recall the fact

1. $5 + 4 = ?$

2. Create or recognize embodiments of the fact

2. Can you use the number line, the rods, the counters, and your fingers to show $5 + 4 = 9$?

3. Understand the concepts in the fact

3. See understanding moves for 5, 4, 9, +, =.

4. Use the fact in simple exercises

4. $\begin{array}{r} 5 \\ 4 \\ + 1 \\ \hline ? \end{array}$

5. Apply the fact

5. Make up a story problem that asks you to use $5 + 4 = 9$.

Level 2: Understanding *why* the fact is true and realizing its significance

6. Show the truth of the fact using objects, models, or other facts

6. Suppose I say that $5 + 4 = 10$. Can you show me I am wrong? Starting with $4 + 4 = 8$, can you show me that $5 + 4 = 9$?

7. Complete related statements of the fact

7. Does $5 + 4 = 4 + 5$? What makes $5 + \square = 9$ true?

Fig. 4

Contexts for Making Moves

Bruner, Dienes, and others have been said to advise elementary school teachers to begin instruction with physical embodiments and progress to pictorial and then symbolic representation. It is advised here that care be taken in following this instructional sequence. Don't stop at the symbolic level. Ask students working at the symbolic level to interpret their work by creating corresponding physical and pictorial representations. When students have completed a page working primarily with symbols, select an occasional item and require them to draw a picture or physically represent what they have done. Children should realize they are going to be required to use a picture, a number line, rods, a geoboard, counting objects, or some other pictorial or physical medium to interpret their symbolic work to someone else. Correct answers to symbolic questions are not enough. Using symbols correctly does not guarantee complete understanding. In fact, many workbook pages can be filled out correctly by a child who is confused or missing the point. Examples of such series of exercises in a primary level textbook and in a middle school text are shown in **figure 5**. In each case, a student can examine the sample exercise (or get help from a neighbor) and complete the exercises without being able to make any other understanding moves for the generalizations being taught.

Students can initiate the kinds of logical exchanges we call moves by asking questions. Task cards in mathematics laboratory settings can initiate moves by asking students to do such things as generate examples of concepts, recall facts, create or examine instances to detect a pattern, reflect on or discover the necessary or sufficient conditions of a concept, paraphrase a procedure, verify or defend a conclusion, and apply generalizations or procedures.

One way to study for an examination in mathematics is to identify the concepts, generalizations, and procedures taught and try to make as many of the moves as possible for each item of knowledge. Here the moves serve as a checklist for students to examine their understandings. A teacher often goes through a similar process when constructing a test.

Do not expect children to attain all Level 1 understandings before any Level 2 understandings are acquired. While instruction frequently moves from Level 1 to Level 2, and from physical to pictorial to symbolic representations, children do not always learn what the teacher intends. If they did, teaching would be easy.

Using Moves for Understanding

It is hoped that the sample outlines for understanding mathematical concepts, generalizations, procedures, and numerical facts will be seen to have practical value for teachers. Moves can easily be used to establish objectives for lessons and learning activities. To illustrate this claim, the moves listed for concepts, generalizations, procedures, and number facts were stated in objective format. From these objects, a teacher can receive guidance in planning lessons, activities, and tests. This can be done by using a listing of the moves and their corresponding questions to create a guide or checklist when planning a lesson or a test. The following is an example of such a checklist for the concept of division as commonly taught to children in grades 3 or 4. It comes directly from the list of moves for understanding a concept given earlier (**fig. 1**).

Can my students—

A. Create examples of division statements using objects or pictures? (from moves 1 and 2)

B. Select examples of division from a set of situations showing examples and nonexamples? (from moves 3 and 4)

C. Write corresponding multiplication (or subtraction) statements for given division statements? (from moves 5, 7, and 8)

D. Make up and solve story problems involving division? (from move 8)

Note that the foregoing checklist is not tied rigidly to each move. Items in the list were generalized from single or multiple moves by using common sense and a little creativity. The moves were used to stimulate the checklist and not to dictate the list. Another teacher might create a different and perhaps more complete checklist. The moves are advocated to help make a checklist "well-rounded" in covering the various aspects of understanding a concept.

Fill in the blanks

3 tens and 7 ones is 37
3 tens and 6 ones is ___
2 tens and 9 ones is ___
.
.
.
9 tens and 1 one is ___

Now try these
___ tens and ___ ones is 47
___ tens and ___ ones is 62
___ tens and ___ ones is 50
.
.
.
___ tens and ___ ones is 33

Fill in the blanks
$3 \cdot (4 + 6) = 3 \cdot 4 + 3 \cdot 6$
$5 \cdot (8 + 2) = 5 \cdot 8 +$ ___
$7 \cdot (1 + 9) =$ ___ $+$ ___
.
.
.
$12 \cdot (15 + 2) =$ ___

Now try these
$4 \cdot ($ ___ $+$ ___ $) = 4 \cdot 5 + 4 \cdot 8$
___ $\cdot ($ ___ $+$ ___ $) = 7 \cdot 2 + 7 \cdot 9$
___ $\cdot ($ ___ $+$ ___ $) = 3 \cdot 1 + 3 \cdot 5$
.
.
.
___ $\cdot ($ ___ $+$ ___ $) = 4 \cdot 8 + 4 \cdot 6$

Fig. 5

A teacher need not feel limited to the moves given in this article for teaching a concept, generalization, procedure, or fact. Neither should a teacher feel compelled to use every move in every teaching situation. Moves are offered as one valuable resource in setting objectives, planning instruction, diagnosing, and evaluating understanding. They are not intended to replace common sense, creativity, or practices that a teacher has found to be successful.

Moves can help a teacher generate questions in instructional as well as testing situations. When a teacher needs to diagnose a student's understanding of a mathematical concept, generalization, procedure, or numerical fact, moves can be called on to provide a comprehensive picture of the student's knowledge. A list of questions similar to those in **figures 1–4** can be posed to diagnose understanding. Before beginning remediation, a teacher may want to ask questions based on a number of the moves to ascertain what the student understands relative to a particular item of knowledge.

Moves could also be selected by a teacher to give directions to an aide or tutor working with a student or a small group. Aides and tutors need to "zero in" to make efficient use of instructional time. Teachers do not give an aide or tutor very specific directions to follow by making comments like "Alice doesn't understand division; please work with her," or "Please help Dan with the rule for finding the area of a triangle; he just doesn't seem to get it." Contrast these directions with "Help Alice create examples for division; statements like fifteen divided by five," and "Dan is not sure what he needs in order to apply the rule for the area of a triangle. Give him some help by reviewing the concepts of base and altitude and by going through some instances. Then see if he can apply the rule on his own."

Research on Using Moves in Teaching for Understanding

Since teachers can use all or some of the moves for teaching a particular concept, generalization, procedure, or numerical fact, when planning lessons and in assessing understandings, it is possible to consider moves in developing a theory of teaching mathematics. Teachers must act. They need prescriptive principles. Consider some of Bruner's (1966) comments on teaching:

1. A theory of instruction is prescriptive in the sense that it sets forth rules concerning the most effective way of achieving knowledge or skill. (p. 40)

2. But theories of learning and of development are descriptive rather than prescriptive. They tell us what happened after the fact: for example, that most children of six do not yet possess the notion of reversibility. A theory of instruction, on the other hand, might attempt to set forth the best means of leading the child toward the notion of reversibility. A theory of instruction, in short, is concerned with how what one wishes to teach can best be learned, with improving rather than describing learning. (p. 40)

3. A theory of instruction must specify the ways in which a body of knowledge should be structured so that it can be most readily grasped by the learner. (p. 41)

4. A theory of instruction should specify the most effective sequences in which to present the materials to be learned. (p. 41)

If moves are used to specify and control teacher actions, it is reasonable to consider or call for research to see if prescriptions for teaching types of mathematical knowledge can be found. Can effective instructional sequences be described in terms of moves? Do moves help structure knowledge in ways most readily grasped by the learner?

Studies by Dossey (1976) indicate teachers are not constrained to choose a particular sequence of moves in teaching mathematical concepts. However, teaching in Dossey's studies was confined to printed programmed material. Students could read over each sequence of moves a number of times—something that does not always characterize classroom teaching. Swank's work (1976) indicates teachers judged by their peers to be superior åmake approximately twice as many moves in teaching concepts as inexperienced teachers and teachers rated lowest by their peers. Swank's results also show some support for concept teaching strategies containing a high number of moves with a high level of student/teacher interaction. While Swank investigated teaching in a classroom setting, he cautions against premature generalization of this finding since it did not hold for students of low ability (p. 109).

Research on classroom teaching is confounded by many variables. Moves in teaching mathematics hold promise of one way to design and control teacher actions so effects of teacher behavior and achievement can be studied.

Research aside, Bruner (1965) sees another area of concern in teaching:

> Perhaps, in discussing the functions of teaching, we should make a special place for . . . teaching people to listen to what they have been doing. (p. 10)

If the set of moves in teaching students to understand types of mathematics is used to record logical interactions in teaching mathematics, we may develop an instrument that can be used by teachers to "listen" to the logical dimension of their teaching.

References

Bruner, Jerome S. *Toward a Theory of Instruction.* New York: W. W. Norton & Company, 1966.

———. *On Knowing.* New York: Atheneum, 1968.

Cooney, Thomas J., ed. *Teaching Strategies: Papers from a Research Workshop.* Athens, Ga.: Georgia Center for the Study of Learning and Teaching Mathematics, 1976. (ERIC no. ED 123 132)

Cooney, Thomas J., Edward J. Davis, and Kenneth B. Henderson. *Dynamics of Teaching Secondary School Mathematics.* Boston: Houghton Mifflin Co., 1975.

Dossey, John A. "The Role of Relative Efficacy Studies in the Development of Mathematical Concept Teaching Strategies: Some Findings and Some Directions." In *Teaching Strategies: Papers from a Research Workshop,* edited by Thomas J. Cooney, pp. 51–80. Athens, Ga.: Georgia Center for the Study of Learning and Teaching Mathematics, 1976. (ERIC no. ED 123 132)

Henderson, K. B. "A Theoretical Model for Teaching." In *Contemporary Thought on Teaching,* edited by Ronald T. Hyman. Englewood Cliffs, N.J.: Prentice Hall, 1971.

Holt, John. *How Children Fail.* New York: Dell Publishing Co., 1964.

Smith, B. Othanel. *Teachers for the Real World.* Washington, D.C.: American Association of Colleges for Teacher Education, 1969.

Swank, Earl W. "An Empirical Comparison of Teaching Strategies Where the Amount of Concept Information and Teacher-Pupil Interaction Is Varied." In *Teaching Strategies: Papers from a Research Workshop,* edited by Thomas J. Cooney, pp. 87–114. Athens, Ga.: Georgia Center for the Study of Learning and Teaching Mathematics, 1976. (ERIC no. ED 123 132)

Van Engen, Henry. "The Formation of Concepts." In *Learning of Mathematics, Its Theory and Practice,* pp. 69–98. Twenty-First Yearbook of the National Council of Teachers of Mathematics (NCTM). Washington, D.C.: NCTM, 1953.

SECTION 2

The Meaning of, and Operations on, Rational Numbers

Introduction

Principles and Standards for School Mathematics (NCTM 2000) recommends that students in grades 6–8 deepen their understanding of, and facility with, fractions, decimals, and percents. They should also develop their ability to solve problems that involve rational numbers. All teachers of mathematics, grades K–12, recognize both the centrality of rational numbers in all sub-areas of mathematics—number, geometry, algebra, probability, and statistics—and the need for work on rational numbers to permeate the curriculum. Despite the importance of rational numbers to the development of mathematical proficiency in the middle years of schooling, they present considerable challenges to students. One cause of students' confusion about rational numbers is the "rush to symbol manipulations," which occurs when students learn algorithms without developing an underlying understanding of the concepts (Lappan et al. 1998). When that happens, students know the rules but do not understand why a rule "works" or how to make sense of situations and choose a specific rule to apply. As a result of learning algorithms this way, students often struggle to explain their reasoning or solve problems that involve more than one step (Wearne and Kouba 2000).

The articles in this section focus on the use of models and representations to help students make sense of and develop proficiency with operations on rational numbers.

"Using Bar Representations as a Model for Connecting Concepts of Rational Number" (Middleton, van den Heuvel-Panhuizen, and Shew 1998) uses a context of submarine sandwiches for students' exploration of fraction concepts. Students develop strategies to make "fair" shares, draw models, and consider ways to name the amount of submarine sandwich each person receives. Problems are included that represent applications of bar models used in the real world.

"Multiplication with Fractions: A Piagetian, Constructivist Approach" (Warrington and Kamii 1998) describes a carefully sequenced set of problems that a teacher used to build her students' understanding of multiplying fractions.

"Measurement and Fair-Sharing Models for Dividing Fractions" (Gregg and Gregg 2007) presents a collection of problems that explore cookie-serving size as a context for division. One sequence of problems leads to the development of a common-denominator algorithm for division. Another sequence helps students understand and construct the traditional algorithm.

Understanding decimals is a stumbling block for upper elementary and middle school students. "Connecting Decimals and Other Mathematical Content" (Thompson and Walker 1996) gives instructional tasks that can, according to the author, "help students connect decimal concepts with decimal symbols, with fraction concepts and symbols, and with place-value concepts and symbols." Hundreds grids, folding strips, and number lines are used to make connections and support students' reasoning. These are all ways of understanding that students need to be facile with decimal interpretation and use.

"Investigating Students' Conceptual Understanding of Decimal Fractions Using Multiple Representations" (Martinie and Bay-Williams 2003) features a task that can be used to assess students' understanding of decimal concepts using a 10-by-10 grid, number line, money, and place-value model. The sixth graders in the sample group had the greatest difficulty with number-line models. The article includes a follow-up assessment and implications for teaching and learning.

References

Gregg, Jeff, and Diana Underwood Gregg. ""Measurement and Fair-Sharing Models for Dividing Fractions." *Mathematics Teaching in the Middle School* 12, no. 9 (May 2007): 490–96.

Lappan, Glenda, James T. Fey, William M. Fitzgerald, Susan N. Friel, and Elizabeth Difanis Phillips. *Bits and Pieces 1: Understanding Rational Numbers*. Palo Alto, Calif.: Dale Seymour Publications, 1998.

Martinie, Sherri L., and Jennifer M. Bay-Williams. "Investigating Students' Conceptual Understanding of Decimal Fractions Using Multiple Representations. *Mathematics Teaching in the Middle School* 8 (January 2003): 244–47.

Middleton, James A., Marja van den Heuvel-Panhuizen, and Julia A. Shew. "Using Bar Representations as a Model for Connecting Concepts of Rational Number." *Mathematics Teaching in the Middle School* 3 (January 1998): 302–12.

National Council of Teachers of Mathematics (NCTM). *Principles and Standards for School Mathematics*. Reston, Va.: NCTM, 2000.

Thompson, Charles S., and Vicki Walker. "Connecting Decimals and Other Mathematical Content." In *Activities for Junior High School and Middle School Mathematics*, Vol. 2, edited by Kenneth E. Easterday, F. Morgan Simpson, and Tommy Smith, pp. 161–65. Reston, Va.: National Council of Teachers of Mathematics, 1999; *Teaching Children Mathematics* 4 (April 1996): 496–502.

Warrington, Mary Ann, and Constance Kamii. "Multiplication with Fractions: A Piagetian, Constructivist Approach." *Mathematics Teaching in the Middle School* 3 (February 1998): 339–43.

Wearne, Diana, and Vicky Kouba. "Rational Numbers." In *Results from the Seventh Mathematics Assessment of the National Assessment of Educational Progress*, edited by Edward A. Silver and Margaret A. Kenney, pp. 163–91. Reston, Va.: National Council of Teachers of Mathematics, 2000.

Using Bar Representations as a Model for Connecting Concepts of Rational Number

*James A. Middleton, Marja van den Heuvel-Panhuizen,
and Julia A. Shew*

Middle grades students should be able to understand, represent, and use numbers in a variety of equivalent forms, including fractions, decimals, and percents. They should develop number sense for fractions and other representations of rational number. Students should also be able to represent such relationships in graphical form (NCTM 1989). This article examines bar models as graphical representations of rational number.

Rationale

Much of the research in the area of children's understanding of rational-number concepts indicates that although learning basic fractions builds on concepts of whole-number arithmetic that children have, by and large, already learned, children tend to have great difficulty putting these ideas together meaningfully (Ohlsson 1988). A few of the difficulties that children experience are summarized in **figure 1** (Marshall 1993; Streefland 1993).

The difficulties in teaching rational numbers can be attributed to a great extent to the overemphasis on the *different* meanings of rational numbers instead of their overall *similarities*. Each meaning of rational numbers has been treated as a separate topic, and each way of representing ratios as a distinct method or set of symbols. Generally, attempts to draw connections among them through appropriate representations have not been widespread. Students must come to understand that fractions, decimals, percents, and ratios have a common underlying meaning and that one can and should move from one to the other when appropriate.

To help resolve these confusions, teachers need some form of representing rational numbers that embodies the relative nature of the quantities but can also be used as a "concrete" model. Pictures have long been used to give students a feel for the magnitude of fractions. Pie charts, pictures of discrete sets of objects, and other ways of representing fractions, such as fraction strips, have been developed specifically for the purpose of communicating rational numbers in a way that is easily understood.

Any appropriate representation must build on our students' prior knowledge—their understanding of sharing, stretching and shrinking, and scaling in the real world. This requirement means that, on the one hand, the model must be concrete for the students in the sense that it is imaginable and self-explanatory, and on the other hand, the model must be as flexible as rational numbers themselves.

The Bar as a Mathematical Model

Figure 2 illustrates how we have used bar models to develop students' understanding of fractions, decimals, percents, and ratios. We generally start with the "real" objects and move down through the abstract representations as students' understanding becomes more sophisticated, but a teacher may wish to introduce the absolute representation at any appropriate time given how students are thinking or the context of the problem. We chose the context of the submarine sandwiches as our students' first formal introduction to fractions because the division into equal parts is linear, so students need to attend to one dimension only, and because the model embodies the common unit, the length. Other linear contexts are also used—graduated measuring cups, routes on a map, and so on—to make connections to the students' real-world understandings.

As students gain familiarity with cutting up sandwiches and other "linear" models, the pictures are then abstracted to a similar but *common* representation, a bar (see **fig. 2a**). But even here, the bar is used in

Difficulty	Example
Overgeneralizing properties of the natural numbers to rational numbers	1/2 + 1/2 = 2/4
Not attending to the "size" of parts	A child's drawing of 2/3: 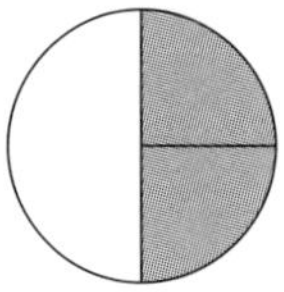
Confusing the different meanings of a fraction in different contexts, which can occur when each meaning is taught as a separate topic	3/5 can mean any of the following: *Part/whole:* Three-fifths of a submarine sandwich *Probability:* The chance of winning is 3 out of 5 (3 winning events out of 5 total events). *Part-part:* The odds of winning are 3:5 (3 winning events to 5 losing events). *Scale factor:* I only need 3/5 as much. Can you reduce it to 60 percent? *Unit of measure:* It takes 5 laps of 3/5 km to finish a 3-km race. *Number on a number line:*  0 3/5 1

**Fig. 1. Some of the difficulties children have learning
rational-number concepts**

a "natural number" way. Each submarine sandwich, or sub, is represented by a separate bar. Students can model any partitioning problem with the bar as a substitute for the real object(s) and count the number of pieces to be distributed across the whole.

The use of a picture to build up reasoning about fractions is helpful in several ways. The bar is easily divided into key "benchmark" fractions, such as 1/2, 1/3, and 1/4, by roughly estimating or measuring. In the instances of 1/2 and 1/4, the symmetry of the bar allows for the development of conceptual strategies that make use of repeated halving. The bar, then, provides a visual indicator of the relative size of these fractions, and it can easily be situated in a context that the students either understand intuitively or can readily access experientially, such as sharing submarine sandwiches or fruit tape, or measurement and distance (see Ball [1993] for a nice description of how she uses pictorial models in her teaching).

The understanding that the bar can be used to represent either context—the numerator (here, the sandwiches) or the denominator (the people)—can be a large leap for some students (see **fig. 2b**). The fraction

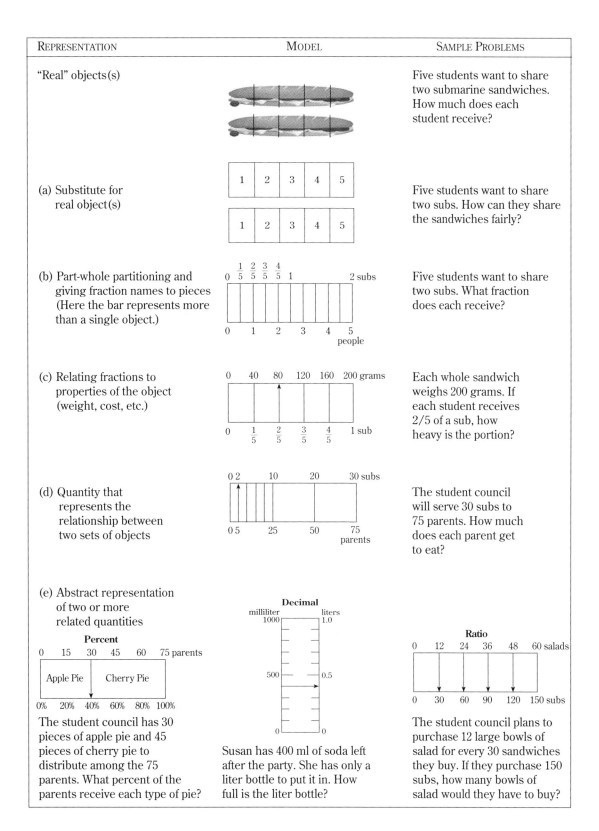

Representation	Model	Sample Problems
"Real" objects(s)		Five students want to share two submarine sandwiches. How much does each student receive?
(a) Substitute for real object(s)		Five students want to share two subs. How can they share the sandwiches fairly?
(b) Part-whole partitioning and giving fraction names to pieces (Here the bar represents more than a single object.)		Five students want to share two subs. What fraction does each receive?
(c) Relating fractions to properties of the object (weight, cost, etc.)		Each whole sandwich weighs 200 grams. If each student receives 2/5 of a sub, how heavy is the portion?
(d) Quantity that represents the relationship between two sets of objects		The student council will serve 30 subs to 75 parents. How much does each parent get to eat?
(e) Abstract representation of two or more related quantities		

(e) Abstract representation of two or more related quantities

Percent

Apple Pie | Cherry Pie

The student council has 30 pieces of apple pie and 45 pieces of cherry pie to distribute among the 75 parents. What percent of the parents receive each type of pie?

Decimal

milliliter — liters

Susan has 400 ml of soda left after the party. She has only a liter bottle to put it in. How full is the liter bottle?

Ratio

The student council plans to purchase 12 large bowls of salad for every 30 sandwiches they buy. If they purchase 150 subs, how many bowls of salad would they have to buy?

Fig. 2. Ways that bar models support students' understanding of different meanings of rational numbers

must be extracted from the number of people by a principle of fair sharing: One piece of each sub is given to each of the five people, resulting in a total of 2/5 of a sub for each. Notice that the countability of the objects is still essential so that the abstraction of the model is not too great. The leap can also be reduced by taking only one sub (see **fig. 2c**) and relating the fraction to a physical property of the context, such as the weight.

The bar can also be used to represent a quantity that may not be countable in the representation itself. In the example of sharing thirty subs among seventy-five people (**fig. 2d**), students must use proportional reasoning to divide the bar equally to discover that five people would have to share two subs among themselves. Here, the student divided the bar first into thirds, and then each third into fifths, the reduced fraction. The student can then begin to see the relationship among 30/75; 20/50; 10/25; and the lowest-terms fraction, 2/5, with the support of the model.

When extended to an abstract representation of the relationship among two or more quantities (**fig. 2e**), the fraction bar helps students connect different notions of rational numbers with a visual indication of the proportions. Because the common notations used to communicate rational numbers—fractions, decimals, percents, and ratios—arise out of the common representation, they can be seen by students as instances of the same mathematical concept. We have found this commonality to be particularly helpful in ameliorating the difficulties associated with teaching the different notations of part-whole relationships—fractions, decimals, and percents.

Such a pictorial tool permits ready access to number sense for students who are more visual thinkers, as well as acts as a flexible visualization tool for children who are more symbolic in thinking. It provides a base for developing conceptual routines for calculation and offers a quick check on the reasonableness of answers. Moreover, it is extended to the use of two-dimensional graphs in algebra, geometry, and statistics contexts.

Vignettes

Sharing submarine sandwiches

This vignette describes the strategies of fifth graders in their first experience with the bar model. It was their first formal experience with fractions in the fifth grade, although their informal knowledge of fractions was fairly detailed for the common benchmark fractions of 1/2, 1/4, and 3/4. The students, working in groups, were asked to solve the problems in the set shown in **figure 3** (van Galen et al. 1977). When the groups were finished, the teacher brought them back together to discuss their strategies. Their solutions are presented in **figure 4**.

During the whole-group session, the children devised various methods for sharing three subs fairly among six students. The solutions offered by Beth and Steve were the most common strategies, and students easily saw that three subs divided into six total pieces made portions the same size as dividing a single sub into two pieces. However, students argued about whether the fraction represented by the portion should be one-sixth or one-half. Beth's group argued that the fraction should be one-half because the subs were cut into six total pieces. Steve's group countered with, "Yeah, but Emmy only gets half of one sub!"

The teacher asked, "Who is right?"

"It depends on whether you think the 'whole' is one sub or all the subs. Beth is right if you are taking a fraction of all the subs, but Steve is right if you are talking about how much of one sandwich she gets."

Later on, Anna offered a very different strategy (see **fig. 4**). The question came up whether her solution was the same as Steve's. Darren used Anna's bar model to demonstrate that 1/3 + 1/6 = 1/2. Darren's explanation illustrates the use of the bar to develop the beginnings of proportional reasoning. Since the bars are of the same length, the "whole" is a constant value and the students needed only to rearrange the pieces to compare the different solutions.

Later, when the class moved on to the problem of sharing three subs among four students, children used similar cut-and-paste strategies to figure out whether different solutions were equivalent. The strategies of Jeff, Anna, and Tim illustrate different ways in which children used the bars to prove that three one-fourth pieces were the same as one three-fourths piece.

These strategies illustrate how pictorial models like the bar can be used as a tool for whole-group communication. The bar is valuable as a model in that it allows students to *show* different levels of solutions and supports different ways of expressing the underlying fractions.

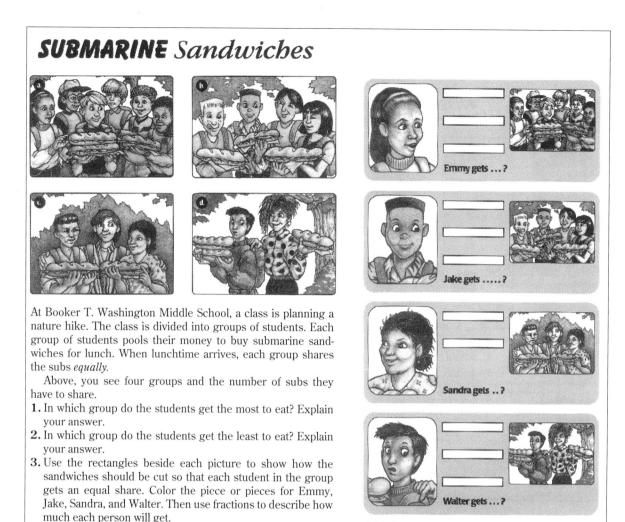

SUBMARINE *Sandwiches*

At Booker T. Washington Middle School, a class is planning a nature hike. The class is divided into groups of students. Each group of students pools their money to buy submarine sandwiches for lunch. When lunchtime arrives, each group shares the subs *equally*.

Above, you see four groups and the number of subs they have to share.

1. In which group do the students get the most to eat? Explain your answer.
2. In which group do the students get the least to eat? Explain your answer.
3. Use the rectangles beside each picture to show how the sandwiches should be cut so that each student in the group gets an equal share. Color the piece or pieces for Emmy, Jake, Sandra, and Walter. Then use fractions to describe how much each person will get.
4. Draw two other pictures of students with submarine sandwiches. Choose your own numbers for students and sandwiches. Show how the sandwiches could be shared equally. Describe with fractions how much each student will get.

Emmy gets ... ?

Jake gets ..... ?

Sandra gets .. ?

Walter gets ... ?

Fig. 3. Fractions of submarine sandwiches

After creating their own individual and small-group strategies, the students shared very different ways of thinking about the problem, and this discussion was important for the students to make a shift to a higher level of reasoning. Jeff saw the fraction as three-fourths of a single sub. Tim may also have perceived the fraction in this way. He initially quipped that not all four students would be able to get that big a portion, forgetting the three "end pieces." However, when Anna created a countable representation and dealt the pieces out, Tim and the rest of the class were able to see the connection between 3 fourths (the three pieces) and 3/4 (the continuous proportion).

Tim: They add up to one, two, that would make half, and then boom! You get three-fourths!

Determining parking-lot use

This vignette is from another fifth-grade class, which had had more experience with rational numbers. The students were accustomed to using the bar model to estimate fractions, but this activity was their first attempt to link their knowledge of fractions with the new concept, percents. The students were presented with

Student	Strategy	Bar Model
Solutions for the problem of sharing three subs among six students		
Beth	Slice all three subs into two pieces, and give half to each student.	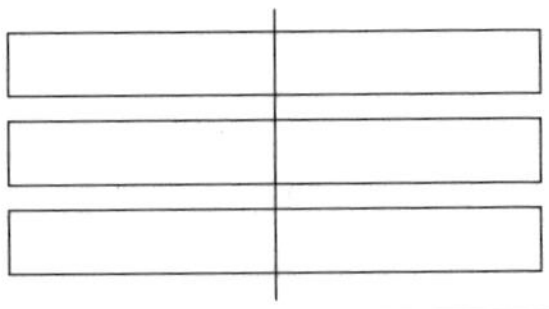
Steve	Slice one sub into two pieces, and give half to Emmy.	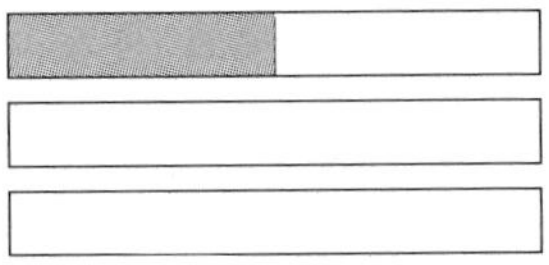
Anna	Slice all three subs into thirds, and then slice one sub into sixths (halving the thirds).	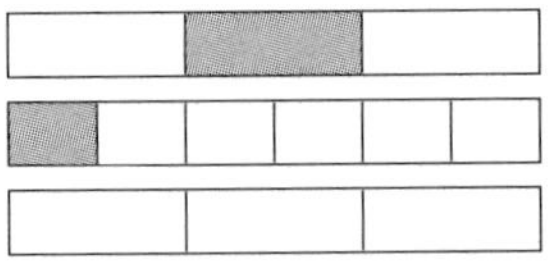
Darren	(Using Anna's solution) Physically move one-sixth of one sub next to one-third of a second sub to make three-sixths.	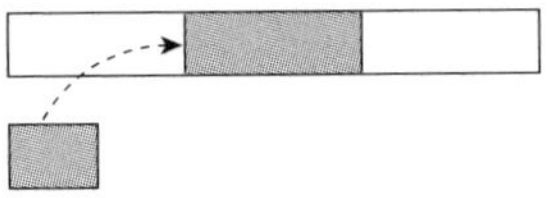
Solutions for the problem of sharing three subs among four students		
Jeff	Slice one sub into a three-fourths piece and a one-fourth piece, and give the larger piece to Jake.	
Anna	Slice all three subs into fourths, and give three one-fourth pieces to Jake. The remaining pieces are dealt out to the other students.	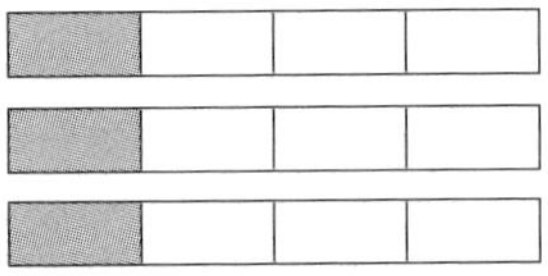
Tim	Slice the three subs into fourths, and give three one-fourth pieces to three students. The remaining pieces are put together to make the last three-fourths portion.	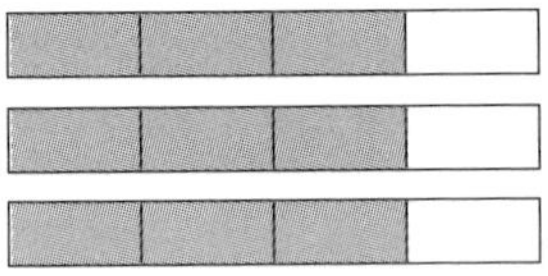

Fig. 4. Fifth graders' strategies using the bar to model part-whole fractions

the page of problems shown in **figure 5** and were working in small groups (van den Heuvel-Panhuizen et al. 1997). Their solution strategies are shown in **figure 6**.

Rae: I took 1/2 and a little bit more . . . I found 24 here [points at line on top bar], and since 40 is half of 80, this [points at 24] is half of here [points at 48 on bottom bar], so this is 48, and a little bit more is 56.

In another group, the reasoning was less visual and more computational; however, it illustrates the connections that the bar can make between computational strategies and visual models.

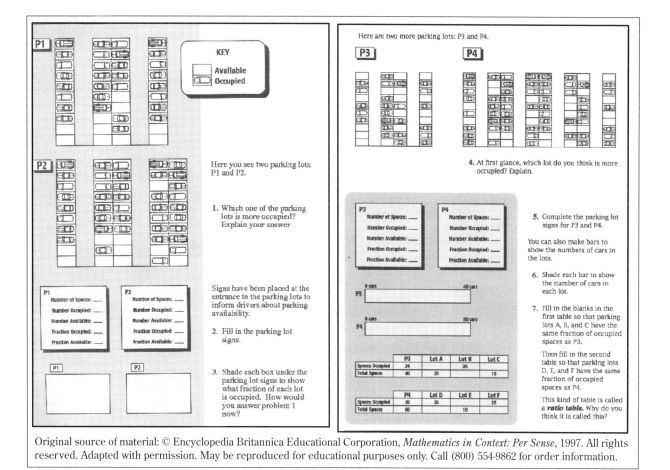

Fig. 5. Parking-lot problems

Breah: We divided the top bar into 5 equal spaces [and colored 3] and colored in 7 [in lot 4].

Cal: 3/5 = 6/10, which is smaller than 7/10, so parking lot 4 is fuller [see **fig. 7**].

Before doing this exercise, Cal thought that parking lot 3 was fuller; he was focusing on the number of free spaces in each lot (sixteen versus twenty-four) rather than the proportion of full spots. He later amended his thinking to include both arguments—that if one were looking for a space to park, the number of spaces would be sufficient to make a decision, but if one were planning to shut down a parking lot, the proportions would be more appropriate.

Notice that here, the bar has evolved from a concrete model of the objects being shared, as in the example of the submarine sandwiches, to a *relative* model that can be used to make comparisons.

As students began to use the bar as a scaling tool, they began to develop general strategies for estimation. The most common strategy that we see in fifth-grade classes is that of repeated halving. For example, the following student was asked to estimate the percent of competitors who dropped out of a half-marathon because of rain. The total number of competitors was 1603, and the number of dropouts was 91.

Student: It is a little bit less than 6 percent.

The student's drawing (**fig. 8**) is a clear example of repeated halving as a general estimation strategy. He found half of the total number of competitors, after first rounding down to 1600, and marked this position on the bar. Then he used his prior knowledge of benchmark percents and fractions, and wrote in the 50 percent to correspond with the 800 competitors. Then he found half of the 800 and marked the bar with 25 percent. Repeating this strategy, again with appropriate rounding, he finally ended up with 100 competitors, which corresponds roughly to 6 percent of the total. Since 91 is slightly less than 100, a quick guesstimate

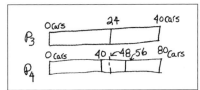

Fig. 6. A visual solution to the parking-lot problem

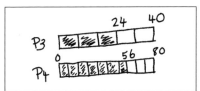

Fig. 7. A more computational solution

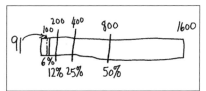

Fig. 8. Estimation using repeated halving

of "It is a little bit less than 6 percent" seems to be a very good, quick conceptual estimate of the actual 5 percent represented by the number.

Other strategies were also used. Many students, like Breah and Cal, used their prior knowledge of benchmark fractions, typically 1/2, 1/4, 3/4, 1/5, and 1/10, to divide up the bars and assign corresponding percents or ratios. Others used a combination of strategies, such as finding three-tenths, or 30 percent, and then halving to find three-twentieths, or 15 percent. The bars became flexible tools for estimation and computation.

Applications of the Bar Model

Extensions of the bar model are found in numerous real-life applications, where they often appear as "double number lines." For example, nearly any tool for converting metric units to United States customary units takes this form. A meterstick-yardstick, for example, can be read as a linear, or ratio, relationship between two measurement systems for length. Other examples are provided in **figure 9**.

Conclusion

Through pairing the fraction bars with ratio tables (Middleton and van den Heuvel-Panhuizen 1995) and other ways of teaching rational numbers, numeric strategies became connected with visual strategies, allowing students with diverse ways of thinking to share their understanding. Often, the connections among ways of representing rational numbers—among a picture, a symbol, and a manipulative activity—build understanding for children (Behr et al. 1992). The bar model is a mathematical representation for teaching rational numbers that makes these translations easier. It is an extension of many things that good teachers already use, such as fraction strips and rulers, but it can be developed to include more complex situations. Although we focus on this one method of representing ratios, we are not advocating imposing the bar on students as "the right way to think about fractions." Instead, we believe that the bar should arise naturally out of good problems that are easily pictured as a linear model, and then it can be developed as a common way for students to show their thinking to facilitate communication. The teacher may wish to provide pictures of bars for students to use, but most often, encourage them to draw the pictures themselves. As students become more familiar with the benchmark fractions, their use of the bars tends to taper off, being reserved for more difficult problems.

We have included two sample problems in **figure 10** for use with students. The first problem can deal with both fractions and ratios—using a ratio relationship to predict one quantity from the value of another, different quantity—and the second deals with reasoning backward with percents. The second problem is rather difficult for many middle-grades students without the support of a picture, but it becomes far more accessible through the use of the bar as a supporting model.

APPLICATION OF BAR MODELS IN THE REAL WORLD	MATHEMATICAL RELATIONSHIP
Bar graphs	Proportions of bars indicate their relative percent or fraction of the total number of observations.
Fill-level indicators on newer vacuum cleaners	Visual indicator of how full the dust collection chamber of a vacuum cleaner is.
Fuel gauges	Visual indicator of how full an automobile fuel tank is; can be paired with fuel capacity in liters or gallons (e.g., 1/2 full = 7 gallons).
Graduated cylinders	1 liter ≈ 1.06 quarts. 1 deciliter = 100 milliliters. 1 milliliter ≈ 0.034 fluid ounces. 355 milliliters ≈ 12 fluid ounces, the capacity of a typical can of soda.
Map scales	1 kilometer ≈ 0.625 mile (around 5 mi/8 km). Older maps also use rods as a unit of measure.
Meterstick/yardstick	1 meter ≈ 3.3 feet. 1 centimeter ≈ 0.4 inch. 1/2 meter = 50 centimeters. 15 meters ≈ 50 feet, the average height of a five-story building.
Speedometer	88 kilometers per hour ≈ 55 miles per hour, a typical highway speed limit.
Status bars on computers	Show how much of a file has been copied, often in bytes and percents.
Tire-pressure gauges	1 kilopascal (Newtons per square meter) ≈ 0.1458 pounds per square inch. 247 kilopascals ≈ 36 pounds per square inch, a typical recommended tire pressure for cars in the United States.

Fig. 9. Real-world applications of bar models

References

Ball, Deborah L. "Halves, Pieces, and Twoths: Constructing and Using Representational Contexts in Teaching Fractions." In *Rational Numbers: An Integration of Research,* edited by Thomas P. Carpenter, Elizabeth Fennema, and Thomas A. Romberg. Hillsdale, N. J.: Lawrence Erlbaum Assoc., 1993.

Behr, Merlyn J., Guershon Harel, Thomas Post, and Richard Lesh. "Rational Number, Ratio, and Proportion." In *Handbook of Research on Mathematics Teaching and Learning,* edited by Douglas A. Grouws. Reston, Va.: National Council of Teachers of Mathematics, 1992.

Marshall, Sandra P. "Assessment of Rational Number Understanding: A Schema-Based Approach." In *Rational Numbers: An Integration of Research,* edited by Thomas P. Carpenter, Elizabeth Fennema, and Thomas A. Romberg, 261–88. Hillsdale, N. J.: Lawrence Erlbaum Assoc., 1993.

Middleton, James A., and Marja van den Heuvel-Panhuizen. "The Ratio Table: Helping Students Understand Rational Number." *Mathematics Teaching in the Middle School* 1 (January–March 1995): 282–88.

National Council of Teachers of Mathematics (NCTM). *Curriculum and Evaluation Standards for School Mathematics.* Reston, Va.: NCTM, 1989.

Problems	Solutions

Problems

Problem 1

John and Margie are driving from Salt Lake City to Reno. Margie's mom tells her that it is about a 10-hour drive. Margie agrees. "Looking at the map, it seems to be about 520 miles," she says.

During the drive, John remarks, "We have driven about 7 hours. I wonder how far we still have to go."

Draw a bar that illustrates the distance from Salt Lake City to Reno. Show on the bar about where John and Margie are and how far they still have to go. Using your drawing, explain how the time and distance that John and Margie have traveled are related to each other.

Problem 2

A department store is having a clearance sale in their electronics department. The sale price of a portable CD player is shown in the price tag pictured.

According to the bar, about what percent do you think the discount was? What was the original price of the CD player?

(a)

Solutions

Problem 1: Solution 1

Here repeated halving is the primary strategy. First draw the halfway point at 5 hours and 260 miles. Then find the third quarter of the journey (7 1/2 hours and 390 miles) and move a little to the left to get an estimate of 360 miles. Subtracting this amount from 520 shows that about 160 miles are left to go.

Problem 1: Solution 2

This strategy is a bit more sophisticated. Find one-tenth of the ratio to determine how far John and Margie had traveled in one hour. Then multiply by seven to get the distance traveled in seven hours.

An alternative would be to divide in half to find the distance traveled in five hours. Find one-tenth of the bar, and double this amount to find the distance traveled in two hours (or just find one-fifth). Add this amount to the distance traveled in five hours to find the distance traveled in seven hours.

Both of these strategies yield the exact solution of 364 miles in 7 hours, with 156 miles to go.

Problem 2: Solution

This strategy involves halving the $96 to get $48, approximately one-third of the original price. Adding the $48 to the $96 approximates the original price of $144.

To estimate the percent of the discount, two methods are common. The first visually recognizes that the sale price is about two-thirds of the total. Most students then either remember that one-third is a little more than 33 percent and estimate that double this amount is about 67 percent, or they divide the 100 percent into thirds and add two of the thirds. The second method we have seen to estimate the percent also involves repeated halving. Students first make a mark for 50 percent and another for 75 percent. Then they make an "eyeball" estimate of about 70 percent, or they keep on halving (e.g., find 62.5 percent, then 69 percent, etc.) until they think that their estimate is close enough to the mark for the sale price.

(b)

Fig. 10. Sample problems (a) and solutions (b)

Ohlsson, Stellan. "Mathematical Meaning and Applicational Meaning in the Semantics of Fractions and Related Concepts." In *Number Concepts and Operations in the Middle Grades,* edited by James Hiebert and Merlyn Behr. Reston, Va.: National Council of Teachers of Mathematics; Hillsdale, N. J.: Lawrence Erlbaum Assoc., 1988.

Streefland, Leen. "Fractions: A Realistic Approach." In *Rational Numbers: An Integration of Research,* edited by Thomas P. Carpenter, Elizabeth Fennema, and Thomas A. Romberg, 289–325. Hillsdale, N. J.: Lawrence Erlbaum Assoc., 1993.

van den Heuvel-Panhuizen, Marja, Leen Streefland, Margaret R. Meyer, James A. Middleton, and James Browne. "Per Sense." In *Mathematics in Context: A Connected Curriculum for Grades 5–8,* edited by National Center for Research in Mathematical Sciences Education and Freudenthal Institute. Chicago: Encyclopaedia Britannica Educational Corp., 1997.

van Galen, Frans, Monica Wijers, Beth R. Cole, and Julia A. Shew. "Some of the Parts." In *Mathematics in Context: A Connected Curriculum for Grades 5–8,* edited by National Center for Research in Mathematical Sciences Education and Freudenthal Institute. Chicago: Encyclopaedia Britannica Educational Corp., 1997.

Multiplication with Fractions: A Piagetian, Constructivist Approach

Mary Ann Warrington and Constance Kamii

On the basis of Piaget's (1954, 1960) constructivism, Kamii (1989, 1994) has demonstrated that children in the primary grades can invent their own procedures for solving multidigit problems with whole numbers. A significant finding of this research is that when children are not taught algorithms, such as those of "carrying" and "borrowing," their number sense and knowledge of place value are far superior to those of students who have been taught these rules. Warrington (1997) extended this work to the fifth- and sixth-grade level and described an approach to "teaching" division with fractions without teaching the algorithm of "invert and multiply." This article describes a constructivist approach to multiplication with fractions.

In a constructivist class, the teacher does not tell children how to solve any problem but, instead, presents problems and encourages children to invent their own ways of solving them. When the children give answers, the teacher tries not to say that the answer is correct or incorrect. Instead, she or he encourages children to agree or disagree with one another and to exchange ideas until agreement is reached about what makes sense. This approach is radically different from traditional instruction in which the teacher is the one who always knows the answer. In a constructivist classroom, the children are empowered by the knowledge that the answers lie within them. They share strategies and solutions, debate with one another, and think critically about the best way to solve each problem.

Warrington was the teacher of a self-contained, fifth- and sixth-grade, multiage, mixed-ability class in an independent school near Boston. Prior to entering her class, the children had been exposed to a variety of teaching practices in mathematics. Some had been taught algorithms, some had invented their own procedures for two years, and some had worked extensively with manipulatives. The culture of the classroom as well as that of the school was one that valued the process of learning, and the children were accustomed to exchanging ideas.

The following description of Warrington's teaching and of her students' responses is written in the first person to communicate what she observed and how she made her decisions. We begin with the questions she posed concerning half of whole numbers and of fractions. We then proceed to questions about a third of whole numbers and of fractions and go on to more complicated problems involving nonunit fractions and mixed numbers.

Half of Whole Numbers and of Fractions

Children construct new knowledge out of what they already know. Therefore, when I introduce a new topic, I begin with the familiar and move forward. Knowing that *half* is the easiest fraction, I began the discussion with the following problem that asked for half of a whole number:

> If Willy had 15 ounces of orange juice in his Thermos, and he drank half of it during lunch, how many ounces of juice did he drink during lunch?

All the students quickly answered this question, and I proceeded to the next one:

> If Willy had drunk one-fourth of 15 ounces during lunch, how much juice would he have drunk?

The children responded rather easily that "cutting" the previous answer "in half" would give the answer of 3 3/4.

I went on to the next problem involving two fractions, which would usually be solved with multiplication:

> If you had half of an apple pie and you ate half of it, how much pie did you eat?

Many students immediately drew pictures, such as the one in **figure 1a**, but a few replied, "You ate a half." This statement brought a dissenting opinion from someone who explained, "You ate half of a half. You only had half of a pie to begin with; so when you ate half of it, you had a fourth left. So you ate one-fourth." The class agreed that this explanation made sense, and I went on to similar problems involving half of the one-fourth that was left over, and then half of the one-eighth that was later left over. Many children drew the kinds of pictures that can be seen in **figures 1b** and **1c**.

I then proceeded to nonunit fractions by asking the following question:

What is half of 3/4?

Three ways were found to solve this problem. The first child called on drew a picture like **figure 2a** and explained, "Three-fourths is the same as 1/4 + 1/4 + 1/4. So I took half of 1/4, which is 1/8, and three times that is 3/8." The next child also broke 3/4 down but thought about it as 1/2 and 1/4 (see **fig. 2b**). He figured out that half of a half is 1/4, which he knew is the same as 2/8. After getting half of 1/4 equals 1/8, he added this amount to 2/8 and got the final answer of 3/8. The third explanation came from a student who decided to "change 3/4 to 6/8 and take half of 6/8, which is 3/8." I was especially impressed with the

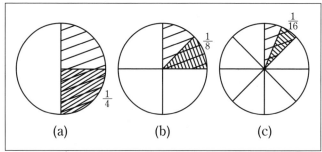

Fig. 1. Students' drawings of (a) half of 1/2, (b) half of 1/4, and (c) half of 1/8

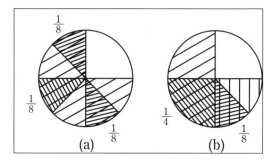

Fig. 2. Two ways of thinking about half of 3/4

ease and efficiency of this third method, and everybody agreed that all three methods made sense. The children's ease can be explained by the fact that they were already good at making equivalent fractions in dealing with addition and subtraction problems.

I decided next to introduce problems involving thirds, sixths, and ninths, which I knew to be more difficult than halves, fourths, and eighths.

A Third of Whole Numbers and of Fractions

As usual, I began with whole numbers, which were easy for the entire class:

If you had 3 pencils and 1/3 of them were blue, how many blue pencils would you have?

Since this problem was handled with ease, I decided to throw in a nonunit fraction in the next problem:

2/3 of 3

The method for solving this problem was simply to take 1/3 of 3 and to double the answer.

The next question I wrote on the chalkboard was the following:

1/3 of 9

The correct answer of 3 came quickly, and I posed the next problem:

1/3 of 1

The responses did not come immediately this time, and many children drew a pie and split it into three parts. A tentative 1/3 was called out, and everybody agreed after all that this response was correct.

I wrote the next problem:

1/3 of 1/3

No immediate responses were forthcoming, and so, as usual, I asked the children to estimate the answer. When an answer is not obvious, I always ask the children to estimate before attempting to get an exact answer. The estimates given were 1/9 and "less than 1/6." The explanation of the child who gave the second estimate was "I'm not sure what the answer is, but I know that it is less than 1/6 because half of 1/3 is 1/6, and 1/3 is smaller than a half; so you're taking even less of the third." Despite the fact that this child did not get beyond an estimate, her reasoning was excellent—something that rarely happens in a traditional classroom in which students merely multiply the numerators and denominators. The child who claimed that the answer was 1/9 reasoned that "If you had 1/3 of something and you took 1/3 of it (see **fig. 3**), you break the 1/3 into 3 parts, and each would be 1/9."

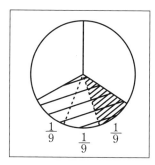

Fig. 3. Thinking about one-third of 1/3

More Complicated Problems with Nonunit Fractions and Mixed Numbers

After a few days of working through several more problems that would usually be solved by multiplying fractions, I presented the class with the following question:

> Michael walked 6 5/8 miles to help raise money for a charitable cause. Ariel walked 1/3 the distance that Michael walked. Shanon walked twice as far as Ariel. How far did Shanon walk?

I began by listing the following estimates that the children offered: 4 1/2, 2 1/3, 4 2/3, and "between 4 and 5." The students proceeded to exact computation, and I later listed on the chalkboard the different answers they got: 4 10/24, 4 5/12, and 4 5/24.

When I asked for an explanation of the first answer, the student responded with, "Well, Michael walked 6 5/8 miles, and Ariel walked only 1/3 of that; so first I took 1/3 of 6, which is 2, and then I took 1/3 of 1/8, which is 1/24." I interrupted here and asked her to explain how she knew that. As she drew a picture like the one in **figure 4**, she explained, "If you had only 1/8 of a pie and you take 1/3 of it, you're breaking that small piece into 3 parts, and if you did that to each piece of the pie, there would be 24 pieces; so 1/3 of 1/8 is 1/24." Her peers and I were all satisfied with this explanation, and she continued with, "If 1/3 of 1/8 is 1/24, then 1/3 of 5/8 would be 5/24."

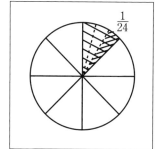

Fig. 4. Thinking about one-third of 1/8

Another child interrupted at this point and asked why this outcome was so. The child at the chalkboard first asked, "Do you understand why 1/3 of 1/8 is 1/24? [A nod indicated yes.] Well, 1/3 of 5/8 is 5/24 because if you take 1/3 of 1/8 for five of those pieces of the pie, you would have 5/24." She continued, "Ariel walked 2 5/24 miles, and Shanon walked twice as far; so you double 2 5/24, and you get 4 10/24, which is the same as 4 5/12." This student had initially not reduced her answer but now made the relationship between her answer and another one that was on the chalkboard. At this point, the student who had given the answer 4 5/24 announced that he wanted to change his answer because "I forgot to double the fraction part."

The children continued to tackle other similar problems in similar ways, and I marveled at their ability to invent their own logical ways of solving complex problems. A few days later, I decided to give the following problem to the class:

> Tobin went apple picking and later baked 4 apple pies. He ate 1/5 of one of the pies and put the remaining pies on his back porch to cool. His sister and her friends came along and ate 1/2 of the pies on the porch. How much pie was left on the porch?

The students were used to estimating and promptly gave the estimates of 2, 1 5/10, and "between 1 1/2 and 2." They then set out to find the exact answer. Many children drew pictures, such as **figure 5**, and one child's answer of 1 9/10 was justified in the following way: "First I took 1/5 away from 4 because Tobin ate 1/5 of a pie; so there were 3 and 4/5 left on the porch. His sister ate half of these; so I took half of 3, which is 1 1/2,

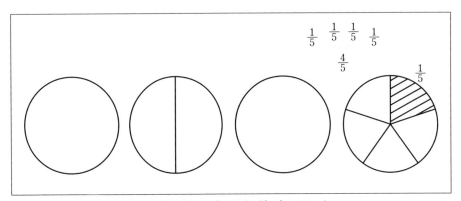

Fig. 5. Thinking about half of 3 4/5 pies

and half of 4/5, which is 2/5. Then I had to add 1 1/2 and 2/5. I changed 2/5 to 4/10 and [changed] 1/2 to 5/10. Four-tenths plus 5/10 is 9/10; so the answer is 1 and 9/10."

When I asked if anyone had solved the problem differently, the following procedure was offered: "I started doing it that way [like the previous student], but I didn't want to find half of 3 4/5; so I figured it was close to 4; so I rounded the 3 4/5 up to 4, and I took half of 4, which is 2. But then there was the 1/5 that Tobin ate; so I took half of that, which is 1/10. I subtracted the 1/10 from 2 and got 1 9/10 pies left over." This solution especially impressed me. Children who are encouraged to think for themselves are not limited by algorithms. Answers to problems lie within them, and my respect for their resourcefulness continues to increase.

A week later, I gave the following problem to the class:

> A half of a pound of jelly beans was in a container. Georgia and Emma ate 2/3 of the jelly beans in the container. How much did they eat?

By now, the entire class could estimate the answer as somewhere between 1/2 and 1/3, often by drawing pictures, such as **figure 6**. When they calculated the exact answer, they used three different strategies. The first one was invented by a child who began by taking 1/3 of 1/2, which she said was 1/6 because "1/3 of 1 equals 1/3; so 1/3 of 1/2 is half of that." She then doubled the 1/6 and got 2/6 equals 1/3. The second child who shared his thinking took 2/3 of 1 (equaling 2/3), and by halving 2/3, he got the same answer of 1/3.

The third strategy shared was characteristic of the brilliant efficiency that one can find in a constructivist classroom. The student realized that she had to find 2/3 of 1/2; so she solved 1/2 of 2/3 and immediately got the answer. Many of her classmates were stunned and impressed with the ease of solving the problem this way, but others were skeptical and asked, "Can you do that?" She said, "Yes, it's the same thing because if you take 1/2 of 12, you get 6; and if you take 12 one-halves, you still get 6." Most of the students were convinced that this explanation was reasonable, but a few continued to feel the need to test it by trying it out on other numbers. As a teacher, I was delighted with the exchange of ideas that took place as a result of this problem and the learning that it fostered. But beyond this pleasure, I was fascinated that a student had independently constructed the commutative property of multiplication with fractions, without any formal instruction on multiplication with fractions. This incident was the first time that I thought about the usefulness of this property with respect to solving problems.

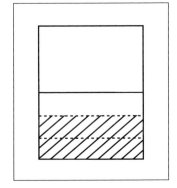

Fig. 6. Thinking about two-thirds of 1/2

Conclusion

The reader must have noticed that none of our students invented anything like the algorithm that is found in textbooks. In fact, the preceding problems were not even presented as multiplication problems. When children later encounter a written form, such as "1/2 × 4/5," the teacher tries to encourage them to relate this form to what they have been doing. So she writes

$$1/2 \times 1$$

on the chalkboard and asks, "What do you think this means?" The usual response is that it means "1/2 one time (equaling 1/2)." Next she writes the following on the chalkboard, asking the class what it means:

$$1/2 \times 2$$

The students typically say that it means "1/2 two times (equaling 1)." The teacher then writes

$$1/2 \text{ of } 2$$

which is familiar and easy (equaling 1). She may then ask what this expression means:

$$1/2 \times 1/2$$

This one is harder, but someone is likely to say that it means "1/2 half a time (equaling 1/4)." The teacher then writes

$$1/2 \text{ of } 1/2$$

which is familiar (equaling 1/4). If the students are in agreement up to this point, she goes on to write pairs of problems on the chalkboard, such as

$$1/2 \times 2/3 \text{ and } 1/2 \text{ of } 2/3,$$
$$1/2 \times 4/5 \text{ and } 1/2 \text{ of } 4/5.$$

The children soon conclude that the pairs must mean the same thing not only because they always result in the same answers but also because if $1 \times 4/5$ equals 4/5, $1/2 \times 4/5$ has to be 2/5. Therefore, "1/2 × 4/5" has to mean "half of 4/5." Likewise, if $1 \times 3/9$ equals 3/9, $1/3 \times 3/9$ has to be 1/9. Therefore, "1/3 × 3/9" has to mean "a third of 3/9."

By telling children that "of means to multiply," we impose an arbitrary definition that makes no sense to them. By giving them the algorithm of multiplying the numerators and the denominators, we impose a rule that does not make sense to students. The children in Warrington's class could simply look at 4/5 and know that half of it was 2/5.

Speaking of algorithms, Mack (1990) stated that children's knowledge of algorithms is often faulty and frequently interferes with their thinking in two ways: "(1) [k]nowledge of procedures often kept students from drawing on their informal knowledge of fractions even for problems presented in the context of real-world situations" (p. 27) and (2) "students often trusted answers obtained by applying faulty procedures more than those obtained by drawing on [their own] informal knowledge" (p. 27).

Traditional instruction is based on the outdated assumption that children must internalize in ready-made form the results of centuries of construction by adult mathematicians. Children will go much further, with depth, pleasure, and confidence, if they are allowed to construct their own mathematics that makes sense to them every step of the way.

References

Kamii, Constance. *Young Children Continue to Reinvent Arithmetic, 2nd Grade.* New York: Teachers College Press, 1989.

———. *Young Children Continue to Reinvent Arithmetic, 3rd Grade.* New York: Teachers College Press, 1994.

Mack, Nancy K. "Learning Fractions with Understanding: Building on Informal Knowledge." *Journal for Research in Mathematics Education* 21(January 1990): 16–32.

Piaget, Jean. *The Construction of Reality in the Child.* New York: Basic Books, 1954.

———. "Problèmes de la Construction du Nombre." In *Problèmes de la Construction du Nombre,* edited by Pierre Gréco, Jean-Blaise Grize, Seymour Papert, and Jean Piaget. Paris: Presses Universitaires de France, 1960.

Warrington, Mary Ann. "How Children Think about Division of Fractions." *Mathematics Teaching in the Middle School* 2 (May 1997): 390–94.

Measurement and Fair-Sharing Models for Dividing Fractions

Jeff Gregg and Diana Underwood Gregg

Van de Walle (2007) describes dividing one fraction by another in this way: "Invert the divisor and multiply is probably one of the most mysterious rules in elementary mathematics" (p. 326). Tirosh (2000) concurs and cites research suggesting that "division of fractions is often considered the most mechanical and least understood topic in elementary school" (p. 6) and that students' performance on tasks involving division of fractions is typically very poor. These claims are reflected in the difficulties that college students experience in courses for mathematics for elementary teachers when they try to explain why the invert-and-multiply algorithm works. See the following problem.

> A new machine can polish 1/2 of the floors in 3/4 of an hour. What fraction of the floors can be polished per hour?

When solving such a problem, we often find that a student will write

$$\frac{1}{2} \times \frac{4}{3} = \frac{4}{6} = \frac{2}{3}.$$

When asked why this procedure works, he or she usually explains, "Well, it's really 1/2 ÷ 3/4, but I flipped the second fraction and then multiplied." When pressed to explain why it is possible to "flip the second fraction and multiply" to obtain the answer to 1/2 ÷ 3/4, the student usually responds, "Because it's a division problem."

One goal in our mathematics courses for elementary teachers is for students to develop a conceptual understanding of the standard algorithms for adding, subtracting, multiplying, and dividing whole numbers, fractions, and decimals. These courses are taught using an "inquiry approach." Class sessions are devoted to small-group work on challenging tasks intended to promote mathematical discussion among peers, followed by whole-class discussions of students' thinking about the tasks. Our role as instructors is to guide these discussions by introducing conventional terminology, symbols, and notation by posing "What if?" questions and counterexamples; by asking students to think about what they have done, about how others have done it, and about how they could have done it differently; and by asking them to consider why what they have done has or has not worked. With regard to helping students understand division of fractions, the challenge has been to develop sequences of activities that will help students (a) appropriately interpret situations that could involve division of fractions, and (b) make sense of algorithmic procedures for dividing fractions.

Using discussions and sample problems in van de Walle (2007) and Fosnot and Dolk (2002) as our starting point, we developed a sequence of activities for what van de Walle calls the "common-denominator algorithm" and a sequence of activities for the "invert-and-multiply algorithm." As van de Walle points out, these two algorithms are related to the two different interpretations of division—measurement and fair sharing. We highlight these interpretations with students when discussing whole-number division. Recall that in the measurement model of division, we know the size of each group and must find the number of groups of that size that can be made from the dividend. A problem that fits this model is the following:

> Ms. Wright has 28 students in her class. She wants to divide them into groups, with 4 students in each group. How many groups will she have?

In other words, "How many 4s are in 28?" In contrast, in the fair-sharing (or partitive) model of division, we know the number of groups to be formed and must determine the size of each group. A problem that fits this model would be this:

> Ms. Wright has 28 students in her class. She wants to divide them into 4 groups. How many students will be in each group?

In the remainder of this article, we will describe the two fraction division sequences we have developed, relate them to the two interpretations of division, and explain the rationale behind them.

The Common-Denominator Algorithm Sequence

We begin this sequence by introducing the idea of serving sizes using the nutrition facts label from the sides of various containers, noting that the serving size is not always a whole number (e.g., the serving size may be 1 1/2 cookies). The first set of problems that we present in the serving-size context is shown in **figure 1**. We explain in problem 2, for instance, that students should express any leftover cookies in terms of the fraction of a serving that they comprise. Students usually do not find this task to be too difficult for problems such as 2, but it becomes decidedly more challenging in problems such as 6 and 7. A typical solution for problem 6 is shown in **figure 2**. Students take one 3/4 serving from each cookie and then three more 1/4 pieces to make a sixth serving. They are left with two 1/4-cookie pieces. The dilemma is how to express the leftover amount. Many students initially say the answer is 6 1/2, which almost always leads to a rich discussion about the units to which the 6 and the 1/2 refer (cf. Perlwitz 2005). It is incorrect to say 6 1/2 servings, but many students struggle initially with viewing the two leftover pieces as 2/3 of a serving.

Note that these problems fit with the measurement interpretation of division because they are asking, "How many 1/2s are in 5?" and "How many 3/4s are in 5?" and so on. We continue working with problems in which both the serving size and the amount given are fractions (see **fig. 3**). We then move to a page of similar problems that contain no illustrations. Students are permitted to use drawings to help them solve the problems, but to move toward a computational algorithm for solving these problems, we encourage them to try to solve the problems without using drawings. The first three problems on this page are the following:

1. A serving is 3 cookies. How many servings can I make from 7 cookies?

2. A serving is 3/8 cookie. How many servings can I make from 7/8 cookie?

3. A serving is 3/11 cookie. How many servings can I make from 7/11 cookie?

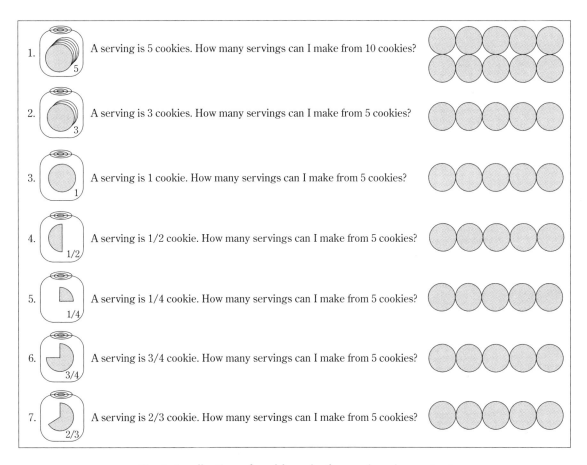

Fig. 1. A collection of problems in the serving-size context

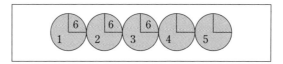

Fig. 2. A typical solution to problem 6 from figure 1

Fig. 3. Problems in which the serving size and the amount given are fractions

This sequence is intended to help students realize that as long as the serving size and the given amount are expressed in the same-sized pieces (e.g., whole cookies, eighth of a cookie, eleventh of a cookie), then the size of the pieces (as expressed by the denominator) is irrelevant. In each case, a serving consists of 3 things of a certain size, and we have 7 things of that same certain size, so how many servings can we make?

At this point, we have not discussed with students that these items may be viewed as division problems, so we present one more page of problems without illustrations. The first five problems on this page are the following:

   1. A serving size is 6 cookies. How many servings can I make from 30 cookies?

   2. A serving size is 7 cookies. How many servings can I make from 30 cookies?

   3. A serving size is 1/2 cookie. How many servings can I make from 30 cookies?

4. A serving size is 1/4 cookie. How many servings can I make from 30 cookies?

5. A serving size is 1/2 cookie. How many servings can I make from 3/4 cookie?

After discussing students' solutions to these problems, we ask, "How can we view these problems as division problems? Can you write a division number sentence for each of these problems?" Students have little difficulty writing the number sentences 30 ÷ 6 and 30 ÷ 7, respectively, for the first two problems. For problem 3, many students figure out that the answer is 60 and many write the number sentence 30 ÷ 1/2, but some students think 30 ÷ 1/2 should be 15. At this point, we discuss the measurement interpretation of division: How many 7s are in 30? How many 1/2s are in 30? (as opposed to how many 2s are in 30?) and so on. Students are then able to interpret problem 5 as being 3/4 ÷ 1/2, or how many 1/2s are in 3/4? We also discuss the idea that the question asked in problem 5 is exactly the same as that asked in problem 1. The only difference is the size of a serving and the amount of cookies we have from which to make servings.

Next we return to a discussion of the units associated with the answer to a problem such as 3/4 ÷ 1/2. Students have little difficulty with the cookie/serving-size context since they have previously used diagrams (as shown in **fig. 4**) to solve such problems. But what about the number sentence 3/4 ÷ 1/2 = 1 1/2? To what does the 1 1/2 refer? The students' drawings and the measurement interpretation of division are helpful when exploring this issue. If the question is "How many 1/2s are in 3/4?" then the answer, 1 1/2, must mean that there are one and a half 1/2s in 3/4. **Figure 4** illustrates this solution if we replace "1 serving" by "1/2 serving." We discuss with our preservice teachers the subtle yet significant challenge that students face in making sense of 3/4 ÷ 1/2 = 1 1/2 in a measurement context: The dividend and the divisor refer to the same-sized unit (e.g., 3/4 of a cookie, 1/2 of a cookie), but the quotient refers to a unit that is the size of the divisor (e.g., 1 1/2 *half* cookies).

We are ready to move toward the common-denominator algorithm for dividing fractions and present the problems shown in **figure 5**. Tim is a pseudonym for an eighth-grade student who constructed this method as he participated in a series of lessons taught by one of the authors. We extend Tim's strategy notationally by writing the following:

$$\frac{3}{4} \div \frac{1}{3} = \frac{9}{12} \div \frac{4}{12} = 9 \div 4 = 2\frac{1}{4}$$

We relate this to the previously discussed idea that if both the serving size and the given amount are expressed in the same-sized pieces, then the denominator is irrelevant. One must focus on the number of pieces in the serving size and the given amount (i.e., the numerator). We also relate the process of getting a common denominator in this algorithm to the need, when solving the problem pictorially, to cut the representations of both the dividend and the divisor into pieces that are the same size (see **fig. 4**). Note that this algorithm is essentially the same as that invented by a seventh grader whom Perlwitz (2004) interviewed. In fact, in many of our classes, the "Tim's Method" page (see **fig. 5**) is not needed because several students have already invented a comparable strategy by the time we reach this point in the sequence.

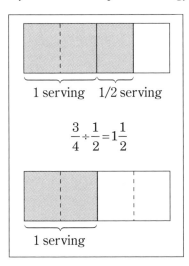

1 serving   1/2 serving

$$\frac{3}{4} \div \frac{1}{2} = 1\frac{1}{2}$$

1 serving

Fig. 4. There are one and a half 1/2s in 3/4.

Tim devised the following method for figuring out the "How many servings?" problems.

Tim said: To figure out a problem like *My serving size is 1/3 cookie. How many servings can I make from 3/4 cookie?* you can first figure out a common denominator for these numbers. By making the 1/3 = 4/12 and the 3/4 = 9/12, the problem is much easier to solve. From the 9/12 I can get 2 whole servings of 4/12 and have 1/12 leftover. The 1/12 that is leftover is 1/4 of a serving, so my answer is 2 1/4. This works with all division with fraction problems.

Do you think Tim's method is valid? Test Tim's method on the tasks below. Then explain why you think this method works with division of fraction problems or why it does not work.

a. 5/8 ÷ 1/2   b. 2 1/4 ÷ 3/8   c. 3/8 ÷ 1/2   d. 9/8 ÷ 2/3

Fig. 5. Tim's method

The Invert-and-Multiply Algorithm Sequence

After applying the measurement interpretation of division to make sense of division of fractions situations, we ask our students if we could apply the fair-sharing interpretation of division to division of fractions. They initially respond no. If one starts by considering a division sentence such as 3/4 ÷ 2/3, it is not clear how such an interpretation might apply. We want to divide 3/4 of a cake equally among 2/3 of a group. What does that mean? We take a similar approach in designing this sequence as in the common-denominator algorithm sequence, that is, we start with situations involving whole numbers and work our way toward those involving fractions.

In particular, we start with problems involving whole-number divisors and unit-fraction dividends followed by whole-number divisors and non-unit-fraction dividends. The following is a typical initial sequence:

1. I have 1/3 of a whole cake. I want to divide it equally into 3 containers. How much cake will be in each container?

2. I have 1/3 of a whole cake. I want to divide it equally into 4 containers. How much cake will be in each container?

3. I have 1/3 of a whole cake. I want to divide it equally into 8 containers. How much cake will be in each container?

4. I have 2/3 of a whole cake. I want to divide it equally into 2 containers. How much cake will be in each container?

5. I have 2/3 of a whole cake. I want to divide it equally into 3 containers. How much cake will be in each container?

6. I have 3/4 of a whole cake. I want to divide it equally into 2 containers. How much cake will be in each container?

Students often use diagrams to help solve these problems. A typical solution for problem 5 is shown in **figure 6**. Students begin by drawing a cake and shading 2/3. Then they cut the 2/3 into three equal parts (represented by the horizontal dashed lines) and determine what fraction of a whole cake each of the three equal parts comprises.

Some students develop nonpictorial strategies for problem 6:

$$\frac{3}{4} = \frac{6}{8} = \frac{3}{8} + \frac{3}{8}$$

This equation shows that each container holds 3/8 of a whole cake. As we discuss students' solutions to these problems, we ask, "What division number sentence could we write for this problem?" Few students have difficulty interpreting these problems as 2/3 ÷ 3, 3/4 ÷ 2, and so on. We discuss that we are now using the fair-sharing interpretation of division, since we are distributing (sharing) a certain amount of cake among some number of containers and want to know how much cake will be in one container.

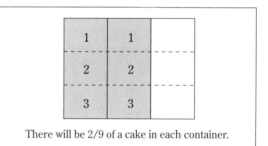

There will be 2/9 of a cake in each container.

Fig. 6. I have 2/3 of a whole cake. I want to divide it equally into 3 containers. How much cake will be in each container?

Next we move to problems with unit-fraction divisors:

1. I have 1/3 of a whole cake. It fills up exactly 1/2 of my container. How much cake will fit in 1 whole container?

2. I have 1/3 of a whole cake. It fills up exactly 1/4 of my container. How much cake will fit in 1 whole container?

3. I have 3/4 of a whole cake. It fills up exactly 1/2 of my container. How much cake will fit in 1 whole container?

For these problems, many students apply a repeated-addition or multiplicative strategy: If 3/4 of a cake fills up 1/2 of the container, then the whole container must hold 3/4 + 3/4 = 2 × 3/4 = 1 1/2 cakes. Although these problems are not difficult for students, the key discussion point is to connect the problems to division and to the problems with whole-number divisors discussed previously. What would be an appropriate division number sentence for problem 3 above? Much as we did in the common-denominator algorithm sequence, we ask students to compare problems with whole-number divisors to problems with fractional divisors. For example, consider the following:

1. I have 3/4 of a whole cake. I want to divide it equally into 2 containers. How much will be in each container?
2. I have 3/4 of a whole cake. It fills up exactly 1/2 of my container. How much cake will fit in 1 whole container?

In both cases, there is an amount of cake that fits into a certain space, and the problem is to determine how much *1 container* will hold. If the first problem is 3/4 ÷ 2, then the second one must be 3/4 ÷ 1/2. Note the ratio aspect:

$$\frac{3/4 \text{ cake}}{2 \text{ containers}} = \frac{\text{how much cake}}{1 \text{ container}}$$

and

$$\frac{3/4 \text{ cake}}{1/2 \text{ container}} = \frac{\text{how much cake}}{1 \text{ container}}$$

We conclude the sequence by moving to cake problems with non-unit-fraction divisors, first using a whole-number, then a unit-fraction, and finally a non-unit-fraction amount of cake:

1. I have 3 whole cakes. They fill up exactly 2/3 of my container.
   a. How much cake will fit in 1/3 of my container?
   b. How much cake will fit in 1 whole container?
2. I have 1/2 of a cake. It fills up exactly 3/4 of my container.
   a. How much cake will fit in 1/4 of the container?
   b. How much cake will fit in 1 whole container?
3. I have 3/4 of a cake. It fills up exactly 2/3 of my container.
   a. How much cake will fit in 1/3 of the container?
   b. How much cake will fit in 1 whole container?

A pictorial solution for problem 3 is shown in **figure 7**. Each question is broken into 2 parts in an effort to foster solution strategies that can be related to the invert-and-multiply algorithm. For example, to find how much cake will fit in 1/3 of a container in problem 3, we can divide 3/4 by 2. Knowing how much fits in 1/3 of a container, we can then multiply by 3 to determine how much 1 container holds. We describe this process notationally as

$$\frac{3}{4} \div \frac{2}{3} = \left(\frac{3}{4} \div 2\right) \times 3.$$

However, when dividing some amount into 2 equal parts (recall that we are using the fair-sharing interpretation of division), each of those 2 parts is 1/2 of the total amount. So dividing by 2 is the same as multiplying by 1/2 (3/4 is *two*-thirds; 1/2 of that amount will be *one*-third). We write

$$\frac{3}{4} \div \frac{2}{3} = \left(\frac{3}{4} \div 2\right) \times 3 = \left(\frac{3}{4} \times \frac{1}{2}\right) \times 3 = \frac{3}{4} \times \frac{3}{2}.$$

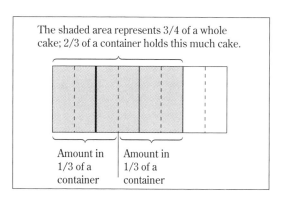

The shaded area represents 3/4 of a whole cake; 2/3 of a container holds this much cake.

Amount in 1/3 of a container | Amount in 1/3 of a container

Fig. 7. If 1/3 of the container holds 3/8 of a cake, 1 container holds 3/8 + 3/8 + 3/8 = 3 × 3/8 = 9/8 = 1 1/8 cakes.

Similarly, if 2/5 of a cake fills 3/4 of a container, and we wanted to know how much 1 container would hold, we could divide 2/5 by 3 to find how much fits in 1/4 of a container and then multiply by 4. We would write

$$\frac{2}{5} \div \frac{3}{4} = \left(\frac{2}{5} \div 3\right) \times 4 = \left(\frac{2}{5} \times \frac{1}{3}\right) \times 4 = \frac{2}{5} \times \frac{4}{3}.$$

Conclusion

We have used the two sequences of problems described here with preservice teachers in both methods and mathematics content courses, and one of the authors has used them in conjunction with the class-room teacher in both a sixth-grade and an eighth-grade class. For both groups, the common-denominator algorithm stemming from the measurement interpretation of division seemed more accessible in terms of students being able to construct the algorithm with a conceptual grounding. Flores, Turner, and Bachmann (2005) describe two teachers who "made the connection between [their] previous understanding of division of fractions in terms of measurement and the standard rule of multiplying by the inverse" (p. 118). However, these teachers simply noted that the result obtained by dividing the numerators in the common-denominator algorithm was the same as that obtained when multiplying the dividend by the inverse of the divisor in the invert-and-multiply algorithm. They did not explain why the invert-and-multiply rule works. Thus, we believe that some sort of invert-and-multiply algorithm sequence of problems is needed.

We interspersed the cake problems in our invert-and-multiply sequence with problems like this:

2/5 of a room can be painted in 3/4 of an hour. How much can be painted in 1 hour?

These problems engendered more ratio interpretations on the part of students. In other words, students reasoned as follows:

$$\frac{\frac{2}{5} \text{ room}}{\frac{3}{4} \text{ hour}} = \frac{? \text{ room}}{1 \text{ hour}}$$

We had done considerable work with ratio tables in which students generated equivalent ratios. So the students could reason that to get from 3/4 hour to 1 hour they would need to multiply by 4/3. (To our delight, one student explained that you would need to multiply by 1 1/3 because in 1 hour there is one 3/4 hour and 1/3 of another 3/4 hour.) To keep the ratio the same, the 2/5 must also be multiplied by 4/3. This gives

$$\frac{\frac{2}{5}}{\frac{3}{4}} = \frac{\frac{2}{5} \times \frac{4}{3}}{\frac{3}{4} \times \frac{4}{3}} = \frac{\frac{2}{5} \times \frac{4}{3}}{1} = \frac{2}{5} \times \frac{4}{3}.$$

Thus, the painting problems resulted in what Tirosh (2000) calls a formal argument for fraction division, one that uses ratios, fraction multiplication, and the principle that the product of reciprocals is 1. We are anxious to continue developing our invert-and-multiply algorithm sequence to examine the influence of the cake problems, the painting problems, and perhaps several other scenarios while helping our students make sense of this algorithm.

References

Flores, Alfinio, Erin E. Turner, and Renee C. Bachmann. "Posing Problems to Develop Conceptual Understanding: Two Teachers Make Sense of Division of Fractions." *Teaching Children Mathematics* 12 (October 2005): 117–21.

Fosnot, Catherine Twomey, and Maarten Dolk. *Young Mathematicians at Work: Constructing Fractions, Decimals, and Percents*. Portsmouth, N.H.: Heinemann, 2002.

Perlwitz, Marcela D. "Two Students' Constructed Strategies to Divide Fractions." *Mathematics Teaching in the Middle School* 10 (October 2004): 122–26.

———. "Dividing Fractions: Reconciling Self-Generated Solutions with Algorithmic Answers." *Mathematics Teaching in the Middle School* 10 (February 2005): 278–83.

Tirosh, Dina. "Enhancing Prospective Teachers' Knowledge of Children's Conceptions: The Case of Division of Fractions." *Journal for Research in Mathematics Education* 31 (January 2000): 5–25.

van de Walle, John A. *Elementary and Middle School Mathematics: Teaching Developmentally*. Boston: Allyn & Bacon, 2007.

Connecting Decimals and Other Mathematical Content

Charles S. Thompson and Vicki Walker

Experiences with many children in the middle grades indicate that they have poor decimal concepts and lack fundamental skills in working with decimal values. For example, when asked to identify which of 0.36 or 0.339 is greater, children frequently choose 0.399 because 339 is great than 36. Other children reason that 0.339 is smaller because it has more decimal places, and they "know" that the values decrease as more decimal places are added. Likewise, children have poor number sense regarding decimal numbers. For example, when asked to round 0.487 to the nearest hundredth, they blithely use the standard rule "round up when the digit to the right is greater than 5," round 0.487 to 0.49, but never think of either 0.487 or 0.49 as being near 1/2 on the number line.

Children often develop misconceptions about decimals because instruction does not promote connections between decimals and other mathematical content. Decimal concepts and symbols need to be related to a variety of fraction ideas and to place value. Connections also need to link decimals with coin and dollar values, metric measurement, and percents.

This article describes instructional activities with decimals that enable children to make connections that are necessary for them to understand and use decimals meaningfully. Decimal concepts and symbols are related to fraction concepts and symbols and to place-value concepts and symbols. Extensive use is made of physical models, diagrams, and number lines. The goal is to enable students to develop decimals as part of an integrated network of number ideas by understanding (1) that decimals are a type of fraction with a different symbolism and (2) that decimals can be meaningfully compared, ordered, and related to common fractions by using fraction ideas and place-value ideas.

Decimals Are Base-Ten Fractions

Decimals can be thought of as parts of a whole, a whole that has been divided into 10, 100, 1000, or some other number of parts that is a power of 10. From this perspective, decimals are special fractions and can appropriately be called decimal fractions, since the word decimal means "based on ten." The following activity focuses on the part-whole aspect of decimal fractions. The special symbols for decimals are addressed in the subsequent activity.

A motivating and intriguing way to help students learn about decimal fractions involves using individually wrapped slices of cheese. Using one slice as the model for one whole, ask each student to cut his or her whole into ten equal-sized strips.

The plastic wrapper can be used as a cutting board (see **fig. 1**). Ask what number name should be given to each of the newly cut strips. Ask students to justify their answers in terms of the pieces of cheese in front of them. Focus on the idea that tenths have been made, since the whole has been cut into ten equal-sized parts. This activity uses children's ideas about fractions, and teachers can have students write fraction symbols (1/10) to match their verbal answers (one tenth). Students can then answer questions related to the number of tenths in five whole slices of cheese (fifty tenths) or in two and one-half slices of cheese (twenty-five tenths).

After the students can answer questions about the tenths strips and justify their answers, ask them to take one of the strips and cut it into ten equal-sized pieces, which

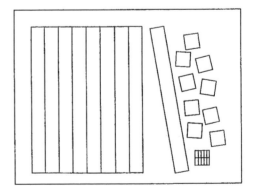

Fig.1. Cutting a cheese slice to show decimals

will be little squares. Follow with the same type of questions as with the tenths: "What names should be given to the new pieces?" (Hundredths) "How do you know?" (One hundred of these pieces are needed to make the whole slice.) "What name would you give to three strips and two little squares?" (3 tenths and 2 hundredths, or 32 hundredths, or 32/100, since each of the three strips has 10 hundredths.)

Students seem to like the challenge of taking one of the hundredths squares and cutting it into ten equal pieces, thereby creating thousandths. The cutting gets tedious at this point, but it is not impossible. The relative sizes of tenths, hundredths, and thousandths become meaningful for students though this activity. They can see the three sizes! They can respond to questions about the values of combinations of the pieces. "What is the value of two strips, one little square, and three tiny pieces?" (213/1000, since each strip contains 100 thousandths, each little square contains 10 thousandths, and 3 extra thousandths are present.) When the discussion is completed, the children enjoy eating their decimal models. For example, ask the students to eat 23 hundredths of their original slice, then 3 tenths, 6 thousandths, and so on, until all the cheese has been eaten.

Decimal Connections with Place Value

In the following activity, children are challenged to extend the place-value notation they have been using for whole numbers to include symbolic representations for decimal fractions. Children manipulate decimal models on a place-value mat (**fig. 2**), verbalize the amounts shown, and later enter the appropriate numerals on a calculator. The materials needed for each pair of children are tagboard decimeter squares to represent the whole, strips 1 cm by 1 dm to represent tenths, squares 1 cm by 1 cm to represent hundredths, three-column place-value mats, and a calculator.

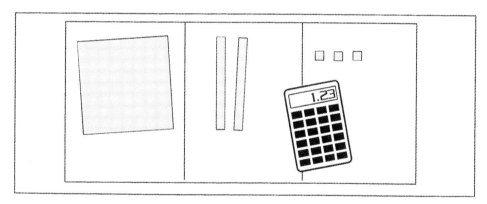

Fig 2. Connecting decimals and place value

Ask the students to compare the strips with the large square and to name them in terms of the large square. Be sure that the students use two characteristics to justify that the strips are tenths: (1) they are equal in size and (2) ten of them make the whole square. Have one student in each pair place one large square in the left column of the place-value mat and one strip in the column immediately to the right. Ask everyone to verbalize the total represented (one and one-tenth) and discuss how to use numbers to write that amount (1 1/10).

Challenge the students with the following idea: "Is it possible to use '11' to stand for the value of the square and the strip? Let's use the '1' on the left to stand for the large square and the '1' on the right to stand for the strip." Students will object, of course, and state that "11" stands for eleven rather than one and one-tenth. One student will usually suggest putting a dot between the 1's (1.1), since many of them have seen decimals written elsewhere. Take this opportunity to challenge them to defend the use of this notation. Ask them to justify that this notation is consistent with the place-value notation that they learned earlier and to identify the meanings of the 1's and the dot. Their explanations should focus on the 1-to-10, right-to-left relationship between adjacent positions in the place-value system. They should also identify that the purpose of the dot, or decimal point, is to separate the whole from the parts.

To test their reasoning and understanding, suggest that if a whole square is cut into eight equal parts and one square and one-eighth of the square are placed on the mat, then 1.1 can be used to represent this amount also. Some children may need hints to help them determine that the reason 1.1 can be used for one and one-tenth but not for one and one-eighth is that a 1-to-10, right-to-left relationship must exist between adjacent positions in the standard place-value system. One hint would be to ask children how the values of the two 1's compare in each of the following numbers: 211, 112, and 1123. (In each example the 1 on the right is worth 1/10 of the 1 on its left.) Another hint would be to have children examine previously used place-value materials, such as base-ten cubes, rods, flats, and big cubes, that model this 1-to-10 relationship.

Following this investigation of the place-value system, the students will have a beginning understanding that 1.1 can be used for one and one-tenth because the tenths are one-tenth in value of the units to the immediate left. This idea will be reinforced throughout the remainder of this activity.

Have the student in each pair who is using the calculator enter 1.1 to match the value of the pieces on the place-value mat. Add one more strip to each mat, and have the student with the calculator enter the corresponding symbols to represent this action: $\boxed{+}\,\boxed{\cdot}\,\boxed{1}\,\boxed{=}$. Have students verbalize the new total on their mats (one and two-tenths) and discuss the calculator representation of this expression (1.2). (The "1" stands for one whole, and the "2" stands for the two tenths. The decimal point separates the whole from the parts, the tenths.) Have the students continue adding strips, or tenths, one at a time to their mats as their partners press the corresponding keys on their calculators, until a total of 1.9 is reached. Consider using the constant feature of many calculators to add 0.1 repeatedly by pressing $\boxed{=}$ after each addition of a tagboard strip. However, many children will benefit from representing the entire action initially by pressing all four keys, $\boxed{+}\,\boxed{\cdot}\,\boxed{1}\,\boxed{=}$, each time.

At this point, add another strip and ask the students to name the total on their mats. (One and ten tenths) Discuss what should be done with the ten strips. (Trade them in for a whole square.) Have students predict what the calculator will do when $\boxed{+}\,\boxed{\cdot}\,\boxed{1}\,\boxed{=}$ is entered. (It automatically "makes the trade," and the display reads simply 2.) Be sure to connect this trading to the cheese activity: it corresponds to reconnecting the ten cheese strips and exchanging them for a new slice. Also, ask the children to check the odometer of their parents' car to see what happens immediately after it changes from a 9 in the tenths place. (The ones digit advances by 1, and the tenths digit changes to 0.)

Continue adding tenths until the children can verbalize the amount on the place-value mats correctly and can predict and justify the calculator's display. Change the activity by having the children add hundredths each time. Begin with one whole, one tenth, and one hundredth on the place-value mat, and ask the students to name this amount. (One and eleven hundredths, since one strip is worth ten hundredths) Ask them how to represent this amount with numbers. (1.11) Have them justify this representation just as they did with 1.1. With a teacher's patience and nudges, they will determine that each "1" in 1.11 is worth one-tenth of the "1" to its left. After they have entered 1.11 on their calculators, have them add one hundredth to their mats and predict what the calculator will display when $\boxed{+}\,\boxed{\cdot}\,\boxed{0}\,\boxed{1}\,\boxed{=}$ is entered. (1.12) Continue adding hundredths to the mat until the students can verbalize and justify the amounts shown and can predict and justify the calculator's representations. When they can, have them place one whole, nine tenths, and five hundredths (1.95) on their mats and add one hundredth at least five times. On the fifth addition, have the children verbalize what they should do with the materials (trade ten hundredths for one tenth and then the ten tenths for a whole) and predict what the calculator will display. (2)

This activity leads to several important outcomes. First, the students learn a new way of representing decimal fractions—for example, representing 1 1/10 as 1.1 and 1 11/100 as 1.11. Second, they learn this concept in a way that can enable them to understand better the consistent 1-to-10 relationship that exists between adjacent positions in the place-value system, for whole numbers and for decimal fractions. Third, they learn how decimal values grow and how their numerical representations change as tenths or hundredths are added repeatedly.

Teachers can broaden students' understand of decimals and place value further by using dollars, dimes, and pennies on place-value mats. Children will already be familiar with the symbolic notation for monetary values, such as $1.23, and will benefit from a discussion about dollars representing wholes, dimes representing tenths, and pennies representing hundredths. Many children will not have thought of dimes and pennies as decimal fractions.

Reasoning about Decimal Concepts

In this activity, students are enticed to connect a variety of ideas about decimal fractions, including various verbal and symbolic representations; relationships among wholes, tenths, and hundredths; and comparisons of decimal values. Two types of writing tasks are posed to students.

The first task involves showing students a 10-by-10 grid with some squares shaded (**fig. 3**). Ask students to name the shaded amount in at least three ways and to explain their answers in terms of the diagram. If thirty-five squares are shaded, the names that students give for the shaded amount might include 0.35, 35/100, 35 hundredths, 1/10 + 1/10 + 1/10 + 5/100, 7/20, and 3 1/2 tenths. The explanations students give often involve comparing the number of shaded squares with the total number of squares. (The fraction 35/100 represents 35 shaded squares out of 100 total squares.) Sometimes they mentally group the squares into sets of ten or five to make comparisons. For example, they justify 3 1/2 tenths by mentally creating and comparing 3 1/2 strips of 10 squares to the total of 10 strips of 10 squares.

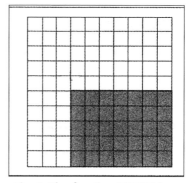

Fig. 3. The fraction 35/100 has many names.

The second task involves having students designate which of two decimals, 0.307 and 0.32, is greater in value and asking them to justify their answers. Give them 10-by-10 grids to use in their justifications. Children are able to draw on their experiences with the cheese slices, the place-value materials, and the previous activity to shade in squares on the grid to represent the two decimal values (**fig. 4**). They then explain that 0.32 represents three strips—tenths—and two more little squares—hundredths—whereas 0.307 represents three strips—tenths—and no complete little squares—hundredths. Hence, 0.32 is greater in value than 0.307.

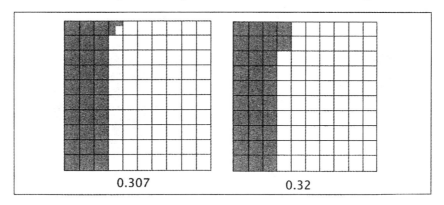

0.307   0.32

Fig. 4. Comparing 0.307 and 0.32 on grid paper

The importance of using physical models and diagrams to represent decimals cannot be overemphasized. The students can base their reasoning on objects and diagrams that they can see, create, and move rather than on abstract definitions and rules, such as the following rule for comparing decimals: "Compare the digits in each place-value position, moving from left to right until the digits differ. At that point, the decimal number having the digit of the greater value is the greater number."

It is important to ask children to communicate their ideas in writing, as described in this activity. When children are asked to write, they are forced to think, to organize their ideas, and to arrange them in a logical sequence. Writing also encourages children to make connections among various ideas to help the reader understand the ideas being expressed.

Connecting Decimals with Common Fractions

For children to develop a good number sense for decimals, they need to relate decimals to such common fractions as 1/4 and 1/8. Stated in another way, children need to connect fractions to their decimal equivalents, such as 1/4 to 0.25. Some students think that 1/8 equals 0.18. Usually common fractions are connected to decimals by using division. For example, to find the decimal equivalent of 1/4, 1 is divided by 4 by using paper and pencil or a calculator; the result is 0.25. Thus, 1/4 is equal to 0.25. But this result is not very satisfying for children. They see the result, but the connection is symbolic rather than conceptual and does not give them an intuitive feeling about the desired relationship nor any understanding of why 1/4 is equal to 0.25.

To make this connection more understandable, use a 10-by-10 square grid divided into 100 parts. The square grid represents the whole, or 1, so each of the 100 equal parts represents one hundredth, 1/100, or 0.01. Ask children to shade one-fourth of the grid. Generally they do this task by drawing a line vertically through the center of the grid and another line horizontally through the center of the grid as shown in **figure 5**. Ask them to name the shaded amount in other ways, particularly by using decimals. By drawing on the previous place-value activities, children frequently name the shaded amount as twenty-five hundredths, that is, twenty-five little squares, or 0.25. Thus they have found that 1/4 equals 0.25. Teachers can help the children connect this result to the previous place-value activity by discussing that a group of twenty-five squares is the same as two strips, or tenths, plus five little squares, or hundredths. Later this process of dividing the one whole into four parts can be connected to the familiar long-division procedure.

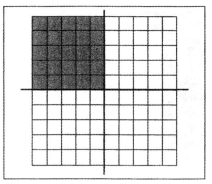

Fig. 5. Connecting 1/4 and 0.25

Next, ask students to shade one-eighth of the grid and to determine a name for 1/8 using decimal notation. The problem this time is that dividing 100 little squares into eight equal groups leaves many partial squares in each group. (See **fig. 6**.) Still, by combining half squares, the students are able to determine that 1/8 is about 12 1/2 little squares, or hundredths, or, by referring back to the cheese slicing, 1 tenth, 2 hundredths, and 5 thousandths, which is 125/1000, or 0.125. If children are asked if this answer makes sense in terms of their results for 1/4, they are usually able to conclude that 1/8 is half of 1/4—they often divide the fourths on the grid into two parts to create the eighths—and so 1/2 of 25 hundredths is 12 1/2 hundredths, which is 0.125.

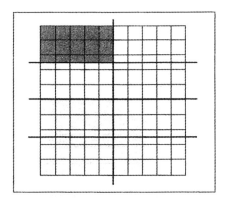

Fig. 6. Connecting 1/8 and 0.125

Additional experiences with other common fractions enable the students to connect those common fractions meaningfully with their decimal equivalents. A good extension activity is finding decimal equivalents for common fractions that have equivalent decimals that repeat indefinitely. Dividing a 10-by-10 grid as was done for 1/4 and 1/8 gives students a good, intuitive idea why the decimal equivalent for 1/3 continues indefinitely. (See **fig. 7**.) The task of showing 1/3 on a 10-by-10 grid translates to dividing the grid into three equal parts. Since 10 strips (tenths) exist originally, 3 of them, since 3 tenths equal 0.3, belong in each group and 1 is left over. That leftover 1 tenth consists of 10 little squares, or hundredths, which can again be placed 3 in each group (3 hundredths equal 0.03, plus the 3 tenths makes 0.33) with 1 left over. The 1 hundredth left over consists of 10 tiny parts, or thousandths, which can again be placed 3 in each group (3 thousandths equal 0.003, plus the previous tenths and hundredths makes 0.333) with 1 left over. Theoretically, this process can continue indefinitely: one piece will always be left over and is traded for 10 of the next

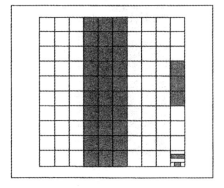

Fig. 7. Connecting 1/3 and 0.3̄33̄

smaller piece, which are shared three to each group; 1 of them is left over; and so on. In this way students obtain an intuitive feeling that 1/3 equals 0.333....

These connections are extremely important because they help students understand that fractions and decimals are just different symbols for representing the same quantity, the shaded part of a grid. This connection is extended in the next activity, which involves placing fractions and decimals on a number line.

Connecting Decimals and Fractions on a Number Line

For students to understand decimals thoroughly, they need to have an understanding of the relative magnitudes of these numbers. That is, they should have a good idea of where decimal values lie on a number line in relation to other decimals. Furthermore, they need to know how the values of decimals compare with common fractions and whole numbers. They need to know, for example, that 0.48 is about 1/2 and is about halfway between 0 and 1. The following activity focuses on the creation of a number line to help students further develop these number relationships.

Begin by giving small groups of students three strips of adding-machine tape, each one meter long, and a meterstick marked in centimeters. Advise them that their task is to create on one of the strips a number line that extends from 0 at one end to 1 at the other end; is divided into hundredths; and has all halves, thirds, fourths, fifths, sixths, eighths, and tenths marked and labeled with numerals. The other two strips may be used by the students to assist them in creating their final product. (See **fig. 8**.)

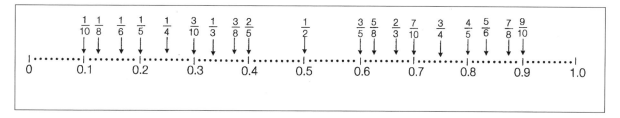

Fig. 8. Connecting common fractions and decimals

Students should be given as little or as much assistance as they need. For example, suggest that the students begin by drawing a line on one strip and marking the tenths and hundredths. They will readily notice that they can do so by using their metersticks. Next, suggest that they fold the other two strips, one to create halves, fourths, and eighths, the other to create thirds and sixths. (See **fig. 9**.) They will have little difficulty with the halves, fourths, and eighths but will probably need some guidance in making the thirds and sixths. Show them how to make thirds by looping over and sliding one end of the tape along the rest until it reaches the approximate midpoint of the remaining part of the tape. Hold the end at that midpoint while making a crease at the other end of the loop. (See **fig. 9**.) A little trial and error may be involved, but the process works well enough. These thirds can be folded in half to create the sixths. After the students have folded the strips to make the fractions requested, they can mark and label the fold lines and transfer these labels to the tape marked in hundredths by laying the tapes side by side.

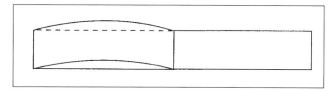

Fig. 9. Folding paper strips into thirds

In the process of making the number lines, the students find that many common fractions correspond exactly to decimals that are either tenths or hundredths. For example, have them explain why 1/2 is the same as 0.5 (0.5 equals 5/10, which means 5 out of 10 parts, which is 1/2) and why 3/4 is the same as 0.75 (0.75

is the same as 75/100, which is equivalent to the fraction 3/4, since 1/4 is 25/100, and 25/100 + 25/100 + 25/100 = 75/100).

After the students have finished their number lines, place the tapes end to end across one wall of the classroom. Presto, they have created a number line that extends from 0 to perhaps 10 and that is marked with common fractions and decimals to hundredths. The points at which the strips connect can be relabeled to read 0, 1, 2, …10. This extended number line can be used to help students think about fractions and decimals as mixed numbers. For example, ask the students to find 4 1/6 on the number line and to rewrite 4 1/6 as a single fraction. The students can count the sixths or multiply 4 × 6, since 6 sixths are in each strip of paper, and determine the answer, 25/6. This process is very meaningful to the students in contrast with the abstract rule, "Multiply the whole number by the denominator of the fraction and add the numerator to the result." In a similar way, students could determine the number of tenths in the number 3.75. (Multiply 3 times 10, since 10 tenths are in each strip of paper, and add 7 tenths, since 7 tenths are in the 0.75 remaining.)

Another extremely valuable activity to complete with the number line connects any decimal with a nice, or common, fraction. Many students do not make these connections naturally, but this skill is necessary for working with decimals meaningfully. It is needed, for example, when finding ratios of body measurements, such as the ratio of foot length to body height. Students divide a foot length—say, 27 centimeters—by a body height—say, 155 centimeters—and obtain 0.1742 as an approximate result. However, they usually do not know how to think of this number as a ratio. Working with the number line just created helps the students make a connection between 0.1742 and the common fraction 1/6. They can approximate 0.1742 as a little less than halfway between 0.17 and 0.18 and notice that 1/6 is approximately equal to 0.17. Hence, the ratio of foot length to body height is about 1 to 6.

The value of creating these number lines is that they help students develop an integrated network of number ideas. The students are enticed to connect fractions and decimals in a new way, on the number line, and this new connection helps them connect the values of these two different types of symbols. They are continuing to develop the ideas that although fractions and decimals are different symbol systems, they both represent part-whole relationships and that their values can be related and sometimes equated.

Conclusion

The instructional activities described herein help students connect decimal concepts with decimal symbols, with fraction concepts and fraction symbols, and with place-value concepts and place-value symbols. Extensive use is made of physical models, diagrams, and number lines. Students are asked to reason, communicate, solve problems, and connect ideas across a variety of mathematical content.

In doing these activities, students develop an understanding of decimals that is meaningful and rich, an understanding that is built with connections among a variety of mathematical ideas. Decimal concepts are remembered because they are part of a network of number ideas rather than isolated bits of information. For students, these decimal concepts have a broad range of applications because they are not tied to abstract rules or to a single physical model or diagram.

Bibliography

National Council of Teachers of Mathematics (NCTM). *Curriculum and Evaluation Standards for School Mathematics.* Reston, Va.: NCTM, 1989.

Van de Walle, John. *Elementary School Mathematics: Teaching Developmentally.* White Plains, N.Y.: Longman, 1994.

Investigating Students' Conceptual Understanding of Decimal Fractions Using Multiple Representations

Sherri L. Martinie and Jennifer M. Bay-Williams

How do you think middle school students would respond if they were asked to determine whether 0.6 is greater than 0.06? More specifically, can you predict the type of errors that students might make when answering this question? What rationales or representations, accurate or inaccurate, do you think students would offer to support their answers? What types of models, such as money or shaded regions of a shape, might students use to illustrate these decimal numbers?

Illogical responses to decimal problems are all too common in middle school classrooms. To students, these responses are not illogical but, rather, their way of making sense of decimal numbers using their prior learning and, sometimes, rote application of rules (Resnick et al. 1989; Wearne and Hiebert 1988). Because students often focus more on procedures or facts than concepts, they misapply procedures for decimal numbers that they have learned to use with whole numbers (Sackur-Grisvard and Leonard 1985; Sowder 1997).

An Instrument to Assess Decimal Understanding

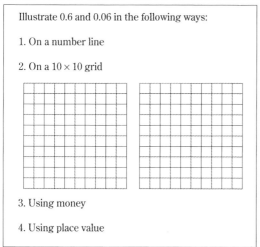

Illustrate 0.6 and 0.06 in the following ways:

1. On a number line

2. On a 10 × 10 grid

3. Using money

4. Using place value

Fig. 1. Assessment of students' understanding of decimal numbers

Despite several weeks devoted to developing decimal concepts, students in our sixth-grade classroom clearly had gaps in their understanding of decimal numbers. To better assess these conceptual gaps, we designed an instrument that asked students to illustrate their understanding of decimal values using four different models (see **fig. 1**). The models involve application of conceptual knowledge of decimals to varying degrees.

How do you think your own students would score on this assessment? Do you think students would score equally well across representations or that they would understand some representations less well than others? Which representations do you predict would be most difficult for your students? Could you analyze a student's work and determine what misconceptions he or she has regarding decimals? We suggest that you test your students by using the tasks in **figure 1** to answer these questions.

Discussion

We administered this instrument to forty-three sixth graders. The students worked individually and had as much time as they needed to complete the questions. An item was scored correct if the student had accurately completed the given representation in a way that correctly identified the size of the two decimal numbers. For example, in the first question, students had to label the number line with a 0 and a 1 and correctly place 0.06 close to 0 and 0.6 slightly to the right of 1/2.

Even though each of these tasks required some conceptual knowledge to represent the answer correctly, students' success with the decimal tasks varied for each representation. Many students could accurately show 0.6 and 0.06 in one or two representations but not the others. The number of students scoring all correct (4) to none correct (0) are shown in **table 1**. Only six students (14%) of those tested were able to represent the

Table 1

Correct Responses on Decimal Questionaire

Number of Correct Responses	Number of Students Responding Correctly	Percent of Students Responding Correctly
4	6	14%
3	14	33%
2	12	28%
1	7	16%
0	4	9%
Total	43	100%

Table 2

Correct Responses for Each Item on the Decimal Questionaire

Items on Questionaire	Number of Students Responding Correctly	Percent of Students Responding Correctly (out of 43 Students)
Number line	11	26%
10 × 10 grid	28	65%
Money	28	65%
Place value	25	58%

decimal numbers in all four situations. Note that 77 percent of the students showed some conceptual understanding of decimals by providing correct responses to one, two, or three of the tasks, but they were not able to represent the numbers correctly for all the models.

Students' success with the different models varied greatly (see **table 2**). Students were correct most often when explaining decimal numbers using the 10 × 10 grid and using money. Although 58 percent of students answered the place-value question correctly, most compared the tenths place of each decimal. Only six stu-

dents (14%) stated that six-tenths is more than six-hundredths or made any quantitative comparison of the two decimals.

The number line was the most difficult of the four models. In fact, of the fourteen students who missed only one representation, eleven missed the number line. The most common error (made by sixteen of the thirty-two students who missed this question) was to label 0 and 1 on the number line, place 0.6 accurately, then incorrectly place 0.06 or leave it off entirely (see **fig. 2**). Notice that the student whose work is shown in **figure 2** considered 0.06 to be halfway between 0 and 0.6, confusing one-tenth the size of 0.6 with one-half the size of 0.6. Another common error was to label 0.06 on the number line to the left of 0.6 but to place both decimal numbers inaccurately between 0 and 1 (see **fig. 3**). Students seemed to understand that 0.06 was smaller than 0.6 but did not indicate the sizes of the decimals in relation to 0 and 1. **Figure 4** shows another common error, which was to identify 0.06 as larger than 0.6,

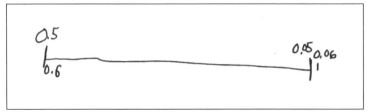

Fig. 2. A student places 0.6 correctly but is unable to place 0.06 correctly.

Fig. 3. This student's solution recognizes that 0.6 is greater than 0.06, but the student does not indicate the relative sizes of the decimal numbers compared with 0 and 1.

Fig. 4. A student places 0.06 to the right of 0.6, apparently based on the misconception that the longer decimal is greater in value.

perhaps with the idea that the longer decimal is larger, as is true with whole numbers. In two of the student samples, students used 0.5 and 0.05 as benchmarks to try to identify the correct placement of 0.6 and 0.06. This approach illustrates students' attempts to apply what they know about the sizes of these decimals, specifically, that 0.5 is one-half and 0.6 is slightly larger than one-half.

Follow-up Assessment on Linear Representation

In the number-line model, students had difficulty labeling endpoints of 0 and 1 and relating the values 0.6 and 0.06 to the endpoints. Because we could not determine whether students were struggling with the number line or with the relative values of the decimals, we designed another assessment that included four number-line tasks of increasing complexity:

1. Draw a number line that shows the numbers 1 through 5.

2. Draw a number line that shows 2.5.

3. Draw a number line that shows 0.4.

4. Draw a number line that shows 0.4 and 0.04.

What percentage of your students would successfully plot the numbers for each of these four tasks? **Figure 5** shows the results for the forty-three sixth graders that we tested.

Most students understood the number line in relation to whole numbers, but many could not place the decimals, especially those less than 1. Only one in five students was able to place 0.04 and 0.4 accurately! Recall that on the first test, 26 percent of students were able to label and place 0.6 and 0.06 correctly. This additional task revealed that students' difficulty with a number-line representation was specific to those decimals less than 1, in particular, those less than 1/10.

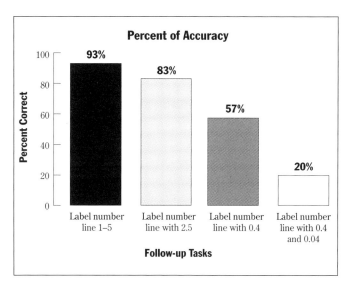

Fig. 5. Results of follow-up assessment using four number-line tasks of increasing complexity

Implications for Teaching and Learning

To make sense of decimals, students need multiple experiences and contexts in which to explore them. Our assessment instrument using four representations indicates that students may appear to understand decimals using some models, but they may lack a profound overall understanding of decimal concepts. In instruction, therefore, teachers must include many representations of decimal concepts to broaden and deepen students' understanding.

Teachers should also use multiple representations to assess students' understanding. Without the number-line question in our assessment instruction, we might have concluded that our students had a sound understanding of decimals and their relative magnitude. Mistakes can reveal student misconceptions or overgeneralizations and provide opportunities for learning, both for the teacher and students. An instrument that asks students to provide different representations and explanations for a particular concept can be an eye-opener for teachers and can guide instructional decisions to enable students to deepen their understanding of concepts. The purpose of our decimal questionnaire was to identify student misconceptions and use that information to guide instructional planning.

Collecting data from students often results in more questions. In our classrooms, the surprising difficulty of the number line led to a follow-up inquiry to find out more about what students could and could not do. The follow-up number-line questions revealed that students' number-line difficulties were specifically related to the size of the numbers, in particular to decimals less than 1/10. We might offer several possible explanations for the students' difficulty with locating numbers less than 1/10 on a number line. One explanation is that students were asked to draw and label all parts of the model, including the 0 and the 1, without any visual organizers already marked for them. This task was also the only one that called for approximation; students might not have been able to estimate approximate positions for the two values, even though they could illustrate exact representations (such as the shading required in item 2, **fig. 1**). Students might also have been inexperienced with number lines. Using the number line to discuss the approximate magnitude of decimal numbers (as well as fractions and percents) is an effective tool for developing students' number sense (Bay 2001). Given that students struggle with the number-line model and knowing that decimals often appear in linear models in real-life situations, such as on a thermometer or metric ruler, we must recognize the importance of including linear models in our teaching of decimal concepts.

Summary

Principles and Standards for School Mathematics (NCTM 2000) states, "Students must learn mathematics with understanding, actively building new knowledge from experience and prior knowledge" (p. 11). With decimals, prior knowledge of whole numbers may cause misunderstandings. For students to fully understand the similarities and differences between decimals and whole numbers, instruction must emphasize conceptual development, including the use of a variety of decimal representations.

References

Bay, Jennifer M. "Developing Number Sense on the Number Line." *Mathematics Teaching in the Middle School* 6 (April 2001): 448–51.

National Council of Teachers of Mathematics (NCTM). *Principles and Standards for School Mathematics*. Reston, Va.: 2000.

Resnick, Lauren B., Pearla Nesher, François Leonard, Maria Magone, Susan Omanson, and Irit Peled. "Conceptual Bases of Arithmetic Errors: The Case of Decimal Fractions." *Journal for Research in Mathematics Education* 20 (January 1989): 8–27.

Sackur-Grisvard, Catherine, and François Leonard. "Intermediate Cognitive Organizations in the Process of Learning a Mathematical Concept: The Order of Positive Decimal Numbers." *Cognition and Instruction* 2 (2) (1985): 157–74.

Sowder, Judith. "Place Value as the Key to Teaching Decimal Operations." *Teaching Children Mathematics* 3 (April 1997): 448–53.

Wearne, Diana, and James Hiebert. "Constructing and Using Meaning for Mathematical Symbols: The Case of Decimal Fractions." In *Number Concepts and Operations in the Middle School*, edited by James Hiebert and Merlyn Behr, pp. 220–35. Reston, Va.: National Council of Teachers of Mathematics, 1988.

Section 3

Ratios, Rate, and Proportional Relationships

Introduction

Proportionality is a central, unifying theme in middle school mathematics (NCTM 2000). It has been called both the capstone of elementary school arithmetic and the cornerstone of high school mathematics (Lesh, Post, and Behr 1988). Although the mechanics of setting up and solving a proportion (i.e., two equivalent ratios with one missing term) are generally straightforward, the notion of proportionality is much more subtle and complex. Facility with proportionality develops through work in many areas of the curriculum, including ratio, rates, proportions, percents, similarity, scaling, linear equations, slope, and probability. (The articles in the Rational Numbers section of this book include examples of ratios and proportional relationships as well.)

Although national and international assessments have identified proportionality as an area of weakness for eighth grade students (Beaton et al. 1996; Sowder et al. 2004; Wearne and Kouba 2000), research has shown that middle-grades students are more successful at solving problems involving proportions when applying strategies that allow them to reason about proportional relationships instead of using algorithmic approaches (i.e., cross multiplication) that have little or no meaning to them (Ben-Chaim et al. 1998; Cramer and Post 1993). Hence the articles included in this section highlight tasks that can be used to help students reason about and make sense of proportional relationships and the related notions of ratio and rates.

The first three articles report research on children's proportional reasoning, make a case for the importance of developing students' mathematical facility in this area over the middle grades, and provide some ways of assessing where your students are in their proportional thinking and reasoning development.

The first article, "Proportional Reasoning" (Cramer and Post 1993), is a report of research on students' proportional reasoning difficulties. The assessments tasks in the article can be used to determine where students are in their facility with solving problems involving proportional reasoning.

The second article "Proportionality: A Unifying Theme for the Middle Grades" (Lanius and Williams 2003) describes the importance of devoting sufficient time to teaching and developing proportional reasoning. A variety of tasks show how proportionality provides a foundation for studying topics including algebra, geometry, measurement, probability, statistics, and number.

The third article "Assessing Proportional Thinking" (Bright, Joyner, and Wallis 2003) includes a set of problems that gives teachers an opportunity to learn whether their students can use additive or multiplicative reasoning appropriately. Common errors, from a sample of 132 eighth and ninth grade students, are described along with instructional implications.

"Problems That Encourage Proportion Sense" (Billings 2001) uses nonnumeric problems to develop proportional reasoning. The tasks allow students to focus on underlying proportional relationships rather than applying quantitative procedures. The problem context in the article uses carafes of coffee that can easily be changed to something more meaningful to students such as pitchers of lemonade or hot chocolate. The additional articles, "Numbers Need Not Apply: Teaching Notes" (Billings 2002b) and "Cocoa: Teaching Notes" (Billings 2002a), can be used directly with students.

"Using Recipes and Ratio Tables to Build on Students' Understanding of Fractions" (Brinker 1998) uses real-world contexts for developing students' understanding of rational number concepts. Students can develop different strategies to multiply fractions and mixed numbers using ratio tables as a tool to organize fractions and ratios.

"The Triple Jump: A Potential Area for Problem Solving and Investigation" (Clarke 1998) explores a set of tasks based on the role of ratios and percentages in triple jump performances. The investigation considers which world-record jumps most closely match the "ideal ratio" for hop:step:jump of 10:8:9.

References

Beaton, Albert E., Ina V. S. Mullis, Michael O. Martin, Eugenio J. Gonzalez, Dana L. Kelly, and Teresa A. Smith. "Mathematics Achievement in the Middle School Years: IEA's Third International Mathematics and Science Study (TIMSS)." Chestnut Hill, Mass.: Center for the Study of Testing Evaluation, and Educational Policy, Boston College, 1996.

Ben-Chaim, David, James T. Fey, William M. Fitzgerald, Catherine Benedetto, and Jane Miller. "Proportional Reasoning among Seventh-Grade Students with Different Curricular Experiences." *Educational Studies in Mathematics* 26 (1998): 247–73.

Billings, Esther M. H. "Problems That Encourage Proportion Sense." *Mathematics Teaching in the Middle School* 1 (September 2001): 1–14.

———. "Cocoa: Teaching Notes." In *Classroom Activities for Making Sense of Fractions, Ratios, and Proportions,* 2002 Yearbook of the National Council of Teachers of Mathematics (NCTM), edited by George W. Bright and Bonnie Litwiller, pp. 38–40. Reston, Va.: NCTM, 2002.

———. "Numbers Need Not Apply: Teaching Notes." In *Classroom Activities for Making Sense of Fractions, Ratios, and Proportions,* 2002 Yearbook of the National Council of Teachers of Mathematics (NCTM), edited by George W. Bright and Bonnie Litwiller, pp. 36–37. Reston, Va.: NCTM, 2002.

Bright, George W., Jeane M. Joyner, and Charles Wallis. "Assessing Proportional Thinking." *Mathematics Teaching in the Middle School* 3 (November 2003): 166–72.

Brinker, Laura. "Using Recipes and Ratio Tables to Build on Students' Understanding of Fractions." *Teaching Children Mathematics* 5 (December 1998): 218–24.

Clarke, Doug. "The Triple Jump: A Potential Area for Problem Solving and Investigation." *Mathematics Teaching in the Middle School* 2 (October 1998): 104–8.

Cramer, Kathleen, and Thomas Post. "Proportional Reasoning." *Mathematics Teacher* 86 (May 1993): 404–7.

Lanius, Cynthia S., and Susan E. Williams. "Proportionality: A Unifying Theme for the Middle Grades." *Mathematics Teaching in the Middle School* 8 (April 2003): 392–96.

Lesh, Richard T., Thomas Post, and Merlyn Behr. "Proportional Reasoning." In *Number Concepts and Operations in the Middle Grades,* edited by James Hiebert and Merlyn Behr, pp. 93–118. Reston, Va.: National Council of Teachers of Mathematics, 1998.

Sowder, Judith T., Diana Wearne, W. Gary Martin, and Marilyn Strutchens. "What Do Eighth-Grade Students Know about Mathematics? Changes over a Decade." In *Results and Interpretations of the 1990–2000 Assessments of the National Assessment of Educational Progress,* edited by Peter Kloosterman and Frank K. Lester, Jr., pp. 105–43. Reston, Va.: National Council of Teachers of Mathematics, 2004.

Wearne, Diana, and Vicky Kouba. "Rational Numbers." In *Results from the Seventh Mathematics Assessment of the National Assessment of Educational Progress,* edited by Edward A. Silver and Patricia A. Kennedy, pp. 163–91. Reston, Va.: National Council of Teachers of Mathematics, 2000.

Proportional Reasoning

Kathleen Cramer and Thomas Post

The attainment of proportional reasoning is considered a milestone in students' cognitive development. According to the NCTM's Curriculum and Evaluation Standards (1989), this ability is "of such great importance that it merits whatever time and effort must be expended to assure its careful development" (p. 82). As teachers and researchers know, students' understanding of proportionality develops slowly over a number of years. This article reports research findings regarding the learning and teaching of proportional reasoning that have potential for making contributions to classroom practice.

Proportional Reasoning

Consider the following proportional situation: Three meters equals 300 centimeters. How many centimeters equal 4.5 meters? The relationship between meters and centimeters is multiplicative and can be expressed in either of two ways:

$$\text{\# of cm} = 100 \ (\text{\# of m})$$

or

$$\text{\# of m} = (1/100) \ (\text{\# of cm}).$$

The critical component in proportional situations is the multiplicative relationship that exists among the quantities that represent the situation (Cramer, Post, and Currier 1993). Because of this relationship, all proportional situations can be expressed through an algebraic rule of the form $y = mx$.

Proportional Reasoning Tasks: Types and Difficulty

Assessing understanding of this multiplicative relationship has been done in various ways. Learning tasks devised in research studies can be a rich source of creative problem sets for classroom instruction and assessment. Research reports not only suggest varieties of tasks but give information about the relative difficulty of the tasks and factors (e.g., context, numerical complexity) that influence difficulty.

The Rational Number Project developed three different types of tasks to assess proportionality: (1) missing value, (2) numerical comparison, and (3) qualitative prediction and comparison (Post, Behr, and Lesh 1988; Heller et al. 1990). Each problem type was posed to students in four different real-world contexts: speed, scaling, mixture, and density (see examples in **fig. 1**).

Missing-Value Problems. In missing value-problems three pieces of numerical information are given and one piece is unknown. Karplus's tall-man–short-man problem is representative of this type of problem (Karplus, Karplus, and Wollman

Problem 1: Missing-value speed
Lisa and Rachel drove equally fast along a country road. It took Lisa 6 minutes to drive 4 miles. How long did it take Rachel to drive 6 miles?

Problem 2: Numerical comparison scaling
Anne and Linda are using different road maps of the city. On Anne's map a road 3 inches long is really 5 miles long. On Linda's map a road 9 inches long is really 45 miles long. Who is using the larger city map?

   a) Anne
   b) Linda
   c) Their maps are the same.
   d) Not enough information
      to tell

Problem 3: Qualitative prediction mixture
If Nick mixed less lemonade mix with more water than he did yesterday, his lemonade would taste _____.

   a) Stronger
   b) Weaker
   c) Exactly the same
   d) Not enough information to tell

Problem 4: Qualitative comparison density
Two friends hammered a line of nails into different boards. Bill hammered more nails than Greg. Bill's board was shorter than Greg's. On which board are the nails hammered closer together?

   a) Bill's board
   b) Greg's board
   c) Their nails are spaced the same.
   d) Not enough information to tell

Fig. 1. Rational Number Project problem types

1974). For the tall-man–short-man task, students are given a chain of six paper clips and told that this chain represents Mr. Short's height in paper clips. The students are also told that Mr. Short measures four large buttons tall. They are then told (not shown) that Mr. Tall is similar to Mr. Short but is six large buttons tall. Students are asked to find the height of Mr. Tall in paper clips and to explain their answers. The information in a missing-value problem can be represented as rates. In the tall-man–short-man task, 6 paper clips/4 buttons is a complete rate and paper clips/6 buttons is an incomplete rate.

Numerical Comparison Problems. In these problems, two complete rates are given. A numerical answer is not required; however, the rates are to be compared. Noelting's (1980) orange-juice task is an example of this type of problem (see **fig. 2**). Students are told that the shaded glasses represent orange-juice mix and that the unshaded glasses represent water. They are asked to imagine that the orange-juice mix and water are poured into a pitcher. Students determine which pitcher has the strongest-tasting orange juice or if the mixtures would taste the same.

Fig. 2. Adapted from Noelting's orange-juice task (1980). Which pitcher will have juice that has the strongest taste? Why? Reprinted with permission of Kluwer Academic Publishers.

In studying the results of these tasks, researchers found that students were more successful when one quantity in a complete rate was an integral multiple of the corresponding given quantity of the other rate, as, for example, two parts of orange-juice mix and five parts of water to six parts to six parts of orange-juice mix and eleven parts of water. When multiples were nonintegral, students often reverted to additive strategies. For example, in solving problem 1 of figure 1 (speed example), students would often conclude that the answer was eight minutes, reasoning that six miles is two more than four miles, so the answer must be two more than six minutes. This typical error in proportional reasoning is discussed at length by a number of researchers (Hart 1981; Noelting 1980).

Qualitative Prediction and Comparison Problems. These types of problems (see problems 3 and 4 in **fig. 1**) require comparisons not dependent on specific numerical values. Such thinking is a part of proportional thinking and, at least for seventh and eighth graders, is not the same as solving numerical-comparison and missing-value problems (Heller et al. 1990). On the one hand, students may use a memorized skill to solve numerical-comparison and missing-value problems. Qualitative-prediction and comparison problems, on the other hand, require students to understand the meaning of proportions. Thinking qualitatively allows students to check the feasibility of answers and to establish appropriate parameters for problem situations. Since this type of thinking is often necessary before actual calculations, the inclusion of such problems in teaching encourages students to use such approaches and improves their calculations and problem solving.

Importance of Context. Researchers found that problem context, as well as the nature of the numerical relationships, influenced problem difficulty. Of the four contexts studied in the Rational Number Project, scaling was significantly more difficult for middle-grades students than the other contexts. This finding was true even though the numbers in the problems were held constant. However, a proportional reasoner should not be radically affected by the awkward numerical relationships or the context in which the problem is posed. Therefore, in both instruction and testing, teachers should vary the numerical relationships and the context of proportional-reasoning problems.

Besides furnishing teachers with creative assessment items, research tasks can also be a rich source of instructional activities. The task presented in **figure 3** can help students develop proportional reasoning and understand the multiplicative relationship inherent in proportional situations. The activity comes from the Rational Number Project and was one of twelve such experiments used by students to highlight the multiplicative relationship in proportional situations. In this activity, students collect data, form a table, and determine an algebraic rule that represents the data. They then transfer the data to a coordinate axis. The rule highlights the multiplicative nature of proportional situations; the graph models the characteristic that in any proportion situation all the rate pairs fall on a straight line crossing the origin. Additional examples for instruction can be found in Cramer, Post, and Behr (1989) and Cramer, Post, and Currier (1993).

Solution Strategies for Proportional Reasoning Tasks

When seventh and eighth graders attempted missing-value and numerical-comparison problems, success rate was low. Analysis of students' correct responses showed four distinct solution strategies: unit rate, factor of change, fraction, and cross product. **Table 1** shows the percent of problems correct by grade level and by solution strategy. Each strategy will be illustrated by using it to solve the following problem:

> Steve and Mark were driving equally fast along a country road. It took Steve 20 minutes to drive 4 miles. How long did it take Mark to drive 12 miles?

The Unit-Rate Strategy. As the name implies, this is a "how many for one?" strategy. It always involves two rates corresponding to a given pair of quantities: 20 minutes/4 miles and its reciprocal 4 miles/20 minutes. The first pair can be represented by the unit rate: 5 minutes per 1 mile; the second by the unit rate: 1/5 mile per 1 minute. Since the question about Mark as for the amount of time to drive twelve miles, the unit rate describing the length of time for one mile is the one used ([5 minutes/1 mile] × 12 miles = 60 minutes). If the questions was "How many miles did Mark drive in 60 minutes?" the other unit rate would be used ([1/5 mile/1 minute] × 60 minutes = 12 miles).

Problem: You are using the overhead projector in your classroom. You place a red Cuisenaire rod on the projector. You measure its image to be 10 cm long. You wonder what will happen to the images of the other rods. Continue to collect data by placing a purple, a dark green, and then a brown rod in the center of the projector. Measure their images to the nearest cm. What patterns to you see? Can you predict the image length for a line segment 21 cm long?

Solution plan: Measure the lengths of rods in cm and record their image lengths. Build a table to show the results.

Rod Color	Rod Length	Image Length
Red		
Purple		
Dark green		
Brown		

Questions:

1. Is it possible to determine the length of the image if you know the length of the rod? If the rod is 10 cm long, how long will its image be?
2. Write a formula that can be used to determine the length of the image given the length of the rod. Use R to stand for the length of the rod and I for the image length. I = _____.
3. Test your formula using the table's number pairs. Use your formula to determine the image length of a 21-cm line segment. _____
4. Graph the data on a pair of coordinate axes and connect the points.
5. Describe the graph. _____

_____

Note to the teacher: Place the projector so the image length is five times the rod length.

Fig. 3. Activity from the Rational Number Project teaching experiment

The Factor-of-Change Strategy. This is a "times as many" strategy. A student using this method would reason as follows: "It takes twenty minutes to drive four miles. Since Mark is driving three times as far, it should take him three times as long. So the answer is twenty minutes times three, or sixty minutes." The ease in using this method is related to the numerical aspects of the problem. Students would be less apt to

TABLE 1
Percent of Correct Solutions for Missing-Value (MV) and Numerical-Comparison (NC) Word Problems

| | Seventh Grade N = 421 | | | | Eighth Grade N = 492 | | | |
Method	MV		NC		MV		NC	
Unit-rate strategy	28*	(15**)	48	(26)	14	(6)	30	(18)
Factor-of-change strategy	17	(5)	12	(5)	7	(3)	8	(2)
Fraction strategy	2	(1)	8	(10)	12	(2)	26	(25)
Cross-product algorithm	3	(4)	1	(1)	33	(45)	10	(15)
Incorrect	50	(75)	31	(57)	35	(44)	32	(40)

* The first entry is an average of three problems: in each problem all numerical values were integral multiples of one another.
** The entry in parentheses is an average for a single problem whose numerical values were not integral multiples of one another.

use this method if the factor to be used was not an integer—for example, if the factor was 2/7, as it would be if the problem had been, "It takes Steve 20 minutes to drive $7n$ miles; how long will it take Mark to drive 2 miles?" (2/7 of 20 is 40/7, or 5 and 5/7 minutes).

The Fraction Strategy. When using rates, the labels for each quantity are usually kept in the expression. This strategy is used when using the unit-rate strategy. If students dropped the labels and used ideas of equivalence, it is a fraction strategy. Students treated the rates as fractions, applying the fraction rule for equivalent fractions (multiply the numerator and denominator by 3) to calculate the answer of 60.

The Cross-Product Algorithm. As with many standard algorithms, this is an extremely efficient but mechanical process devoid of meaning in the real world. To solve the problem about Steve and Mark, a student sets up a proportion, forms a cross product, and solves the resulting equation by division:

$$\frac{20 \text{ minutes}}{4 \text{ miles}} = \frac{? \text{ minutes}}{12 \text{ miles}}$$

$$20 \text{ minutes} \times 12 \text{ miles} = ? \text{ minutes} \times 4 \text{ miles}$$

$$\frac{20 \text{ minutes} \times 12 \text{ miles}}{4 \text{ miles}} = ? \text{ minutes}$$

$$60 = ?$$

The unit-rate strategy was used most by seventh graders in the Rational Number Project. The unit rate seemed to be an intuitive approach building on students' real-life experiences, whereas the cross-product algorithm used most often by eighth grades seemed more contrived. (What meaning does 20 minutes × 12 miles have?) The more intuitive unit-rate and factor-of-change strategies related more meaningfully to the situation. On the one nonproportional problem included on the assessment, eighth graders were less successful: close to 30 percent inappropriately applied the cross-product algorithm to this task. Seventh graders, who had not learned this algorithm, were more successful and solved the nonproportional problem using other problem-solving strategies. Knowing how to do a procedure does not mean that a student knows when it can be applied, and value is found in intuitive methods.

Since most students not instructed in the cross-multiplication algorithm used the unit-rate and factor-of-change strategies to solve proportion problems, teachers may capitalize on these natural thought patterns and begin instruction focusing on these strategies. A sample lesson can be found in a *Mathematics Teacher* article by Cramer, Bezuk, and Behr (1989).

Conclusion

Research can have a positive effect on classroom practice. This article suggests that research tasks can and should be used in classrooms. They can function as instructional activities as well as assessment tools. The types of problems generated by research inform teachers of the different ways in which understanding can be assessed. Being a proportional reasoner means more than applying the cross-product algorithm. Students should be able to solve multiple problem types, including missing value, numerical comparison, qualitative comparison, and qualitative prediction.

Just as researchers analyze the effect of different variables on performance, teachers can consider these same variables as they teach and assess. Two important variables include context and the presence of integral multiples. Instruction should start with familiar contexts and extend to less familiar ones. With the availability of calculators, proportional problems should include "nasty" numbers so that students can encounter nonintegral relationships early on.

Research suggests teaching multiple strategies, including unit rate, factor of change, fractions, and the cross-product algorithm. Teachers should begin instruction with more intuitive strategies, such as the unit rate and factor of change.

These teaching suggestions emphasize learning concepts over learning procedures. As textbooks often focus on procedural knowledge, teachers will have to go beyond the content of textbooks to offer meaningful instruction for this important domain.

References

Cramer, Kathleen, Nadine Bezuk, and Merlyn Behr. "Proportional Relationships and Unit Rates." *Mathematics Teacher* 82 (October 1989): 537–44.

Cramer, Kathleen, Thomas Post, and Merlyn Behr. "Interpreting Proportional Relationships." *Mathematics Teacher* 82 (September 1989): 445–53.

Cramer, Kathleen, Thomas Post, and Sara Currier. "Learning and Teaching Ratio and Proportion: Research Implications." In *Research Ideas for the Classroom: Middle Grades Mathematics*, edited by Douglas Owens, pp. 159–78. Reston, Va.: National Council of Teachers of Mathematics and Macmillan, 1993.

Hart, Kathleen. "Ratio and Proportion." In *Children's Understanding of Mathematics* 11–16, edited by Kathleen Hart, pp. 88–101. London: John Murray, 1981.

Heller, Patricia, Thomas Post, Merlyn Behr, and Richard Lesh. "Qualitative and Numerical Reasoning about Fractions and Rates by Seventh- and Eighth-Grade Students." *Journal for Research in Mathematics Education* 21 (November 1990): 388–402.

Karplus, Elizabeth, Robert Karplus, and Warren Wollman. "Intellectual Development beyond Elementary School IV: Ratio, the Influence of Cognitive Style." *School Science and Mathematics* 74 (October 1974): 476–82.

National Council of Teachers of Mathematics (NCTM). *Curriculum and Evaluation Standards for School Mathematics*. Reston, Va.: NCTM, 1989.

Noelting, Gerald. "The Development of Proportional Reasoning and the Ratio Concept: Part 1—the Differentiation of Stages." *Educational Studies in Mathematics* 11 (May 1980): 217–53.

Post, Thomas, Merlyn Behr, and Richard Lesh. "Proportionality and the Development of Prealgebra Understandings." In *The Ideas of Algebra, K–12*, 1988 Yearbook of the National Council of Teachers of Mathematics (NCTM), edited by Arthur Coxford, pp. 78–90. Reston, Va.: NCTM, 1988.

Proportionality: A Unifying Theme for the Middle Grades

Cynthia S. Lanius and Susan E. Williams

The mathematics studied in high school and beyond is organized around large themes, such as algebra, geometry, trigonometry, calculus, statistics, and so on. Even though the boundaries between these topics blur at times, the themes give connections and structure to the mathematics studied. For example, a huge body of knowledge is recognized as algebra. Students know that they are doing algebra when they formulate and solve equations, even when they perform these tasks in geometry or calculus class. In contrast, the study of mathematics in the middle grades, with the exception of prealgebra, lacks an overarching theme. Most middle grades courses, generally known merely as sixth-, seventh-, or eighth-grade mathematics, lack big ideas and tend to be a mass of discrete topics with little connection or continuity. The notion that prealgebra is a course to be done right before algebra, as opposed to a long-term theme to be developed over several years, is a prime example of this situation.

NCTM's *Principles and Standards for School Mathematics* warns against a fragmented curriculum and calls for the integration of middle-grades mathematics curriculum and instruction (NCTM 2000). We might ask, however, "integrated around what?" One overarching concept with the potential to unite, relate, and clarify many important, complex middle-grades topics into a cohesive theme is proportionality.

Proportionality is an essential concept that arguably does not receive enough attention. According to Hoffer and Hoffer (1988), "Proportional reasoning is generally regarded as one of the important components of formal thought acquired in adolescence. . . . Failure to develop in this area by early to middle adolescence precludes study in a variety of disciplines requiring quantitative thinking and understanding, including algebra, geometry, some aspects of biology, chemistry and physics" (p. 303). Almost every page of *Principles and Standards* stresses the importance of proportionality in grades 6–8. Proportionality is clearly not "fluff" mathematics. It is broad, deep, and significant enough to unify many concepts into a major theme of middle-grades mathematics.

What Is Proportionality?

Proportionality, proportional reasoning, and *proportion* are terms that are closely associated in the literature. Throughout this article, *proportionality* refers to a special quality of a relation such that it can be written in the form of a *proportion,* namely,

$$\frac{a}{b} = \frac{c}{d}.$$

Proportional reasoning refers to a mathematical way of thinking in which students recognize proportional versus nonproportional situations and can use multiple approaches, not just the cross-products approach, for solving problems about proportional situations. Proportionality can be illustrated in many ways, for example: (1) algebraically, as linear functions in the form of *y = mx;* (2) geometrically, as a line that passes through the origin; and (3) in words, such as "Elena earns $250 every 2 weeks." Nonproportionality can be expressed similarly, for example: (1) algebraically, as any other kind of function; (2) geometrically, as any graph other than a line through the origin; and (3) in words, such as "Elena earns $250 every 2 weeks plus a one-time signing bonus of $300." Consider the following statements: "Mona saves $5 per week." "The temperature is dropping 3 degrees every 2 hours." "To make punch, you add 3 parts juice to 2 parts water." In other words, Mona's savings are proportional to the number of weeks she saves. The temperature is dropping proportionally to the time passing. The amount of water and juice are proportional to each other in the punch, and both are proportional to the total amount of punch.

Proportion Problems in Everyday Life

Questions often arise from proportional situations. In fact, many contend that people face proportion-related problems most frequently in their lives, such as "How much would Mona save in 3 years? How long will it take her to save $1000?" "How many degrees will the temperature fall in 8 hours? How long will it take to drop 20 degrees?" "How much water is needed for 5 gallons of punch? If you have 2 pints of juice, how much water do you need?" To answer these questions, our first inclination might be to teach students to create proportions and solve using cross products; for example:

$$\frac{x \text{ degrees}}{8 \text{ hours}} = \frac{3 \text{ degrees}}{2 \text{ hours}}$$

$$\frac{3 \text{ parts juice}}{2 \text{ parts water}} = \frac{2 \text{ parts juice}}{x \text{ parts water}}$$

Why not use this approach? It is quick and certain—practically mindless—which is exactly the point.

Lesh, Post, and Behr (1988) warn that if students are taught merely to use an algorithm, such as cross multiplication, they may not develop proportional reasoning even if they can use the algorithm effectively. Does the cross-multiplication process build understanding of proportionality? How, for example, would we explain a unit of degree × hours that we obtain when we cross multiply? Can middle-grades students justify why cross multiplication is mathematically correct, or is it, to them, merely a magical spell that mysteriously results in the answer? When students do not understand the cross-multiplication algorithm, they tend to apply it indiscriminately in a multitude of situations, not all of which are proportional. For example, a common student mistake is to apply the algorithm to the multiplication of fractions, as shown below:

$$\frac{2}{3} \times \frac{3}{4} = \frac{8}{9}$$

Let us look at approaches to working with proportion-related problems that might help to develop this theme of proportionality in an integrated way. Consider the water-to-juice situation discussed above and expressed in **table 1**. Remember that the proportions for the punch are 3 parts juice to 2 parts water.

Table 1

The Water-to-Juice Scenario: 2 Parts Water to 3 Parts Juice

Parts Water	Parts Juice	Parts Punch
2 or (2 × 1)	3 or (3 × 1)	5 or (5 × 1)
4 or (2 × 2)	6 or (3 × 2)	10 or (5 × 2)
6 or (2 × 3)	9 or (3 × 3)	15 or (5 × 3)

Students can immediately see connections to the multiplication that they learned in the elementary grades and gather that proportionality is closely related to multiplication. They can look for patterns and make predictions, both of which are important skills that they developed in elementary school. They can build skills working with fractions. For example, after students have generated the table for 2, 4, and 6 parts water, they can then easily generate values for 1, 3, 5, and so on by observing the pattern (see **table 2**). If I use 1 part water (2 × 1/2), from the pattern, I can determine the amount of juice needed by multiplying 3 × 1/2, or 1.5, and together, the water and juice will produce 5 × 1/2, or 2.5, parts punch. Finding parts juice and parts punch for 3 and 5 parts water can be done similarly.

Table 2
Generating Values for 1, 3, and 5 Parts Water

Parts Water	Parts Juice	Parts Punch
1 or (2 ×?)	(3 × ?)	(5 × ?)
2 or (2 × 1)	3 or (3 × 1)	5 or (5 × 1)
3 or (2 × ?)	???	???
4 or (2 × 2)	6 or (3 × 2)	10 or (5 × 2)
5 or (2 × ?)	???	???
6 or (2 × 3)	9 or (3 × 3)	15 or (5 × 3)

The next step might be to express the proportional relation algebraically by observing the pattern (see **table 3**). Notice how easily the notion of two related variables can now be introduced:

$$\text{\# parts juice} = 1.5 \times \text{\# parts water, or } (j = 1.5w)$$
$$\text{\# parts punch} = 2.5 \times \text{\# parts water, or } (p = 2.5w)$$

Table 3
An Algebraic Approach

Parts Water (w)	Parts Juice (j)	Parts Punch (p)
1	1.5	2.5
2	3	5
3	4.5	7.5
4	6	10
5	7.5	12.5
6	9	15
# parts water	1.5 × # parts water	2.5 × # parts water

We can now use these algebraic equations to solve other problems, such as "How much punch can you make using 25 quarts of water?"

Note that this way of presenting proportionality not only builds on the concepts that students learned in elementary school but also extends to the mathematics that they will learn in algebra. In fact, Lesh, Post, and Behr call proportionality a "cornerstone of higher mathematics, and the capstone of elementary concepts" (1988).

When learning a new mathematical concept, seeing counterexamples, as well as examples, is important. Let us look again, then, at the degrees-dropping relation. The temperature drops 3 degrees per hour. Given that the temperature is 99 degrees at 3:00 p.m., when will the temperature be 80 degrees if it continues to drop at the same rate?

We can express the temperature over time as a linear function, but is it a proportional relation? Consider **table 4**. Those who understand proportional reasoning can see that time and number of degrees dropped follow the same pattern as before and are proportional, but the change in temperature does not follow the pattern and is not proportional. We can use this information to formulate rules about when a relationship is proportional and when it is not.

TABLE 4
Temperature over Time as a Linear Function, but Is It Proportional?

Time	No. Degrees Dropped	Temperature
1 hour or (1×1)	3 or (3×1)	96° or $(? \times 1)$???
2 hours or (1×2)	6 or (3×2)	93° or $(? \times 2)$???
3 hours or (1×3)	9 or (3×3)	90° or $(? \times 3)$???

This introduction touches on the many and varied ways that proportionality can be developed in the middle grades as an integrated theme.

Why Use Proportionality as a Middle-Grades Theme?

Many reasons emerge as a rationale to develop proportionality as a theme in the middle grades, including those outlined in the following paragraphs.

Proportionality is complex and requires significant time and attention to master.

Proportionality is not a concept that students can master in a short time. As Lesh, Post, and Behr (1988) have noted, "Mathematics education research clearly shows that the evolution of proportional reasoning is characterized by a gradual increase in local competence" (p. 116). Hoffer and Hoffer (1988) maintain, "Not only do these skills emerge more slowly than originally suggested, but there is evidence that a large segment of our society never acquires them at all" (p. 303).

Topics in proportionality become more and more complex as students move through middle school. For example, when students first see **figure 1**, they will see that the shaded rectangle is 3/5 of the large rectangle, but can they also see a quantity that is 5/3? If we change the referent unit to the shaded part, then the large rectangle is 5/3 of that unit. If we change the referent unit again to the unshaded part, then how much is the shaded part? Given the complex nature of proportionality and the importance of devoting an extensive amount of time to attaining understanding of this concept, a major, multigrade strand organized around proportionality is necessary.

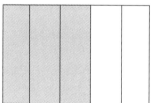

Fig. 1. Quantity depends on referent unit

Proportionality involves topics with which students have great difficulty.

Many, if not all, of the proportionality topics have long presented major difficulties to middle-grades children; sometimes these difficulties persist throughout the higher grades. Hoffer and Hoffer (1988) note, "The acquisition of proportional thinking skills in the population at large has been unsatisfactory" (p. 303). Post, Behr, and Lesh (1988) warn that ratios and proportions represent a crucial point at which many types of mathematical knowledge are required, and a point beyond which students' mathematical understanding will be greatly hampered if they do not attain conceptual understanding. Once again, given the importance of the concepts and the difficulties that students have with the concepts, we can see the logic of developing a major strand that gives significant time to the topics in a unified, coherent way throughout the middle grades.

> **Proportionality provides a framework for studying topics in algebra, geometry, measurement, and probability and statistics—all of which are important topics in the middle grades.**

Proportionality is so far-reaching in scope that it has connections to most, if not all, of the other foundational middle-grades topics and can provide a context for their study.

Algebra

Another topic that is an important unifying theme for the middle grades is algebraic reasoning. Preparing students to think algebraically and starting as early as possible are essential. Proportional reasoning and algebraic reasoning support and depend on each other. *Principles and Standards* (2000) suggests that linear functions be connected with proportionality and includes the following problem:

> Charles saw advertisements for two cellular telephone companies. Keep-in-Touch offers phone service for a basic fee of $20.00 a month plus $0.10 for each minute used. ChitChat has no monthly basic fee but charges $0.45 a minute. Both companies use technology that allows them to charge for the exact amount of time used; they do not "round up" the time to the nearest minute, as many of their competitors do. Compare these two companies' charges for the time used each month. (p. 222)

Students can see that one model, ChitChat, is proportional, and one, Keep-in-Touch, is not.

Geometry

Similarity and scale factor are topics in geometry that readily come to mind when thinking of proportionality. Geometry provides many applications for proportionality. A typical problem might be as follows:

> A certain rectangle has a length and width that are whole numbers of inches, and the ratio of its length to its width is 5 to 4. Its area is 500 square inches. What are its length and width?

Measurement

Relationships among units and conversions from one unit to another in the same system are proportionality topics. Problems involving rates arise from measurement. The relation 1 inch = 2.54 centimeters is proportional, as is 1 meter = 100 centimeters. Are centigrade-to-Fahrenheit conversions proportional?

Probability and statistics

Since probabilities are ratios, problems involving probability require the use of proportional reasoning at many levels. For example, consider the following problem:

> The boy-to-girl ratio in a band is 3/5. Both a boy and a girl leader are randomly chosen. If the band has 45 boys, what is the probability that a particular girl in the band will be selected to lead?

> **Proportionality has many important connections outside mathematics.**

Proportions may be the most commonly applied mathematics in the real world. Sometimes, for a given mathematical topic, a teacher may have to search for applications outside mathematics, but not with proportionality. According to Hoffer and Hoffer (1988), "Because the use of ratios and proportional thinking occurs in many practical situations, these skills should be developed carefully in the school program" (p. 303). A few examples of how we use proportionality outside mathematics are as follows:

- Shopping: Is 3 for $0.79 or 7 for $1 the better buy?
- Cooking: If 1 1/2 cups of sugar in a recipe serves 4 people, how much sugar is needed to serve 6 people?

- Carpentry: If you need 70 planks for 30 feet of fencing, how many planks will you need for 75 feet of fencing?
- Travel: If 1 inch represents 20 miles on a map, how many inches represent 85 miles? If you use 20 gallons of gas to travel 850 miles, how much gasoline will you need to travel 1,000 miles?

Conclusion

Many other issues need to be addressed before proportionality can be developed as a theme in the middle grades. For example, what type of professional development would be required for teachers to be prepared to teach and assess this material effectively? Clearly, however, given the low levels of proportional reasoning that students currently attain, serious thought should be given to designing the middle-grades curriculum around an intensive and extensive theme of proportionality.

References

Hoffer, Allan, and Shirley Hoffer. "Ratios and Proportional Thinking." In *Teaching Mathematics in Grades K–8,* edited by Thomas Post, pp. 285–312. Boston: Allyn & Bacon, 1988.

Lesh, Richard, Thomas Post, and Merlyn Behr. "Proportional Reasoning." In *Number Concepts and Operations in the Middle Grades,* edited by James Hiebert and Merlyn Behr, pp. 93–118. Reston, Va.: National Council of Teachers of Mathematics, 1988.

National Council of Teachers of Mathematics (NCTM). *Principles and Standards for School Mathematics.* Reston, Va.: NCTM, 2000.

Assessing Proportional Thinking

George W. Bright, Jeane M. Joyner, and Charles Wallis

Proportional thinking is an important part of mathematics in the middle grades and "connects many of the mathematics topics studied in grades 6–8" (NCTM 2000, p. 217). Partly in response to this need, NCTM's 2002 Yearbook, titled *Making Sense of Fractions, Ratios, and Proportions* (Bright and Litwiller 2002; Litwiller and Bright 2002), addressed proportional reasoning across the grades but with special emphasis on the teaching and learning of this important area in the middle grades.

Proportional or multiplicative reasoning is in contrast to additive reasoning. Additive reasoning involves using counts—for example, sums or differences of numbers—as the critical factor in comparing quantities. Multiplicative or proportional reasoning involves using ratios as the critical factor in comparing quantities. Two examples illustrate these differences in thinking and reasoning.

In measurement, if two rectangles have the same width, then the rectangle with the greater length has the greater area, so the larger rectangle can be identified by comparing the lengths directly. However, if the lengths and widths of two rectangles are both different, then the product of the two values must be computed to determine which has the greater area. Students who are reasoning additively, however, may try to coordinate some kind of comparison of lengths and widths without ever finding the product of these values. For example, they might say something like "Rectangle A is much longer and rectangle B is only a little wider, so rectangle A must be bigger."

In data analysis, additive reasoning is used to compare absolute frequencies (i.e., counts of the number of times particular data values occur), whereas multiplicative reasoning is used to compare relative frequencies (i.e., percentages of occurrence of particular data values). When two data sets have equal n's, additive reasoning is typically adequate for comparing the distributions. For example, to compare the performance of two equal-sized teams of golfers, students might count the number of players on each team who scored below par or scored between 80 and 90. However, when two data sets have unequal n's, multiplicative reasoning is required. For example, to compare the performance of two golf teams with different numbers of members, students would need to compute the proportion of players who scored below par or scored between 80 and 90. Use of additive and multiplicative reasoning in data analysis is discussed in greater detail in *Navigating through Data Analysis in Grades 6–8* (Bright et al. 2003).

Items to Assess Proportional Reasoning

To assess students' proportional reasoning, it is important to create settings in which they can apply additive and multiplicative reasoning both correctly and incorrectly. It is also important to use multiple methods of assessment, for example, multiple-choice and constructed-response items, because different methods are likely to reveal different information about students' thinking. As part of our current work with teachers, we created a sample assessment that permits teachers to get a sense of how students use additive and multiplicative reasoning. Our goals in organizing this assessment were to provide teachers with an example of assessing a particular type of reasoning and to help teachers generate student data that could be examined to understand the process of classroom assessment. See Bright and Joyner (1998) for details about classroom assessment.

The proportional reasoning assessment consists of four multiple-choice items and one constructed-response item (**fig. 1**). The correct answers to the multiple-choice items are marked with two asterisks (**). The items were adapted from a variety of sources (e.g., Rachlin and Preston 2001).

To answer item 1 correctly, students need to know, or make the assumption, that a copier changes both dimensions equally. In this problem, the 200 percent option doubles both the length and the width, so that the ratio of length to width remains constant. Because each dimension doubles, the area of the copy is four times the area of the original. The solution requires proportional reasoning in that the ratios of length to width are the same for both the original and the copy. Some students might reason, however, that the smaller (or larger) figure is more square just because it is smaller (or larger). This thinking would be evidence of

For each problem, circle the correct answer.

1. Mrs. Allen took a 3 inch by 5 inch photo of the Cape Hatteras Lighthouse and made an enlargement on a photocopier using the 200% option. Which is "more square," the original photo or the enlargement?

   A. The original photo is "more square."
   B. The enlargement is "more square."
   C. The photo and the enlargement are equally square. **
   D. There is not enough information to determine which is "more square."

2. The Science Club has four separate rectangular plots for experiments with plants:

   | 1 foot by 4 feet | 7 feet by 10 feet |
   | 17 feet by 20 feet | 27 feet by 30 feet |

   Which rectangle is most square?

   A. 1 foot by 4 feet   B. 7 feet by 10 feet
   C. 17 feet by 20 feet   D. 27 feet by 30 feet **

3. Sue and Julie were running equally fast around a track. Sue started first. When Sue had run 9 laps, Julie had run 3 laps. When Julie completed 15 laps, how many laps had Sue run?

   A. 45 laps   B. 24 laps
   C. 21 laps **   D. 6 laps

4. At the midway point of the basketball season, you must recommend the best free-throw shooter for the all-star game. Here are the statistics for four players:

   Novak: 8 of 11 shots   Peterson: 22 of 29 shots
   Williams: 15 of 19 shots Reynolds: 33 of 41 shots

   Which player is the best free-throw shooter?

   A. Novak   B. Peterson
   C. Williams   D. Reynolds **

5. Write your answers below the problem.

   A farmer has three fields. One is 185 feet by 245 feet, one is 75 feet by 114 feet, and one is 455 feet by 508 feet. If you were flying over these fields, which one would seem most square? Which one would seem least square?

   Explain your answers.

   Answers: The 455 × 508 field is most square, and the 75 × 114 field is least square, because the ratio 455/508 is closest to 1, and the ratio 75/114 is closest to 0.

Fig. 1. Items to assess proportional reasoning

a lack of proportional reasoning. Of course, an incorrect answer to this item might also reflect a misunderstanding about how a photocopier works rather than confusion about proportional reasoning.

The sizes of the plots in item 2 are chosen so that the length is 3 feet longer than the width. Because the difference of length and width is constant, the ratio of width to length approaches 1 as the sizes of the length and width increase. In this special situation, the plot that is the most square has the longest width, because the ratio of width to length is closest to 1. Here again, students might reason that the smallest (or largest) plot is most square. The problem does not have the option "All are equally square," although such an option might be very attractive to students who are able to reason only additively.

Item 3 is an additive-reasoning problem. Sue is 6 laps ahead of Julie and stays 6 laps ahead, because they were running equally fast. However, students might inappropriately apply proportional reasoning and choose the incorrect answer of A, 45 laps.

Item 4 allows for several different kinds of reasoning. Students might look for (a) the least difference between shots made and shots attempted (8 of 11 shots), (b) the greatest difference between shots made and shots attempted (33 of 41 shots), (c) the ratio of shots made to shots attempted being closest to 1 (33 of 41 shots), (d) the least difference when shots made and shots attempted are in the same "decade" (15 of 19 shots with a difference of 4, as opposed to 22 of 29 shots with a difference of 7), or (e) simply choosing the player who made the most free throws (33 of 41 shots). Notice that the correct answer could be generated with more than one kind of reasoning.

Item 5 allows students to reason in their own way, without trying to understand only specified answers. As we looked at students' work, we saw how they interpreted the idea of "most square" and how they applied that meaning to their reasoning. Students could find the least or greatest difference, the least or greatest ratio of length to width, or apply visual comparisons by choosing the biggest or smallest square.

Students' Responses

We have administered these items in five classes of eighth- and ninth-grade students from both urban and rural settings in North Carolina; the total number of students was 132. The classes included several levels of eighth-grade mathematics, eighth-grade algebra, and ninth-grade algebra. **Tables 1** and **2** contain the number (percentage) of students who chose each answer for the entire sample of 132 students; ** indicates the correct answer for each item.

Table 1
Responses on Multiple-Choice Items

Choice	Item 1	Item 2	Item 3	Item 4
A	27 (20.4%)	16 (12.1%)	48 (36.3%)	53 (40.1%)
B	11 (8.3%)	24 (18.2%)	0 (0.0%)	3 (2.3%)
C	78 (59.1%)**	3 (2.3%)	78 (59.1%)**	15 (11.4%)
D	15 (11.4%)	89 (67.4%)**	5 (3.8%)	60 (45.4%)**
Blank	1 (0.8%)	0 (0.0%)	1 (0.8%)	1 (0.8%)

Table 2
Responses on Open-Ended Item

Choice	Most Square Field	Least Square Field
75 × 114	69 (52.3%)	37 (28.0%)**
185 × 245	10 (7.6%)	59 (44.7%)
455 × 508	49 (37.1%)**	14 (10.6%)
Blank	4 (3.0%)	22 (16.7%)

Figure 2 contains responses of some of the eighth-grade students; their responses reflect the range of responses that we found across all the students. Six of these 14 students (students 8–13) responded to all four multiple-choice items correctly, and two more students (students 6 and 7) missed only the first item. As noted earlier, responses to the first item might be confounded by a misunderstanding about how a photocopier works rather than confusion about proportional reasoning. On the basis of responses to the multiple-choice items, then, these middle-grades students seem to have a reasonable grasp of proportional reasoning. The teacher might proceed with an assumption that the students not only can deal reasonably well with situations that require multiplicative reasoning but also know when to use additive reasoning and when to use multiplicative reasoning. The responses about the most square and least square field, however, reveal how these students are actually reasoning.

Five students (7, 8, 12, 13, and 14) identified the correct fields for "most square" and "least square"; three students (8, 12, and 13) were among the six who answered all the multiple-choice items correctly. Explained another way, three of the six students (9, 10, and 11) who answered all the multiple-choice items correctly were not able to identify correctly the most square and least square fields. The response of student 12 is shown in **figure 3**; an error appears in the response to the second part of the task, as the student writes "most" instead of "least." Interestingly, of 132 students, only 11 students answered all questions correctly and also gave an explanation that reflected proportional reasoning.

Across all 14 students, two common errors were found. Five students (2, 3, 4, 5, and 10) used the difference between length and width as the determining factor for "squareness." This error reflects the use of additive reasoning. The explanation given by student 7 is ambiguous; it might reflect the use of either differences or ratios, because the phrase "closest together" has more than one interpretation. The ambiguity here illustrates very well the fact that probing is often needed to know what a student is thinking.

Five students (1, 6, 8, 9, and 11) argued that squareness was determined by the size of the field. These explanations are somewhat ambiguous about any use of proportional reasoning, although it seems unlikely. The response of student 6 simply refers to the sizes of the fields. The explanation given by student 8 is unusual and unexpected, but it also refers solely to the size of the fields. Note that the product of the dimensions (i.e., area of the field) is responsive only to the size of the numbers, not to their ratio.

Only student 12 used the word "ratio," but even this explanation is somewhat unclear. We have to read quite a bit into the response to infer that this student really used proportional reasoning correctly. The

Student	Item 1	Item 2	Item 3	Item 4	Most Square	Least Square	Explanation
1	a	b	c	d	75×114	455×508	The larger the number the more it is not square, but the smaller the number the more it is square.
2	d	b	c	c	75×114	185×245	[Most square] because their measurements have the least amount of difference. [Least] because this field's measurement has the most amount of difference. For something to be square the measurements have to be as close together as possible.
3	a	b	a	a	75×114	185×245	Most square because it has the least amount of difference. Least square because it has the largest difference.
4	d	b	c	c	75×114	185×245	The field with least difference between its two measurements (__ by __) is the squarest and the field with the most difference is the least square.
5	a	d	c	a	75×114	185×245	I subtracted the numbers on my calculator. For [most square] I found the least number, and for [least square] I found the greatest.
6	a	d	c	d	185×245	455×508	The first field would look the most square because it is the smallest so it wouldn't be that noticeable. The third field is so big it would look rectangular.
7	a	d	c	d	455×508	75×114	Because the two numbers have to be the same to be a square so the closest together will be closer to a square. The opposite for the least square.
8	c	d	c	d	455×508	75×114	If [you] times both numbers, you will have the highest number out of the rest. If you times both numbers you will have the lowest number out of all.
9	c	d	c	d	455×508	185×245	Because if you are flying over then the bigger fields will look more square and there is a better proportion.
10	c	d	c	d	75×114	185×245	If you take the first field and subtract 185 from 245 you get 60. If you do the same for the second you get 39. And the third was 53. So 39 is the least number which would be the most square and the 60 would be the most and seem less square.
11	c	d	c	d	455×508	185×245	Because if you are flying the bigger fields look more square.
12	c	d	c	d	455×508	75×114	Two numbers have to [be the] same to be a square. The most square one has the most ratio of the two numbers and the least square has the least ratio of the two numbers.
13	c	d	c	d	455×508	75×114	I got these answers by dividing each one to get a percent, trying to find the closest one to 100%.
14	a	d	a	d	455×508	75×114	The one that is 455×508 is the biggest because 455 is 89% of 508 and 75×114 is the smallest because 75 is only 65% of 114.

Fig. 2. Students' responses to proportional reasoning items

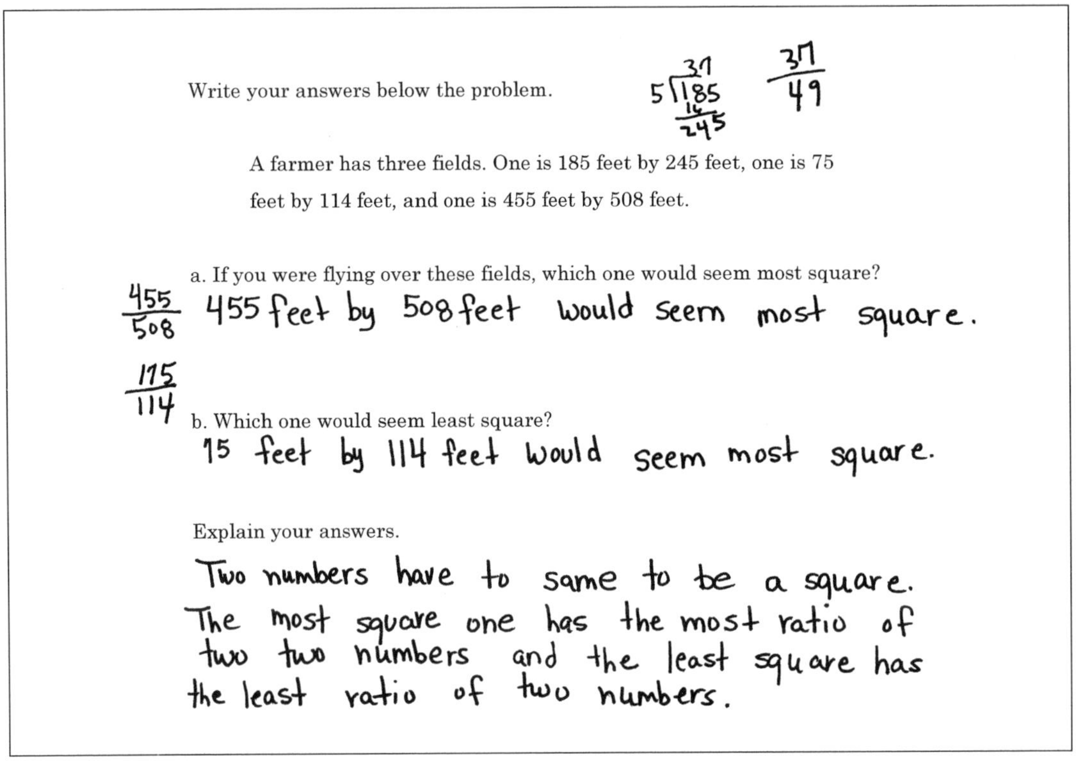

Write your answers below the problem.

$$5\overline{)185}$$ $$\frac{37}{49}$$

A farmer has three fields. One is 185 feet by 245 feet, one is 75 feet by 114 feet, and one is 455 feet by 508 feet.

a. If you were flying over these fields, which one would seem most square?

$\frac{455}{508}$ 455 feet by 508 feet would seem most square.

$\frac{115}{114}$

b. Which one would seem least square?

75 feet by 114 feet would seem most square.

Explain your answers.

Two numbers have to same to be a square. The most square one has the most ratio of two two numbers and the least square has the least ratio of two numbers.

Fig. 3. Multiplicative reasoning by student 12

notion that "the most square one has the most ratio of the two numbers" is correct or incorrect depending on the order in which the two numbers are taken. Stated correctly, it would read, "The most square field has the greatest ratio, that is, a ratio closest to 1, when the smaller dimension is divided by the larger dimension." In contrast, the student who computes the ratios by consistently dividing the larger dimension by the smaller dimension would look for the field with the least ratio. Because student 12 correctly identified the fields that are least square and most square, one might assume that the ratio was computed by taking the dimensions in the order given in the problem.

Many teachers are comfortable making these kinds of inferences about what students write, but it is important to recognize that the inferences are judgments made about students' thinking rather than precise evidence. In our work with teachers, we try to help teachers understand how many inferences they commonly make in the process of understanding what students say and write.

Instructional Implications

The students' responses to the proportional reasoning assessment reinforce the fact that different assessment methods reveal different information about students' thinking. It is possible, for instance, that in easy situations—represented by multiple-choice items—students may reason in a sophisticated way. In more difficult situations—represented by the constructed response item—students may revert to more primitive strategies of reasoning. It is possible that the use of additive reasoning in answering item 5 is simply reverting to familiar reasoning patterns. Perhaps these students had not had much experience solving open-ended, multiplicative-reasoning problems or these problems in any format. In any event, it is clearly important to have a wide view of how students are reasoning, which requires a variety of assessment methods.

The students' responses may also indicate that even students who respond correctly on several multiple-choice items do not have deep understanding of multiplicative reasoning. They may select correct answers in forced choice situations by eliminating the incorrect answers, but they may not be able to apply the concepts spontaneously in problem-solving situations. Clearly, this outcome is not acceptable for a mathematics curriculum. It is important that students be able to apply their knowledge in different situations. Measuring learning in only one situation, such as in multiple-choice tests, is too limiting. If we look only at these responses, we may make inferences that are too generous, both about what students know and the range of application of their knowledge. These inferences might need to be tempered by asking students to respond to other kinds of questions.

Some of the specific responses—for example, bigger dimensions mean more square—need to be explored to find out what students really know and what they really intend to communicate with those words. One key element of classroom assessment is knowing what questions to ask and when to ask them to reveal what students truly understand. It is not easy to ask good probing questions and know how to manage discourse so that students learn how to reflect on their own learning and make sense of what others say. Our own experiences in the classroom suggest that it also takes time to learn how to listen and make sense of what students say and do, so that appropriate follow-up questions and tasks can be designed and used effectively.

One way to help students reflect on their meaning, while providing useful information to the teacher about what the students know and can do, would be to ask students to explain their multiple-choice responses. This reflection will help reveal what students were really thinking. Ask students why they did not choose the other options on the multiple-choice items. Did they explicitly decide to eliminate some choices or did they work each problem and then choose the option that matched their answer? These two strategies show different kinds of mathematical (and test taking) reasoning.

These students might also be helped by a whole-class discussion of solutions to the problems included in the assessment. Having students share their reasoning is an effective way to help the group negotiate some common meaning for what proportional reasoning really is and when it is or is not appropriate to use. In particular, discussion of item 3 (which requires additive reasoning) might reveal information about how students decide when not to use multiplicative reasoning.

Because classroom assessment should influence instruction and promote student learning, teachers should use what they have learned about their students' thinking to select instructional activities that help students develop multiplicative reasoning and understand the difference between additive and multiplicative reasoning. In addition to the ideas suggested below, teachers may want to examine activities in the Navigations books (e.g., Friel et al. 2001) or in the Balanced Assessment Project materials (1999).

The Mr. Tall/Mr. Short task shown in **figure 4** (Khoury 2002) has a long history as a tool for revealing whether students are thinking additively or multiplicatively or are in transition between the two kinds of thinking. Students' typical responses to this task show either additive reasoning, multiplicative reasoning, or transition from additive to multiplicative reasoning. Having students share their solutions is one way to help them see the underlying mathematical differences between additive and multiplicative reasoning.

Another traditional problem is comparison of flavors when various combinations of orange juice concentrate and water are mixed together (e.g., 3 scoops of concentrate and 2 cups of water versus 2 scoops of concentrate and 4 cups of water). In these situations, students are expected to compare the ratios of concentrate to water (e.g., 3/2 versus 2/4) to see which ratio is greater; that is, students can treat the ratios as fractions. Billings (2002) and Roy (2002) provide variations of this idea with problems in which numbers are not used. Kent, Arnosky, and McMonagle (2002) also discuss the importance of understanding ratios in developing multiplicative reasoning. In particular, Roy's task involves making tables of values of water and lemonade mix for two recipes, then representing these values graphically to connect the slopes of the resulting lines with the strength of flavor of the two recipes.

Cai and Sun (2002) highlight the ratio (e.g., 12:4), the ratio operation (e.g., 12 ÷ 4), and ratio value (e.g., 3) as important ideas that students need to understand and connect conceptually. For teachers, it is obvious that 12:4 = 12 ÷ 4 = 3, but students may not see this connection so clearly. Merely using different words to describe these different ideas might help students make the connection that a ratio should be connected to the corresponding division problem as well as to the quotient of that division. It might also help students to use what they know about fractions and division to help them develop understanding of ratio, and subsequently, proportions.

Scale drawings—for example, taking a shape drawn on a grid and doubling (or halving) all of the dimensions—can engage students in multiplicative reasoning. Students could explore the differences in shape when only the horizontal (or only the vertical) dimension is doubled. Weinberg (2002) provides an activity

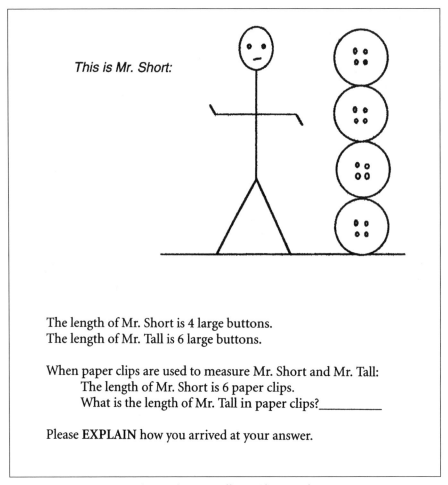

This is Mr. Short:

The length of Mr. Short is 4 large buttons.
The length of Mr. Tall is 6 large buttons.

When paper clips are used to measure Mr. Short and Mr. Tall:
    The length of Mr. Short is 6 paper clips.
    What is the length of Mr. Tall in paper clips?_____

Please **EXPLAIN** how you arrived at your answer.

Fig. 4. The Mr. Tall/Mr. Short task

in which students measure objects in both centimeters and inches, create a table of values, and then graph the data. The slope of the resulting line represents the scale factor, 1 inch = 2.54 centimeters.

In our view, classroom assessment should involve understanding students' thinking; it is not about assigning grades, although assigning grades is an important part of a teacher's work. Classroom assessment is useful as a way to gather information about how students are thinking, but that information must then be used to inform instruction and facilitate students' learning. And isn't that what good teaching is really about?

References

Balanced Assessment Project. *Middle Grades Assessment (Package 1 and Package 2).* White Plains, N.Y.: Dale Seymour Publications, 1999.

Billings, Esther M. H. "Cocoa." In *Classroom Activities for Making Sense of Fractions, Ratios, and Proportions,* 2002 Yearbook of the National Council of Teachers of Mathematics (NCTM), edited by George W. Bright and Bonnie Litwiller, pp. 38–40. Reston, Va.: NCTM, 2002.

Bright, George W., and Jeane M. Joyner, eds. *Classroom Assessment in Mathematics: Views from a National Science Foundation Working Conference.* Lanham, Md.: University Press of America, 1998.

Bright, George W., and Bonnie Litwiller, eds. *Classroom Activities for Making Sense of Fractions, Ratios, and Proportions,* 2002 Yearbook of the National Council of Teachers of Mathematics (NCTM). Reston, Va.: NCTM, 2002.

Bright, George, Wallece Brewer, Kay McClain, and Edward S. Mooney. *Navigating through Data Analysis in Grades 6–8*. Reston, Va: National Council of Teachers of Mathematics, 2003.

Cai, Jinfa, and Wei Sun. "Developing Students' Proportional Reasoning: A Chinese Perspective." In *Making Sense of Fractions, Ratios, and Proportions,* 2002 Yearbook of the National Council of Teachers of Mathematics (NCTM), edited by Bonnie Litwiller and George W. Bright, pp. 195–205. Reston, Va: NCTM, 2002.

Friel, Susan N., Sid Rachlin, Dot Doyle, Claire Mygard, and David Pugalee. *Navigating through Algebra in Grades 6–8*. Reston, Va.: National Council of Teachers of Mathematics, 2001.

Kent, Laura B., Joyce Arnosky, and Judy McMonagle. "Using Representational Contexts to Support Multiplicative Reasoning." In *Making Sense of Fractions, Ratios, and Proportions,* 2002 Yearbook of the National Council of Teachers of Mathematics (NCTM), edited by Bonnie Litwiller and George W. Bright, pp. 145–152. Reston, Va.: NCTM, 2002.

Khoury, Helen A. "Exploring Proportional Reasoning: Mr. Tall/Mr. Short." In *Making Sense of Fractions, Ratios, and Proportions,* 2002 Yearbook of the National Council of Teachers of Mathematics (NCTM), edited by Bonnie Litwiller and George W. Bright, pp. 100–102. Reston, Va.: NCTM, 2002.

Litwiller, Bonnie, and George W. Bright, eds. *Making Sense of Fractions, Ratios, and Proportions,* 2002 Yearbook of the National Council of Teachers of Mathematics (NCTM). Reston, Va.: NCTM, 2002.

National Council of Teachers of Mathematics (NCTM). *Principles and Standards for School Mathematics*. Reston, Va.: NCTM, 2000.

Rachlin, Sid L., and Ron V. Preston. "Algebraic Concepts and Relationships: Instructor's Materials." Greenville, N.C.: The Middle Math Project, East Carolina University, 2001. www.math.ecu.edu /midmath/curriculum.

Roy, Francine Cabral. "Lemonade Mix." In *Classroom Activities for Making Sense of Fractions, Ratios, and Proportions,* 2002 Yearbook of the National Council of Teachers of Mathematics (NCTM), edited by George W. Bright and Bonnie Litwiller, pp. 49–51. Reston, Va.: NCTM, 2002.

Weinberg, Suzanne Levin. "Centimeters and Inches—A Different Look at Proportional Reasoning." In *Classroom Activities for Making Sense of Fractions, Ratios, and Proportions,* 2002 Yearbook of the National Council of Teachers of Mathematics (NCTM), edited by George W. Bright and Bonnie Litwiller, pp. 52–55. Reston, Va.: NCTM, 2002.

Problems That Encourage Proportion Sense

Esther M. H. Billings

A few years ago, a former student, whom I will call Carol, asked me to help her review for a standardized mathematics test. She had solved some proportion problems on her own and wanted me to check her work. One of the problems was similar to the following: "John drove 60 miles in 2 hours. If he continues to drive at this same speed, how long will it take him to drive 40 additional miles?" To solve the problem, Carol set up two ratios, solved for the unknown using an application of the standard algorithm for proportions, and determined that driving the additional 40 miles would take John 3 hours (see **fig. 1**).

$$\frac{60}{40} = \frac{x}{2}$$
$$40x = 120$$
$$x = 3$$

Fig. 1. Carol's solution strategy

I suggested that Carol forget about her calculations for a moment and think about the problem directly. I asked her whether driving 40 miles would take John more or less time than driving the initial 60 miles would. She immediately replied that because 40 miles was a shorter distance than 60 miles, driving that distance would take less time, specifically, less than 2 hours. She also commented that because 40 miles was a bit more than half of 60 miles, driving that distance would take a bit more than 1 hour, which is half of the 2 hours needed to drive 60 miles. Using her proportion sense, or what others have called qualitative-based reasoning, Carol determined that her answer had to be between 1 and 2 hours and concluded that her initial answer of 3 hours did not make sense and could not be correct. Carol set up the proportion equation again and found that John would need 1 hour and 20 minutes to drive 40 miles. She was now confident that her answer had to be correct. Carol's use of proportion sense was essential to her understanding of the proportional situation of the time required for John to drive a certain distance.

NCTM's *Principles and Standards for School Mathematics* (2000) emphasizes the importance of developing and nurturing middle school students' proportional reasoning abilities. One of the ways to do so is to help students understand how to coordinate the various quantities in the ratios that are being compared so that relationships between these quantities can be explored and extended. The ability to reason about quantities and the various relationships that quantities share in proportional situations is what I call *proportion sense.*

This article describes four problems that encourage the use and development of proportion sense. These problems were created during a research study with prospective elementary school teachers (Billings 1998). As part of the study, the participants solved a variety of proportion problems. Excerpts from their solution strategies are presented to show how these problems created a rich environment for proportion sense to emerge and develop. Pseudonyms have been given to the participants in the study.

Using Nonnumeric Problems to Encourage Proportion Sense

When solving numeric proportion problems, many students are so concerned with getting an answer that they fail to consider the reasonableness of their answers. Many attempt to apply the standard algorithm or some other quantitative procedure without truly understanding why the algorithm or procedure is appropriate (Cramer and Post 1993). As teachers, we face the challenge of making proportions meaningful for our students. Because students tend to "misuse" numbers by applying them to some formula, we must help them focus on underlying proportional relationships and create an environment that nurtures proportion sense. One way that we can help students cultivate proportion sense is to strip problems of numbers, that is, provide nonnumeric proportion problems that force students to examine the relationships between variables directly.

Nonnumeric biking-speed problem

Consider the following nonnumeric proportion problem that involves two girls biking on a path:

> Catherine and Rachel like to ride their bicycles along the bike path in Forever Green Park. Today, they both started riding at the beginning of the trail; each rode continuously at a constant speed, making no stops, to the end of the trail. Rachel took more time than Catherine to reach the end of the path. Which girl was biking faster? Why? Explain your answer.

This problem context is similar to any standard problem that could be found in a chapter of a middle school textbook dealing with proportions. In this setting, however, students are asked to make a conclusion about a relationship—which girl was riding faster—rather than calculate a numerical answer—the speed or distance traveled by one or both of the girls.

The fourteen prospective teachers who participated in the study all used their proportion sense to reason that Catherine rode her bike faster than Rachel. They concluded that because the bikers did not make any stops and rode the same distance, they must have taken different amounts of time to reach the end of the path. Consequently, the girls had to be riding at different speeds. For example, Grace explained the problem this way:

> Catherine made it to the end first, so she had to have been moving faster. . . . She was able to reach the end of the path first. Rachel must have been moving slower; otherwise, she would have arrived at the same time or before Catherine.

Because the problem is open ended, however, it also allows students to further analyze unstated assumptions that could affect the proportional relationship. For example, Bill said that Catherine was biking faster, "assuming she didn't take a shortcut." He noted that a decrease in the total distance that Catherine was biking would affect the amount of time needed to reach the end of the trail. In a class discussion, Bill's observation offered an opportunity to discuss the role of distance in this problem. Students could see that if the girls rode two different distances, the length of time required to reach the end of the path would not be sufficient information to determine who was the faster biker. Mary found another example of an unstated assumption in this problem. She observed, "They both started riding at the beginning of the trail, but they didn't say they both started at the same time, which may mean that one may have started before the other." She realized that if the time in the problem did not mean actual time spent riding, then it could not be used as a means for comparison either.

This problem not only focuses on the relationship between time and speed but also allows students to analyze other factors, such as distance and starting time, that might affect whether the relationship is truly proportional. This seemingly simple problem provided an opportunity to reason about the relationship between variables that could both directly and indirectly affect the bikers' speeds.

Nonnumeric piano-string-vibration problem

Another example of a problem that promotes proportion sense was modified from a standard textbook problem involving piano strings.

> The frequency of vibrations of a piano string increases as the length decreases. Which piano string would vibrate more slowly, a 36-inch string or a 24-inch string? Why? Explain your answer.

Here, the statement of the problem gives numerical values, but not enough values are given to calculate an exact answer. As a result, the student must analyze the relationship between the length of the string and the frequency of the string's vibration. Again, all the prospective teachers reasoned that the 36-inch string would vibrate more slowly. Joan's response is typical of this type of reasoning:

> So it would be a 36-inch string that is vibrating more slowly because the less string, the more it vibrates. A 36-inch string would vibrate more slowly for that reason. The shorter the length, the more vibrations. The longer the length, the less vibrations.

In this problem, students must focus on the underlying proportional relationship that connects the various quantities and determine how an increase or decrease in one quantity, in this instance, the length of the string, directly affects the behavior of another quantity, the frequency of the vibrations.

Nonnumeric coffee-taste problem

In addition to modifying standard textbook proportion problems, I also developed a series of nonnumeric problems. These problems show a picture of two carafes of coffee and indicate which carafe contains stronger-tasting coffee. In addition, the problems state that some change is made to the carafes, such as adding a cup of water or adding a spoonful of instant coffee. The objective is to identify, if possible, the carafe that contains the stronger-tasting coffee after the change has been made. Once again, these problems require students to reason about the relationships that exist between the amount of water or coffee and the taste of the coffee, thus cultivating students' proportion sense in a different context. See **figure 2** for an example of this type of problem.

The prospective teachers also answered this question correctly by reasoning about the effects of adding more coffee and water to the coffee mixtures in the carafes. They realized that as the amount of coffee increased, the concentration of the mixture also increased. Likewise, as the amount of water added to a mixture increased, the concentration of the mixture decreased. For example, Lucy explained the relationship as follows:

> [Carafe B] is already weaker to start off with, and then you're still going to add more water to it; you're not even adding any coffee at all. And [carafe A] is already strong, and you're just adding coffee to it, which is going to make it stronger.

Making a mathematically meaningful comparison between carafes in a different and slightly more complicated situation (see **fig. 3**) proved more challenging for the study participants. Most of the prospective teachers successfully identified the initial volume of the liquid as a necessary component in determining the relationship between the addition of more coffee and the taste of the coffee. Bill reasoned as follows:

> If they both taste the same, I would assume they would both have the same ratio of water to coffee, [and you are] adding one spoon of coffee to each. In carafe A, it would be diluted more. In carafe B, there would be less water to dilute the coffee; therefore, it would be stronger.

Misconceptions about the proportional relationships also emerged. Several prospective teachers reasoned incorrectly, as Grace did when she said, "The coffee tastes the same; add coffee to both. So it's always the same . . . because you're adding the same amount to each and they started out the same." Grace, like several others, was operating under the assumption that in adding the same amount of coffee to both carafes, the relative relationship of the taste also remained the same. These students disregarded the initial volume of liquid in the carafes, not realizing that this variable was essential in analyzing the situation. They realized that an increase in the amount of coffee caused an overall increase of stronger-tasting coffee in each carafe, but they failed to compare the overall strength of the coffee *between* carafes, an important component in this proportional situation. Their reasoning appears to focus on doing the "same thing" to both carafes. This reasoning illustrates the teachers' misunderstanding of the notion that simultaneously increasing the value of one quantity in a pair of corresponding ratios can affect the relationship between the two ratios. Their reasoning can be summarized as follows:

Below it is indicated which carafe contains the stronger coffee. Determine which carafe will contain the stronger coffee after the alterations have been made. Explain how you came to your answer.

Carafe B contains weaker coffee than carafe A. Add one spoon of instant coffee to carafe A and one cup of water to carafe B.

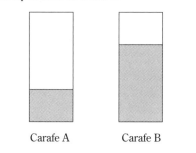

Fig. 2. Nonnumeric coffee-taste problem 1

Below it is indicated which carafe contains the stronger coffee. Determine which carafe will contain the stronger coffee after the alterations have been made. Explain how you came to your answer.

Carafe A and carafe B contain coffee that tastes the same. Add one spoon of instant coffee to both carafe A and carafe B.

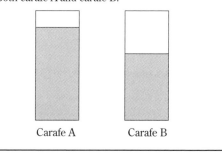

Fig. 3. Nonnumeric coffee-taste problem 2

If $\dfrac{a}{c} = \dfrac{b}{d}$ $(c, d \neq 0)$, then $\dfrac{a+1}{c} = \dfrac{b+1}{d}$ $(c, d \neq 0)$, when the values of a, b, c, and d are unknown.

However, altering corresponding values in a ratio changes not only the ratio itself but also the relationship between the ratios.

This nonnumeric proportion situation exposed certain assumptions that the teachers made about the relationships that exist between the quantities in a proportional setting. If the problem had involved numerical quantities and asked the teachers to calculate a numerical answer rather than to directly reflect on the relationship between the quantities in the ratios, this fundamental misunderstanding may not have emerged. When such misconceptions emerge as students solve this type of nonnumeric problem, the opportunity arises to discuss the importance of also comparing the relationship between the new ratios, such as, in this instance, comparing the altered carafes of coffee. The discussion will help students strengthen their proportion sense.

Nurturing Proportion Sense in a Variety of Proportion Situations

The four nonnumeric problems presented in this article were all designed to deepen students' understanding of the underlying concepts that influence the relationships in proportional situations. Because nonnumeric problems demand that students examine relationships, having students solve these types of problems, especially when the concept of proportions is being introduced, can be beneficial. Many traditional proportion word problems can be altered to focus primarily on the underlying proportional relationship, as was done in the bicycle and piano-strings problems. Simply modify the proportion problem in such a way that some of or all the numerical quantities are deleted but the relationship between the variables is still clear, then ask a question that requires the students to focus on the proportional relationship inherent in the problem.

Nonnumeric problems offer a different type of context in which to examine the underlying relationships that connect the variables in proportional situations. If your students cannot relate to carafes of coffee, alter the context to something that has more meaning to them, such as pitchers of hot chocolate or lemonade. These problems can also be extended to include additional scenarios in which students are asked to contrast the results of adding quantities of some type of variable to various mixtures, then to compare concentrations.

By presenting students with different nonnumeric proportion problems, especially as they are introduced to proportions, we will help them focus on the underlying relationships and anticipate how an increase or decrease in one variable affects another variable, as well as alters the ratio. Exposing students to nonnumeric proportion situations is essential in helping them develop proportion sense.

Using Numeric Problems for Proportion Sense

Developing proportion sense is not limited to these types of nonnumeric problems. Most of the proportion problems that students face in their studies will involve numbers. Teachers can build students' proportion sense and understanding of proportions in numeric situations. One way to incorporate numeric problems is to first discuss and solve a nonnumeric problem, such as the bicycle or piano-string problems presented previously. Then, extend the discussion by posing a similar numeric problem. This approach allows students to apply their developing proportion sense in a concrete, numeric setting.

We can also encourage our students to use proportion sense and focus first on underlying relationships in numeric proportion situations. For example, the problem that introduced this article asks students to determine the length of time John needs to drive 40 miles given that he has driven 60 miles in 2 hours. Instead of immediately encouraging the use of some quantitative strategy, such as the standard algorithm or some other solution strategy, begin by asking the students, "Do you think John will drive the 40 miles in more or less than 2 hours? Why do you think so?" This type of question communicates to our students that we want them to make sense of the problem and their proposed answers. In addition, the question emphasizes the importance of reflecting about the nature of the underlying relationships in the problem first. After students have concluded that driving the 40 miles would take less time because the distance is shorter, you might ask, "Could anyone make a reasonable estimate about how long John would take to drive 40 miles? Why is your estimate reasonable?" After reflecting about the relationships, students could then be asked to think about what solution strategy might be appropriate to solve this problem and to determine the exact amount of time required to drive the 40 miles.

Summary

Research has shown that emphasis on the standard algorithm for solving proportions—equating two ratios with one unknown, cross-multiplying, and solving for the unknown—has limitations in encouraging students to reason proportionally (Post, Behr, and Lesh 1988). However, this standard algorithm is a procedure that middle school students are taught in a traditional curriculum. Although this algorithm can be useful and efficient for solving proportion problems, it may suggest to students that they simply memorize the procedure; they do not necessarily have to reason about the various quantities that constitute the ratios, nor directly reason about how one variable is related to another. In contrast, when students are expected to reason about the relationships between the variables and use proportion sense, they can then begin to make more sense of the standard algorithm and other strategies for solving numeric proportion situations.

Most of the proportion problems that students encounter are quantitative, and their knowing how to solve proportion situations numerically is important, but students must also be able to reason directly about the relationships that exist between the quantities in these situations. As students solve numeric proportion problems, teachers must ask questions that will help them continue to reflect about the underlying relationships that exist in the problem. If we encourage this type of reflection, students will begin to form the habit of asking themselves questions about underlying proportional relationships, thus strengthening their proportion sense. Students who actively use proportion sense can make sense of the relationships in the problem and verify that their final answers make sense after applying some quantitative strategy, such as the standard algorithm, or unit-rate method. Emphasizing proportion sense can also help students make sense of, and draw mathematical meaning from, ratio and proportion situations. As their proportion sense grows, students deepen their understanding of ratios and proportions and become better mathematical thinkers.

References

Billings, Esther. "Qualitative-Based Reasoning of Preservice Elementary School Teachers in Proportional Situations." Ph.D. diss., Northern Illinois University, 1998.

Cramer, Kathleen, and Thomas Post. "Proportional Reasoning." *Mathematics Teacher* 86 (May 1993): 404–7.

National Council of Teachers of Mathematics (NCTM). *Principles and Standards for School Mathematics.* Reston, Va.: NCTM, 2000.

Post, Thomas, Merlyn Behr, and Richard Lesh. "Proportionality and the Development of Prealgebra Understandings." In *The Ideas of Algebra, K–12*, 1988 Yearbook of the National Council of Teachers of Mathematics (NCTM), edited by Arthur F. Coxford, pp. 78–90. Reston, Va.: NCTM, 1988.

Numbers Need Not Apply: Teaching Notes

Esther M. H. Billings

GRADE RANGE: 5–8
MATHEMATICAL TOPICS: proportions, ratios, multiplicative reasoning, proportion sense

Discussion of the Mathematics, with Answers and Solutions

These problems help cultivate students' proportion sense, that is, the ability to reason about quantities and the various relationships that quantities share with other quantities in proportional situations. Students often focus on the numerical quantities in a proportion problem and try to apply some known strategy to these quantities without really understanding why or if their strategy is appropriate for the situation. One way to help students understand proportional relationships is to provide "numberless" problems that encourage direct reasoning about the relationship between variables, how one variable affects another, and what these relationships indicate about the proportional situation. Most students are fairly successful in correctly identifying the answers for these problems. However, they may have trouble identifying the pertinent variables that directly affect the proportional relationship.

Answers

1. Catherine. Since Catherine arrives at the end destination first, she is riding faster because she covers the same distance as Rachel in a shorter time period. (Of course, this answer assumes that each girl rides the same distance and that neither took a short cut.)

2. 36-inch string. As the length of a piano string becomes shorter, its frequency of vibration (the speed at which the string moves back and forth) becomes faster. We could also say that the longer the piano string is, the slower its frequency of vibration. Choose the longer string, since it vibrates more slowly.

3. This problem provides a nice opportunity to talk about assumptions and the role of different variables. One possible answer is to assume that the walls they are building are the same thickness or depth (e.g., 2 blocks deep). In this case, since they use the same number of identical blocks, the only variables that vary are the height and length of the wall. Then, if Maria's wall is taller, Ann's wall is longer, since the volume of blocks used to build the wall is conserved. Another answer is to conclude that more information is needed, since the problem does not explicitly state that the walls are the same thickness (depth). Consequently, Maria's wall might be taller, but we can't say for sure that Ann's wall will be longer (in length) or thicker (in depth). For example, if each girl uses 24 blocks, Maria's wall could be 4 blocks high, 2 blocks thick, and 3 blocks long, and Ann's, 3 blocks high, 4 blocks thick, and 2 blocks long, making it shorter (in height and length) but thicker (in depth) than Maria's. (Ann's wall could also be 1 block high, 4 blocks thick, and 6 blocks long, making it thicker in depth, shorter in height, and longer in length.)

Credit

Billings, Esther M. H. "Qualitative Based Reasoning of Preservice Elementary School Teachers in Proportional Situations." Ph.D. diss., Northern Illinois University, 1998. *Dissertation Abstracts International* 59 no. 09A (1998): 3383.

Name   Date

Numbers Need Not Apply

1. Catherine and Rachel like to ride their bikes along a bike trail. Today they started riding at the same time at the beginning of the trail. Each rode continuously at a constant speed (making no stops) to the end of the trail. Rachel took more time than Catherine to reach the end of the trail. Which girl was biking faster? Explain your answer.

2. The frequency of vibrations of a piano string increases as the length decreases. Which piano string would vibrate more slowly, a 36-inch string or a 24-inch string? Explain your answer.

3. Maria and Ann each have the same number of identical wooden (cube) blocks. Each girl is told to build a wall, using all of the blocks, so that there are no "holes" in the wall. Maria's wall is taller than Ann's. What can we say about Ann's wall? Explain your answer.

Cocoa: Teaching Notes

Esther M. H. Billings

GRADE RANGE: 5–8
MATHEMATICAL TOPICS: proportion, ratio, multiplicative reasoning, proportion sense

Discussion of the Mathematics, with Answers and Solutions

These problems help cultivate students' proportion sense, that is, the ability to reason about quantities and the various relationships that quantities share with other quantities in proportional situations. Since no scale is given for the volume of cocoa or concentration of cocoa mix to water in each thermos, encourage students to think generally about the scenarios, especially extreme cases (a very large amount of hot cocoa versus a minute amount of hot cocoa; very "thick" hot cocoa versus very weak and diluted hot cocoa) and the relative relationships between thermoses.

Answers

1. Thermos A. Adding mix to A makes it even stronger-tasting and adding water to B further dilutes it.

2. Thermos B. Though the initial taste is the same, the volumes differ. Adding cocoa mix to a mixture of lesser volume will have a greater effect on the overall taste, so B now contains the cocoa with the stronger chocolate taste.

3. Thermos B. Since both thermoses contain the same volume, there is more cocoa mix per unit of water in B, since it is initially stronger-tasting. Each thermos of cocoa becomes stronger-tasting. The relationship between thermoses remains the same, since B was initially stronger-tasting.

4. Indeterminate, since we don't know how much stronger B is than A. The cocoa becomes stronger-tasting in A and weaker-tasting in B after alterations are made. However, we cannot conclude if the concentrations of cocoa have altered enough to change the relationship between thermoses. Depending on the initial ratios of scoops of cocoa mix to cups of water, different outcomes are possible. For example, if A starts with 1 scoop of mix and 2 cups of water and B with 9 scoops of mix and 2 cups of water, B still contains stronger-tasting cocoa after the alterations. But if A initially contains 4 scoops of mix and 2 cups of water and B contains 5 scoops of mix and 2 cups of water, making the alterations would make A contain the stronger-tasting cocoa.

An informal argument also works. (Reasoning informally may also help provide a starting place to choose appropriate numerical examples to show the indeterminacy of the situation.) If the cocoa in B is very "thick" and chocolatey, adding one cup of water may only change the consistency slightly. The cocoa in A may be so weak that you can hardly taste a chocolate flavor, so adding one scoop of mix may only slightly alter the flavor and consistency. Consequently, the cocoa in B would still be stronger-tasting. However, the two thermoses may also contain cocoa that tastes almost the same, with the cocoa in B only slightly stronger-tasting. Making the alterations could cause a change in taste so that A now contains hot cocoa with a stronger chocolate taste.

Credit

Billings, Esther M. H. "Qualitative Based Reasoning of Preservice Elementary School Teachers in Proportional Situations." Ph.D. diss., Northern Illinois University, 1998. *Dissertation Abstracts International* 59, no. 09A (1998): 3383.

Name   Date

Cocoa

1. Thermos A contains cocoa with a stronger chocolate taste. If one scoop of cocoa mix is added to Thermos A and one cup of hot water is added to Thermos B, which thermos contains the cocoa with the stronger chocolate taste? Explain your answer.

Thermos A   *Thermos B*

2. Thermos A and Thermos B contain cocoa that tastes the same. If one scoop of cocoa mix is added to both Thermos A and Thermos B, which thermos contains the cocoa with the stronger chocolate taste? Explain your answer.

Thermos A   *Thermos B*

Cocoa (continued)

3. Thermos A contains cocoa with a weaker chocolate taste. If one scoop of cocoa mix is added to both Thermos A and Thermos B, which thermos contains the cocoa with the stronger chocolate taste? Explain your answer.

Thermos A   *Thermos B*

4. Thermos B contains cocoa with a stronger chocolate taste. If one scoop of cocoa mix is added to Thermos A and one cup of hot water is added to Thermos B, which thermos contains the cocoa with the stronger chocolate taste? Explain your answer.

Thermos A   *Thermos B*

Using Recipes and Ratio Tables to Build on Students' Understanding of Fractions

Laura Brinker

I recently worked with a teacher in a combined fourth- and fifth-grade class as she taught a unit on fractions and mixed numbers. All the problems given to students during this unit were situated within various real-world contexts. One part of the unit required students to increase and decrease the number of servings of different recipes. We were both amazed at the number of different strategies that the students used to multiply fractions and mixed numbers without any direct instruction on the standard algorithms! Although many of their solutions may seem long or inefficient by traditional standards, it was clear that they had a good understanding of the processes being used and that they rarely made mistakes.

This article describes three students' strategies for multiplying fractions and mixed numbers when increasing the number of servings of various recipes. All three students had had some prior instruction in adding and subtracting fractions, but none had had any formal instruction in multiplying or dividing fractions. Their solutions for solving these different recipe problems illustrate an implicit understanding of the distributive property.

Three main factors that contributed to the students' ability to solve recipe problems are discussed in detail. One was their informal knowledge of such benchmark fractions as 1/2, 1/3, and 1/4. A second factor was the use of recipe contexts that were familiar and meaningful to them. Finally, the use of a ratio table to organize their operations with fractions facilitated their solution processes.

Students' Informal Knowledge

Several recent studies illustrate that students in the elementary grades already possess a great deal of intuitive knowledge about fractions and ratios (Empson 1995; Lamon 1993; Mack 1990; Streefland 1993). Both Empson and Streefland found that students could successfully add and compare fractions within the context of "equal sharing." Also, Streefland (1991) found that a knowledge of relationships among fractional amounts can provide a basis for students to multiply fractions and mixed numbers without direct instruction. For example, students can use their informal knowledge to reason that doubling a half of the whole completes the whole or that tripling a fourth of the whole yields three-fourths. They can reason about these problems without knowing the standard algorithm for multiplying simple fractions.

Recipe Context

The NCTM's *Curriculum and Evaluation Standards for School Mathematics* (1989) recommends that students solve mathematics problems that are situated in real-world contexts. Recipes present natural situations for the development of students' understanding of rational-number concepts. **Figure 1** shows, in table form, the ingredients needed in a recipe for chocolate-chip cookies.

Many cooking recipes involve fractional amounts of ingredients. For example, this chocolate-chip-cookie recipe requires 3/4 of a cup of brown sugar for five dozen cookies. Increasing or decreasing the number of servings of a recipe can introduce other fractions or mixed numbers. If the number of servings of chocolate-chip cookies is halved, then the amount of brown sugar needed also needs to be halved, to only 3/8 of a cup. If the number of servings is tripled, then the amount of brown sugar is also tripled, to 2 1/4 cups. Most students can do these computations by making sense of the fractional amounts as quantities or by modeling the context of the measuring cup.

The author wishes to thank Teri Kuhs and Ed Dickey for their thoughtful critiques on earlier drafts of this article, and Teri Hedges for providing a wonderful classroom atmosphere to explore children's thinking about fractions.

Number of dozens of cookies	5
Sticks of butter	2
Cups of sugar	3/4
Cups of brown sugar	3/4
Eggs	2
Teaspoons of vanilla	1
Teaspoons of salt	1/2
Teaspoons of baking soda	1
Cups of flour	2 1/4
Cups of chocolate chips	2

Fig. 1. Ingredients needed to make sixty chocolate-chip cookies

Increasing and decreasing recipes provide a context not only for operations with fractions but also for thinking about the concept of ratios or fixed relationships. For example, the number of cups of flour needed in a typical chocolate-chip-cookie recipe, 2 1/4 cups, is triple the number of cups of brown sugar regardless of the change in the number of servings of the recipe. If the recipe is quadrupled, 3 cups of brown sugar and 9 cups of flour are needed; the number of cups of flour is still triple the number of cups of brown sugar.

Another important feature of using the recipe context to teach the multiplication of fractions and mixed numbers is the use of concrete referents with which students are familiar, such as teaspoons and cups. These referents help students make sense of their solutions and may also help them avoid the temptation to apply previously learned standard algorithms incorrectly. For example, students are less likely to add the numerators and denominators when tripling 1/2, thus getting the incorrect answer of 3/6, if they are tripling 1/2 of a unit they know, such as cups, miles, and so on. Most students know that if they triple 1/2 cup of something, they will end up with more than one cup.

Ratio Table

A ratio table is a useful tool for organizing ratios and operations with fractions. A ratio table is a pictorial model that allows students to represent fractions and ratios. **Figure 2** shows an example of a table of ingredients for a chicken recipe from an introductory unit on fractions called "Some of the Parts" in a new middle school curriculum, *Mathematics in Context: A Connected Curriculum for Grades 5–8* (Van Galen et al. 1997). When subsequent columns are added to list changes in the amounts of ingredients, a ratio table is formed, as shown in **figure 3**.

The context of cooking for different numbers of people is intended to give students opportunities to use their informal strategies to multiply and divide fractions as the number of servings of a given recipe is increased or decreased. Although the concept of ratio is not made explicit in the curriculum unit, the notion of increasing (or decreasing) the amount of ingredients as the number of servings is increased (or decreased) implicitly addresses the idea of ratio as a constant relationship.

Number of servings	8				
Number of boneless chicken-breast halves	8				
Jars of salsa verde	1				
Cups of light sour cream	1				
Cups of half and half	1/2				
Corn tortillas	12				
Cups of shredded cheddar cheese	4				
Cups of grated parmesan cheese	1/3				

Fig. 2. Table of ingredients for the chicken-and-tortilla-casserole recipe

Number of servings	8	16	4	20	28
Number of boneless chicken-breast halves	8	16	4	20	28
Jars of salsa verde	1	2	1/2	2 1/2	3 1/2
Cups of light sour cream	1	2	1/2	2 1/2	3 1/2
Cups of half and half	1/2	1	1/4	1 1/4	1 3/4
Corn tortillas	12	24	6	30	42
Cups of shredded cheddar cheese	4	8	2	10	14
Cups of grated parmesan cheese	1/3	2/3	1/6	5/6	1 1/6

Fig 3. Additional columns added to the chicken-and-tortilla-casserole recipe

Instruction

Instruction in this particular fourth-fifth–grade mathematics class focused on problem solving and on op-portunities for students to share solution strategies. The teacher introduced the ratio table near the middle of the unit on fractions. Students were initially presented with a ratio table in the form of a partial recipe as shown in **figure 4**. Students were asked to determine the number of teaspoons of oregano needed for twenty-four pizzas if 1/2 teaspoon of oregano is needed for four pizzas. These ratio-table solutions were given to students only *after* they had had ample opportunity to answer this question by using their own strategies. The teacher, in this instance, was careful not to prescribe strategies for students to use. The ratio-table strategies were presented as a way to organize computations with fractions. Thereafter, the students were responsible for deciding which computations to use for each recipe problem, which often looked very different.

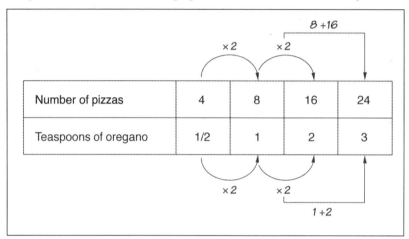

Fig 4. Partial recipe from "Some of the Parts" (Van Galen et al. 1997)

Most students in the class could enlarge and reduce recipes when they worked with benchmark frac-tions, such as 1/4, 1/3, and 1/2. They used various strategies, such as repeated addition, to double and triple these fractional amounts. The teacher decided that we should challenge them by using more difficult frac-tions and mixed numbers. The new problems that we gave them involved multiplying a fraction by a mixed number and multiplying two mixed numbers. In the next section, solutions given by Julie, Frank, and Dixie for solving these types of problems highlight the different strategies used and illustrate their understanding of the distributive property.

Julie's strategies

Julie, a fourth-grade student, did not have much experience or success in computing with fraction symbols prior to this instructional sequence. She often relied on concrete materials, such as fraction strips, and on her own drawings of the problem contexts to solve fraction problems. For example, during an interview before the introduction of the ratio table, Julie was asked to solve the following problem:

> To make Sloppy Joe sandwiches for 3 people, Bob needs a half-pound of ground beef. If Bob decides to make enough Sloppy Joe sandwiches for 15 people, how many pounds of ground beef will he need?

As illustrated in **figure 5**, Julie solved this problem by drawing five 3s on a piece of paper and making sets of two 3s. She counted two sets of two 3s to get two pounds and had one 3 left over. She knew that that would be 1/2 pound, and she got 2 1/2 pounds for 15 people. If Julie had used a ratio-table approach, her solution might have looked like the one in **figure 6**.

As the unit progressed, Julie became more proficient with fractions and could use relationships between fractions (for example, half of 1/3 is 1/6) to solve recipe problems. One recipe problem that involved increasing the num-ber of servings from two to three required 1/3 cup of yogurt for two servings. To find the amount of yogurt needed for three servings, Julie first halved the

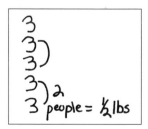

Fig. 5. Julie's solution to the Sloppy Joe problem

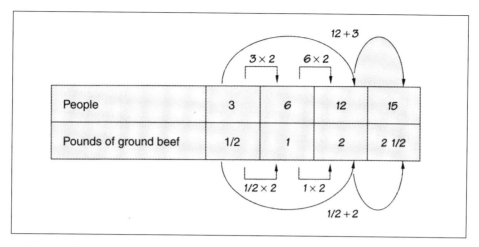

Fig. 6. Julie's solution to the Sloppy Joe problem in a ratio-table format

amount of yogurt needed for two servings to get the amount needed for one serving. Then she added the amount of yogurt required for one serving to that required for two servings to figure the total for three servings.

During an interview following the fraction unit, Julie was asked to solve the following problem:

A fruit-punch recipe that serves 10 people requires 1 1/3 cups of lemonade. Trudy wants to make enough to serve 75 people. How many cups of lemonade will she need?

The solution to this problem involves multiplying 1 1/3 cups by 7 1/2. Julie used the distributive property to perform several steps in her solution process. First she multiplied 1 1/3 by 7, then she multiplied 1 1/3 by 1/2. Finally, she added the two products. **Figure 7** shows the three representations that Julie used to solve this problem. The drawing on the right shows the ratio table that she made to list the number of people and cups of lemonade. As each computation was completed, she recorded her results in the columns of the ratio table.

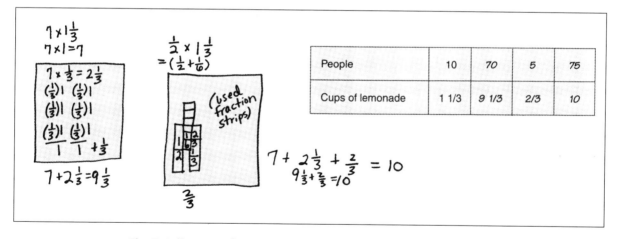

Fig. 7. Julie's use of a ratio table to solve the fruit-punch problem

The drawing on the left in **figure 7** illustrates Julie's strategy for multiplying 1 1/3 by 7. She first multiplied 7 by 1 to get 7. To multiply 7 and 1/3, she drew three tally marks for three 1/3s to get one whole and three more tally marks to get another whole, after which she was left with 1/3 remaining. She then added those wholes with the 1/3 left over to get 2 1/3. She added that quantity to 7 to get 9 1/3.

The middle drawing in **figure 7** illustrates Julie's continued use of the distributive property as she multiplied 1 1/3 by 1/2. She knew that half of 1 was 1/2. From previous problems, she knew that 1/2 of 1/3 was 1/6. To add 1/2 and 1/6, she used a set of fraction strips that had been introduced earlier in the unit.

Students had not been given explicit instructions on how to use the fraction strips, but Julie had used this strategy in her small-group work. She lined up the 1/6 strip with the 1/2 strip. She then lined up the 1/3 strip with the 1/6 division line and got 2/3. Finally she added 9 1/3 and 2/3 to get 10.

Frank's strategies

Frank, a fifth-grade student, also used modeling strategies to solve fraction problems. He used the ratio table in various ways to facilitate his solutions to the recipe problems involving mixed numbers. One problem involved multiplying 4 1/2 by 2 1/2 to determine the number of teaspoons of salt needed for eighteen servings if 2 1/2 teaspoons are needed for four servings. He first multiplied 2 1/2 by 4 to get 10 teaspoons of salt for sixteen servings. Next he halved the number of teaspoons of salt in the recipe to get the amount for two servings, or 1 1/4 teaspoons. He then added the "16 servings" column and the "2 servings" column to get the "18 servings" column. **Figure 8** shows Frank's solution with the ratio table.

To solve the fruit-punch problem, Frank also used a ratio table, then implicitly applied the distributive property in his solution. When the problem was first read to him, he immediately said, "Ratio table." When asked why he liked using the ratio table, he responded, "You can do almost anything with a ratio table."

Dixie's strategies

Dixie, also a fifth-grade student, had used several strategies to solve fraction problems before solving the recipe problems. For example, to solve the Sloppy Joe problem, she said that she knew that 15 divided by 3 was 5. She multiplied 5 by 1/2 by first multiplying 4 by 1/2 to get 2 and then adding another 1/2 to get 2 1/2. To triple 3/8 on another problem, Dixie used a repeated-addition strategy, first adding 3/8 and 3/8 to get 6/8, then adding 3/8 to 6/8 to get 9/8, and then rewriting 9/8 as 1 1/8.

When the ratio table was introduced as a way to organize operations with the fractions involved in the recipe problems, Dixie used it to solve problems involving more complex fractions and mixed numbers. She demonstrated a great deal of creativity by solving the problem in many ways by using the ratio table. For example, one problem involved increasing the amount of sugar (2/3 cup) in a recipe for four servings to an amount of sugar for twenty-two servings, which in essence involves multiplying 2/3 by 5 1/2. This problem, if presented only as a numerical computation, might traditionally be taught by telling students to rewrite 5 1/2 as an improper fraction, or 11/2, and then multiply 2 by 11 and 3 by 2 to get 22/6 or 3 2/3. Dixie not only solved this problem by implicitly applying the distributive property, she also solved it four other ways!

Figure 9 shows Dixie's first solution to this problem with the ratio table. She first multiplied 2/3 by 5 to get the amount of sugar needed for twenty servings, using an additive strategy that she had commonly used before, and wrote that amount, 3 1/3 cups, in the second column. She then reasoned that to get the

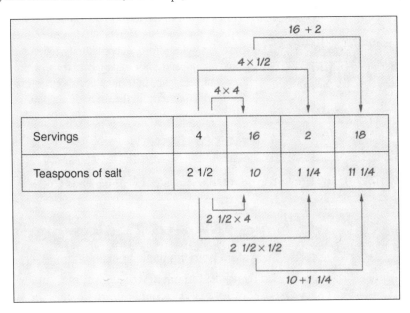

Fig. 8. Frank's use of the ratio table

amount of sugar needed for twenty-two servings, she would need to take half of the amount needed for four servings. She then added the amount of sugar needed for twenty servings to the amount of sugar needed for two servings to get 3 2/3, which is the amount of sugar needed for twenty-two servings. This strategy shows Dixie's understanding of mixed numbers and multiplication and her intuitive understanding of the distributive property. In more formal notation, her strategy might look something like the following:

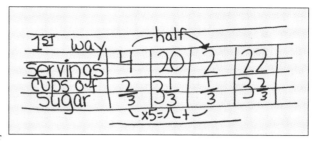

Fig. 9. Dixie's use of the ratio table

$$\frac{2}{3}\left(5+\frac{1}{2}\right)=\left(\frac{2}{3}\times 5\right)+\left(\frac{2}{3}\times\frac{1}{2}\right)=3\frac{1}{3}+\frac{1}{3}=3\frac{2}{3}$$

This strategy is valid for multiplying a fraction by a mixed number and also illustrates the importance of the distributive property.

Dixie's four other strategies involved doubling, halving, and tripling, and her facility with the ratio table helped her organize her steps.

Conclusion

The strategies used by Julie, Frank, and Dixie illustrate the potential for students to invent procedures for solving fraction and mixed-number multiplication problems. The ratio table was offered as a tool to organize their computations, and it was used flexibly by the students to solve the recipe problems. They were not given direct instruction on procedures to solve these problems, yet their invented strategies showed sophisticated thinking about concepts that are often considered difficult to teach or difficult for students to retain. Moreover, many of these strategies afford an opportunity for students to think about, and gain experience with, a property they will see again in a more abstract context—the distributive property in the study of algebra.

References

Empson, Susan B. "Research into Practice: Using Equal Sharing Situations to Help Children Learn Fractions." *Teaching Children Mathematics* 2 (October 1995): 110–14.

Lamon, Susan J. "Ratio and Proportion: Connecting Content and Children's Thinking." *Journal for Research in Mathematics Education* 24 (January 1993): 41–61.

Mack, Nancy K. "Learning Fractions with Understanding: Building on Informal Knowledge." *Journal for Research in Mathematics Education* 21 (January 1990): 16–32.

National Council of Teachers of Mathematics (NCTM). *Curriculum and Evaluation Standards for School Mathematics.* Reston, Va.: NCTM, 1989.

Streefland, Leen. *Fractions in Realistic Mathematics Education: A Paradigm of Developmental Research.* Dordrecht, Netherlands: Kluwer Academic Publishers, 1991.

——— "Fractions: A Realistic Approach." In *Rational Numbers: An Integration of Research*, edited by Thomas P. Carpenter, Elizabeth Fennema, and Thomas A. Romberg, pp. 289–326. Hillsdale, N. J.: Lawrence Erlbaum Associates, 1993.

van Galen, Frans, Monica Wijers, Julia A. Shew, Beth R. Cole, Jonathan Brendefur, and Laura Brinker. "Some of the Parts." In *Mathematics in Context: A Connected Curriculum for Grades 5–8*, edited by National Center for Research in Mathematical Sciences Education and Freudenthal Institute. Chicago: Encyclopaedia Britannica Educational Corporation, 1997.

The Triple Jump: A Potential Area for Problem Solving and Investigation

Doug Clarke

Many teachers comment that interesting applications of ratio are hard to find. Teachers also find that many students have difficulty with proportional reasoning in general, and ratio in particular. In this article, I talk through a process that led to the discovery of the role of ratios and percentages in discussions about triple jump performances, and to a range of tasks that provide important information about students' understanding of key concepts in mathematics.

Using Current Events as Springboards for Mathematical Investigations

I have had an interest for a while in developing problem-solving tasks and investigations from current events and students' interests. A colleague showed me the sketch below from *The Age* (p. 465).

The article talked about the impending visit of the world long jump record holder to Melbourne. As you can see, it showed Mike Powell leaping lengthwise over two cars. The cars appear to be Mercedes Benz. The mathematics teacher in me immediately saw the potential for a mathematical investigation: Could Mike Powell actually jump two Mercedes Benz cars?

For the next week or so, whenever I saw a stationary Mercedes at a shopping centre, I would jump out of my car, ask the driver of the Mercedes to hold the other end of the tape, and help me to measure the length, width, and height of the car. Each driver seemed somewhat surprised, but I guess if I ever owned a Mercedes (and given that I work in education, this seems fairly unlikely), I would be somewhat suspicious of someone who wanted my help to measure my car!

The different sorts of Mercedes varied in measurements, but the "sporty" ones had a length of 4.4 m and a height of about 1.4 m. Since Powell's world record jump was 8.95 m, it became clear therefore that he could jump the length of two such Mercedes, but could he clear the height?

The investigation then took me to a variety of books on biomechanics, in a vain search to find a scale drawing of the "flight path" of a long jumper. My plan was that the cars could be superimposed on such a sketch, in order to determine whether Powell would clear the cars. Even though I was unable to find such a scale drawing, I am confident by looking at pictures and videos of long jumpers in action that Mike Powell would most likely crash straight into the back of the first car, as his take-off angle would not enable him to gain enough height.

Before I leave Mike Powell, I want to mention that I was sharing this activity with a group of American teachers, and, given my strange Australian accent, they thought that I was referring to "*my pal*, the world long jump record holder!" Several commented later that it must be very good to have the world record holder as a pal!

Moving On to Triple Jump

In the course of reading about the biomechanics of long jumps, I discovered an interesting table in the book *Triple Jump* (McNab 1977), part of which is reproduced in **table 1**.

As the table indicates, ratios were expressed as percentages. An interesting discussion point with students is the reasons why percentages were chosen to show these ratios. Given the complicated numbers involved in the three components of the triple jump, percentages enable the ratios to be presented in a clearer way, and also comparisons over the years can be more easily made. Some students also notice that the percentages do not necessarily add up to 100, leading to a discussion of round-off error.

Table 1
Phase Distances and Ratios

Athlete	Year	Hop Distance (m)	Step Distance (m)	Jump Distance (m)	Ratio	Total Distance (m)
Da Silva (Brazil)	1955	6.27	4.98	5.31	38%:30%:32%	16.56
Ryakhovskiy (U.S.S.R.)	1958	6.46	4.96	5.15	39%:30%:31%	16.57
Fyedoseyev (U.S.S.R.)	1959	6.50	4.82	5.38	39%:29%:32%	16.70
Schmidt (Poland)	1960	6.00	5.01	6.01	35%:29%:35%	17.02
Saneyev (U.S.S.R.)	1968	6.30	5.05	6.04	36%:29%:35%	17.39
Saneyev (U.S.S.R.)	1972	6.50	4.93	6.01	37%:28%:34%	17.44
De Oliveira (Brazil)	1975	6.08	5.37	6.43	34%:30%:36%	17.88

From reading some background information, it is clear that the ratio of hop:step:jump is of considerable interest to those involved in analyzing the triple jump and in enhancing performance. The various texts on triple jumping techniques discuss a range of preferred ratios for the triple jump. One proposed "ideal ratio" is 10:8:9. One might consider which of the world record jumps most nearly matches this ratio—not easy mathematics for students.

A Powerful Problem-Solving Task

The following problem-solving task turns out to be mathematically powerful, and I found that I learned a lot about the students with whom I used it, as they shared their methods (and frustrations!).

Using ample amounts of liquid paper, I presented students with the table in **table 2**, adapted from the first, with a challenge to fill in the gaps. I have replaced the gaps with lines here for clarity.

Although at first it may appear that I applied the liquid paper randomly, each line of the table provides a new challenge and connects important mathematical concepts. In discussing some of the methods, it should be noted that a whole variety of methods was used by students. The "official" answers, of course, can be found in **table 1**.

Some comments on each line:

(*a*) Da Silva: Clearly, the simplest method is to add the decimals together.

(*b*) Ryakhovskiy: Subtraction of the hop and step from the total jump gives the jump distance.

(*c*) Fyedoseyev: Since the percentages should add to 100, this line should be straightforward.

(*d*) Schmidt: This is the line which provides the first major challenge for most students. Interestingly, most secondary teachers solve this problem in a way that is quite different from that of most students and preservice students. Most secondary teachers with whom I have used the task solved the problem by expressing it algebraically as a ratio:

$$6.00:35\% \text{ as } x:29\%$$

Table 2
Phase Distances and Ratios with Some Missing Information

Athlete	Year	Hop Distance (m)	Step Distance (m)	Jump Distance (m)	Ratio	Total Distance (m)
Da Silva (Brazil)	1955	6.27	4.98	5.31	38%:30%:32%	——
Ryakhovskiy (U.S.S.R.)	1958	6.46	4.96	——	39%:30%:31%	16.57
Fyedoseyev (U.S.S.R.)	1959	6.50	4.82	5.38	___:29%:32%	16.70
Schmidt (Poland)	1960	6.00	——	6.01	35%:29%:35%	——
Saneyev (U.S.S.R.)	1968	——	5.05	——	36%:29%:35%	17.39
Saneyev (U.S.S.R.)	1972	6.50	——	6.01	37%:___:___	17.44
De Oliveira (Brazil)	1975	——	——	6.43	___:___:36%	——

and so on. This method works well, but I found few students who were comfortable with it.

A preferred method among students was what one person called the "unitary method." That is, if I can find 1 percent of the total jump, then I can find any other percentage (29%, 100%, etc.). Dividing 6.00 by 35 gives 1 percent of the total jump, so 29 percent of the total jump will be (6.00/35) × 29. Some readers may have been using this method for years, but since it was shown to me, I have found many situations in which it renders a solution far easier than more conventional methods.

(e) Saneyev (1): A similar method to the previous one is useful. Finding 1 percent of the jump (5.05/29) enables 36 percent to be obtained ([5.05/29] × 36).

(f) Saneyev (2): This involves two of the types of problems presented earlier in the table.

(g) de Oliveira: This problem was included to remind students (and teachers) that not all problems provide sufficient information for a solution to be determined. Apart from finding the total distance, the rest must be speculation. Interestingly, several students (trained by previous experience that every problem must be solvable!), continued patterns evident in the previous lines of the table to estimate their answers for the final line of the table.

A New World Record

In August 1995, England's Jonathan Edwards broke his own world record for the triple jump in the World Athletic Championships in Gothenburg, Sweden. On August 7, he actually broke it twice, first leaping 18.16 m and then 18.29 m.

The *Herald Sun* (August 9, 1995) gave the breakdown of the three phases as 6.45 m (Hop), 5.55 m (Step), and 6.29 (Jump). (See **fig. 1**.)

Teachers I have worked with have used this jump and the relevant data in several different ways:

- Some teachers have gathered the students out in the corridor (or outside), and, using masking tape, encouraged students to estimate each part of the jump. "Walk to where you think 6.45 m would be." Students do so, the correct distance is measured, and students then consider their accuracy. This spot is marked with masking tape, and then the next challenge is posed: "Walk to where you think the step would have landed: 5.55 m." This process is continued until the three parts of the jump are marked. Given that most school classrooms are around 7–8 metres long, the students get a sense of what a giant triple jump this was.

- What are the percentages in this case? Since the total jump is 18.29 m, the percentages work out to be 35 percent, 30 percent, and 34 percent (once again, round-off error gives a total of 99%).

- 18.29 m was a phenomenal jump. How close was the ratio to the ideal 10:8:9?

- What about your own triple jump? Some teachers have combined mathematics with physical education in encouraging students to measure each other's triple jumps and express the ratios in the same form as the table. A humorous note was that one teacher reported that some of his students were straining to jump as far as they could "to make our ratios the same as the champions!" The fact that a very small triple jump could still be the ideal ratio (e.g., 100 cm:80 cm:90 cm) appeared to escape them.

- Willie Banks of the United States held the world record for the triple jump for many years. I was unable to find the breakdown of his best jump (June 16, 1995), but the total was 17.97 m. Using both

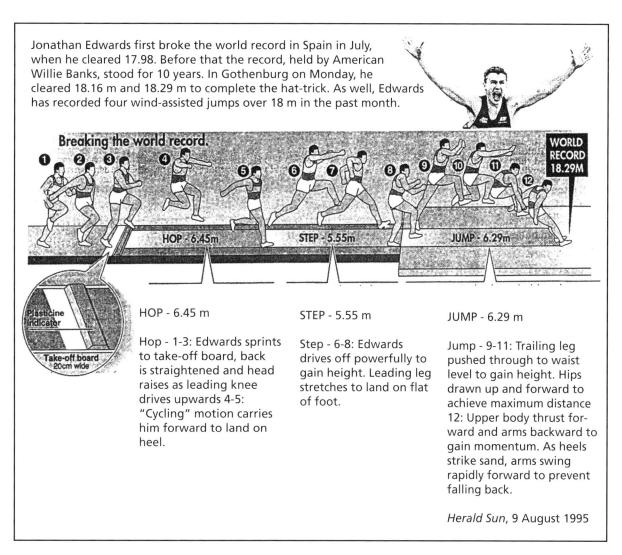

Jonathan Edwards first broke the world record in Spain in July, when he cleared 17.98. Before that the record, held by American Willie Banks, stood for 10 years. In Gothenburg on Monday, he cleared 18.16 m and 18.29 m to complete the hat-trick. As well, Edwards has recorded four wind-assisted jumps over 18 m in the past month.

Breaking the world record.

WORLD RECORD 18.29M

HOP - 6.45m   STEP - 5.55m   JUMP - 6.29m

Plasticine indicator

Take-off board 20cm wide

HOP - 6.45 m

Hop - 1-3: Edwards sprints to take-off board, back is straightened and head raises as leading knee drives upwards 4-5: "Cycling" motion carries him forward to land on heel.

STEP - 5.55 m

Step - 6-8: Edwards drives off powerfully to gain height. Leading leg stretches to land on flat of foot.

JUMP - 6.29 m

Jump - 9-11: Trailing leg pushed through to waist level to gain height. Hips drawn up and forward to achieve maximum distance 12: Upper body thrust forward and arms backward to gain momentum. As heels strike sand, arms swing rapidly forward to prevent falling back.

Herald Sun, 9 August 1995

Fig. 1. A hat trick of world records

(1) the table, and (2) the ideal ratio 10:8:9, estimate the hop, step, and jump components in this triple jump.

In Summary

This article describes a process by which I learned a great deal about an Olympic event that doesn't get much attention. In using an admittedly contrived mathematical problem, I learned much about my students' understanding of mathematics (decimal addition and subtraction, percentages, ratios, estimation, and the connections between mathematical concepts) and their preferred methods of solving problems. Several mature-age preservice students commented during this and similar investigations that they were pleased that their methods were valued and in many cases were more efficient and more easily understood than the more traditional methods. I encourage readers to try out some of these ideas and to share your experiences with me.

References

The Age. Melbourne, Australia, 24 February 1993.

Clarke, Doug. "The Triple Jump." *Australian Mathematics Teacher* 52 (June 1996): 4–7.

Herald Sun. Melbourne, Australia, 9 August 1995.

McNab, T. *Triple Jump*. London: British Amateur Athletic Board, 1977.

SECTION 4

Numbers and Number Theory

Introduction

In the National Council of Teachers of Mathematics (NCTM) publication *Principles and Standards for School Mathematics* (NCTM 2000), the middle school section includes the following question and follow-up (p. 262):

> What should reasoning and proof look like in grades 6 through 8?
>
> In the middle grades, students should have frequent and diverse experiences with mathematics reasoning as they—
>
> • examine patterns and structures to detect regularities;
>
> • formulate generalizations and conjectures about observed regularities;
>
> • evaluate conjectures;
>
> • construct and evaluate mathematical arguments.

Number patterns and number theory in particular provide a context for these important mathematical thinking experiences.

Number theory is a fascinating part of mathematics and an area through which teachers can help students get a glimpse of the beauty of mathematics. In the first set of standards, *Curriculum and Evaluation Standards for School Mathematics* (NCTM 1989), the authors of the middle school sections included the following (p. 91):

> Number theory offers many rich opportunities for explorations that are interesting, enjoyable, and useful. These explorations have payoffs in problem solving, in understanding and developing other mathematical concepts, in illustrating the beauty of mathematics and in understanding the human aspects of the historical development of number.

The authors included the following lovely number theory challenge (p. 93):

> **Find five examples of numbers that have exactly three factors. Repeat for four factors, then five factors. What can you say about the numbers in each of your lists?**
>
> Students might give 4, 9, 25, 49, and 121 as examples or numbers with exactly three factors. Each of these numbers is the square of a prime.
>
> Without an understanding of number systems and number theory, mathematics is a mysterious collection of facts. With such an understanding, mathematics is seen as a beautiful, cohesive whole.

In this section, we include articles that promote students' engagement with numbers and their characteristics and properties. The articles in the section offer tasks that engage students in examining number patterns, making conjectures from those patterns, and seeking "proof" that their conjectures are valid.

As a tribute to a wonderful teacher and researcher, Alba Thompson, who was involved in developing the *Curriculum and Evaluation Standards for School Mathematics* and whose untimely death was a loss to mathematics education and all who knew her, we start with the article "Developing Students' Mathematical Thinking" (Thompson 1985). This article includes two number problems in the text and three additional problems in the work sheet. All five problems engage students in observing patterns, making conjectures, and seeking arguments to support their conjectures.

"Foxy Fives" (Schell 1999), engages students in using mathematics operations and grouping symbols to make different totals from a set of five numbers—the foxy five. Each of the three activities gives practice in mathematical reasoning as well as computation involving all four operations. Through these three activities, students learn to use and understand a number of useful mathematics vocabulary words as well as to gain practice using and computing answers involving numerical operations and expressions.

The set of problems in "Stamp Collector's Nightmare, Phase Two" (Willcutt 1983) spans the simple to the complex and can thus be used at many different grade levels. This is a patterning problem in which conditions are established on what each row and column may or may not have.

One of the exciting times in a mathematics classroom is when students find multiple ways to solve a "big" problem. The article "The Sum of 1 + 2 + ... + 99 + 100" (Anderson 1983) gives the reader such a problem and includes four different and interesting ways students have found to easily get this sum. Use this one with your students and challenge them to find as many different ways to easily find the sum as they can. The discussion of the various ways they find can be both motivational and instructive.

"Adding à la Gauss" (Martinez-Cruz and Barger 2004) starts with the same task of adding the number from 1 to 100, but branches into tasks involving adding consecutive even numbers, triangular numbers, and others. The activity pages give three sets of interesting tasks that promote reasoning with numbers.

References

Anderson, Delores. "The Sum of 1 + 2 + ... + 99 + 100." *Arithmetic Teacher* 31 (November 1983): 50–51.

Martinez-Cruz, Armando M., and Ellen C. Barger. "Adding à la Gauss." *Mathematics Teaching in the Middle School* 10 (October 2004): 152–55.

National Council of Teachers of Mathematics (NCTM). *Curriculum and Evaluation Standards for School Mathematics.* Reston, Va.: NCTM, 1989.

———. *Principles and Standards for School Mathematics.* Reston, Va.: NCTM, 2000.

Schell, Vicki. "Foxy Fives." In *Activities for Junior High School and Middle School Mathematics*, Vol. 2, edited by Kenneth E. Easterday, F. Morgan Simpson, and Tommy Smith, pp. 146–49. Reston, Va.: National Council of Teachers of Mathematics, 1999; *Mathematics Teacher* 73 (October 1980): 601–04.

Thompson, Alba G. "Developing Students' Mathematical Thinking." *Arithmetic Teacher* 33 (September 1985): 20–23.

Willcutt, Bob. "'Stamp Collector's Nightmare,' Phase Two." *Arithmetic Teacher* 31 (September 1983): 43–46.

Developing Students' Mathematical Thinking

Alba G. Thompson

A useful strategy in solving problems is "look for a pattern." In using this strategy, we start with simple cases or versions of the problem and from these cases discover a pattern or rule that can be applied to find the general solution.

The Staircase Problem

Consider, for example, the following problem:

> Ten blocks are needed to make a staircase of four steps (as shown in **fig. 1**). How many blocks are needed to make ten steps? How many blocks are needed to make fifty steps?

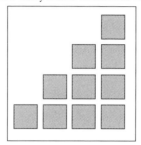

Fig. 1. A 4-step staircase

For a four-step staircase, we use one block for the first step, two blocks for the second (second column from the left), three blocks for the third step, and so on. Thus the total number of blocks needed is found by adding

$$1 + 2 + 3 + 4 = 10.$$

To construct a ten-step staircase, we can add blocks to the four-step staircase, beginning with a column of five blocks to form the fifth step, followed by six blocks to form the sixth step, and so on, until we have ten steps. The number of blocks needed for ten steps is

$$1 + 2 + 3 + 4 + 5 + 6 + 7 + 8 + 9 + 10 = 55 \text{ blocks.}$$

We see a pattern in the process of constructing the staircase: The number of blocks needed to add another step corresponds to the ordinal number of the new step. Thus we can add the whole numbers from 1 to 50 to find the number of blocks needed for a fifty-step staircase. However, unless we know a formula for obtaining this sum directly, calculating it would be tedious. If we are not familiar with such a formula, we can again look for a possible pattern in the data:

For 4 steps   10 blocks are needed

For 10 steps   55 blocks are needed

Can we detect a relationship between the number of steps and the number of blocks needed? It is difficult to detect a pattern with only two instances. Let us look at some more special cases We pick cases for which the calculations are not cumbersome, and we record our data in a table similar to **table 1**.

At this point, we try to find a relationship between the number of a steps and the number of blocks. It may not be obvious, so its discovery may take a while. Guessing and testing our guess is a good way to start. We think of how four is related to ten, five to fifteen, seven to twenty-eight, and so on. After several trials we may notice that $(4 \times 5)/2 = 10$, likewise $(5 \times 6)/2 = 15$. We have a rule that seems to work! Let us test it: $(6 \times 7)/2 = 21$, $(7 \times 8)/2 = 28$, $(8 \times 9)/2 = 36$, $(9 \times 10)/2 = 45$, and $(10 \times 11)/2 = 55$. It works for all the cases in our table. We conjecture that the number of blocks needed for n steps is given by $n(n + 1)/2$. At this point, we are reasonably confident that the number of blocks needed for fifty steps is $(50 \times 51)/2 = 1275$. But we are not certain of this result.

The exploration of patterns calls for the careful analysis of regularities that may occur in a series of instances. As in the previous example, we search for regularities for the purpose of making a conjecture or hypothesis that may lead to the formulation of a generalization. We need to be cautious, however, for the conjecture may hold true for each of the instances examined but may not be true in general. Only when the conjecture is proved can we formulate a generalization. The validity of the conjecture must be established through either (1) induction, by showing that it holds in the first case and showing that, if it holds for all the cases preceding a given one, then it also holds for that case; or (2) deduction, by deriving it from known facts through logical reasoning. Only then can the conjecture be stated as a generalization. However, it suffices to find a single instance for which the conjecture is not true to dismiss its validity.

How can we be sure that our conjectured relationship between the number of steps in a staircase and the number of blocks needed is valid? We conjectured that the number of blocks is given by $n(n + 1)/2$, where n is the number of steps. As we saw in the process of constructing the staircase, if we want n steps, the number of blocks we need is the sum of the first n natural numbers, that is

$$1 + 2 + 3 + \ldots + (n - 2) + (n - 1) + n.$$

Notice that if we add the first to the last added, the sum is $n + 1$. Adding the second addend to the one before the last, we get $2 + (n - 1) = n + 1$. Adding the third addend to the second from the last gives $3 + (n - 2) = n + 1$. We can continue to pair off the addends in this manner, and we observe that the sum of each pair is $n + 1$. With n addends where n is even, we have $n/2$ pairs, each adding to $n + 1$. So we obtain $(n + 1)n/2$. With n addends where n is odd, we have $(n - 1)/2$ pairs, each adding to $n + 1$, plus the middle number, that is $n (n + 1)/2$. So, in the case of n odd, the total sum is

$$\frac{(n+1)(n-1)}{2} + \frac{(n+1)}{2}.$$

Simplifying this expression, we obtain

$$\frac{(n+1)(n-1)+(n+1)}{2} = \frac{(n+1)[(n-1)+1]}{2}$$
$$= \frac{(n+1)n}{2},$$

which was our conjecture. We now have a generalization for the sum of the first n numbers, as well as a solution to our original problem.

The Region Problem

Let us look at another situation.

> Consider the circles shown in **figure 2**. If we pick two points on the first circle and connect them with a line segment, into how many regions is the circle divided? If we pick three points on the second circle and connect each of these points to each of the other points with line segments, into how many regions is the circle divided? Let's continue the process with four and five points.

Table 1

Extending Figure 1

Number of steps	Number of blocks
1	1
2	3
3	6
4	10
5	15
6	21
7	28
8	36
9	45
10	55

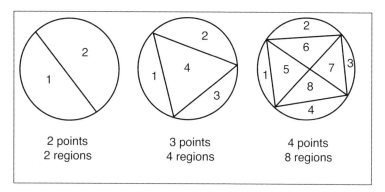

Fig. 2. How many regions?

We record our responses in a table listing the number of points and the corresponding number of regions. The entries in our able should be as shown in table 2.

Table 2

Extending Figure 2

Number of points	Number of regions
2	2
3	4
4	8
5	16

Let's carefully examine the entries in the table. Can we see a pattern? Does a relationship exist between the number of points and the number of regions? What is our conjecture?

On the basis of the conjecture, how many regions should we expect when six points are connected with a line segment? Let's check for six points. We need to be careful to count all the regions but count each one only once. Does our conjecture hold true for six points?

After examining the table, you may have discovered that the number of regions is given by $2^{(n-1)}$, where n is the number of points. This is true for $n = 1, 2, 3, 4$, or 5. According to this rule of correspondence, when six points are connected, the number of regions should be $2^{(6-1)} = 32$. But it is not! Checking empirically for six points, we see that the number of regions is 30 or 31, not 32! See **figure 3**. This single case for which the conjectured relationship does not hold is sufficient to reject the conjecture as not true in general. Thus we cannot generalize.

More Problems

The processes of searching for patterns, making and testing conjectures, and formulating generalizations, although not unique to mathematics, are essential in mathematical thinking and in the generation of mathematical knowledge. Problems in which these processes are useful in arriving at solutions should be collected and presented periodically. In addition to specific types of problems, laboratory or exploratory activities can be used effectively to develop students' skills in using these processes. Three examples of such activities are given on the worksheet.

These activities are not novel ones, and the reader may be familiar with them. They have been chosen from various sources (e.g., Cooney, Davis, and Henderson [1983]; Lester and Charles [n.d.]; Mason, Burton, and Stacey [1982]). The purpose is to stress the activities' pedagogical value, since each one emphasizes an important aspect of mathematical proof. Activity 1 leads to a conjecture that can be proved inductively. The conjecture resulting from activity 2 can be proved deductively. These two activities lead to the formulation of generalizations (see the Appendix). Finally, the conjecture in the third activity can be rejected. Teachers can begin a discussion of historical interest after activity 3 by pointing out that the French mathematician Marin Mersenne (1588–1648) claimed that $2^p - 1$ would be prime only for values of $p = 2, 3, 5, 7, 13, 17, 19, 31, 67, 127,$ and 257. It has been shown that $2^p - 1$ is not prime when $p = 67$ or 257 and that it is prime when $p = 61, 89,$ and 107.

Closing Comments

Most students enjoy searching for patterns, particularly numerical ones. However, in solving problems many students have difficulty deciding when and how to use this technique as a strategy.

Students need practice in searching for patterns, conjecturing, and generalizing much like they need practice in other areas of mathematics. The skillful use of these methods requires that students not only know *how* to use them but be able to decide *when* to use them. It is unlikely that sporadic and incidental exposure to these processes will increase students' skill in using them or their appreciation of their role in mathematical thinking. It is important to make the development of students' skills in the use of these processes a cognitive objective of the mathematics program.

Besides knowing what to do, students need to know why, and under what conditions, they should use these processes. The role of the teacher is to demonstrate and stress the rationale underlying the selection of the processes so that students can learn about their uses and benefits. Teacher-led discussions should help students understand the conditions in a mathematical task that suggests the use of these processes. In additional, modeling by the teacher, showing how the processes should be monitored and assessed as they are used, is essential.

As mathematics teachers, we should not only strive to give students ample practice in the use of these processes but also initiate discussions that are aimed at helping students think about when, why, and how to use them. Only when students can make these decisions on their own will they be truly skillful in applying them.

References

Cooney, Thomas, Edward Davis, and Kenneth Henderson. *Dynamics of Teaching Secondary School Mathematics.* Prospect Heights, Ill.: Waveland Press, 1983.

Lester, Frank, and Randall Charles. *Mathematical Problem Solving Project Tests.* n.d.

Mason, John, Leone Burton, and Kay Stacey. *Thinking Mathematically.* London: Addison-Wesley Publishers, 1982.

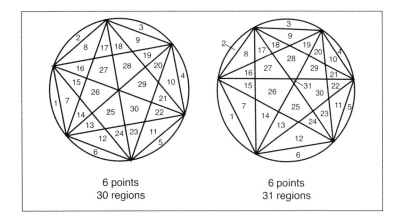

Fig. 3. Can you predict these results from the pattern in figure 2?

Appendix

Activity 1

Materials: one sheet of paper (waxed paper works better than regular paper)
Directions
1. Fold the paper once, crease it along the fold, open it up, and record in a table the number of regions created.
2. With the paper opened, make another fold that intersects the first to make the maximal number of regions possible. Record the number of regions made in the table.
3. Repeat the process for a third fold that intersects the first two. Record the number of regions.
4. Try to discover a relationship between the number of folds and the number of regions, and predict the result for four folds. Test your prediction by folding again and counting the regions.
5. Can you guess the number of regions created after ten folds? Look for a relationship between the number of folds and the number of regions. Can you tell how many regions will be made after *n* folds? Write the conjecture.

Activity 2

Materials: pencil and paper
Directions
1. Pick any five consecutive integers and find their sum. Keep a record of the integers and their sum.
2. Repeat the directions in step 1 for another set of five consecutive integers.
3. Repeat the process two or three more times.
4. Examine the sums. Can the sums be found without adding? Can you make a conjecture? Write it.

Activity 3

Materials: pencil and paper
Directions:
1. Consider the expression $2p - 1$, where p is a prime.
2. Let p take the values 2, 3, 5, 7, and so on.
3. Notice that in each case, the value of the expression is an odd number. What else do you notice about these values?
4. Can you make a conjecture about the value of the expression in step 1? Write it.
5. On the basis of your conjecture, what can you predict about the number $2^{11} - 1$? Check your prediction. Is your conjecture true? Why?

Solution to activity 1

Number of folds	Number of regions
1	2
2	4
3	7
4	11
5	16
6	22

The number of regions is given by $(n^2 + n + 2)/2$, where n is the number of folds. This relationship can be proved by induction. It works for $n = 1$: $f(1) = (1^2 + 1 + 2)/2 = 2$. Assuming that $f(n)$ is true for $n = 1$, $2, 3, \ldots, n$, we can show $f(n + 1)$ is true:

$$f(n +1) = f(n) + (n +1).$$

Each new fold increases the number of regions by an amount equal to the ordinal number of the fold. Substituting for $f(n)$, we get

$$f(n+1) = \frac{(n^2 + n + 2)}{2} + (n+1)$$
$$= \frac{(n^2 + n + 2 + 2n + 2)}{2}$$
$$= \frac{(n^2 + 3n + 4)}{2},$$

which is what we would get if we had substituted $(n + 1)$ for n in $f(n)$, that is

$$f(n+1) = \frac{\left[(n+1)^2 + (n+1) + 2\right]}{2}$$
$$= \frac{(n^2 + 2n + 1 + n + 1 + 2)}{2}$$
$$= \frac{(n^2 + 3n + 4)}{2}.$$

Solution to activity 2

Any five consecutive integers can be represented by

$$x, (x + 1), (x + 2), (x + 3), (x + 4).$$

Their sum is

$$x + x + 1 + x + 2 + x + 3 + x + 4 = 5x + 10 = 5(x + 2).$$

The sum of any five consecutive integers can be calculated by adding 2 to the first number and multiplying by 5.

Comments on activity 3

Students are likely to notice that the value of $2^p - 1$ for $p = 2, 3, 5,$ and 7 is odd in each case, before they notice that it is a prime number. The teacher will probably need to stress the question in step 3 of the activity. Because of the magnitude of the numbers involved for large values of p, it is advisable to allow the students to use calculators.

Foxy Fives

Vicki Schell

Grade Levels: 7–12

Materials: One set of activity sheets and one deck of Foxy Five cards per student. To make a deck of cards, cut sixty-two 2 1/4–by–3 1/2-inch rectangles from posterboard (or for a thinner card, cut from a three-by-five-inch file card; blank decks are also commercially available). Mark three cards with the number "1," three with the number "2," continuing through "10"; mark each number from 11 through 17 on two cards each; and for numbers 18 through 25, mark one card each.

Objectives: To provide experience in observing the relationships among numbers, to provide drill in basic arithmetic operations, and to provide experience in applying the order of operations to a set of numbers.

Background: Playing the Foxy Fives game is my foxy way of sneaking in drill and review to general mathematics classes. The deck consists of cards numbered from 1 to 25. Each player is dealt five cards, and one card is turned up in the center. The object of the game is to combine the five cards in any order and, using any of the four basic operations, to obtain the number on the center card. The students should be familiar with the basic game before trying any variations. As an alternative approach, these activities can be done without cards by selecting the numbers in some random procedure (using a spinner is such an option), but the students seem to find it easier having the cards at hand.

Directions: Distribute the card decks and activity sheets (one at a time) to each student. Have the students complete each sheet before going on to the next one.

Sheet 1: This initial activity familiarizes the students with the basic procedure of the Foxy Fives game. It may be helpful to do this sheet as a class group, using an overhead the first few times the game is played. It is interesting to compare results of different students as a means of reinforcing the fact that there is often more than one possible solution to a problem.

Sheets 2 & 3: These sheets reinforce the discovery that the same Foxy Five numbers will produce a different total depending on how the numbers are combined, as well as providing additional practice in number manipulation.

Solution Guide: There are, of course, many possible solutions for each of the given problems. I include here one solution for each.

Answers

Sheet 1: (1) $10 - (6 + 3 + 1) + 5 = 5$;
(2) $11 + 1 - 9 - (8 \div 8) = 2$;
(3) $11 - [(20 - 15) \times 3 - 10] = 6$;
(4) $(11 + 3) - 12 + 18 - 12 = 8$;
(5) $(4 + 16) \div 10 - (25 - 24) = 1$;
(6) $17 - 17 + (14 - 13) \times 7 = 7$;
(7) $(9 - 9) + (5 \times 4) + 2 = 22$;
(8) $(7 - 6) + [3 - (10 \div 5)] = 2$;
(9) $5 - [(11 + 21) \div 8] + 6 = 7$;
(10) $(17 - 1) \div 1(6 - 2) \times 2 = 8$;
(11) $(10 + 1) - 11 + (9 - 4) = 5$.

Sheet 2: (2) $9 - \{14 \div [(19 + 3) \div 11]\} = 2$;
(3) $11 - [(19 + 9) \div 14] \div 3 = 3$;
(4) $19 - 9 + 11 - 14 - 3 = 4$;
(5) $9 - \{14 - [(11 + 19) \div 3]\} = 5$;

(7) $14 \div \{[(3 + 19) - 9] - 11\} = 7$;
(8) $9 - [(11 \times 3) \div (14 + 19)] = 8$;
(9) $11 \times 3 - (14 + 19) + 9 = 9$;
(10) $19 - 9 + 11 - 14 + 3 = 10$.

Sheet 3: (1) $[(11 + 3) - (2 \times 7)] \div 5 = 0$;
(2) $[(2 \times 5) + (7 - 3)] - 11 = 3$;
(3) $5 - [(11 + 3) \div 7 + 2] = 1$;
(4) $[(5 + 3) - (11 - 7)] \div 2 = 2$;
(5) $[(5 + 3) \div (11 - 7)] \times 2 = 4$;
(6) $2 \times 3 \times 5 \times 7 \times 11 = 2310$;
(7) $11 \times 7 \times 5 \times (3 + 2) = 1925$;
(8) $[(11 - 3) \times (5 + 7) \times 1 \div 2 = 48$;
(9) $5 - \{3 - [(11 - 2) - 7]\} = 4$;
(10) $11 \times 7 \times 5 \times 3 - 2 = 1153$.

SHEET 1

Foxy Fives

Directions:

- Deal yourself the following Foxy Five hands. Use each card once (and only once) to make the given total.

- Write out your combination, being sure to introduce parentheses where needed to show order of operations.

Example:

| Hand: | 7, 8, 1, 9, 9 | total: 16 $(9 \div 9) \times (7 + 8 + 1) = 16$ |

1.   1, 5, 3, 6, 10   total: 5 _____

2.   8, 11, 9, 1, 8   total: 2 _____

3.   11, 10, 5, 20, 3   total: 6 _____

4.   12, 18, 3, 11, 12   total: 8 _____

5.   4, 16, 10, 24, 25   total: 1 _____

6.   17, 14, 7, 17, 13   total: 7 _____

7.   2, 9, 5, 9, 4   total: 22 _____

8.   3, 6, 10, 5, 7   total: 2 _____

9.   8, 6, 11, 5, 21   total: 7 _____

10.   6, 1, 2, 2, 17   total: 8 _____

11.   10, 4, 1, 11, 9   total: 5 _____

SHEET 2

Foxy Fives

Directions:
- Deal yourself the following Foxy Five hand:

  11, 14, 3, 19, 9.

- With this hand, make the totals from 1 to 11. Write each combination as an equation. Be careful of the order of operations!

1. $(11 + 14 - 19 + 3) \div 9 = 1$

2. _____

3. _____

4. _____

5. _____

6. $11 - [(19 + 9) \div 14 + 3] = 6$

7. _____

8. _____

9. _____

10. _____

11. $[9 - (19 - 14) - 3] \times 11 = 11$

SHEET 3

Foxy Fives

Directions:

- Deal yourself the following Foxy Five hand: 2, 3, 5, 7, 11. (Notice that these are the first 5 prime numbers!)

- With this hand, find the following totals. Write each combination as an equation. Be careful of the order of operations!

1. What is the smallest whole number that you can find, using these five numbers and each arithmetic operation exactly once? _____

2. Find the smallest odd prime number. _____

3. Find the smallest odd natural number. _____

4. Find the smallest prime number. _____

5. Find the smallest composite natural number. _____

6. What is the largest composite natural number you can find? _____

7. What is the largest odd natural number you can find? _____

8. Find the largest even natural number possible, using each operation only once. _____

9. Find a natural number using only subtraction. _____

10. Find the largest prime number possible with these five numbers. _____

Stamp Collector's Nightmare, Phase 2

Bob Willcutt

Problems that span the simple to the complex and that can therefore be used with many different groups of students, problems that have a strong motivational thrust, and problems that are full of many different kinds of mathematics are very special problems. When I discover such a problem, I like to share it with others in the hope that the challenges, frustrations, and satisfactions that go with it will be shared also. One such problem is the old problem of placing stamps on a grid. Ernest Ranucci (1968) deserves the credit for the basic version of this problem, which he entitled "The Stamp Collector's Nightmare."

It all begins with a 4-by-4 grid and an unlimited supply of 1¢, 2¢, 3¢, 4¢, and 5¢ stamps (**fig. 1**). The problem, at the first level, is as follows:

> You are to arrange sixteen stamps on the grid so that no two stamps of the same value are in the same row or the same column. Thus, if you choose to place a 5¢ stamp in the upper left-hand corner, you cannot place another 5¢ stamp in the first column or the first row, as shown in **figure 2**.

With younger children (and some older people, too) I have found it very important actually to take the time to cut out "stamps" from oak tag so that the children can literally move the stamps around to find solutions. Many students are not ready to go to the more abstract solution process of simply writing numbers in the blank grid to find a solution. Actually moving physical objects seems to be a more realistic problem-solving process for many students than writing and erasing numbers on a grid. Of course, for those students who are ready to operate at a more abstract level, the paper-and-pencil process is appropriate.

Many different solutions are possible for this first-level condition of no duplicate stamps in any row or column. One such solution is shown in **figure 3**.

A solution under this first-level condition is a worthy accomplishment for some students. For others, we will begin to extend the basic ideas. For example, what is the maximum total cash value for the sixteen stamps placed on the grid? The solution shown in **figure 3** has a cash value of 49¢, but this is not the

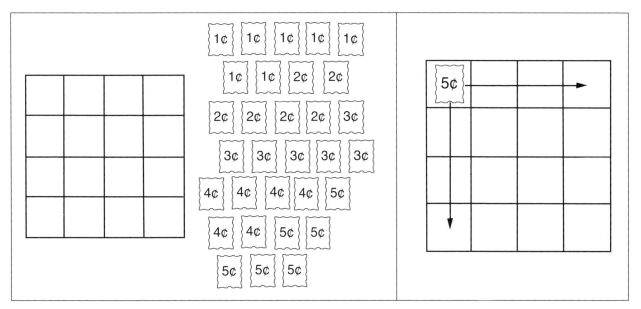

Fig. 1   **Fig. 2**

maximum value. The depth of the problem increases, for in order to obtain the maximum, 56¢, strategies or a system would be helpful. How can you arrange the stamps to obtain the maximum total? Which stamps do you want to use? What is the greatest number of 5¢ stamps that you can use? Why? If you can find the maximum sum, can you also tell me the minimum sum? The question of a minimum sum gives students a good chance to engage in the solution process of using the information gained from a related problem to find the solution to a new problem. Most students can quickly show the minimum sum to be 40¢.

Now, for many students, we are ready to move on to what I will call the second level. The same conditions that applied to the first level will apply again, that is, no duplication of stamp values in any row or column. A new condition is also included. No two stamps of the same value can be placed on either of the two major diagonals, as shown in **figure 4**. Now, we have an overall condition of no duplications in any row, column, or along either major diagonal.

Again, the use of physical representations for the stamps can be very helpful for many students. And again, a plan or strategy can be helpful. Still, a trial-and-error approach will work, as such an approach often does. One possible solution for this second-level condition is shown in **figure 5**. This is a perfectly good solution, and it does appear to be somewhat systematic. Can you see any orderliness in this arrangement?

What about the maximum and minimum sums for the second-level condition? Is it possible to obtain a maximum sum of 56¢ and a minimum sum of 40¢, as was done in the first-level condition? In order to do so, no 1¢ stamps can be used in a maximum solution and no 5¢ stamps can be used in a minimum solution. Students can find that, indeed, the maximum sum is 56¢ and, therefore, the minimum sum is 40¢.

Second-level conditions may be a suitable ending point for many students and, if so, going on to the following extensions would not be appropriate. I find, however, that we underestimate the potential of many students as well as their eagerness for depth. In fact, many students can readily predict the third-level conditions.

For the third level, we maintain the existing conditions of the second level and add the following restrictions: No two stamps of equal value can be located along any diagonal. We will define diagonals to include the two major diagonals and all partial diagonals (sometimes referred to a broken diagonals), as illustrated in **figure 6**. Therefore, under the third-level conditions, we have no duplications in any row, column, or on any diagonal (including major and partial diagonals).

Now, because of the number of restrictions, the difficulty level has increased a great deal. Using physical objects, determining strategies, involving patterns, learning from previous solutions, and relying on a trial-and-error process emerge as possible problem-solving techniques. Is there a pattern? Can it be done? What about maximum and minimum sums? Why can't the maximum sum be 56¢? How do you get the maximum sum (or minimum sum) from just any solution? Under the third-level conditions, solutions can be shown for a maximum (50¢) and a minimum (46¢).

Although we have reached another stopping point for some students, many problem-solving techniques have been included up to this point, as well as a good deal of plain, old addition and multiplcation in finding the maximum and minimum sums. Even the original problem is full of good mathematics and excitement. For those who are ready for more adventures, however, we continue into even more intriguing aspects of this originally simple problem.

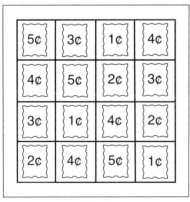

Fig. 3.

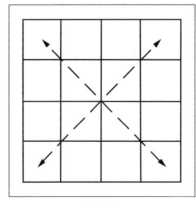

Fig. 4.

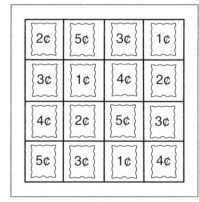

Fig. 5.

What happens if we changed the size from a 4-by-4 arrangement to a 5-by-5 arrangement? At the same time, we will add an additional stamp value, namely, an unlimited number of 6¢ stamps. Now, a new dimension of the original problem emerges.

If we can extend the grid from a 4-by-4 to a 5-by-5, why not continue to extend the size of the grid indefinitely, always adding an additional stamp value as the size of the grid increases? The door is open to a great deal of mathematics. We now have three different levels of conditions as well as maximum and minimum sums on n-by-n grids using $(n + 1)$ values for stamps. What started out as a very simple problem has now become a rather complex one.

Partial diagonals

be	ch
cfi	bgl
hkn	ejo
lo	in

a	b	c	d
e	f	g	h
i	j	k	l
m	n	o	p

Fig. 6.

To give generalized solutions to all these extensions would surely take the fun and satisfaction (as well as the frustration) away from too many people. It does seem appropriate, however, to mention a few experiences I have encountered as I have worked with students solving this now somewhat complicated problem.

To begin with, let's consider the first-level condition. This is an easy one. A rather straightforward solution process emerges, for the restraining conditions are at a minimum. For example, given a 13-by-13 grid, a maximum solution under the first level is not very complicated. One such possible solution is shown in **figure 7**. The total sum can be found by using the idea of summing consecutive natural numbers along with simple multiplication. Thus, first-level generalizations are not that complicated.

13-by-13, First level: maximum sum

2	3	4	5	6	7	8	9	10	11	12	13	14
3	4	5	6	7	8	9	10	11	12	13	14	2
4	5	6	7	8	9	10	11	12	13	14	2	3
5	6	7	8	9	10	11	12	13	14	2	3	4
6	7	8	9	10	11	12	13	14	2	3	4	5
7	8	9	10	11	12	13	14	2	3	4	5	6
8	9	10	11	12	13	14	2	3	4	5	6	7
9	10	11	12	13	14	2	3	4	5	6	7	8
10	11	12	13	14	2	3	4	5	6	7	8	9
11	12	13	14	2	3	4	5	6	7	8	9	10
12	13	14	2	3	4	5	6	7	8	9	10	11
13	14	2	3	4	5	6	7	8	9	10	11	12
14	2	3	4	5	6	7	8	9	10	11	12	13

Fig. 7.

Second-level conditions are a different story. For me, this level is even more complicated than the solution for the third level, as consistent patterns are not readily apparent. Solutions appear to be possible for all grids. The difficult aspect of this level is contained in the maximum (or minimum) sum idea. For example, second-level solutions for three different grids are shown in **figure 8**. None of these are maximum or minimum solutions, however. The challenge at this level appears to be finding solution patterns that will yield maximum sums but not using 1¢ stamps and, likewise, minimum sums by not using the largest-valued stamp available. Such solutions do exist for grids of sizes 4-by-4 through 15-by-15 and probably for all grids.

6-by-6 Second level						7-by-7 Second level							8-by-8 Second level							
1	2	3	4	5	6	1	2	3	4	5	6	7	6	4	8	9	1	2	3	7
2	3	7	1	4	5	3	4	5	6	7	8	1	4	5	6	7	8	9	1	2
6	5	4	3	2	7	5	6	7	8	1	2	3	9	1	2	3	4	5	6	8
3	6	2	5	1	4	7	8	1	2	3	5	6	5	6	7	8	9	1	2	3
4	1	5	2	6	3	2	3	4	5	6	7	8	8	9	1	2	3	4	5	6
5	4	6	7	3	2	4	5	6	7	8	3	2	2	3	4	5	6	7	8	9
						6	7	8	9	2	4	5	7	8	9	1	2	3	4	5
													3	2	5	6	7	8	9	1

Fig. 8.

As is the case in the third level, a trial-and-error solution process becomes unwieldy as the size of the grid increases. The need for a pattern or a systematic method of placing the numbers becomes very apparent. Thus, problem solving involving patterns and logical strategies becomes very dominant. Without a systematic procedure, solutions become few and far between and frustrations increase.

Level-three solutions do fall into a neat pattern and become very predictable. The stumbling block often comes in assuming that all grids have solutions. A quick examination of 2-by-2 and 3-by-3 grids will show you that these two grids have no solutions possible under level-three conditions. And with that knowledge, finding other pairs of grids that do not have solutions becomes easier. Systematic solution processes, such as the one in **figure 9**, become a must if any degree of efficiency is to exist.

Many different solution strategies exist. Chess players often comment on the moves of the knight fulfilling level-three conditions. Maximum- and minimum-solution sums can also be generalized for those grids that do have solutions under level three. But enough hints: the satisfaction comes from solving the problem by yourself, not by being told how to solve it. We have now taken a simple problem involving a 4-by-4 grid and a group of stamps and have looked at many possible extensions. This problem is full of problem-solving strategies, motivation, challenges, imagination, frustration, and even basic-skill work with simple addition and multiplication. And for those hearty souls who want to go deeper, what would happen if you extend this entire problem to three-dimensional grids? The possibilities seem almost endless, but such an extension will have to wait for another time. I hope you and your students will find the satisfaction that many of my students and I have found in working with the "Stamp Collector's Nightmare."

11-by-11, Level three: maximum sum										
2	3	4	5	6	7	8	9	10	11	12
4	5	6	7	8	9	10	11	12	2	3
6	7	8	9	10	11	12	2	3	4	5
8	9	10	11	12	2	3	4	5	6	7
10	11	12	2	3	4	5	6	7	8	9
12	2	3	4	5	6	7	8	9	10	11
3	4	5	6	7	8	9	10	11	12	2
5	6	7	8	9	10	11	12	2	3	4
7	8	9	10	11	12	2	3	4	5	6
9	10	11	12	2	3	4	5	6	7	8
11	12	2	3	4	5	6	7	8	9	10

Fig. 9

References

Ranucci, Ernest. *Four by Four*. Boston: Houghton Mifflin Co., 1968.

The Sum of 1 + 2 + ... + 99 + 100

Delores Anderson

What is the sum of the first one hundred counting numbers? This is the problem that I assigned to my gifted seventh-grade class. This is the problem that was solved by the great mathematician Carl Friedrich Gauss when he was eleven years old. It did not take Gauss much time to find the pattern to present the answer to his teacher.

Gauss probably used one of the two methods described by Seymour and Shedd in their book *Finite Differences: A Problem-Solving Technique* (1973, pp. 22–23).

Method One

Write the numbers in order from 1 to 100. Pair them as shown in **figure 1**. The sum of each of the fifty pairs is 101. Thus the sum of the first one hundred counting numbers is 101×50, or 5050.

$$1 + 2 + 3 + 4 + \ldots + 97 + 98 + 99 + 100$$

Fig. 1.

Method Two

Write the numbers in order from 1 to 100, and write the numbers in reverse order for 100 to 1 below them, as in **figure 2**.

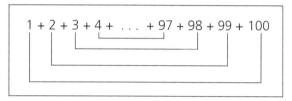

Fig. 2.

The sum of each one of the one hundred pairs is 101. Half of these pairs contain the counting number from 1 to 100. Thus the first one hundred counting numbers is

$$\frac{100 \times 101}{2}, 5050.$$

In general, the sum of the first n counting numbers is

$$\frac{n(n+1)}{2}.$$

After I had stated my problem for my seventh-grade class, they soon realized that there must be some pattern by which to get the answer. Several students discovered the first method. I let them explain this method to the class. I showed the class the second method. Then one of the students, Sonja Jarrett, told me that she had found another method. It is her method that I want to share with others.

Sonja's method

She had listed the numbers in columns by groups of ten and had added the ten columns, as in **figure 3**. She saw the pattern that the sums of the successive columns increase by 100.

1	11	21	31	41	51	61	71	81	91
2	12	22	32	42	52	62	72	82	92
3	13	23	33	43	53	63	73	83	93
4	14	24	34	44	54	64	74	84	94
5	15	25	35	45	55	65	75	85	95
6	16	26	36	46	56	66	76	86	96
7	17	27	37	47	57	67	77	87	97
8	18	28	38	48	58	68	78	88	98
9	19	29	39	49	59	69	79	89	99
<u>10</u>	<u>20</u>	<u>30</u>	<u>40</u>	<u>50</u>	<u>60</u>	<u>70</u>	<u>80</u>	<u>90</u>	<u>100</u>
55	155	255	355	455	555	655	755	855	955

Fig. 3.

This pattern can easily be explained, as shown in **figure 4**. And, of course, the sum of the totals, $55 + 155 + \ldots + 855 + 955$, is 5050.

1 +	10 =	11	11 +	10 =	21	and so	81 +	10 =	91
2 +	10 =	12	12 +	10 =	22	the pattern continues	82 +	10 =	92
3 +	10 =	13	13 +	10 =	23		83 +	10 =	93
4 +	10 =	14	14 +	10 =	24		84 +	10 =	94
5 +	10 =	15	15 +	10 =	25		85 +	10 =	95
6 +	10 =	16	16 +	10 =	26		86 +	10 =	96
7 +	10 =	17	17 +	10 =	27		87 +	10 =	97
8 +	10 =	18	18 +	10 =	28		88 +	10 =	98
9 +	10 =	19	19 +	10 =	29		89 +	10 =	99
10 +	10 =	20	20 +	10 =	30		90 +	10 =	100
55 +	100 =	155	155 +	100 =	255		855 +	100 =	955

Fig. 4.

Sonja surprised me with her discovery of a third method for finding the sum of $1 + 2 + 3 + 4 + \ldots + 97 + 98 + 99 + 100$. The students in my class enjoyed the challenge of the problem. We spent almost an entire class period looking for different ways of getting the answer and developing the general formula for the first n counting numbers.

Reference

Seymour, Dale, and Margaret Shedd. *Finite Differences: A Problem-Solving Technique*. Palo Alto, Calif.: Creative Publications, 1973.

Adding à la Gauss

Armando M. Martinez-Cruz and Ellen Barger

Carl Friedrich Gauss (1777–1855), considered the greatest mathematician of modern times, was born to a poor family in Brunswick, Germany. Although his father worked several unprofitable jobs to earn a meager living and assumed that Carl would follow in his footsteps, his mother insisted that her son receive an appropriate education. Young Gauss demonstrated amazing intellect at an early age. He was just three years old when he corrected a mistake in his father's weekly payroll computation. By the time he was nine, his schoolmasters admitted, "There was nothing more they could teach the boy" (Burton 2003, p. 509).

Over the course of his lifetime, Gauss made many significant contributions to mathematics. Perhaps one of the most interesting, however, was a problem-solving approach he developed in fourth grade. Gauss was in his first arithmetic class when he was presented with the problem, "Find the sum of all the numbers from 1 to 100." According to Burton (2003), this problem was intended to keep the class busy. Gauss handed in the answer (5,050) a few moments after the problem was presented, with no sign of the calculation or the method he used to arrive at the sum. You can imagine that his teacher must have been bewildered. Without using any kind of calculating device or even a pencil and paper, a nine-year-old boy added 100 numbers quickly and effortlessly. Gauss confessed later that he noticed that the sum contained 50 pairs of terms that added to 101. Hence, the sum of the first 100 counting numbers would be 50×101, or 5,050.

Approach 1: The Pairing Numbers Method

A model of this type of reasoning demonstrates that the sum of the first and last terms is equal to the sum of the second and the second-to-last terms. We can continue to pair the terms to make sums of 101 until we get to the middle of the sequence. The last pair of terms, 50 and 51, is consecutive. Each term in the first half of the sequence can be paired with a term in the second half of the sequence, and all the pairs equal the sum of the outermost pair. (See **fig. 1**.) We call this method of adding "à la Gauss," and it can be used to add many different sequences of numbers.

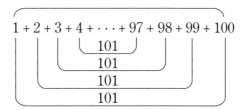

Fig. 1. An illustration of the problem solved by Gauss

Example 1

Find the sum of the first ten even counting numbers. (See **fig. 2**.) This method of adding à la Gauss is handy for finding sums of arithmetic sequences, especially when an even number of terms is in the sequence. When we attempt to find the sum of an odd number of terms, the middle term will be alone, without a partner. The middle term of the sequence will represent one-half of a pair that has the same sum as the first and last terms. For example, imagine that we decided to find the sum of the first fifteen even counting numbers. The first seven terms would pair with the last seven terms, leaving the eighth term without a partner.

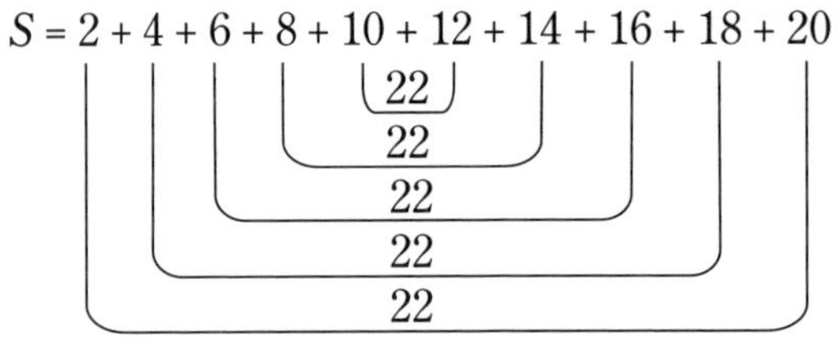

$$S = 2 + 4 + 6 + 8 + 10 + 12 + 14 + 16 + 18 + 20$$

$$\boxed{22}$$
$$22$$
$$22$$
$$22$$
$$22$$

$$5(2 + 20) = 110$$

Fig. 2. Finding the sum of the first ten even counting numbers

Example 2

Determine the sum of the first fifteen even counting numbers. (See **fig. 3.**)

$$S = 2 + 4 + 6 + 8 + 10 + 12 + 14 + 16 + 18 + 20 + 22 + 24 + 26 + 28 + 30$$

There are 7 pairs pf (30 + 2) plus the lonely 16, but 16 is half of 32, so we have 7 1/2 pairs of 32.

$$15 \text{ terms} \rightarrow 7 \text{ 1/2 pairs of } (2 + 30) = S$$

$$7 \text{ 1/2}(32) = 240$$

Fig. 3. Finding the sum of the first fifteen even counting numbers

Approach 2: The Lining-up Numbers Method

Another way of looking at the à la Gauss method of adding the terms of a sequence eliminates the worry of working with an odd number of terms and finding the middle of the sequence. We can display the sum in two different ways to make the pairing and the counting of pairs easier (see **fig. 4**). Recall the original problem, "Find the sum of all the numbers from 1 to 100." Now we will list the numbers twice. First, we list them like we did before, then we list the terms in reverse order. Then we simply add the two equalities vertically. Notice here that 101 is the sum of the outermost pair (1 and 100), and that 100 represents how many numbers we are adding; when divided by 2, we have 50 pairs, each totaling 101.

$$S = \quad 1 + 2 + \quad 3 + \quad 4 + \quad 5 + \ldots + 96 + \quad 97 + \quad 98 + 99 + 100$$
$$S = 100 + 99 + \quad 99 + 97 + 96 + \ldots + \quad 5 + \quad 4 + \quad 3 + 2 + \quad 1$$

$$2S = 101 + 101 + 101 + 101 + 101 + \ldots + 101 + 101 + 101 + 101 + 101$$

$$2S = 100(101)$$

Since we want a single sum, we divide by 2.

$$\frac{2S}{2} = \frac{100(101)}{2}$$

$$S = 50(101)$$

$$S = 5{,}050$$

Fig. 4. Illustrating the lining-up numbers method

The Pythagoreans were familiar with this formula more than 2,500 years before Gauss suggested it. "In fact, they used it as a password in their secret society: the sum of the numbers from one to any number is equal to one half of the last number times the last number plus one" (Mlodinow 2001, pp. 110–11). Using geometry and viewed as by the Pythagoreans, the formula can be seen as a triangular number. Pythagoreans perceived integers as pebbles, which they laid out in certain geometric shapes. They found that some numbers could be formed by laying out the pebbles in rows (1, 2, 3, etc.) to form triangles (1, 3, 6, 10, 15, etc.). **Figure 5** shows these examples.

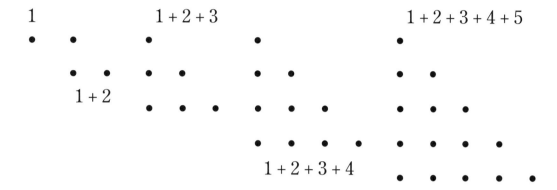

Fig. 5. The first five triangular numbers

The Pythagoreans noted that triangular numbers are the sum of consecutive numbers. For instance, the triangular number 10 is the sum of 1 + 2 + 3 + 4 (the fourth triangle in **fig. 5**). Similarly, we can determine the nineteenth triangular number by adding these numbers: $1 + 2 + 3 + 4 + \cdots + 19 = 19 \times 20/2 = 190$.

This solution strategy is and was quite interesting for it suggested using rectangles. For instance, the fourth triangular number (1 + 2 + 3 + 4 = 10) is half of the pebbles in a 4 × 5 rectangle (see **fig. 6**). So in a rectangle n by$(n + 1)$, we have two triangles, each with $n(n + 1)/2$ pebbles (see **fig. 7**).

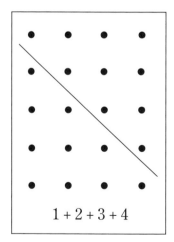

Fig. 6. An illustration showing that triangular number 10 is one-half the pebbles in a 4 × 5 rectangle

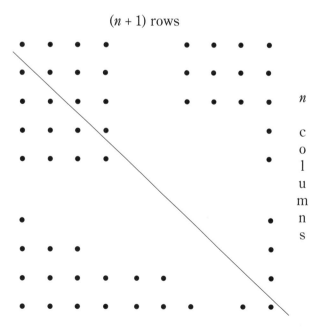

Fig. 7. The nth triangular number, $n(n + 1)/2$

Conclusion

Other interesting stories can be found about children contributing to mathematics. The lesson to learn is that if your students come up with an idea to solve a problem, share it with the class. It may provide insight on how to solve other problems, just like young Gauss.

Teacher notes

Problem 6 in Student Activity 1 is at times difficult for students, especially when it comes to determining how many numbers there are from 13 to 19. Students tend to respond that there are 6, which comes from computing 19 − 13. However, that is not the case. There are 7 numbers, which occurs when subtracting 19 − 12. Have students write all the numbers from 13 to 19, then count them. A useful example that we present to students is to think how many pages of a book they read if starting on page 1 and ending on page 2.

Students tend to mix the concepts of multiples and factors. The activities proposed in this article may serve to alleviate this difficulty. In our classes, we use several ideas to solidify the concept of multiple. One approach consists of using multiplication tables to produce the multiples of a given number. For instance, in Student Activity 3 we discuss the multiples of 6: 6, 12, 18, 24, ... With older students, we discuss the idea of multiples that occurs with an ATM. When people withdraw money, the machine typically displays a message that reads "Enter the quantity to be withdrawn as a multiple of 20." The quantities that can be withdrawn are 20, 40, 60, and so on.

A third alternative when adding multiples of a given number is to add them, which applies the method of young Gauss. For instance, suppose that we want to add the first 100 multiples of 7. It would appear as shown below.

$$7 + 14 + 21 + 28 + \cdots + 700$$

Few students notice that 7 can be factored. Hence, we can rewrite it as shown here.

$$7 + 14 + 21 + 28 + \cdots + 700 = 7(1 + 2 + 3 + \cdots + 100)$$

Using the answer found by young Gauss, we know that the quantity in the parentheses is 5,050. Therefore, the sum is $7 \times 5{,}050$. In short, when adding multiples of a given number, factor the number and compute the sum of what is in parentheses—which is a sum of consecutive numbers.

The lining-up numbers method can be used to deduce a formula for the general case of adding the first n counting numbers. In other words, suppose that we want to compute

$$S = 1 + 2 + 3 + \cdots + n.$$

Reverse the numbers being added, and write them under the first sum:

$$S = 1 \ + \ 2 \ + \ 3 \ + \cdots + \ n$$
$$S = n + (n-1) + (n-2) + \cdots + 1$$

Next, add by columns to obtain $2S = (n + 1) + (n + 1) + (n + 1) + \cdots + (n + 1)$. To determine how many columns we have, we use the top sum. Notice that it goes from 1 up to the end and that those numbers can be used to easily identify (and number) the columns. So the last number being added (n) indicates how many columns we have and also how many factors
($n + 1$) are obtained. Therefore, $2S = n(n + 1)/2$.

Again, notice how this formula reflects the particular cases: ($n + 1$) is the sum of the outermost pair, whereas $n/2$ is the number of pairs being added, as shown in **figure 7**.

References

Burton, David M. *The History of Mathematics: An Introduction*. 5th ed. New York: McGraw-Hill, 2003.

Mlodinow, Leonard. *Euclid's Window. The Story of Geometry from Parallel Lines to Hyperspace*. New York: Touchstone, 2001

Name   Date

Student Activity 1

1. You have probably heard "The Twelve Days of Christmas": "On the first day . . . my true love gave to me. . . ." Think about the 4th day, for example. The singer gets not just 4 gifts, but 4 + 3 + 2 + 1 gifts. How many gifts did the singer receive on the 4th day?

2. How many gifts did the singer receive on each of the 12 days? Record your totals (sums) in the table.

Day	1	2	3	4	5	6	7	8	9	10	11	12
Gifts												

3. Each day, the number of gifts is the arithmetic sequence $1 + 2 + 3 + 4 + 5 + \cdots + n$, where "$n$" is the number of days. Can you find a faster way to count your gifts? Explain your method.

4. Imagine that you were getting gifts not just for 12 days, but for 100 days. How many gifts would you receive?

5. How many gifts would the generous gift-giver have to give for the whole year?

6. Now suppose that you decided to return the gesture of gift giving for one week after the 12. How many gifts would you have to give on day 19?

Name   Date
_____

Student Activity 2

Find the sum indicated by using the Pairing Numbers Method.

1. Find the sum of the first 20 multiples of 4 by doing the following:
    a) List all the numbers being added for this problem.

    $$4 + 8 + 12 + 16 + ?$$

    b) What is the 20th multiple of 4? Could you have found it without listing all the 19 previous multiples? If you answer yes, explain how to find it.

    c) Pair the numbers as young Gauss did. How many pairs do you have?

    d) What is the sum of the outermost pair?

    e) Using the information in 1c and 1d, what is the sum of the first 20 multiples of 4?

2. Use the steps above to compute the sum of the first 50 multiples of 5.

Name   Date

Student Activity 3

Find the sum indicated by using the Lining-up Numbers Method.

1. Find the sum of the first 19 multiples of 6 by doing the following:
   a) List all the numbers being added in the following sum.
   $$6 + 12 + 18 + 24 + ?$$

   b) What is the 19th multiple of 6? Could you have found it without listing all 18 previous multiples? If you answer yes, explain how to find it.

   c) Write the sum in the order given (we got you started). Below it, write the sum, listing the numbers is reverse order.
   $$S = 6 + 12 + 18 + \cdots$$
   $$S =$$

   d) What is the sum of each column?

   e) How many columns do you have?

   f) Use the information in 1d and 1e to find the total of $2S$.

   g) What is the sum of the first 19 multiples of 6?

SECTION 5

Patterns and Functions

Introduction

Patterns and functions are a unifying concept in school mathematics. According to the National Council of Teachers of Mathematics (NCTM 2000, p. 227), "a major goal in the middle grades is to develop students' facility with using patterns and functions to represent, model, and analyze a variety of phenomena and relationships in mathematics problems or in the real world." Despite the centrality of these ideas to middle grades mathematics, research suggests that this is not an easy topic for students. For example, students have difficulty moving flexibly among different representations of functions (Knuth 2000) and in providing explanations and justifications for their strategies and solutions (e.g., Blume and Heckman 2000).

In order to overcome the challenges that students face in the domain, the instructional experiences in which they engage need to focus on helping them develop a conceptual understanding of function, the ability to represent a function in a variety of ways, and fluency in moving among different representations of function (Kalchman and Koedinger 2005). The tasks and activities in this section are intended to provide teachers with the raw material for designing such instruction. They build on and extend students' facility in thinking and reasoning proportionally.

"Building Explicit and Recursive Forms of Patterns with the Function Game" (Rubenstein 2002) focuses on how input and output tables generated from the function game can help students build, distinguish, and translate between recursive and explicit forms of a function rule. The functions explored include both linear and quadratic.

"Developing Algebraic Reasoning through Generalization" (Lannin 2003) describes the strategies that students use as they attempt to create algebraic generalizations for the Cube Sticker Problem. The task focuses on linear change and features a fanciful task that can be physically modeled.

"Promoting Multiple Representations in Algebra" (Friedlander and Tabach 2001) features the Savings Task in which various parts of the problem situation are presented in different representations so as to encourage the simultaneous use of several representations. The task focuses on a series of linear relationships.

References

Blume, Glendon, and David Heckman. "What Do Students Know about Algebra and Functions?" In *Results from the Sixth Mathematics Assessment of the National Assessment of Educational Progress*, edited by Margaret A. Kenney and Edward A. Silver, pp. 255–77. Reston, Va.: NCTM, 2000.

Friedlander, Alex, and Michal Tabach. "Promoting Multiple Representations in Algebra." In *The Roles of Representation in School Mathematics*, 2001 Yearbook of the National Council of Teachers of Mathematics (NCTM), edited by Albert A. Cuoco, pp. 173–85. Reston, Va.: NCTM, 2001.

Kalchman, Mindy, and Kenneth R. Koedinger. "Teaching and Learning Functions." In *How Students Learn: History, Mathematics, and Science in the Classroom*, edited by M. Suzanne Donovan and John D. Bransford, pp. 351–96. Washington, D.C.: National Academies Press, 2005.

Knuth, Eric. "Understanding the Connection between Equations and Graphs." *Mathematics Teacher* 93 (January 2000): 48–53.

Lannin, John K. "Developing Algebraic Reasoning through Generalization." *Mathematics Teaching in the Middle School* 8 (March 2003): 342–48.

National Council of Teachers of Mathematics (NCTM). *Principles and Standards for School Mathematics*. Reston, Va.: NCTM, 2000.

Rubenstein, Rheta N. "Building Explicit and Recursive Forms of Patterns with the Function Game." *Mathematics Teaching in the Middle School* 7 (April 2002): 426–31.

Building Explicit and Recursive Forms of Patterns with the Function Game

Rheta N. Rubenstein

The function game is a powerful and motivating tool for engaging middle-grades students in mental mathematics, problem solving, communication, and inductive reasoning (Rubenstein 1996). The game can also be used to help students achieve the goals of NCTM's Algebra Standard for grades 6–8; that is, to "represent, analyze, and generalize a variety of patterns with tables, graphs, words, and, when possible, symbolic rules" (NCTM 2000, p. 222). (For a simple electronic version of the game, use the applet on the CD-ROM in Cuevas and Yeatts [2001].) This article will show how the function game format serves as a launchpad to help students build, distinguish, and translate between two basic forms of patterns.

To play the function game, also known as "guess my rule," "the computer game," or "the input/output game," the teacher or a student acts as the "computer." Players—the whole class or a smaller group—offer one input number at a time. The "computer" follows some fixed but secret rule to produce the related "output." The input numbers and associated output results are recorded on a table. For example, for a game in which the rule is "the output is 3 times the input plus 1," the table of a game in progress might look like the table to the right:

INPUT	OUTPUT
7	22
12	37
10	31
25	76

The object is to guess the rule. To keep the game open, if a player knows the rule, he or she is asked not to state it. Instead, the player may demonstrate his or her knowledge by telling the output for a given input. (If the player is wrong, he or she either does not know the rule or miscalculated. If the player is right, he or she probably knows the rule.) When a number of people know the rule, someone is invited to state it. Sometimes, alternative versions are given. For example, a student may state the rule above as "double the number, add it again, then add 1." Then students are challenged to decide why that rule and "triple the input plus 1" are always equivalent.

One strategy students usually figure out after playing a few games is to use 0 for an input. Another strategy is to give input values that are whole numbers in consecutive order. More astute players who are trying to guess the rule above might produce a table that looks like the table to the right:

INPUT	OUTPUT
0	1
1	4
2	7
3	10

At this point, students usually figure out a pattern in the output column of "add 3 to the previous number." This strategy gives students a way to build chains of consecutive output results but stumps them when they try to determine the output for an input of, say, 30. To find that result, students need a rule that moves directly from input to output. The same problem occurs when presenting students with a sequence and asking them to continue it. For example, students are often able to find the next three terms in the sequence 12, 24, 48, 96 by recognizing that each term is twice the previous term. They have trouble, however, giving a formula for the tenth term or, more abstractly, the nth term (e.g., $6 \cdot 2^n$). As one common example, when students are presented with the sequence 1, 4, 9, 16, 25, 36, 49, 64, . . . , rather than seeing the perfect squares jump off the page, many see that they can move from term to term by adding the next odd number. For example:

$$1 + 3 = 4, \quad 4 + 5 = 9, \quad 9 + 7 = 16, \quad 16 + 9 = 25$$

The students' pattern is beautiful, but perfect squares ought to be such "good friends" that students recognize them immediately, especially when a whole group appears together!

These examples show that students look for patterns in at least two distinct ways. The following paragraphs describe how to help students move between these two perspectives.

Functions, Sequences, and Recursive versus Explicit Rules

Although the function game can be played with all kinds of input numbers, such as fractions, integers, and so on, when the input consists of whole numbers (0, 1, 2, 3, . . .), the function can be thought of as a sequence. A rule for the sequence can be expressed recursively or explicitly. Consider, for example, the game above with the output 1, 4, 7, 10, ... Using the students' generally intuitive notion of "adding 3," we can build a recursive, or step-by-step, rule:

$$\text{start} = 1$$
$$\text{next} = \text{current} + 3$$

The first step tells how the sequence begins. It anchors the later steps. The second step tells how to go from one output to the next. The metaphor I share with students is that once I know how to begin, I can just "look over my shoulder" at the previous number to figure out how to find the next number. We often need a conversation at this point to convince students that both parts of the "rule" are necessary. "Why do I need to know the starting number? Suppose the first number were 10 rather than 1. Then what would the following numbers be? Is the sequence the same?" Ultimately, students recognize that the "start" matters.

The "start, next, current" notation is used in *Mathematics in Context* (Encyclopaedia Britannica Educational Corporation 1998). Other publishers use "next = now + 3" or "new = old + 3." In all these textbooks, the notation has been designed to be student friendly, unlike the more abstract and traditional subscripted sequence or function notations, such as the following:

$$t_1 = 1 \quad f(1) = 1$$
$$t_n = t_{n-1} + 3 \qquad f(x) = f(x - 1) + 3$$

The rule that makes this round of the function game easy to play, however, is simply $y = 3x + 1$, or output = 3(input) + 1. This rule is an *explicit* (or *closed* or *direct*) rule. With an explicit rule, one can take any input and find the corresponding output directly.

Students need to be able to distinguish these two ways of thinking about rules, that is, using a step-by-step, or recursive, form versus using a direct, or explicit, form. When students talk about a problem, they need to know if one person is offering an explicit rule while another is using a recursive rule. For example, consider asking students to describe patterns for the even numbers 2, 4, 6, 8, 10, ... One student may say, "add 2" and another may say, "multiply by 2." They appear to be in conflict! Students must realize that "add 2" is part of a recursive rule: "Start at 2 and add 2 to the previous number to get the next." In contrast, "multiply by 2" is an explicit rule: "Multiply the input by 2 to get the output."

After struggling for some time with teaching this distinction, I discovered that the function game table helps tremendously. As shown in **figure 1**, a recursive rule goes from output to output down the right-hand column. An explicit rule goes from input to output across the table. The table clarifies the two types of rules and how they each work. In particular, when students are asked to find rules for sequences presented simply as consecutive terms, they typically do not see the "input," or term, number and have difficulty using this "hidden" number in building a rule. The input/output table makes the input explicit.

Input	Output	
0	1	Start at 1
1	4	+3
2	7	+3
3	10	+3
x	$y = 3x + 1$	

Recursive Rule ↓

Explicit Rule →

Fig. 1. Distinguishing recursive and explicit rules

Using Game Tables to Build Explicit Rules from Recursive Rules

Because so many students have a natural inclination to look first for recursive rules, finding explicit rules may be hard for them. Again, the function game table can build a bridge between the two forms. Assume that students have been asked to solve the following problem: "A construction crew at an agricultural fair is building square animal pens. How many panels does the crew need to build a line of 30 pens?" The problem may be modeled with toothpicks, as shown in **figure 2**. Note that students are working with the same pattern shown earlier, but this time in a geometric context. They are asked to include a third column (as shown in **figure 2a**) to show how the recursive rule, "add 3 to the previous number," can be used to find an explicit rule. The third column shows the structure of the pattern explicitly. After seeing an example or two, students usually begin to realize that they are just adding more 3s to the starting value. The number of 3s added is one less than the input number because the 3 is not added the first time. Consequently, an explicit formula for the output can be derived: $4 + (n - 1)3$.

For many students, the $(n - 1)$ idea is difficult. For these students, we offer another solution method, shown in **figure 2b**. At this point, ask, "If you can add 3 to move forward, what must you do to move backward?" Students realize that they must subtract 3. With this part of the rule in mind, they move backward one row from the starting row to consider an input of 0. The output for 0 must be $4 - 3 = 1$. As shown in

No. of Pens	No. of Panels (or Toothpicks)	Pattern A	
1	4	4	4
2	7	$4 + 3 =$	$4 + 1(3)$
3	10	$4 + 3 + 3 =$	$4 + 2(3)$
4	13	$4 + 3 + 3 + 3 =$	$4 + 3(3)$
5	16	$4 + 3 + 3 + 3 + 3 =$	$4 + 4(3)$
n			$4 + (n - 1)3$
30			$4 + (29)3 = 91$

(a)

No. of Pens	No. of Panels (or Toothpicks)	Pattern B	
0	1	1	
1	4	$1 + 3$	$1 + 1(3)$
2	7	$4 + 3 + 3 =$	$1 + 2(3)$
3	10	$4 + 3 + 3 + 3 =$	$1 + 3(3)$
4	13	$4 + 3 + 3 + 3 + 3 =$	$1 + 4(3)$
5	16	$4 + 3 + 3 + 3 + 3 + 3 =$	$1 + 5(3)$
n			$1 + n(3)$
30			$1 + (30)3 = 91$

(b)

$$1 \quad 1+3 \quad 1+3+3 \quad 1+3+3+3 \quad 1+3+3+3+3$$
Case 0   1   2   3   4

(c)

Fig. 2. Using tables to build explicit rules from recursive rules

figure 2c, the "0 case" can be envisioned geometrically. Imagine just one toothpick at the left of the display. Then, for each successive square, add three toothpicks in the form of a backward C. Many students benefit by seeing geometrically the connection between the numerical pattern and its physical construction. Now we can create a formula in which the number of 3s added is precisely the number of squares, or the input number. The formula is $1 + 3n$.

The particular problem illustrated asks students to find the output for the thirtieth case. With a general formula now in hand, they can substitute and evaluate for $n = 30$ or any other input.

Investigating Whether Rules Are Equivalent

Students are often surprised that more than one way may exist to express a rule. This situation is an opportunity to use graphs and algebra to enhance their learning. Graphing either of the two rules in **figure 2** produces points that fall on a line (see **fig. 3**). The line has a slope of 3 and a y-intercept of 1. As with all rules that produce points on a line, the slope is the value added to each successive term in the recursive rule (in this case, the three panels added repeatedly) and the y-intercept is the output produced when the input is 0. (In this case, the single vertical toothpick needed before three panels completes the first pen.) After investigating several such linear rules, students begin to recognize these connections, deepening their understanding of important algebraic ideas.

1. Graph the data from the agricultural pen pattern (fig. 2).

   Let the x-axis show the number of pens scaled by ones.

   Let the y-axis show the number of panels scaled by ones.

2. What is the shape of the graph?

3. What are its characteristics? Slope? y-intercept?

4. What do the graph's characteristics have to do with the original pattern?

Sample graph:

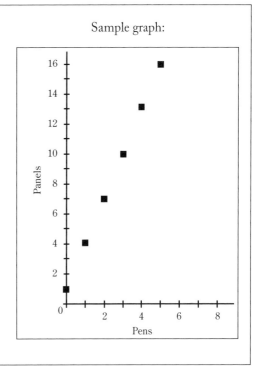

Fig. 3. Graphing points of a linear function

When two rules produce the same graph, we have evidence that they are, in fact, two forms of the same rule. To be perfectly sure, however, we need to use algebra to prove the equivalence. For example, using the rules in **figures 2a** and **2b**, we can show equivalence using the distributive property and adding like terms:

$$4 + 3(n - 1) = 4 + 3n - 3 = 1 + 3n$$

Unfortunately, not all patterns can be as easily derived as the case of the line illustrated above is. Sometimes, a geometric approach works better. Recall the earlier discussion that when shown the sequence of perfect squares, students often see only the recursive pattern, that is, next = current + next odd number.

Figure 4 offers an activity to help students recognize the equivalence of their recursive rule ("adding the next odd") and the explicit rule, n^2. Students are usually surprised and intrigued that they can physically see the successive odd numbers of a recursive rule being added to produce the squares of an explicit rule.

Investigating Patterns with Calculators

Calculators can also be used to help students explore linear and geometric sequences. One of the calculators that is helpful in exploring recursive sequences is the TI-73. With such a calculator, students can create recursive sequences using the constant feature. As shown in **figure 5a**, a student can SET an operation as a constant along with a value, for example, +3, which corresponds to our earlier example. Then, when the student presses 1 CONST, the calculator automatically prints and computes 1 + 3 and shows 4. The screen also displays $n = 1$, indicating the *first* use of the built-in constant. As the constant key is pressed repeatedly, successive terms in the sequence appear, along with their term numbers (n). **Figure 5b** shows the same procedure for producing a geometric sequence.

Students may like to verify that the same sequence is produced when using the explicit form of a rule. This time, they may use the Y= menu to enter a formula, as shown in **figure 6**. Using TBLSET, students can set the table to increment x values by ones. Finally, they can produce the table and compare the values produced explicitly with those produced recursively.

Summary

Familiarity with numerical patterns is fundamental to students' number sense, problem solving, mental mathematics, modeling, and algebra concept learning. Being able to recognize, distinguish, and symbolize these patterns in both explicit and recursive forms is part of basic mathematics literacy. The function game and its input/output tables can be effective tools in helping students to achieve these goals.

References

Cuevas, Gilbert J., and Karol Yeatts. In *Navigating through Algebra in Grades 3–5*, edited by Gilbert J. Cuevas and Peggy A. House. Reston, Va.: National Council of Teachers of Mathematics, 2001.

Encyclopaedia Britannica Educational Corporation. "Building Formulas." In *Mathematics in Context*. Chicago: Encyclopaedia Britannica Educational Corporation, 1998.

National Council of Teachers of Mathematics (NCTM). *Principles and Standards for School Mathematics*. Reston, Va.: NCTM, 2000.

Rubenstein, Rheta N. "The Function Game." *Mathematics Teaching in the Middle School* (November–December 1996): 74–78.

Materials: Square color tiles

1. Start with 1 color tile. How many odd numbers have you used? What is the area of the square?

2. Add 3 more tiles of another color along the right and bottom edges to produce a square. How many odd numbers have you added so far? What is the area of the square?

3. Add 5 more tiles of another color along the right and bottom edges to produce a square. How many odd numbers have you added so far? What is the area of the square?

4. Continue adding 7, then 9 more tiles.

5. Describe your findings.

Partial response:

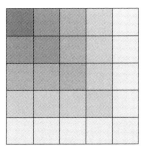

First number:	1 = 1
First two numbers:	1 + 3 = 4
First three numbers:	1 + 3 + 5 = 9
First four numbers:	1 + 3 + 5 + 7 = 16

The sums of consecutive odd numbers are perfect squares. You are adding enough to match each existing edge plus one more to fill in the corner of the new square.

Fig. 4. The sum of consecutive odds equals a perfect square.

Press Set Constant, select Single mode, and set C1 = +3.

Press 1, then CONST (constant). The calculator automatically prints and calculates +3 and tells the value for n of the term. Successively pressing CONST produces successive terms in the sequence.

(a)
Linear sequence

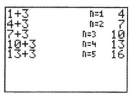

Press Set Constant, select Single mode, and set C1 = *2.

Press 2.5, then CONST (constant). The calculator automatically prints and calculates *2 and tells the n of the term. Successively pressing CONST produces successive terms in the sequence.

(b)
Geometric sequence

Fig. 5. Using the TI-73 constant feature to produce linear and geometric sequences recursively

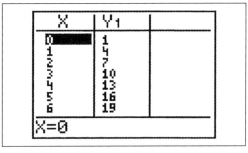

Fig. 6. Using the TI-73 table feature to produce sequences explicitly

Developing Algebraic Reasoning through Generalization

John K. Lannin

NCTM's (2000) recommendations for algebra in the middle grades strive to assist students' transition to formal algebra by developing meaning for the algebraic symbols that students use. Further, students are expected to have opportunities to develop understanding of patterns and functions, represent and analyze mathematical situations, develop mathematical models, and analyze change. By helping students move from specific numeric situations to develop general rules that model all situations of that type, teachers in fact begin to address the NCTM's recommendations for algebra. Generalizing numeric situations can create strong connections between the mathematical content strands of number and operation and algebra (as well as with other content strands). In addition, these generalizing activities build on what students already know about number and operation and can help students develop a deeper understanding of formal algebraic symbols.

My research has examined the various strategies that students use as they attempt to generalize numeric situations and articulate corresponding justifications. Knowledge of students' algebraic reasoning can assist teachers in identifying common errors and guiding students toward an understanding of what constitutes a valid and a useful algebraic generalization.

Background on Generalizing Mathematical Situations

An excellent introductory situation for middle school students to generalize is the Cube Sticker problem (see **fig. 1**). This situation can be generalized using a variety of rules, each providing insight into the connections between the arithmetic and geometric relationships that exist in the situation. The following paragraphs describe how I present such situations to students to give them the opportunity to create and discuss their own rules as they attempt to construct generalizations.

A company makes colored rods by joining cubes in a row and using a sticker machine to place "smiley" stickers on the rods. The machine places exactly 1 sticker on each exposed face of each cube. Every exposed face of each cube has to have a sticker; this rod of length 2, then, would need 10 stickers.

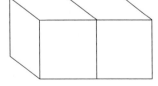

1. How many stickers would you need for rods of lengths 1–10? Explain how you determined these values.
2. How many stickers would you need for a rod of length 20? Of length 56? Explain how you determined these values.
3. How many stickers would you need for a rod of length 137? Of length 213? Explain how you determined these values.
4. Write a rule that would allow you to find the number of stickers needed for a rod of any length. Explain your rule.

Fig. 1. The Cube Sticker problem (adapted from NCTM 2000)

When introducing this problem, I spend a few minutes discussing the problem situation (what we are trying to find, what information is useful, and so on, to help students understand the nature of the problem). Then, I allow students to work individually on the problem for about ten minutes to enable each student to develop at least one strategy for finding the number of stickers.

After working individually, students share their thinking in small groups and discuss the validity of each strategy, along with its advantages and disadvantages. A whole-class discussion about each student's strategy is helpful to demonstrate the variety of possible solution strategies and to develop classroom expectations for what constitutes an efficient generalization and what constitutes a valid generalization.

Two important characteristics of the Cube Sticker problem facilitate generalization. First, the problem requires students to find the number of stickers for rods of different lengths before asking them to construct a general rule. This progression helps students identify which factors vary and which remain the same when calculating the number of stickers on a rod. Second, by requiring students to find the number of stickers for relatively short rods, followed by the number of stickers for much longer rods, the problem forces students to move beyond using drawing and counting strategies toward identifying a general relationship that exists in the situation.

Students' Strategies for Developing Generalizations

When students try to formulate generalizations for situations, such as the Cube Sticker problem, they bring both powerful reasoning and misconceptions regarding the application of mathematical operations to the problem. I invite you to think about how you would find the number of stickers for rods of various lengths before reading the descriptions that follow.

Figure 2 lists students' strategies that other researchers (Stacey 1989; Swafford and Langrall 2000) and I have observed. Note, however, that students often use more than one of these strategies as they attempt to generalize this situation. The following sections elaborate on these strategies.

Strategy	Description
Counting	Drawing a picture or constructing a model to represent the situation and counting the desired attribute
Recursion	Building on a previous term or terms in the sequence to construct the next term
Whole-object	Using a portion as a unit to construct a larger unit using multiples of the unit. This strategy may or may not require an adjustment for over- or undercounting.
Contextual	Constructing a rule on the basis of a relationship that is determined from the problem situation
Guess and check	Guessing a rule without regard to why the rule may work
Rate-adjust	Using the constant rate of change as a multiplying factor. An adjustment is then made by adding or subtracting a constant to attain a particular value of the dependent variable.

Fig. 2. Student strategies for generalizing numerical situations

Counting

A possible statement given by a student who uses the counting strategy is, "Make a rod of that length and count the number of stickers that you would need." This statement describes the level of problem solving at which every student should begin, that is, by building a rod and counting the number of stickers. As teachers, however, we must encourage students to move beyond counting by asking such questions as "Building and counting would be difficult for a rod of length 137. Can you use what you know about shorter rods to find a way to calculate the number of stickers on a rod of length 137?"

Recursion

A student using a recursive strategy has constructed a relationship for building a rod of a given length from a rod with a length that is 1 cube shorter than the desired rod. When using this strategy for the Cube Sticker problem, a student might state, "To find the number of stickers, start with 6 stickers for the first one and add 4 stickers for every cube that you add to the rod, because you can peel the sticker off the end of the old rod and place it on the new cube. Then, you need only 4 more stickers for the new rod" (see **fig. 3**).

A recursive strategy is a powerful means for finding the number of stickers if we know (or can find) the number of stickers on the previous rod. This rule is relatively simple to demonstrate on a computer spreadsheet (see **fig. 4**). The rule also provides a strong connection to the concept of slope (i.e., it describes the increase in the number of stickers when the length of the rod increases by 1), but for longer rods, this strategy is not as efficient as an explicit rule. This strategy can lead to the development of an explicit rule if the student can connect the number of times that he or she adds 4 (one less time than the length of the rod) and the number of stickers for a rod of length 1, which is 6. The resulting rule is $6 + 4(n - 1)$, where n is the length of the rod. Some middle school students have difficulty moving beyond the use of a recursive strategy in this situation, possibly because they do not have a strong understanding of the connection between addition and multiplication. I have witnessed middle school students enter 6 into their calculators and add 4 repeatedly to find the number of stickers for rods of length 137.

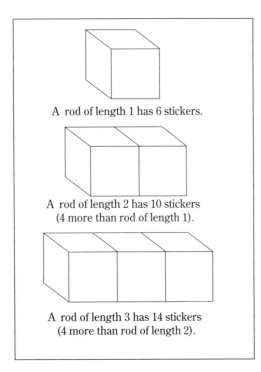

A rod of length 1 has 6 stickers.

A rod of length 2 has 10 stickers (4 more than rod of length 1).

A rod of length 3 has 14 stickers (4 more than rod of length 2).

Fig. 3. A recursive strategy involves building on the previous rod.

Length of Rod	Number of Stickers
1	6
2	=B2+4
3	=B3+4
4	=B4+4
5	=B5+4
6	=B6+4
7	=B7+4
8	=B8+4
9	=B9+4
10	=B10+4
11	=B11+4
12	=B12+4
13	=B13+4
14	=B14+4
15	=B15+4

Fig. 4. Use of a recursive formula on a spreadsheet

Whole-object

The use of the whole-object method is often a mistaken attempt to directly apply proportional reasoning to this situation. A student using this strategy might state, "Because a length-10 rod has 42 stickers, you could multiply 42 by the number of times that 10 goes into the length of the rod. For example, for a rod of length 20, you could multiply 42 (the number of stickers in a rod of length 10) by 2 (the number of rods of length 10 that are in a rod of length 20)." We need to encourage students to count the number of stickers for a rod of length 20 and examine why this strategy results in the incorrect number of stickers. Often, students are unaware that when they use this method, they are counting the extra stickers where the two length-10 rods are joined.

Some students who use this strategy will also adjust for overcounting of the stickers by subtracting the two extra stickers that would be counted when the two rods of length 10 are connected. This method correctly counts the number of stickers for a rod of length 20, but students may have difficulty using this strategy to create a rule that would find the number of stickers for a rod of any length; the strategy is confusing to apply to rods with lengths that are not multiples of 10.

Contextual

The contextual strategy is useful because it links the student's rule to the situation and allows for the immediate calculation of the number of stickers for a rod of any length. A student who uses this strategy might say, "All of the middle blocks have only 4 stickers, and the number of middle blocks is 2 less than the length of the rod [see **fig. 5**]. To find the number of middle blocks, subtract 2 from the length of the rod and multiply that number by 4. Then, add 10 to that total because the 2 blocks on the end have 5 stickers each." (This generalization is one of many such explicit rules that could be constructed for this situation.) This strategy helps students make a connection to a general relationship that exists for all rods of length 2 or more. (Note that explaining how this rule can be related to a rod of length 1 is difficult, although the rule results in the correct number of stickers for that situation, as well.) The blocks on the ends of the rod will always have 5 stickers, and the blocks connecting them (if any) will always have 4 stickers.

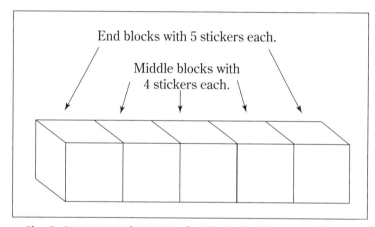

Fig. 5. A contextual strategy for the Cube Sticker problem

Guess and check

The final strategy offers no connection to the context or the number sequence generated for the number of stickers. A student who uses this strategy might state, "I tried a few rules and came up with multiply by 4 and add 2." Although the rule is correct for this situation, it provides no insight into the relationship between the rule and the context and, therefore, is difficult to justify.

Rate-adjust

The rate-adjust strategy is related to the contextual method but uses abstract reasoning regarding the number sequence generated for the number of stickers. A student using this strategy could state, "Because the number of stickers increases by 4 each time [from a rod of length n to a rod of length $n + 1$], you know that you have to multiply the length of the rod by 4. Then, to get 6 stickers for the rod of length 1, you multiply 1 by 4, but you have to add 2 [to make 6 stickers]. You should multiply the length of the rod by 4 and add 2 to find the number of stickers." This strategy requires the understanding that the expression $4n$ increases by 4 as n increases by 1, an important connection to the concept of slope.

Once the rate of change (four stickers added per cube) is identified, it is used to find the correct number of stickers for a rod of length 1, recognizing that the same rule will also result in the correct number of stickers for a rod of any length. This strategy is relatively easy to apply to linear situations, but it is difficult to apply to nonlinear situations; therefore, I encourage students who use this strategy to also develop rules using the contextual strategy.

Student justifications

The following paragraphs discuss the types of justifications that students provide and how teachers can help students recognize what constitutes a valid justification for a generalization.

Avoiding the pitfalls of proof by example

Trying to justify a general situation by demonstrating that the rule results in the correct values for a few individual cases is a common error that occurs throughout grades K–12 (Hoyles 1997). Often, teachers model this type of reasoning. For example, when teaching a traditional algebra course, I remember illustrating the distributive property by calculating 4(5 + 7) and 4(5) + 4(7), noting that these two expressions resulted in the same value, and moving on. Such a misuse of examples can lead to student misunderstanding about what constitutes a valid justification for a general statement. What can we do to counter this type of misconception? An excerpt from a lesson that I taught demonstrates my attempt to deal with this situation:

Teacher: Jason, please explain your rule.

Jason: I multiplied by 4, and I added 2. It was like a guess and check.

Teacher: OK, so you guessed and it worked for the first [example].

Jason: Yeah, and I checked it for others and it worked.

Teacher: And it worked for the second [example], and it worked for the third [example]. Is it always going to work?

[I then asked for a show of hands of students who agreed with Jason's reasoning and those who did not. The class was divided almost evenly between these two groups.]

Teacher: Lisa, what do you think?

Lisa: Well, I don't really understand what he is doing. I don't think that it will work every time. It may work for a few, but it may not work for some numbers.

My purpose in polling the class was to see how prevalent this misconception was. Then, I solicited further input from particular students who disagreed, and Lisa provided a counterargument (that we do not know whether this rule really works for all values) for Jason's faulty justification. Jason had no means of supporting his argument further, and for subsequent problems, no student offered this type of argument during a whole-class discussion.

Despite this discussion, many students continued to use proof by example when questioned individually. Further discussion about this type of justification is necessary to help students understand the need to establish a general relationship. The resilience of this error demonstrates that teachers should proceed with caution when faced with this type of argument.

Linking rules to the problem context

Linking the rule to a general relationship that exists in the problem situation, such as the explanations provided for the recursive and contextual strategies, is an acceptable means of justifying a generalization. In classroom discourse, teachers must consistently follow each student's valid or invalid justification by questioning the entire class to see whether others accept the student's justification. In doing so, we can establish the class expectation that all generalizations must be adequately justified. Similarly, we can continue to question students' attempts to provide justification by example by stating, "This rule appears to work for the examples that have been provided. Now we need to understand why this rule will always work." Many students will also reinforce this idea by asking others to explain why a rule works. The emphasis must be placed on understanding why the rule results in the correct values, as well as on finding a correct rule.

Teachers must also require students to explain each component of their rules. Students tend to provide rules without any explanation of what the various parts of their rules represent in relation to the context of the situation. For the Cube Sticker problem, students often state that their rule is to "Multiply the length of a rod by 4 and add 2." Although this rule results in the correct number of stickers when given the length of the rod, it supplies little insight into the situation. Such questions as "Why are you multiplying by 4?" "What does multiplying the length of the rod by 4 calculate?" and "Why are you adding 2 to the length of the rod?" require students to connect each part of the rule to the situation and thus help others achieve a deeper understanding of the generalization.

Using proof by induction

A third type of justification, an informal proof by induction, is sometimes offered by students who use the rate-adjust strategy. For the Cube Sticker problem, a student using this justification might say, "I know my rule works for a rod of length 1 because I tested it, and it gave me 6. I know that it will work for all other rods because if I increase the length of the rod by 1, the number of stickers increases by 4." A student providing this type of argument should also explain how he or she knows that the increase will be 4, establishing a strong connection to the concept of slope.

Formalizing and Extending Students' Understanding of Generalization

One of the advantages of generalizing numeric situations is that the variables actually represent varying quantities (as opposed to the view often promoted of a variable as a single unknown value in an equation, such as $2x + 3 = 11$). The introduction of formal notation can help students see algebraic symbols as representing varying quantities. For example, the contextual description provided earlier could easily be translated into the explicit rule $S = 4(n - 2) + 10$, where S is the number of stickers and n is the length of a rod.

Teachers can ask questions about what n represents in this situation and what values are appropriate for substituting for n, such as "Can n be 3/4?" Also, we can ask students whether we could construct a rod that contains exactly 40 stickers, for example, to encourage them to think about the output values of this function. By asking these types of questions, we can begin to address the concepts of domain and range that will be introduced later in formal algebra.

The recursive rule could also be written informally using notation that some middle and secondary school textbooks use (see, for example, Coxford et al. [1998]; Romberg et al. [1998]). Students could write the rule as follows: "Start: 6, NEXT = NOW + 4." This notation describes both the initial value in the sequence and the relationship between the current term and the next term in the sequence. Further discussion about when the recursive rule is easier to use and when an explicit rule is easier to use helps students develop a deeper understanding of the advantages and disadvantages of reasoning recursively and explicitly.

Extending the Cube Sticker situation to related situations involving the joining of other prisms, such as triangular or pentagonal prisms, can encourage students to further reflect on the mathematical power of various strategies. For example, the recursive rule could be modified to generate a new rule if the triangular prisms were joined at their bases. The starting value would change to 5 for a rod of length 1. The NOW-NEXT rule would be changed to NEXT = NOW + 3, because 3 more stickers are needed each time the rod is increased in length by 1. The contextual rule described earlier could also be quickly reapplied to this situation, resulting in the explicit rule $S = 3(n - 2) + 8$. Extending the situation in this manner can help students extend their thinking about how their generalizations can be applied to related situations.

Conclusion

Generalizing numeric situations gives students an opportunity to engage in discussions about important mathematical ideas. As seen in the Cube Sticker problem, these situations often connect many mathematical strands and emphasize the need to formulate and validate conjectures. They encourage students to view variables as dynamic quantities that can be used to make sense of their environment.

One of the difficulties students face is that they may not have been asked to justify general statements in the past, and they often resort to justification through the use of examples. We must help students recognize the importance of linking their rules to the context of the situation and not promote the proof-by-example justification commonly used by students.

References

Coxford, Arthur F., James T. Fey, Christian R. Hirsch, Harold L. Schoen, Gail Burrill, Eric W. Hart, and Ann E. Watkins. *Contemporary Mathematics in Context*. Chicago: Everyday Learning, 1998.

Hoyles, Celia. "The Curricular Shaping of Students' Approaches to Proof." *For the Learning of Mathematics* 17 (February 1997): 7–16.

National Council of Teachers of Mathematics (NCTM). *Principles and Standards for School Mathematics*. Reston, Va.: NCTM, 2000.

Romberg, Thomas A., Gail Burrill, Mary A. Fix, James A. Middleton, Joan D. Pedro, Margaret R. Meyer, Sherian Foster, and Margaret A. Pligge. *Mathematics in Context*. Chicago: Encyclopaedia Britannica, 1998.

Stacey, Kaye. "Finding and Using Patterns in Linear Generalizing Problems." *Educational Studies in Mathematics* 20 (1989): 147–64.

Swafford, Jane O., and Cynthia W. Langrall. "Grade 6 Students' Preinstructional Use of Equations to Describe and Represent Problem Situations." *Journal for Research in Mathematics Education* 31 (January 2000): 89–112.

Promoting Multiple Representations in Algebra

Alex Friedlander and Michal Tabach

Many teachers and researchers know that the presentation of algebra almost exclusively as the study of expressions and equations can pose serious obstacles in the process of effective and meaningful learning (Kieran 1992). As a result, mathematics educators recommend that students use various representations from the very beginning of learning algebra (National Council of Teachers of Mathematics [NCTM] 2000).

The use of verbal, numerical, graphical, and algebraic representations has the potential of making the process of learning algebra meaningful and effective. In order that this potential be realized in practice, we must be aware of both the advantages and disadvantages of each representation:

- *The verbal representation* is usually used in posing a problem and is needed in the final interpretation of the results obtained in the solution process. The verbal presentation of a problem creates a natural environment for understanding its context and for communicating its solution. Verbal reasoning can also be a tool for solving problems and can facilitate the presentation and application of general patterns. It emphasizes the connection between mathematics and other domains of academic and everyday life. But the use of verbal language can also be ambiguous and elicit irrelevant or misleading associations; it is less universal, and its dependence on personal style can be an obstacle in mathematical communication.

- *The numerical representation* is familiar to students at the beginning algebra stage. Numerical approaches offer a convenient and effective bridge to algebra and frequently precede any other representation. The use of numbers is important in acquiring a first understanding of a problem and in investigating particular cases. However, its lack of generality can be a disadvantage. A numerical approach may not be very effective in providing a general picture; as a result, some important aspects or solutions of a problem may be missed. Thus, its potential as a tool for solving problems may be sometimes quite limited.

- *The graphical representation* is effective in providing a clear picture of a real valued function of a real variable. Graphs are intuitive and particularly appealing to students who like a visual approach. But graphical representation may lack the required accuracy, is influenced by external factors (such as scaling), and frequently presents only a section of the problem's domain or range. Its utility as a mathematical tool varies according to the task at hand.

- *The algebraic representation* is concise, general, and effective in the presentation of patterns and mathematical models. The manipulation of algebraic objects is sometimes the only method of justifying or proving general statements. However, an exclusive use of algebraic symbols (at any stage of learning) may blur or obstruct the mathematical meaning or nature of the represented objects and cause difficulties in some students' interpretation of their results.

The importance of working with various representations is a result of these and other advantages and disadvantages of each representation and of the need to cater to students' individual styles of thinking. Thus, both curriculum developers and teachers should be aware of the need to work in an environment of multiple representations—that is, an environment that allows the representation of a problem and its solution in several ways (usually some or all of the four representations mentioned above). Although each representation has its disadvantages, their combined use can cancel out the disadvantages and prove to be an effective tool (Kaput 1992). Similarly, the Representation Standard for grades 6–8 in the new *Principles and Standards for School Mathematics* relates to the solution of algebraic problems in general and of situations based on linear functions in particular by addressing the following recommendation (NCTM 2000, p. 281):

Students will be better able to solve a range of algebra problems if they can move easily from one type of representation to another. In the middle grades, students often begin with tables of numerical data to examine a pattern underlying a linear function, but they should also learn to represent those data in the form of a graph or equation when they wish to characterize the generalized linear relationship. Students should also become flexible in recognizing equivalent forms of linear equations and expressions. This flexibility can emerge as students gain experience with multiple ways of representing a contextualized problem.

More specifically, Ainsworth, Bibby, and Wood (1998) mention three ways that multiple representations may promote learning: (*a*) it is highly probable that different representations express different aspects more clearly and that, hence, the information gained from combining representations will be greater than what can be gained from a single representation; (*b*) multiple representations constrain each other, so that the space of permissible operators becomes smaller; (*c*) when required to relate multiple representations to each other, the learner has to engage in activities that promote understanding.

With algebra learning, the use of computers contributes considerably to the promotion of multiple representations (Heid 1995). As students work with spreadsheets and graph plotters, algebraic expressions become a natural requirement and provide an effective means for obtaining a numerical and graphical representation of the relevant data. In a learning environment that lacks computers, drawing graphs or producing extended lists of numbers tends to be tedious and unrewarding.

In the process of solving a problem, isolating representations can be difficult. Thus in most situations, any approach is accompanied by verbal explanations or by numerical computations. In this article we restrict ourselves to the use of representations as *mathematical tools* (and less as means of communication) in the context of beginning algebra. The use of a sequence or a table to answer a question will be an example of a numerical approach, whereas the use of verbal reasoning (possibly including some computations and numbers) will be considered a verbal approach. The use of graphs or algebraic expressions is easier to define and detect.

We cannot expect the ability to work with a variety of representations to develop spontaneously. Therefore, when students are learning algebra in either a technologically based or a conventional environment, their awareness of and ability to use various representations must be promoted actively and systematically. We describe some ways in which tasks can be designed to promote the use of multiple representations. The following section presents, as an example, an activity taken from a beginning algebra course for seventh-grade students and discusses its potential to achieve this goal. We also report some findings about students' use of representations in an assessment task given at the end of one week of work on the activity.

Designing Tasks

In our attempts to promote student thinking and actions in a variety of representations, we found some effective types of tasks and questions. Our analysis of the structure of an activity called Savings illustrates the claim that tasks can be designed to encourage the simultaneous use of several representations.

Describing the problem situation

Questions, tasks, or even more complex activities are usually presented in one representation, and they may, or may not, require the solver to make a transition to another representation. For example, students may decide to solve a verbally posed problem graphically or algebraically. (In some classrooms, the use of verbal reasoning to solve an algebra problem has not yet received full legitimization.)

We found that presenting various parts of a problem situation in different representations encourages flexibility in students' choice of representations in their solution path and increases their awareness of their solution style. The presentation of a problem in several representations gives legitimization to their use in the solution process. Moreover, to understand and solve such a problem, most students perform frequent transitions between representations and perceive them as a natural need rather than as an arbitrary requirement. Posing a problem in several representations is particularly suitable for situations that require the parallel investigation of several methods, quantities, and so on. **Figure 1** presents the Savings problem situation. In this activity, students investigate the weekly changes in the savings of four children, where the savings of each child is presented in a different representation.

Posing Investigative Questions

The presentation of the problem situation is followed by a variety of questions aimed at leading students through their investigations. These questions are posed for a variety of reasons. The following categories of tasks are examples of ways to design activities that relate to our agenda of multiple representations. We illustrate each category by a sample of questions from the Savings activity.

Getting acquainted with the initial representation

The first questions require students to analyze each component in its original presentation and make some extrapolations or draw some conclusions. At this stage many students avoid any transitions from one representation to another. In our example, we posed questions about the savings of each child. First, we asked for the amount of money at the end of a week that was specifically included in the data. We then asked students to extrapolate to a week not represented. Finally, we asked for the week corresponding to a given amount of money.

- Describe in words how the savings of each child changes through the year.
- Given the graphs of the savings of all four children throughout the year, identify each graph and find the meaning and the value of each intersection point.

The savings of Dina, Yonni, Moshon, and Danny changed during the last year, as described below. The numbers indicate amounts of money (in dollars) at the end of each week.

Dina: The table shows how much money Dina had saved at the end of each week. The table continues in the same way for the rest of the year.

Week	1	2	3	4	5	6	7	8	9 ...
Amount	7	14	21	28	35	42	49	56	63 ...

Yonni: Yonni kept his savings at $300 throughout the year.

Moshon: The graph describes Moshon's savings at the end of each of the first 20 weeks. The graph continues in the same way for the rest of the year.

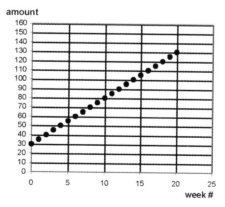

Danny: Danny's savings can be described by the expression $300 - 5x$, where x stands for the number of weeks.

Fig. 1. Savings—problem situation

Explicit requests for transitions between representations

At the next stage, we require students to work in a specific representation. The following two activities illustrate this stage.

Exploratory questions

Finally, we ask students more complex and open-ended questions. At this stage, we expect them to choose their own method of representation and solution path. In our activity, we asked the students to compare the savings of the four children.

> • Compare the savings of two out of the four children.
>
>   Use words like "the savings increase (or decrease),"
>
>   "the savings increase or decrease at a rate of …,"
>
>   "who has a larger (or smaller) amount at the beginning (or end)," and
>
>   "larger (or smaller) by … , double … , equal."
>
>   Use tables, graphs, expressions, and explanations.
> • Add another child to your comparison.

Posing Reflective Questions

Reflection has several important aspects. It helps students become aware of the possiblity of using various representations, exposes them to the advantages and disadvantages of these possibilities, and acquaints them with various ways of presenting the solution to a problem. Reflective questions allow students to distance themselves from actions undertaken previously and hence lead them to evaluate their own and others' actions. Moreover, the ability to reflect on the solution of a problem increases considerably the solver's mathematical power (Hershkowitz and Schwarz 1999). As with multiple representations, we cannot rely exclusively on a spontaneous development of the ability to reflect. The following types of tasks are examples of ways to design activities that make reflection an integral part of the solution process.

Description of work

The requirement to describe one's work is attached to many questions. This "habit" is more than routine, and its importance is beyond the need to document the solution. It allows students to reevaluate their solution strategies and eventually to consider other possibilities. Sometimes we make the task more specific by attaching to the text of a problem a blank page called *Work Area*, with the words *Tables, Graphs, Expressions*, and *Descriptions* on various parts of the page. In this example, the use of any particular representation is recommended, but optional. At other times, we directly ask students to mention the representation they used on each occasion.

Commenting on others' work

Presenting the work of one or several (fictional) students reduces the burden of getting involved in the actual process of solving a problem and allows students to relate to, and reflect on, particular aspects of the solution. Here is an example:

Ran wanted to find how much Dina had saved by the end of the 15th week. Vered suggested continuing the table a little more.

Week	11	12	13	14	15
Amount	77	84	91	98	105

She looked at the table and found that the amount is $105. Motty claimed that he had another way. Since Dina had no savings at the beginning of the year and her savings increased by 7 each week, she would have 7 times the number of weeks—that is, $7 \cdot 15 = 105$. Do you think that both methods are correct? Which method do you prefer?

Asking students to design their own questions

Another possible way to raise awareness of the potential of various representations is to give a problem situation in one or multiple representations (possibly collected from students' previous work) and ask students to design (and solve) a question that in their view can be answered by using the given representation. In our activity, for example, we can pose this task and enclose the tables, graphs, expressions, or verbal descriptions of the savings of all four children.

Asking for reflection on mathematical concepts

Journal items are particularly appropriate for asking students to reflect on possible ways to answer the posed questions and to describe their solution. Thus, toward the end of our activity, we require students to construct a concept map on ways to represent data and solutions. They were also encouraged to discuss the advantages and disadvantages of using a particular representation.

Allowing time for reflection

The solution of complex problems over a longer period of time (in our situation, five lessons spread through one week) creates, of itself, further opportunities for spontaneous or induced reflection.

In the next section, we consider the use of various representations in the solution of a task by two classes of beginning algebra students, who worked on Savings and other similar activities.

Assessing Students' Use of Representations

After a week of investigating the Savings activity (including one lesson of work with Excel), the teachers of two seventh-grade beginning algebra classes gave an assessment task related to the same context. The task was given about two months after the beginning of the course to seventy students who worked in pairs and without computers. Although the assessment of the students' work had a wider scope, we present here only some findings that relate to their use of representations. At the initial stage of the task, the savings of two children during a year were described in a table and a graph. Then, the students were required to answer a sequence of questions and were specifically instructed, both orally and in writing, to show their work and to mention the representation they used in each answer. **Figure 2** presents the first seven (of ten) questions in this task.

The teachers mentioned algebraic expressions at the beginning of the task as one of the four possible representations but did not actually give any. Our impression from the students' classroom work indicated that at this stage of the course, they preferred numerical or verbal solutions and made a more limited use of graphs, and even less use of algebraic expressions. We wanted, however, to have a more detailed picture of students' preferences and flexibility in their choice of representations. According to our (expert) view, different questions in the task favor different representations. Thus, the first two questions clearly favor the use of the given table of numbers, whereas to find the largest difference between their savings (question 4), the use of graphs is more advantageous. In our opinion, the other questions could be answered with a reasonable investment of effort by choosing from several possible representations.

The table and the graph below describe the savings of Danny and Moshon during the year.

Week #	Savings Danny's	Savings Moshon's	Week #	Savings Danny's	Savings Moshon's
0	300	30	26	170	160
1	295	35	27	165	165
2	290	40	28	160	170
3	285	45	29	155	175
4	280	50	30	150	180
5	275	55	31	145	185
6	270	60	32	140	190
7	265	65	33	135	195
8	260	70	34	130	200
9	255	75	35	125	205
10	250	80	36	120	210
11	245	85	37	115	215
12	240	90	38	110	220
13	235	95	39	105	225
14	230	100	40	100	230
15	225	105	41	95	235
16	220	110	42	90	240
17	215	115	43	85	245
18	210	120	44	80	250
19	205	125	45	75	255
20	200	130	46	70	260
21	195	135	47	65	265
22	190	140	48	60	270
23	185	145	49	55	275
24	180	150	50	50	280
25	175	155	51	45	285
			52	40	290

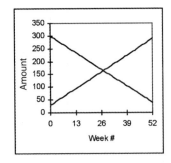

Fig. 2. Savings—assessment task data

Describe the work that you do to answer the questions below. Please describe in detail all your (right or wrong) attempts, and the representations (table/expressions/graph/words) that you use to answer each question.

Important Remark:

The solution process is more important than the final result. A detailed description of your work will improve your assessment.

The questions:

1. How much had Moshon saved after half a year? And how much did Danny have at the same time?
2. After how many weeks did each of the two children have $210?
3. When was the difference between their savings $60? In whose favor was the difference?
4. Find the week with the largest difference between their savings.
5. Find the week when their savings were equal.
6. Find the week when the savings of one were double that of the other. In whose favor?
7. Danny and Moshon decided to pool their savings in order to buy a $400 walkie-talkie. Find the week in which they can realize their intention.

Fig. 2. (cont.) The first seven questions

As expected, the use of the table of numbers was dominant. However, each question attracted various representations. To find the savings after half a year (question 1), the majority of students made direct use of the given table, as in the following solution:

• We looked at Danny and Moshon's table and found the savings for the 26th week because 52 ÷ 2 = 26.

  52 weeks in a year
  2 divided by 2 for half a year
Moshon's savings in the 26th week are $160 and Danny's savings are $170.

Using the table to answer question 1 seems natural and simple. The following two examples show, however, that the approaches to the solution were quite varied. Some pairs of students preferred the algebraic expressions (first example) or graphs (second example).

• After half a year, Moshon had $160. During the first week, Moshon had $30, and each week he added $5. Therefore we made the expression $30 + 5x$. x is the number of weeks and in order to compute [the amount after] half a year, the expression will be $30 + 5 \cdot 26$ and in order to calculate on a calculator we need [to keep] the order of operation. Thus, we found $5 \cdot 26 = 130$ and added $30 = 160$.
• We marked the midpoint of the horizontal axis and drew a line upwards (until our line intersects Danny's and Moshon's points). From Danny's and Moshon's points we drew a horizontal line to the vertical axis. We discovered that Danny had $175 by the middle of the year and Moshon had only $160.

Question 7 related to the possibility of Danny's and Moshon's reaching a common sum of $400 and attracted many verbal solutions, like the not completely correct reasoning in the following example.

> • Danny and Moshon will never get the walkie-talkie because when Danny will have $300 (his largest amount) Moshon will have only $30 and when Moshon will have $290 (his largest amount) Danny will have only $40 and therefore the largest amount that they can reach is $330.

An analysis of the students' answers to all seven questions showed that students were remarkably flexible in their use of representations. Only five pairs of students were consistently numerical. All the others used two, three, or four representations (31, 37, and 12 percent, respectively). Sometimes, a pair used more than one representation to answer a question. Such transfers between representations usually occurred when work with the initially chosen representation seemed too difficult or unrewarding. The following two answers to question 3 (finding cases when the difference between the savings is $60) illustrate this situation.

> • We compared the expressions: Moshon $30 + 5x$ and Danny $300 - 5x$ and then … ah … then we switched to an unsystematic and silly search of each number in the table (the results: the 21st, and the 33rd week).

In this example, the pair of students attempted to answer the question algebraically, but a lack of knowledge about how to use this tool forced them to switch to the numerical approach, in spite of their awareness of its disadvantages. In the next example, another pair makes a transition from a numerical to a graphical representation. The students make the transition to graphs when their initial attempt provides an incomplete answer.

> • On the 21st week Danny had $60 more than Moshon. On the 33rd week Moshon had $60 more than Danny did. We looked for a difference of less than $100 and when we found them, we looked in Moshon's column [to find] when do we have to add or subtract $60 to get Danny's amount in the same week. We found in Danny's column $195 and in the same week we found there in Moshon's column $135. Then we saw in the graph that the same case happens, only that [the amount of] Moshon is larger by $60 than Danny's amount.

Table 1 presents the distribution of the students' choice of representations on each of the first seven questions. Besides the obvious dominance of the numerical representation, it should be noted that some questions attracted a relatively large proportion of other representations. Thus, about 20 percent of the answers to question 5 (finding when the savings are equal) were based on graphs, and more than half of the answers to question 7 (finding when the total savings exceed $400) were either verbal or algebraic.

Conclusion

Many mathematics educators recommend using multiple representations in algebra. We have tried to illustrate some concrete ways of enhancing students' awareness of these advantages and their ability to use them in their routine work. The design of the Savings activity helped us illustrate our belief that the promotion of multiple representations depends in the first place on the presentation of a problem situation and on the nature of the questions asked. These should suggest, legitimize, recommend, and some times even require more than one representation. To internalize the principle of multiple representations, student reflection on these actions is also needed and should be promoted by the task design.

The Savings activity and its follow-up task were conducted as regular classroom activities and were not planned and carried out as research. However, the analysis of students' responses supports our claim that suitable problem posing and questioning—and systematic encouragement of students' experimentation with various representations—can increase the awareness of, and the ability to use, various representations in the solution of a problem.

TABLE 1

Choice of Representation as a Percent of Total Responses* for Each Question and the Assessment Task as a Whole

Question	Numerical	Verbal	Graphical	Algebraic	Unidentifiable
1	68	0	5	16	11
2	74	3	5	13	5
3	71	10	7	7	5
4	51	14	19	0	16
5	61	5	24	0	10
6	59	13	13	2	13
7	25	41	8	13	13
Total	60	13	12	7	8

*The total number of students was 70 (35 pairs). However, if two representations were used in a pair's answer to a question, each representation was counted separately in the corresponding column.

The predominant use of the numerical representation was expected. We relate this preference to the students' early stage in their learning of algebra and to the fact that in many situations the nature of a task makes the use of a numerical approach mathematically sound.

The good news, however, is that if students are given an appropriate learning environment, they will be able and willing to employ a wide variety of solution tools and paths. In our analysis of students' work, we found that the choice of a representation can be the result of the task's nature, personal preference, the problem solver's thinking style, or attempts to overcome difficulties encountered during the use of another representation. Frequently, the choice of representation is influenced by a combination of several factors. To answer a question, students may choose a representation on the basis of their analysis of the problem and personal preference, and they may switch to another representation at a later stage as a result of difficulties in the solution process.

References

Ainsworth, Shaaron E., Peter A. Bibby, and David J. Wood. "Analysing the Costs and Benefits of Multi-Representational Learning Environments." In *Learning with Multiple Representations*, edited by Maarten W. van Someren, Peter Reimann, Henry P. A. Boshuizen, and Ton de Jong, pp. 120–34. Oxford, U. K.: Elsevier Science, 1998.

Heid, M. Kathleen. *Algebra in a Technological World. Curriculum and Evaluation Standards for School Mathematics* Addenda Series, Grades 9–12. Reston, Va.: National Council of Teachers of Mathematics, 1995.

Hershkowitz, Rina, and Baruch Schwarz. "Reflective Processes in a Mathematics Classroom with a Rich Learning Environment." *Cognition and Instruction* 17 (1999): 65–91.

Kaput, James J. "Technology and Mathematics Education." In *Handbook of Research on Mathematics Teaching and Learning*, edited by Douglas A. Grouws, pp. 515–56. New York: Macmillan, 1992.

Kieran, Carolyn. "The Learning and Teaching of School Algebra." In *Handbook of Research on Mathematics Teaching and Learning*, edited by Douglas A. Grouws, pp. 390–419. New York: Macmillan, 1992.

National Council of Teachers of Mathematics (NCTM). *Principles and Standards for School Mathematcs*. Reston, Va.: NCTM, 2000.

SECTION 6

Linear Equations

Introduction

In the years since the second volume of *Activities for Junior High School and Middle School Mathematics* (Easterday, Freeman, and Smith 1999), the change in the importance of algebra in the curriculum for these students is significant. More states are expecting that substantial numbers of students will have an experience with algebra equivalent to a traditional Algebra 1 high school course by the end of eighth grade. In all states the algebraic reasoning strand across grades K–8 has taken on more importance, and the expectations for engaging students in such thinking and reasoning have been substantively raised (Reys 2006). Algebra for all is the call—and the earlier the better. In order to make progress toward these goals in meaningful ways, we need to give students educative experiences that promote students' learning to think and reason in algebraic situations grounded in contexts that support such progress. Practice with particular algebraic manipulations absent any sense of when the manipulation might be useful seems doomed to leave students short of what *Principles and Standards for School Mathematics* (NCTM 2000, p. 223) sets as expectations: "Students in the middle grades should learn algebra both as a set of concepts and competencies tied to the representation of quantitative relationships and as a style of mathematical thinking for formalizing patterns, functions, and generalizations.... It is essential that they become comfortable in relating symbolic expressions containing variables to verbal, tabular, and graphical representations of numerical and quantitative relationships." The argument that all is not well in the teaching and learning of algebra is echoed in the following quote from Smith (2003, p. 139): "… the need for radical change in the way algebra is taught is evident in both the attitudes and accomplishments of our students."

The articles selected for this section on linear equations all present tasks that have the potential to engage students in algebraic explorations. These tasks can help you engage students in algebraic thinking, reasoning, and generalization as students are learning algebraic techniques for representing, generalizing, and solving algebraic equations. Four stages characterizing students' progress in algebra were articulated by James Kaput (1999, 2000) as (1) generalizing arithmetic—generalizing about operations and operations associated with numbers; (2) generalizing numerical patterns—expressing regularity in numbers and functional relationships; (3) formalizing generalizations—modeling; and (4) generalizing systems—abstracting from computations and relations. The tasks in this section focus mainly on the first two stages of this progression of sophistication—generalizing arithmetic and generalizing numerical patterns. In several of the tasks, students engage in learning to write and solve linear equations.

"Representation in Realistic Mathematics Education" Meyer (2001) presents an instructional sequence that allows students to explore algebraic situations involving equality relationships. These are good tasks to pose with students who are moving toward formal equation solving in linear algebra.

"The Chicken Problem" (Reeves 2000) is similar in content to the Meyer (2001) article mentioned above. Here the move to algebra is highlighted in the five mathematical task sequences that are presented.

"Revisiting a Difference of Squares" (Slavit 2001) looks at algebra through the lens of the difference of squares. Two tasks are posed in the article: the first explores differences of squares, and the second gives the more advanced challenge of factoring cubes.

The article "New Approaches to Algebra: Have We Missed the Point?" (Thornton 2001) presents examples of tasks that approach the introduction to algebra in three different ways—a patterns approach, a symbolic approach, and a functions approach—and examines what each contributes.

References

Easterday, Kenneth E., F. Morgan Freeman, and Tommy Smith. *Activities for Junior High School and Middle School Mathematics*, Vol. 2. Reston, Va.: National Council of Teachers of Mathematics, 1999.

Kaput, James J. "Teaching and Learning a New Algebra." In *Mathematics Classrooms That Promote Understanding*, edited by Elizabeth Fennema and Thomas A. Romberg, pp. 133–55. Mahwah, N.J.: Lawrence Erlbaum Associates, 1999.

———. *Transforming Algebra from an Engine of Inequity to an Engine of Mathematical Power by "Algebrafying" the K–12 Curriculum*. Dartmouth, Mass.; National Center for Improving Student Learning and Achievement in Mathematics and Science, 2000. ERIC Document Reproduction No. ED 441664.

Meyer, Margaret R. "Representation in Realistic Mathematics Education." In *The Roles of Representation in School Mathematics*, 2001 Yearbook of the National Council of Teachers of Mathematics (NCTM), edited by Albert A, Cuoco, pp. 238–50. Reston, Va.: NCTM, 2001.

National Council of Teachers of Mathematics (NCTM). *Principles and Standards for School Mathematics*. Reston, Va.: NCTM, 2000.

Reeves, Charles A. (Andy). "The Chicken Problem." *Mathematics Teaching in the Middle School* 5 (February 2000): 398–402.

Reys, Barbara J., ed. *The Intended Mathematics Curriculum as Represented in State-Level Curriculum Standards: Consensus or Confusion?* Greenwich, Conn.: Information Age Publishing, 2006.

Slavit, David. "Revisiting a Difference of Squares." *Mathematics Teaching in the Middle School* 6 (February 2001): 378–81.

Smith, Erick. "Stasis and Change: Integrating Patterns, Functions, and Algebra throughout the K–12 Curriculum," In *A Research Companion to "Principles and Standards for School Mathematics,"* edited by Jeremy Kilpatrick, W. Gary Martin, and Deborah Schifter, pp. 136–50. Reston, Va.: National Council of Teachers of Mathematics, 2003.

Thornton, Stephen J. "New Approaches to Algebra: Have We Missed the Point?" *Mathematics Teaching in the Middle School* 6 (March 2001): 388–92.

Representation in Realistic Mathematics Education

Margaret R. Meyer

This article will explore a theory of mathematics learning and instruction and show how representation in middle school algebra might develop in an instructional sequence based on this theory. This theory, which is called Realistic Mathematics Education (RME), has evolved over the past thirty years of developmental research. RME represents a significant departure from traditional ideas about learning and teaching mathematics that can best be seen by examples that illustrate its principles.

Principles of Realistic Mathematics Education

RME is based on five related principles of learning and instruction. The formulation of these principles here represents a synthesis of statements that appear in several sources (de Lange 1987, 1992; Treffers 1991). The five principles may be stated as follows:

1. Learning mathematics is a constructive activity, in contrast to one in which the student absorbs knowledge that has been presented or transmitted. Such construction becomes possible when the starting point of instructional sequences is experientially real to students, allowing them to engage immediately in mathematical activity that is personally meaningful.

2. The learning of a concept or skill is accomplished over a long period of time and moves through different levels of abstraction. The initial, informal mathematical activity should constitute a concrete basis from which students can abstract and construct increasingly sophisticated mathematical concepts. Students bridge the gaps between concrete and increasingly abstract levels through their creation and use of models, drawings, diagrams, tables, or symbolic notations.

3. Students' learning of mathematics and progress through levels of understanding are promoted through reflection on their own thoughts and those of others. Students must have the opportunity at critical points to reflect on what they have learned and to anticipate where the instructional sequence is heading.

4. Learning takes place not in isolation but rather in sociocultural contexts. Consequently, interaction should be an essential component of instruction. Instructional activities should encourage students to reflect, to explain and justify solutions, to understand other students' solutions, to agree and disagree with one another, and to question alternatives.

5. Mathematical understanding is structured and interconnected. Real phenomena, in which mathematical structures and concepts manifest themselves, usually contain mathematics from multiple disciplinary strands. As a result, learning strands should be intertwined rather than independent.

An Instructional Sequence Based on RME

Perhaps the most obvious difference between an instructional sequence based on RME and a more traditional sequence is their starting points. In explaining algebraic representation, most traditional algebra texts start with abstract expressions involving variables and rapidly move to formal equations and their manipulation. After attaining some degree of facility in manipulating equations, the student of algebra is invited to apply these skills to context-based problems.

Materials based on RME, however, reverse the progression. Instead of starting in the abstract realm and moving toward the concrete application, the mathematics starts in contexts (principle 1) and gradually progresses to formal symbolism (principle 2). This shift allows students to engage in meaningful, preformal algebraic activity in earlier grades than they traditionally have. Through a structured instructional sequence, students explore and rediscover significant mathematics that anticipates the more formal representations found in traditional algebra.

The remainder of this article will explore the variety of representations that emerge from two algebra units in the middle school curriculum *Mathematics in Context*, which is based on the principles of RME. "Comparing Quantities" (Kindt et al. 1998) is a unit for grade 6, and "Get the Most Out of It" (Roodhardt et al. 1998) is for grade 8. The following representations of linear relationships will be examined: pictures, invented symbols, combination charts, tables, and algebraic symbols. The focus of the discussion will be on the progressive formalization of students' representations and their relationship to standard algebraic notations.

Pictures

Figure 1 shows a problem that "Comparing Quantities" represents in pictures. Although the balanced scales imply an equality of measure that could be represented in equations, this is purposely not done. Since the authors include this problem on page 2 of the unit, they clearly do not expect students to use any formal algebraic procedures to solve it. Instead, they anticipate that students will approach the problem in whatever way they understand. Solutions reveal a variety of representations that preview more formal representations and strategies that will come later in the instructional sequence.

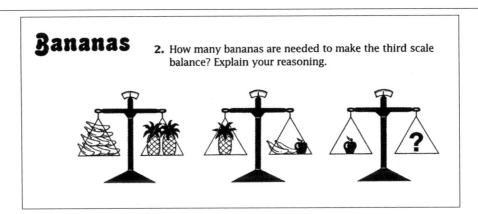

Fig. 1

Some students solve this problem using pictures, as illustrated in **figure 2**. Other students use words in equations, in the manner shown in **figure 3**.

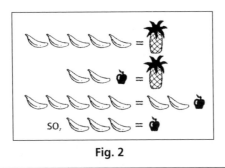

Fig. 2

10	bananas	= 2 pineapples, so
5	bananas	= 1 pineapple
1	pineapple	= 2 bananas + 1 apple
5	bananas	= 2 bananas + 1 apple, so
3	bananas	= 1 apple

Fig 3

This informal process is very close to a formal solution involving variables and equations. Other students assign an arbitrary weight to the pile of bananas—for example, they might say, "Suppose the bananas weigh 10 pounds," and reason from there, using words.

Figure 4 shows a problem that is stated only through pictures. This problem can be solved using a number of different equivalent representations, but for some students the most obvious strategy involves the pictures. They notice that if they cover up (or take away) a cap and an umbrella from each row, then the difference in price ($4.00) is the difference between the cap and the umbrella.

Other students see the two rows of pictures as forming a series that can be continued by producing a third row containing all caps. **Figure 5** shows the result.

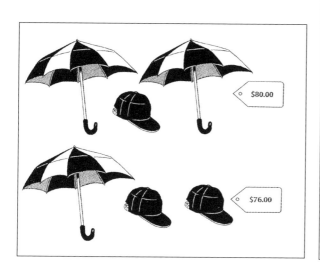

Fig. 4.

Fig. 5.

When asked to describe what they have done, the students give explanations such as the following: "When one of the umbrellas in the first row is replaced with a cap, the total goes down by $4.00. So I replaced the umbrella in the second row with a cap, and now I have 3 caps totaling $72.00. Now I can find the cost of one cap by dividing." In a similar manner, they might start from the lower row in figure 4 and produce a new row above the upper one, containing three umbrellas for a total price of $84.00.

Invented Symbols That Resemble Variables

When working with the pictures, some students represent a cap with the letter C and an umbrella with the letter U. This is a shorthand notation that emerges quite naturally. It takes too much effort to draw an umbrella, so they use a U instead. They might even write $3U$ to represent UUU, but it means three umbrellas—not three times the price of one umbrella, as it would if U were being used as a variable. Students even use this invented notation to create "equations" that are in the same form as they would be with variables. Using this notation, they translate the picture "sentences" into the statements shown below.

$$2U + 1C = 80$$
$$1U + 2C = 76$$

This invented notation leads students toward using U more abstractly, implicitly representing the cost of an umbrella. The invented notation often leads them to perform operations on the equations that mirror standard operations on equations. For example, students might add the two equations to get

$$3U + 3C = 156.$$

This operation is supported by the context, and the result is meaningful. It is also reasonable within the context to divide this equation by 3 to get

$$1U + 1C = 52.$$

Then, by taking just a few more steps, students can find the cost of one cap. These preformal representations of variables and operations on equations emerge from the context and are prompted by the pictures and a desire to be economical with words, pictures, and symbols. It probably does not occur to the student that these symbols might have power beyond the context. The symbols simply provide a faster way to represent the situation than pictures or words do.

Combination Charts

The unit "Comparing Quantities" introduces the use of combination charts as a representational strategy that is quite useful for solving this type of problem. A combination chart would represent the problem of the caps and umbrellas, as shown in **figure 6**.

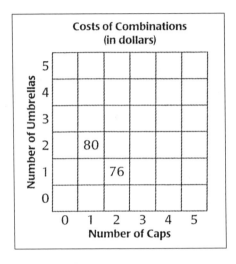

Fig. 6.

In general, a combination chart shows totals for all combinations of two values. In this problem, the values are the costs for caps and umbrellas. By exploring many combination charts representing different contexts, students learn that each chart contains many patterns in the numbers. They discover that they can use these patterns to solve problems that they can express as two numbers in a combination chart. For example, students soon see that each combination chart has consistent diagonal patterns. By studying the chart shown in **figure 6**, for example, they learn that when they move down and to the right, the number decreases by 4. They can exploit this pattern to find other numbers on the diagonal and finally to arrive at the cost of three caps when they reach the edge of the chart. Such playing with patterns can be done without any reference to caps and umbrellas. However, in the context, the diagonal pattern of *moving down and to the right decreases the number by 4* is analogous to reducing the number of umbrellas by one while increasing the number of caps by one and lowering the total cost by $4. Also, finding the number on the edge of the chart where it shows a combination of three caps and no umbrellas is analogous to drawing a new picture equation that shows three caps equal to $72.00. By the same token, a picture equation showing that three umbrellas is equal to $84.00 is analogous to moving up and to the left on the chart, with an increase of $4, to find the combination for three umbrellas and no caps. **Figure 7** shows the two approaches.

Tables

"Comparing Quantities" introduces another representational strategy for solving problems of this type. This strategy uses what the unit calls "notebook" notation, since it is introduced in the context of writing down information in a notebook. A waiter is taking orders and tallying costs in a restaurant. **Figure 8** presents the problem, using both pictures and notation.

Some students solve the problem using the pictorial representations, whereas other students don't see them as containing useful information. The totals for orders 4 and 5 in the notebook can be found by the

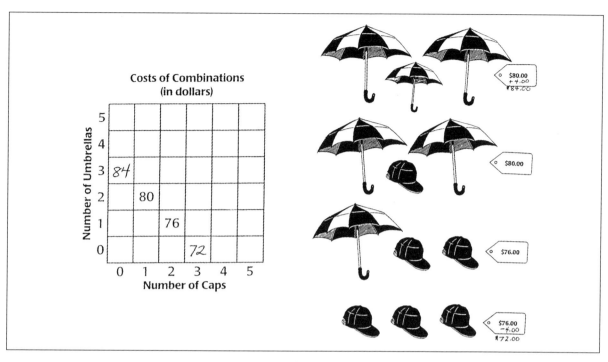

Fig. 7

simple division of previous orders (1 and 3). Total prices for orders 6 and 7 are somewhat more difficult to determine but quickly become apparent when students recognize each of them as the sum of two earlier orders (order 4 + order 5 = order 6, and order 3 + order 4 = order 7). Teachers may see the first three orders, for which prices are given, as a 3 × 3 matrix and may recognize that the missing totals for the other orders can be found by using the results of elementary row operations (dividing by a scalar, adding rows, etc.). Students are unaware of this matrix format. They see the rows and columns on Mario's pad simply as a shorthand way of writing the information of the problem.

Classroom interaction (principle 4) reveals that students do in fact see the difference between this problem and the one involving the caps and umbrellas. They recognize that there are three prices to find here instead of just two. Students often ask if a combination chart could be used to represent the combinations of information about tacos, drinks, and salads.

Fig. 8

Some even try to imagine a three-dimensional equivalent to the combination chart but quickly realize that such a thing would be impractical, even if it were theoretically possible. This reflection on the instructional sequence illustrates principle 3 of RME.

Equations

The instructional sequence described above concludes with a section in which variables and equations are introduced more formally by relating them to combination charts and the notebook notation. The equations are always related to a familiar context that supports their meaning, and as a result, equations are seen as just one more way to represent information. The fact that equations can be explored for their own sake, apart from context, is something that comes in later study. At this point in grade 6, a preformal use of equations with understanding is the goal of instruction.

The expanded notion of equation as a representation is seen in the following problem from the grade 8 unit "Get the Most Out of It":

> Eighth-grade students from Wingra Middle School are going on a camping trip. There will be 96 people going, including the students and teachers. All the luggage, gear, and supplies are already packed into 64 equal-sized boxes. Now the organizers want to rent the right number of vehicles to take everyone to the campsite. They can choose between two different types of vehicles from a car rental agency:

Minivan: seats 6 people   Van: seats 8 people
Cargo space: 5 boxes   Cargo space: 4 boxes

A formal algebraic approach would focus on the simultaneous solution of the two equations that describe the situation: $6M + 8V = 96$ and $5M + 4V = 64$. However, in the preformal approach adopted by RME, students use the representations they have learned so far and clues from the context.

Questions follow that encourage students to explore different combinations of vans and minivans and the resulting numbers of people and packages that can be transported, with the idea of eventually finding the smallest number of minivans and vans that are needed. These explorations are all performed by examining the meanings supplied by the context. For example, the unit suggests that if students consider just the people, they will see that 4 minivans can be exchanged evenly for 3 vans. "Why does this work?" the unit asks the students, and then it directs them as follows: "List all the possible combinations of minivans and vans that carry exactly 96 people." This effort might result in a table such as that shown in **figure 9**. Similar questions related to an even exchange between minivans and vans for the boxes and all possible combinations will lead students to the solution that 8 minivans and 6 vans make up the smallest number of vans and minivans needed to carry 96 people and 64 boxes.

The next strategy that students encounter is a graphical one. Using the table in **figure 9** and the one resulting from the students' examination of the combinations of minivans and vans needed to carry exactly 64 boxes, students produce the graphical representation of the problem shown in **figure 10**. A specific question directs students to discover that in the context of the problem, most of the points on either line are not solutions, because you can rent only whole vehicles.

Students can also solve the van and minivan problem using combination charts. The chart in **figure 11a** is designed to show the number of people carried by various combinations of minivans and vans. The number 96 is written in the appropriate cells because the problem requires that exactly that many people be transported. The chart in **figure 11b** is designed to show the number of boxes carried by various combinations of minivans and vans. Here, the number 64 is written in, because the problem requires that that many boxes be transported. The similarity between the combination charts and the graphical solution is of course no accident. The representations reflect the same relationships between minivans and vans in the numbers of boxes and people that they can carry. In **figure 10,** the even exchange between minivans and vans is reflected by the slopes of the two lines. The line that represents people reflects the exchange of four minivans for three vans by the slope of $-3/4$ for the graph of $6M + 8V = 96$. In the combination chart, the combinations totaling 96 are 3 down and 4 to the right of each other (or 3 up and 4 to the left).

Minivans	Vans
16	0
12	3
8	6
4	9
0	12

Fig. 9

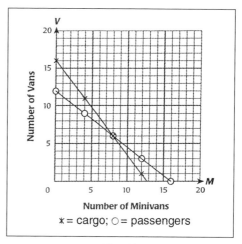

Fig. 10

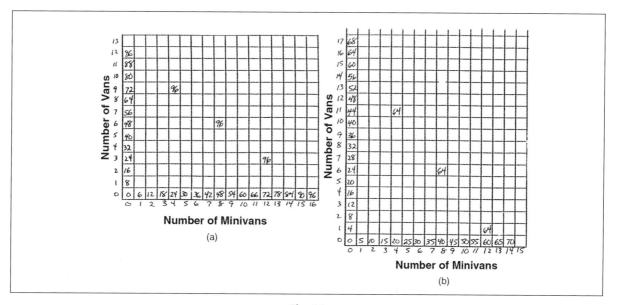

Fig. 11.

The final strategy presented in the context of this problem involves the following two equations:

$$6M + 8V = 96$$
$$5M + 4V = 64$$

The numbers and letters are clearly attached to the context, and students can express their meaning. For example, in the equation $6M + 8V = 96$,

6 stands for six people in each minivan.

M stands for the number of minivans.

8 stands for the number of people in each van.

V stands for the number of vans.

96 stands for the total number of people who must be carried.

The mathematical structure of this set of equations is identical to that of the set of equations for the caps-and-umbrellas problem. The linear equations for both problems represent the context. However, an interesting thing happens when students apply one of the strategies that the sixth-grade unit used for solving that earlier problem, as shown:

$$(5M + 4V = 64) \times 2 \quad \longrightarrow \quad 10M + 8V = 128$$
$$6M + 8V = 96 \quad \longrightarrow \quad 6M + 8V = 96$$
$$4M = 32$$
$$M = 8$$

Substituting the value for M in the second equation results in $V = 6$, a value that students can check against the previous solutions. Some students may object that the equation $10M + 8V = 128$ that resulted from doubling the first equation appears to have changed meaning within the context. They may point out that the minivan can still hold only 5 boxes—not 10—and that the van can still hold only 4 boxes—not 8—as suggested by the new equation. A subtle rewriting can restore their concrete understanding of meaning in the context. When the equation is written $5(2M) + 4(2V) = 128$, these students should see that it is the number of vehicles that has been doubled—not the number of boxes that the vehicles can hold. Now, the operation on the equation appears reasonable, both from a mathematical point of view and in the context. Most students at this level would never notice any problem with the doubled equation. They are not bound by the context, and they accomplish a transition to the abstract without confusion.

The Five Principles Revisited

We have explored a variety of representations that emerge from a sequence of linear problems that are based on concrete situations, in keeping with the tenets of RME. The first principle of RME was manifest in the way in which the contexts stimulated these representations. These concrete contexts allowed students to engage in meaningful mathematical activity from which their understanding could grow. The second principle of RME was embodied in the progressive levels of abstraction reflected by the pictures, charts, tables, and equations presented in the units and in students' solutions to problems. Teachers should note that even after students have encountered formal equations, it is not unusual for them to operate with preformal models. It is always preferable for a student to use a less formal strategy with understanding than a more formal one without understanding. The third and fourth principles are most evident in classroom interactions, and as a result, they are difficult to illustrate here. It is clear, however, that reflection and interaction can enhance students' understanding and appreciation of many of the representations shown in this article. Finally, the fifth principle is illustrated by the connections between the two units.

The reader might wonder about the learning outcomes of the instructional sequence described here. At a minimum, the instructional sequence appears to allow students to engage in significant mathematics with understanding at earlier grade levels than more traditional programs do. It would also seem reasonable to conjecture that students gain from this sequence a deeper understanding than students ordinarily achieve of the connections among representations, in whatever form, and the context they reflect. A related outcome is also possible—that is, that students can model contexts with symbols, which they in turn can use to solve problems related to those contexts. This expectation that mathematics is about "making sense" is often suspended or forgotten when students move to abstract representations too quickly and without the grounding provided by realistic contexts. Another possible outcome of the instruction is an understanding that situations presented in problems can often be represented in different ways and that the different representations suggest different strategies for solutions. These learning outcomes are currently only conjectures, if not high hopes. Nevertheless, they are plausible, significant, and worthy of investigation.

References

de Lange, Jan. *Mathematics Insight and Meaning*. Utrecht, Netherlands: Vatgroep Onderzoek Wiskundeonderwijs en Onderwijscomputercentrum, 1987.

———. "Higher Order (Un-)Teaching." In *Developments in School Mathematics Education around the World: Proceedings of the Third UCSMP International Conference on Mathematics Education*, edited by Izaak Wirszup and Robert Streit, pp. 49–72. Reston, Va.: National Council of Teachers of Mathematics, 1992.

Kindt, Martin, Mieke Abels, Margaret R. Meyer, and Margaret A. Pligge. "Comparing Quantities." In *Mathematics in Context*, edited by the National Center for Research in Mathematical Sciences Education and the Freudenthal Institute. Chicago: Encyclopaedia Britannica Educational Corporation, 1998.

Roodhardt, Anton, Martin Kindt, Margaret A. Pligge, and Aaron Simon. "Get the Most Out of It." In *Mathematics in Context*, edited by the National Center for Research in Mathematical Sciences Education and the Freudenthal Institute. Chicago: Encyclopaedia Britannica Educational Corporation, 1998.

Treffers, Adri. "Didactical Background of a Mathematics Program for Primary Children." In *Realistic Mathematics Education in Primary School*, edited by Leen Streffland, pp. 21–56. Utrecht, Netherlands: Freudenthal Institute, 1991.

The Chicken Problem

Charles A. (Andy) Reeves

The problem shown in **figure 1** (Burrill 1998) struck me immediately as one to try with my sixth graders. Before reading further, try to solve the Chicken Problem yourself.

Reprinted with permission from the Mathematics in Context® program, 1999, Encyclopedia Britannica, Inc.

Fig. 1. The Chicken Problem

The Chicken Problem involves algebraic reasoning. Its solution is accessible through arithmetic, but once you have studied systems of equations in algebra, you would probably solve it using formal algebra (i.e., using variables and a systematic approach). One formal solution using algebra is demonstrated in **Appendix 1**. Algebraic-reasoning problems like the Chicken Problem are now appearing in textbook series for the middle grades, offering students the chance to approach such problems at an intuitive level before they study the abstractions of formal algebra. Including these types of problems seems to be a promising step toward reaching the "algebra for all" goal that is sweeping the country. I wondered how my sixth graders would approach this problem without my intervention.

The students were invited to try the problem over the Thanksgiving holidays, pretending that the chickens were turkeys. They were encouraged to get help from their family members. Students who produced easy-to-follow, systematic solutions would be given a chance to explain their reasoning to the rest of the class after Thanksgiving.

What Happened?

Twenty-two students (50%) attempted the problem; twelve found the correct answer, and four of those produced easy-to-follow, systematic solutions. Matt Brooks's work is shown in **figure 2** and Joanna Whitney's, in **figure 3**. Notice that Matt did the problem without using variables by numbering the boxes and using arithmetic. It was obvious to me in checking his paper that Matt understood what he was doing. Joanna used variables, but I was not quite as sure that she understood her approach using formal algebra. Laila Chatelain produced a solution similar to Matt's, and Dominic Griffin's was like Joanna's.

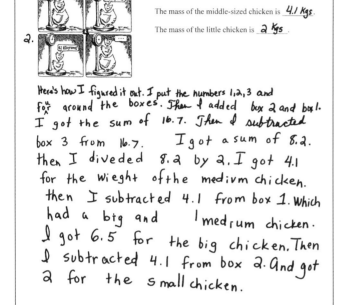

Fig. 2. A solution to the Chicken
Problem that does not use variables

Fig. 3. A solution to the Chicken
Problem that uses variables

The four successful students explained their solutions to the rest of the class the following week, but I neglected to ask them to concentrate on their strategies rather than their computations, so the class heard four explanations that emphasized arithmetic rather than a strategy. I refrained from summarizing any of their explanations, wanting to know instead whether students could learn from one another how to think in this manner. One thing was clear, however; all four students knew exactly how to solve the problem, even if they had received help initially.

An Extension

Later I redesigned the problem, replacing the numbers and rearranging the four frames. This new version of the problem was given to the students over the Christmas holidays with the same instructions.
Only six students turned in papers after the holidays, with five students having correct solutions. Of those five, three used a systematic approach. Two of the three, Steven Hill and Myles O'Keefe, were not in the group of four who had solved the problem this way originally, so I knew that at least six students in the class could use such an approach. All three explained their solutions to the class again, but this time I stressed explaining their strategies rather than their computations. The explanations were more focused, and I hoped now that most students in the class had learned how to solve the problem from listening to their peers.

Yet Another Extension

Toward the end of the year, I again replaced the numbers and rearranged the frames of the second version of the Chicken Problem, resulting in a problem identical to the original except for the numbers, and offered it to the students. This time, of the thirty-three students who turned in papers, sixteen did the problem correctly and twelve used a systematic approach. Leo Khin's work is shown in **figure 4**. I was disappointed that of the thirteen who used such an approach, only four used variables, even though they had previously seen other students explain this problem's solution using variables. Several students who had used variables in solving the problem previously did not use them for this last version.

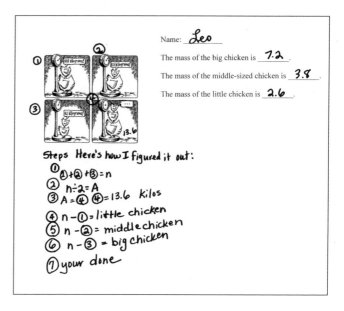

Leo's paper and presentation deserve special mention. He demonstrated a good feel for variables and casually used the term in his explanation to other students, but he did not use the variables consistently. The circled numerals represent the four numbers that he assigned to each of the frames. He used *n* to stand for the mass of all the chickens in the first three frames; then A to represent *n*/2, which is the answer to frame 4. In his steps 4–6, however, Leo used *n* instead of A to show how to get each individual chicken's mass from frames 1–3. I could tell that Leo knew what he was doing from his explanation to other students and that his use of variables will be refined over time. He is fearless about, and confident in, his ability to handle mathematics.

Fig. 4. Leo Khin's solution to Chicken Problem III

Summary

Altogether, thirteen students (about 30%) successfully used an easy-to-follow, systematic approach at least once in the three attempts at the Chicken Problem. Twenty-four students (over 50%) got the problem right, by hook or by crook, at least once. The number that tried the problem went from 22 (50%) to 33 (75%) from the first to the third version. The experiment was a qualified success. Perhaps you can improve on the situation if you attempt the problem with your students.

Reflections

This series of problems left me with the following observations:

- Some students can learn to solve problems like this one from listening to one another and to their parents. Not all the solutions will be efficient. The problem itself, as a precursor to systems of equations, is within the reach of sixth graders.

- If students are to teach problem-solving strategies to others, they should be asked to emphasize strategies rather than computations. They should be encouraged to explain their approaches without using numbers.

- Students will not automatically learn to use variables even after hearing their classmates use them as shortcuts. The use of variables will have to be encouraged by the teacher if that outcome is a goal of an algebraic-thinking strand.

Try to find problems like the Chicken Problem and use them with your students. Begin with one such problem, and modify it over time. **Figure 5** contains four such problems that you can reproduce for classroom use. These problems are courtesy of an enrichment program called Sunshine Math. (See **Appendix 2** for information about this program.) An article in the May 1999 issue of *Mathematics Teaching in the Middle*

School (Meyer 1999) discusses another algebraic-reasoning problem and shows various ways that students might approach it. This kind of activity may nudge students to see algebra as merely the next step in acquiring a set of tools to solve interesting problems.

References

Burrill, Gail. "Changes in Your Classroom: From the Past to the Present to the Future." *Mathematics Teaching in the Middle School* 4 (November–December 1998): 184–90.

Meyer, Margaret R. "Multiple Strategies = Multiple Challenges." *Mathematics Teaching in the Middle School* 4 (May 1999): 519–23.

The total price of a dictionary and an almanac is $32. The total price of 2 dictionaries and 3 almanacs is $86. What is the price of each book?

Answer: The cost of a dictionary is _____. The cost of an almanac is _____.

Consider the pattern of buildings shown, made from blocks.

a. How many blocks would the 4th building require? _____
b. How many blocks would the 5th building require? _____
c. How many blocks would the 25th building require? _____

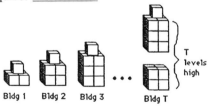

Bldg 1   Bldg 2   Bldg 3   Bldg T

How many blocks would it take to make building *T* in the pattern above, where *T* can be any whole number?

Answer: To make building *T*, I need this many blocks: _____

Maria likes to weigh her toy animals. She found that the animals below balanced the gram weights in her science kit. Three elephants and 2 donkeys balanced 28 grams; two elephants and 1 donkey balanced 17 grams. Maria says she can now tell how much both animals weigh. Are you as clever as Maria?

Answer: An elephant is _____ grams; a donkey is _____ grams.

The scale below shows three helium balloons attached to a scale, with two cans of unknown weight *x*. The helium balloons pull *up* on the scale, and so have a negative weight which has previously been measured as –5 because each one exactly balances a 5 gram weight. The cans push *down* on the scale and so have a positive unknown weight. Use your ingenuity to find the weight of one can.

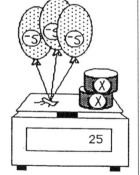

Answer: *x* = _____ grams.

Fig. 5. Four algebraic-thinking problems from the sixth-grade level of Sunshine Math

Appendix 1

The following is an algebraic approach to the original Chicken Problem:

Let x, y, and z be the masses of the small, medium, and large chickens, respectively. Then

$$y + z = 10.6,$$

$$x + z = 8.5,$$

and

$$x + y = 6.1$$

are three equations in three unknowns from the first three frames. Add the left sides and the right sides of the three equations to get

$$y + z + x + z + x + y = 25.2,$$

or

$$2(x + y + z) = 25.2,$$

or

$$x + y + z = 12.6,$$

which is the sum of the masses of all three chickens and the answer to the problem as pictured. To find the mass of each type of chicken, use the original equations in combination with the last one. To find x, subtract $y + z$ and 10.6 from the left and right sides of $x + y + z = 12.6$, respectively, to get $x = 2.0$. Similarly, $y = 4.1$, and $z = 6.5$.

Appendix 2

Sunshine Math is a grades K–8 enrichment program designed to be run by school volunteers and supported by teachers and administrators. The nonprofit program can be purchased by contacting Jean Chance at the PAEC Clearing House, 753 West Boulevard Street, Chipley, FL 32428; (850) 638-6131; e-mail: chancej@ paec.org. The current cost is about $12 per grade level or $100 for the grades K–12 set.

Revisiting a Difference of Squares

David Slavit

While on a drive, three-year-old Rudi sees a cow and yells out, "Horsey! Horsey!" Although the word is wrong, this child has correctly abstracted his experiences with similar animals into one general idea and called it "horsey." Rudi has made an important generalization that allows him to think about all such animals as a single group.

Middle school algebra can present similar challenges in the mathematical life of a student because numerous aspects of algebra require similar reasoning and generalization. For example, algebra is usually the first class that requires students to transform their computational and pattern-based views of arithmetic into a more structured understanding using algebraic symbols. Although algebra involves many concepts (Kaput 1995), such as functions, variables, and solving equations, this articles focuses on the kind of algebraic thinking that develops from a series of related arithmetic experiences, which are then generalized into more abstract ideas (Slavit 1999). To achieve the goal of making algebra accessible for everyone, we must tap students' knowledge and awareness of arithmetic while making the transition to more formal and abstract understanding. This article discusses a classroom activity that uses a common factoring pattern to develop this kind of algebraic understanding. Student-centered classroom investigation and discussion are central to the approach.

Algebra as Generalized Arithmetic

The idea of algebra as generalized arithmetic involves structural understanding of arithmetic operations when acting on arbitrary quantities. This aspect of algebra requires a general understanding of arithmetic that is *grounded in a series of computations*, then abstracted into a single idea. In any prealgebra or beginning-algebra course, plenty of opportunities exist to discuss this kind of algebraic reasoning, because factoring patterns are abstractions of arithmetic operations.

Teachers can design tasks that allow students to develop both a knowledge of common factoring patterns and related symbolic manipulations and an understanding of algebra as generalized arithmetic. The following equation is the basis for designing such tasks:

Concrete Computations + Thinking = Algebra as Generalized Arithmetic

The activity described in this article shows how this transition can be accomplished in middle-grades classrooms.

Using the Difference of Squares

Ask your students to do the following activity:

1. Pick any two consecutive numbers.

2. Square each, and find the difference (ignoring the sign).

3. Add the two original numbers.

4. Explain why the answers in steps 2 and 3 are the same.

I have on several occasions given this problem to middle school students and preservice elementary school teachers. The first reaction that I receive when students complete steps 2 and 3 is often amazement, followed by confusion. I treasure this reaction, which reveals that I have captured the students' interest and have developed a genuine problem-solving situation. Students who are comfortable with variables and symbolic manipulation usually solve the problem using an appropriate algebraic equation, for example,

$$(n + 1)^2 - n^2 = n^2 + 2n + 1 - n^2 = 2n + 1 = (n + 1) + n.$$

The work of Keith (pseudonyms are used throughout), a middle school student, illustrates how his computations led him to develop his symbolic explanation (see **fig. 1**). Keith investigated the problem using the numbers 3 and 4, from which he derived a "general computation" using x and $x + 1$. This problem-solving episode occurred during a seventy-minute period and after just two weeks of instruction that focused on symbol manipulation.

A solution such as that in **figure 1** can set the stage for a discussion of the power of algebraic symbols; however, I delay this discussion while other students explore the problem using a more arithmetic approach, one that is also at the heart of algebra as generalized arithmetic. This approach usually involves repeating steps 1–3 for several pairs of consecutive numbers. **Figure 2** shows a sample of the results of this approach after the students have organized their data. Invariably, several students try to find a pattern in the various computations that they used to test the validity of statement 4 above. The students often have some interesting observations, but they usually cannot adequately explain the underlying reasons for the similarities in the results of the computations contained in statements 2 and 3.

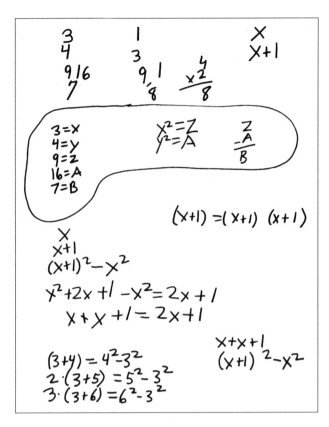

Fig. 1. One middle school student's solution

Because further investigation of patterns may be necessary for these students, I pose a similar task designed to supply scaffolding for the students' thinking. However, instead of using two consecutive numbers, we use two numbers that differ by two (e.g., 4 and 6). Their investigations may lead to information similar to that in **figure 3**. If necessary, we repeat this process for numbers that differ by three, but many students make this exploration on their own.

At this stage, the students are in a position to cross the algebraic divide. Encourage a discussion in which students examine a holistic view of all the computations and attend to the patterns found in them. In my view, this ability to understand patterns is the core of algebraic reasoning of this kind. I ask students what specific observations they made that allowed them to express the general rule. In response, I have received such comments as "The second one was the sum of the numbers times 2, so I guessed that the third one is the sum of the numbers times 3."

The discussion can continue using such language, and the students can discover the general pattern in the computation. At times, students may invent their own language to discuss their discoveries. Lydia used

$4^2 - 3^2$ = 16 − 9 = 7	4 + 3 = 7	
$5^2 - 4^2$ = 25 − 16 = 9	5 + 4 = 9	
$6^2 - 5^2$ = 36 − 25 = 11	6 + 5 = 11	
$10^2 - 9^2$ = 100 − 81 = 19	10 + 9 = 19	

Fig. 2. Student investigation of the difference-of-squares factoring pattern in which the numbers differ by 1

$4^2 - 2^2$ = 16 − 4 = 12	4 + 2 = 6	(12 ÷ 2 = 6)
$5^2 - 3^2$ = 25 − 9 = 16	5 + 3 = 8	(16 ÷ 2 = 8)
$6^2 - 4^2$ = 36 − 16 = 20	6 + 4 = 10	(20 ÷ 2 = 10)

Fig. 3. Student investigation of the difference-of-squares factoring pattern in which the numbers differ by 2

the notion of "start-off numbers" to explain how she understood the general computational aspects of the difference-of-squares factoring pattern (see **fig. 4**). Although algebraic understanding has emerged, the need to express the ideas with formal algebraic symbols may still exist. If so, ask the students to use variables to write the results of the three investigations. Their equations for each investigation, respectively, may resemble the following:

$$a^2 - b^2 = a + b$$
$$a^2 - b^2 = 2(a + b)$$
$$a^2 - b^2 = 3(a + b)$$

Appropriate discussion or student insight can guide students to realize that $a - b = 1, 2,$ and 3, respectively, and eventually to form a conjecture about the general factoring pattern:

$$a^2 - b^2 = (a + b)(a - b)$$

Slowly and with guidance, the students make an algebraic leap. Further, they require very little knowledge of symbolic manipulation to produce the expression; the construction is grounded in their arithmetic experiences.

Students may also approach the problem in rather unexpected ways. Sherrie, a preservice teacher, used her understanding of multiplication as repeated addition to construct a solution. As her work indicates, she first expressed 3^2 and 4^2 as sums (see **fig. 5**). She then realized that a set of three 1's and an extra 4 would remain when she took the difference of these sums. The difference would be $3 + 4$, a result that she generalized to all numbers. Although she did not immediately realize the symbolic connection with her computations when it was discussed in class, she was able to make the connection in a later portfolio entry. An understanding of algebra as generalized arithmetic, as well as its relationship to algebraic symbols, often take time to develop.

When we review the kinds of understanding that developed from this problem, the true power of using students' computations and intuitions is revealed. On one level, the students developed a meaningful way to remember the factoring pattern of the difference of squares. More important, the students were given a chance to explore and analyze numeric computational patterns that led to algebraic forms.

A geometric interpretation can introduce greater depth to the task. Have the students cut an arbitrarily sized square with a side of length a, then draw in its lower-left portion a smaller square with

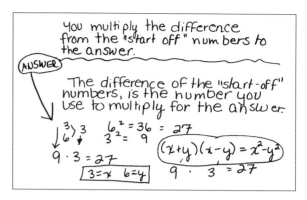

Fig. 4. Lydia's solution

Something I Am Proud Of:

Choose two consecutive numbers:
3 and 4
Add them together:
3 + 4 = 7
Square each of the numbers:
9 and 16
Subtract the lowest from the highest:
16 − 9 = 7
Why is the number the same?

They are the same
because 4 squared can   and 3 squared can
be represented as   be represented as
4   3
4   3
4   3
4

4 − 3 = 1
4 − 3 = 1 } equals 3
4 − 3 = 1
4 − 0 = 4 equals 4

and 4 + 3 = 7

I was really proud of this when I first solved it in class. (However, after seeing it solved using an algebraic equation, I felt as if I had proven the quantitative amount of 17 by taking my shoes off.)

I think it means that I saw a relationship between a number and its square. But one operation was addition and the other subtraction. So I wrote it out and in doing the subtraction, recreated the original 2 numbers, that when added together gave the sum.

I still DO NOT understand the algebraic equation used to solve the problem, but at least I found an answer.

Fig. 5. Sherrie's initial portfolio entry

a side of length *b*, shading all the figure except the smaller square of side *b* (see **fig. 6**). Students could use graph paper, but doing so may lead to investigations dealing with specific calculations rather than to a more general approach to the task. First, ask the students how this object relates to the results of their arithmetic investigations of this pattern. With guidance, the discussion will turn to the fact that the use of the shaded region can be found by performing the calculation $a^2 - b^2$.

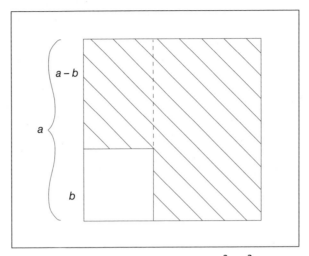

Fig. 6. Geometric interpretation of $a^2 - b^2$

How could this region be shown to have a length of $(a + b)(a - b)$? Give students time to analyze their drawings, and provide scissors to allow them to manipulate portions of the figure and investigate the situation dynamically. By sliding and rotating the larger shaded rectangle, we see that the shaded portion of the square is a rectangle of dimension $(a + b)$ by $(a - b)$. If given time, one or more of your students may make this exciting observation. (See **fig. 7**.)

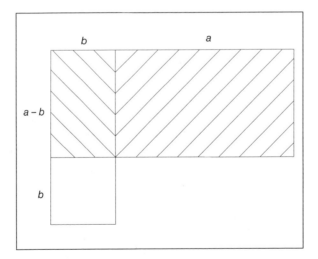

Fig. 7. A transformation illustrating that $a^2 - b^2 = (a + b)(a - b)$

Finally, the following task could be used in an advanced discussion of factoring cubes.

1. Find a prime number that is one less than a cube.
2. Find another prime number that is one less than a cube.
3. Explain!

Solution: Any number that is one less than a cube can be represented algebraically as $x^3 - 1$. Consider the factoring pattern $x^3 - 1 = (x - 1)(x^2 + x + 1)$. This number is prime only if either one of the factors is equal to 1, but $x^2 + x + 1$ cannot equal 1 for any value for which $x > 0$. The only way for one of the factors to be equal to 1 is when $x - 1 = 1$, which is true only when $x = 2$. Therefore, $2^3 - 1 = 7$ is the only prime number that is one less than a perfect cube.

Concluding Remarks

Cai (1998) observed that sixth-grade students in the United States usually prefer arithmetic approaches to algebraic ones. Teachers of beginning-algebra students can take advantage of these tendencies by creating situations that allow students to generalize a given computational pattern. This article has described one such task to develop algebraic understanding in middle-grades students. The complexity of algebra makes it exciting, difficult, pleasing, and cohesive. The key to developing algebraic thought in these activities is to provide the students with sufficient information and an intriguing activity, then engage them in appropriately guided discussion. Students can make the leap from arithmetic to algebra if they are given enough rope to help them swing across. In this task, that assistance was the presence of a series of related computations that could be generalized into a single idea, then represented by a single algebraic expression.

References

Cai, Jinfa. "Developing Algebraic Reasoning in the Elementary Grades." *Teaching Children Mathematics* 5 (December 1998): 225–29.

Kaput, James J. "A Research Base Supporting Long-Term Algebra Reform?" In *Proceedings of the Seventh Annual Meeting of the North American Chapter of the International Group for the Psychology of Mathematics Education,* edited by Douglas T. Owens, Michelle K. Reed, and Gayle M. Millsaps, pp. 71–94. Columbus, Ohio: ERIC Clearinghouse for Science, Mathematics, and Environmental Education, 1995.

Slavit, David. "The Role of Operation Sense in Transitions from Arithmetic to Algebraic Thought." *Educational Studies in Mathematics* 37, no. 3 (1999): 251–74.

New Approaches to Algebra: Have We Missed the Point?

Stephen J. Thornton

Curriculum movements in the United States and Australia, characterized by such documents as *Curriculum and Evaluation Standards for School Mathematics* (NCTM 1989) and *A National Statement on Mathematics for Australian Schools* (AEC 1991), have challenged the conventional view of algebra as formal structure, arguing that algebra is fundamentally the study of patterns and relationships. Increased emphasis has been given to developing an understanding of variables, expressions, and equations and to presenting informal methods of solving equations. The emphasis on symbol manipulation and on drill and practice in solving equations has decreased (NCTM 1989).

Has the net effect of these changes been merely to replace one kind of procedural knowledge with another? This article looks at three approaches to algebra: (1) a patterns approach, in which students are asked to generalize a relationship; (2) a symbolic approach, in which students learn to manipulate algebraic expressions; and (3) a functions approach, which emphasizes generation and interpretation of graphs. This article examines the nature of thinking inherent in each approach and asks whether any or all of these approaches are, in themselves, sufficient to generate powerful algebraic reasoning.

The Patterns Approach, or "Matchstick Algebra"

The patterns approach to algebra in the middle school is typified by the matchstick pattern shown in **figure 1**. Faced with this problem, students almost invariably describe the rule as "add 3." Most students look at the table of values horizontally, observing that each time a square is added, the number of matches needed increases by three. Well-intentioned teachers often help students find a general rule from this observation, saying, for example, that if one adds 3 each time, the rule is of the form $m = 3s + k$, and suggesting that students try a few numbers to determine the value of the constant.

The students regard this approach as good teaching because it helps them obtain the correct answer. The teacher is similarly reinforced in the belief that he or she is acting in the students' best interests, because the students are able to find the rule for this pattern and, perhaps, even

Examine the following pattern, complete the table, and find a rule that shows how the number of matches (m) depends on the number of squares (s).

s	1	2	3	4	5	100
m	4	7	10			

Rule: $m =$ _____

Fig. 1. Matchstick pattern

a general rule for other linear cases. The ability to find these rules is, arguably, a useful skill, but do the students understand any more about the nature of algebra than if the subject had been introduced in a formal, symbolic way? Students who use this heuristic to find the constant and thus the general rule have, in reality, looked at the specific rather than the general. They have not necessarily acquired any well-developed notion of the general nature of the pattern but have merely learned a procedure to develop a correct symbolic expression. The algebraic essence of the problem is absent.

The Matchstick Pattern Problem is not about finding a general rule. The answer to the problem, that is, the rule itself, is unimportant. The problem is really about alternative representations. It is a visualization exercise in which different ways of looking at the pattern produce different expressions. Visualizing the pattern in different ways and writing corresponding algebraic relationships help students understand the nature of a variable and become familiar with the structure of algebraic expressions. This particular pattern can be visualized in at least four different ways (see **fig. 2**).

Writing down the number pattern in a table, an activity commonly found in textbooks and on worksheets, does not help students visualize the generality inherent in the matchstick constructions. A much more constructive approach is to ask students to build one element of the pattern physically and explain how it is put together, not in terms of numbers but in terms of its underlying physical structure. The different algebraic structures then have direct physical meanings.

Numerous other visual approaches to algebra are possible (Nelsen 1993). For example, students could be asked to visualize the pattern shown in **figure 3** in different ways so as to generate a relationship between the number of shaded squares (b) and the length of the side of the white square (n). Again, at least four different representations are possible (see **fig. 4**). The point of the exercise is not to obtain the answer $b = 4n + 4$ or any of its variants but rather to understand how the pattern can be visualized and how these different visualizations can be described symbolically. If we are to foster powerful algebraic thinking in our students, we must encourage a variety of well-justified generalizations of the pattern. Rather than be an end in itself, the purpose of generating rules is to develop insight into patterns and relationships. As Gardner (1973, p. 114) writes, "There is no more effective aid in understanding certain algebraic identities than a good diagram. One should, of course, know how to manipulate algebraic symbols to obtain proofs, but in many cases a dull proof can be supplemented by a geometric analogue so simple and beautiful that the truth of a theorem is almost seen at a glance."

The Symbolic Approach, or "Fruit Salad Algebra"

The formal, symbolic approach to algebra, in which variables are defined as letters that stand for numbers, has been criticized as lacking meaning (Chalouh and Herscovics 1988) and has been identified as the source of many difficulties faced by beginning algebra students (Booth 1988). Olivier (1984) used the term "fruit salad algebra" to describe an approach to algebra in which students choose variables as objects or labels rather than as numbers. The fruit-salad approach to algebra is illustrated by such questions as the following (Haese et al. 1991, p. 198):

Pattern built of one match plus three for each square, or $m = 3s + 1$

Pattern built of four matches for the first square plus three for each subsequent square, or $m = 4 + 3(s - 1)$

Pattern built of two horizontal rows joined by vertical links, or $m = 2s + (s + 1)$

Pattern built of four matches for each square, with the overlapping match removed from all but one of the squares, or $m = 4s - (s - 1)$

Fig. 2. Different ways to visualize the matchstick pattern

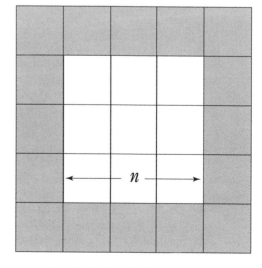

Fig. 3. A visualization exercise

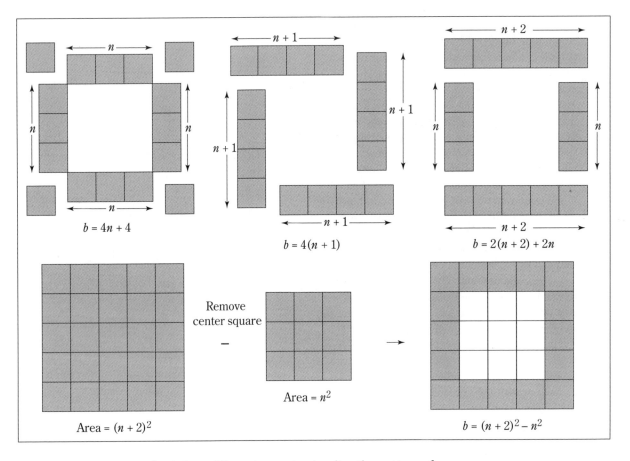

Fig. 4. Four different ways to visualize the pattern of squares

Three people have two apples and a banana each, and two other people have an apple and three bananas each.

(1) How many apples and bananas did they have altogether?

(2) Expand and simplify $3(2a + b) + 2(a + 3b)$.

(3) What do you notice about (1) and (2)?

This approach provides concrete models for symbols, which can lead students to short-term success, but the confusion of variables with objects can also lead to widespread misunderstanding (MacGregor 1986). To help alleviate this confusion, some much more effective and powerful models, such as algebra tiles, have been developed to give concrete meaning to symbolic manipulation.

No matter how effective the model or context is, a potential danger is that the fundamental meaning and purpose of symbolic manipulation may be lost. The essence of symbolic manipulation lies not in obtaining an answer to a specific question but rather in helping make sense of an observation. Each different representation produced through symbolic manipulation can reveal a different insight into the situation being considered. For example, Crossfield (1997) describes using colored numbers in his classroom as a strategy for helping students develop general results. His students observe, for example, that if two square numbers are subtracted, the result can only be a prime number if the two squares are consecutive squares, and even then only if the sum of their square roots is a prime number. In every other case, a composite number results. The result that $a^2 - b^2 = (a + b)(a - b)$ shows that if $a - b \neq 1$, the result cannot be prime.

Calendar patterns (Olssen 1995) also present an ideal context in which to emphasize the meaning and purpose of symbolic manipulation. In one exercise, a square of four numbers is selected at random from any month of a calendar (see **fig. 5**). Multiplying the two shaded numbers along each diagonal in **figure 5** and then subtracting their products produces the result 10 × 16 − 9 × 17 = 7. Every square of four numbers, taken from any month, will result in a difference of products equaling 7. As it does in the exercise with colored numbers, the algebraic justification for this observation lends meaning and purpose to the processes of symbolic manipulation. One of the most significant features of this problem is the position of each number in the calendar in relation to the others (see **fig. 6**). Thus, $d + 1$ and $d + 7$ have not only a numerical significance but also a positional significance. Identifying algebraic symbols both numerically and visually enhances students' algebraic thinking. An almost endless supply of similar results can be found embedded in a simple calendar.

Symbolic manipulation has a purpose. The search for concrete models in algebra should not mask the fundamental purpose of symbolic manipulation as communicating insight into generality by enabling an expression to be written in different ways. Each different form of an expression should reveal a different feature, leading to the discovery, communication, and proof of general results.

The Functions Approach, or "Taxicab Algebra"

The functions-and-graph approach to algebra is characterized by the problem shown in **figure 7**. This approach emphasizes a realistic application of graphs and encourages students to represent situations in words, symbols, graphs, and tables. Yet seldom do teachers or textbooks ask students to discuss the different insights that can be gained from each of these representations.

The four representations lead to twelve possible transitions between representations, as shown in **figure 8**. By far, the most common path around this diagram is counterclockwise, moving from words to numbers to graphs to symbols. Seldom do we expect students to move directly from words to symbols or from tables to words. Yet all twelve of the possible transitions add to students' understanding of the nature of functions and relationships. For example, the ability to recognize that the relationship in the Taxicab Problem can be written as $c = 180 + 120k$, without having to draw a graph or a table of values, shows insight into the relationship between cost and distance. Understanding why this symbolic representation is useful—because it makes the problem easier to solve using a spreadsheet or programmable calculator or

December 1998			1	2	3	4	5
6	7	8	9	10	11	12
13	14	15	16	17	18	19
20	21	22	23	24	25	26
27	28	29	30	31		

Fig. 5. Calendar pattern to show symbolic manipulation

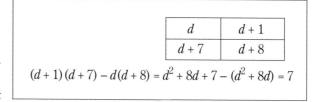

$$(d + 1)(d + 7) − d(d + 8) = d^2 + 8d + 7 − (d^2 + 8d) = 7$$

Fig. 6. Position of each number in the calendar in relation to other numbers

A certain taxicab company charges $1.80 as an initial "pickup" fee, then $1.20 per mile. Complete the table below, represent the total charge graphically, and write down an algebraic expression for the total charge in terms of the number of miles traveled.

Distance (miles)	5	10	15	20
Cost ($)				

Fig. 7. The Taxicab Problem

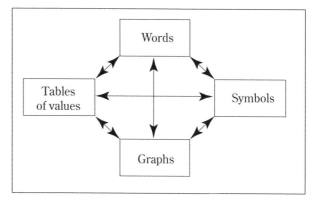

Fig. 8. Transitions between representations of algebraic situations

to work the question backward—shows an even greater degree of insight into the situation itself and into the power of algebraic thinking. The ability to represent a relationship graphically, in a table, as a function, and in words, and the thinking required to convert directly from one representation to another in every possible permutation is to promote the development of different insights into the situation being studied.

Conclusion

The reform of school mathematics curricula has tended to deemphasize the formal, symbolic approach to algebra and emphasize patterns and functions as central themes of middle school mathematics (NCTM 1989). Clearly, all three approaches—patterns, symbols, and function—are of central importance; however, an unquestioning acceptance of these approaches to algebra, even as outlined in current curriculum documents, can still fail to develop powerful algebraic thinking in our students. We must examine the fundamental nature of algebra before we can help our students use algebra for a purpose. The power of algebra lies in its capacity to develop and communicate insight by representing situations in alternative ways. Whether developed through alternative visualizations, symbolic manipulation, or a functional approach, each of these alternative representations leads to new insights into mathematical relationships. As teachers of algebra, our role is to help students take advantage of the insights illuminated by these alternative representations.

References

Australian Education Council (AEC). *A National Statement on Mathematics for Australian Schools.* Carlton, Victoria, Australia: Curriculum Corporation, 1991.

Booth, Lesley R. "Children's Difficulties in Beginning Algebra." In *The Ideas of Algebra, K–12*, 1988 Yearbook of the National Council of Teachers of Mathematics (NCTM), edited by Arthur F. Coxford, pp. 20–32. Reston, Va.: NCTM, 1988.

Chalouh, Louise, and Nicolas Herscovics. "Teaching Algebraic Expressions in a Meaningful Way." In *The Ideas of Algebra K–12*, 1988 Yearbook of the National Council of Teachers of Mathematics (NCTM), edited by Arthur F. Coxford, pp. 33–42. Reston, Va.: NCTM, 1988.

Crossfield, Dan. "(Naturally) Numbers Are Fun." *Mathematics Teacher* 90 (February 1997): 92–95.

Gardner, Martin. "Mathematical Games." *Scientific American* (October 1973).

Haese, Robert, Kim Harris, Sandra Haese, Brenton Webber, and Diane Howarth. *Mathematics for Year 8.* 3rd ed. Adelaide, Australia: Haese & Harris, 1991.

MacGregor, Mollie E. "A Fresh Look at Fruit Salad Algebra." *Australian Mathematics Teacher* 42 (3) (1986): 9–11.

National Council of Teachers of Mathematics (NCTM). *Curriculum and Evaluation Standards for School Mathematics.* Reston, Va.: NCTM, 1989.

Nelsen, Roger B. *Proof without Words: Exercises in Visual Thinking.* Washington, D.C.: Mathematical Association of America, 1993.

Olivier, Alwyn I. "Developing Basic Concepts in Elementary Algebra." In *Proceedings of the Eighth International Conference for the Psychology of Mathematics Education*, edited by Beth Southwell, Roger Eyland, John Conroy, and Kevin Collis, pp. 110–15. Sydney, Australia: International Group for the Psychology of Mathematics Education, 1984.

Olssen, Kevin. *Working Mathematically: Investigations.* Carlton, Victoria, Australia: Curriculum Corporation, 1995.

SECTION 7

Measurement

Introduction

Look around you and let your mind explore what would be different if we had not developed ways to measure different kinds of phenomena. A moment of such reflection should convince you that understanding what it means to measure and becoming skilled at measuring different kinds of phenomena is important for our students. Unfortunately, many of our students first engage measurement through practicing the use of measurement tools without understanding what it means to "measure," why tools are useful, and how tools can be used.

This set of articles starts with three papers that report research on students' learning of measurement concepts and procedures as well as examples of tasks to use with students. The additional articles include mathematical tasks that can help give your students a different and powerful experience in learning to measure. The tasks engage students in the fundamental ideas of choosing a measurement unit that is practical for measuring specific attributes of phenomena, iterating that unit, and partitioning the unit to get a closer estimate of the measurement. For example, measuring time (in the early grades), angles, length, area, and volume—in fact, making a measurement in general—requires an appropriate unit of measure that can be "matched" to the aspect of the phenomena we want to measure and then iterating this unit of measure to "match" the phenomena while keeping count of the numbers of unit iterations needed. For example, to measure length we need a unit that can "match" length. We need to choose a version of such a unit that, through iterating the unit, can come close to matching the length of the object we are measuring. We would not choose a yard to be the unit of measure if we are measuring the length of sticks of butter. We might choose an inch or a centimeter. However, we would need multiple copies of the unit to match the length of the stick of butter. But what if the match is not exact? Then we need the idea of partitioning into equal-sized pieces to make subunits that help make a closer match to the length of the stick of butter. We can get as close as we need to in our matching with units and partitions of units, but we cannot guarantee that the measure is the exact measure. Measuring is inherently an approximation.

This section contains ten articles with rich mathematical tasks or sequences of tasks that can help your students make sense of these ideas. The first three articles can help you assess your students' facility with measurement tasks. Overall, the articles are ordered so that the mathematical ideas investigated grow in sophistication and cognitive demand.

The first article in this section, "Which Comes First—Length, Area, or Volume?" (Hart 1984), is a report on what is known from research on children's understanding of length, area and volume measurements. We include it here to give you ways to think about how to engage your students in measurement activities as well as some assessment items that you can use to determine where your students are in understanding these three basic kinds of measurements.

"Understanding Students' Thinking about Area and Volume Measurement" (Battista 2003) gives a researcher's comments on difficulties to look for in your students as they engage with area and volume measurements.

"Assessment in Action: Mrs. Grant's Measurement Unit" (Steele 2002) has a series of measurement tasks that can be used to assess students' knowledge as well as advance students' understanding of linear measurement. The article makes the point that continual assessment as a part of instruction helps a teacher in planning and helps students know what they are accomplishing.

"Packing the Packages" (NCTM 2002) explores volume and adds work on measuring surface area. The activity includes cost analyses for making containers of different shapes. This gives students examples of practical applications of measurement of length, area, and volume.

"Spatial Visualization: What Happens When You Turn It?" (Chávez, Reys, and Jones 2005) begins early work on measuring volume or capacity by engaging students in building prisms from cubes, turning the prisms so that they stand on different faces, and exploring how to examine them to count the number of cubes used to build the prism. These spatial visualization and measurement experiences are important for students' growth in "reading" diagrams they encounter in text materials. Research shows that students who do not have such experiences are unable to imagine the structure of the prism from its picture and, therefore, have trouble finding a measure of the volume of the prisms presented as pictures in text materials.

"How Many Times Does a Radius Square Fit into the Circle?" (Flores and Regis 2003) builds on the estimation techniques in "Measuring Montana" (Hodgson et al. 2003). Through this task students can build a better understanding of π as well as finding the area of a circle.

References

Battista, Michael. "Understanding Students' Thinking about Area and Volume Measurement." In *Learning and Teaching Measurement*, 2003 Yearbook of the National Council of Teachers of Mathematics (NCTM), edited by Douglas H. Clements, pp. 122–42. Reston, Va.: NCTM, 2003.

Chávez, Óscar, Robert Reys, and Dusty Jones. "Spatial Visualization: What Happens When You Turn It?" *Mathematics Teaching in the Middle School* 11 (November 2005): 190–95.

Flores, Alfinio, and Troy P. Regis. "How Many Times Does a Radius Square Fit into the Circle?" *Mathematics Teaching in the Middle School* 8 (March 2003): 363–67.

Hart, Kathleen. "Which Comes First—Length, Area, or Volume?" *Arithmetic Teacher* 31 (May 1984): 16–18.

Hodgeson, Ted, Linda Simonson, Jennifer Luebeck, and Lyle Anderson. "Measuring Montana: An Episode in Estimation." In *Learning and Teaching Measurement*, 2003 Yearbook of the National Council of Teachers of Mathematics (NCTM), edited by Douglas H. Clements, pp. 220–28. Reston, Va.: NCTM, 2003

National Council of Teachers of Mathematics. "Packing the Packages." *Student Math Notes*, September 2002.

Steele, Diana F. "Assessment in Action: Mrs. Grant's Measurement Unit." *Mathematics Teaching in the Middle School* 7 (January 2002): 266–72.

Which Comes First—Length, Area, or Volume?

Kathleen Hart

If teachers of mathematics were asked to choose the five or six most important topics in the school mathematics curriculum, then measurement would very likely appear on every list. When teaching such a broad topic as measurement, the teacher must give considerable thought to sequencing the presentation of concepts, skills, and processes with the topic so as to make learning both efficient and enjoyable. It was a concern with this goal that prompted the staff of the research project Concepts in Secondary Mathematics and Science (CSMS) at Chelsea College, University of London, to determine a hierarchy of measurement skills and ten other mathematical strands the commonly appear in the British secondary school curriculum (age 11 to 16 years). Details of all the hierarchies are contained in a book (CSMS 1980) and a research monograph (Hart 1980). This article will focus on the work in measurement.

The research had three phases: (1) the writing of the word problems, (2) interviews using these problems, and (3) testing with written tests containing the same problems. The hierarchies of concepts and skills were related to a particular topic in the solution of measurement exercises.

These problems embodied key ideas in the particular topic and were not presented to students immediately after a topic had been taught. Computations were kept to a minimum, and the problems were designed to test basic knowledge of measurement ideas rather than measuring skills.

Thirty students (aged 12–15 years) were interviewed for each topic. They were asked to work out the problems and to describe the methods they had used. Their replies were tape-recorded. It was noticed that the responses often relied on naïve methods or strategies employed in primary school rather than algorithms that had been part of the secondary school teaching.

The written test was given to a sample of English children, representative of the normal distribution of IQ scores, from different schools and different age levels. In the case of measurement, twenty schools provided pupils: 169 aged 12+, 444 aged 13+, and 373 aged 14+. The schools that volunteered to take part in the research were in both urban and rural areas.

The measurement investigation was limited to assessing children's ability to solve word problems on the topics of length, area, and volume. Several of these problems were adapted from Piaget's *The Child's Conception of Geometry* (1960). Most of the other items would be recognizable to teachers as the type of measurement questions given to children aged 12–15. A number of technical words used in measurement, such as *area, perimeter,* and *volume,* were described (with illustrations) on the first page of the test.

Results from the test were used to form the hierarchy. First, items were ranked according to facility, the percentage of children obtaining the correct answer. Then, the items were grouped in set of approximately the same difficulty. If a child was successful in one item in a group, then the child was likely to be successful on the others. Items for which this was not true were discarded (see Hart [1980] for a more detailed description of the procedure). Children were judged successful at a particular level if they solved two-thirds of the items at that level. The term *hierarchy* presupposes that children who succeed on a harder group of items also succeed on all easier groups. In the measurement hierarchy, 97 percent of the sample had this type of response pattern.

Piaget and other researchers in Geneva have presented a theory of cognitive development based on children's responses to tasks presented in a clinical interview. The responses were divided into categories representative of certain stages of development: preoperational (aged 1.5–7), concrete operational (7–11), and formal (11 and older). Although the ages suggested by Piaget have been questioned by many researchers, the order of the three stages has generally been accepted. Some research (Hughes 1979) had tended to show that although a child may respond to one task at the concrete operational level, the *same* child may respond to a different task at a different level. Thus, some evidence indicates that the stage may not be the general developmental level but instead dependent on the task. Piaget's tasks to assess conservation of length, area, and volume were based on the child's ability to reason that the measurement was unchanged by displacement.

Length

The length of a line segment is obtained by counting the number of times a unit of measurement can be repeated placed along the segment, the number of units being dependent on the size of the unit itself. The use of a standard unit for length (the centimeter, for example) eases communication. The length of a line segment is not changed if the segment is moved or if the endpoints are not aligned. An understanding of this latter concept was tested on the CSMS paper by presenting two examples (**fig. 1**).

The success rate for the problem in **figure 1a** was between 72 and 82 percent, whereas for the problem in **figure 1b** it was between 42 and 52 percent. In the interviews, the children who said C and D were the same length almost always quote a number as in this example:

Child: They're the same. It doesn't matter what angle they are just as long as they're 5—4 squares.

Interviewer: So you counted the squares?

Child: Yes, and if they end on, you know, the end, it's the same.

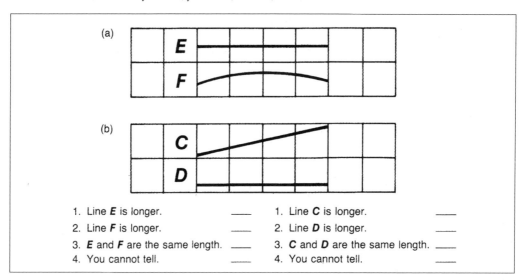

1. Line **E** is longer.   ____   1. Line **C** is longer.   ____
2. Line **F** is longer.   ____   2. Line **D** is longer.   ____
3. **E** and **F** are the same length. ____   3. **C** and **D** are the same length. ____
4. You cannot tell.   ____   4. You cannot tell.   ____

Fig. 1

This desire to use numbers to support an argument at the expense of all other considerations was apparent when the two different units were used to measure the same paths. For example, consider the item in **figure 2**.

Although 90 percent of the same gave the correct answer to questions 1 and 3, 50 percent of the children aged 12, 34 percent of those aged 13, and 27 percent of those aged 14+ said C was longer than B in question 2. Most of those who provided this answer gave the reason as "15 is more than 14 1/2," even when asked "15 what? 14 1/2 what?" These errors point to a fundamental misunderstanding of the nature of measurement, possibly reflecting a too-early insistence that a number is always the answer to be sought without emphasis on the unit employed.

Area

In the measurement of area a square unit is usually employed, which can be used two ways:

• By covering a shape with square tiles

• By drawing a shape on square paper and counting the number of squares covered

John measures the lengths of paths **A** and **B** using a walking stick. Then he measures the lengths of paths **C** and **D** using a metal rod. His answers are as follows:

Path **A** 13 walking sticks Path **C** 15 rods
Path **B** 14½ walking sticks Path **D** 12½ rods

Draw a ring around the answer you think is true in each question.

(1) Path **B** is longer than Path **A**.   True   False   Cannot tell

(2) Path **C** is longer than Path **B**.   True   False   Cannot tell

(3) Path **D** is longer than Path **C**.   True   False   Cannot tell

Fig. 2

Both of these involve counting, although in the case of the rectangle they lead naturally to the statement of the formula area = length × width. The tiling can be extended to including matching parts of squares to make whole units. Children were confused when they asked for the number of squares needed to tile a rectangle when two different sizes of squares were provided. Although 87 percent of the total population could state how many 1-cm squares were needed to cover a rectangle 4 cm by 2 cm, 60 percent of the same population simply doubled the answer when asked for the number of tiles of size 1/2 cm × 1/2 cm needed, although both sizes of tiles were shown.

Although the formula for the area of a rectangle is taught in the English primary school (7–11 years), considerable evidence suggests that the counting method is used by children far into the secondary school. It is interesting to note the difference in performance on the area questions in **figure 3**. One is tiled and the other is not, which suggests that the first problem was solved by counting and the second was not. The success rate on (a) was 78, 87, and 94 percent for children aged 12, 13, and 14, respectively, whereas on (b) it was 31, 39, and 48 percent.

One of the items designed to test children's ideas of the conservation of area is shown in **figure 4**. The success rate was 80, 85, and 85 percent for children aged 12, 13, and 14, respectively. On a question as to whether the perimeters were the same, however, 36 percent (age 12), 29 percent (age 13), and 20 percent (age 14) replied that they were.

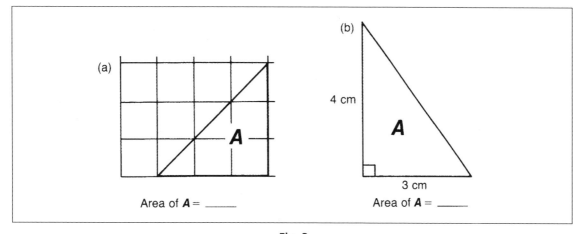

Fig. 3

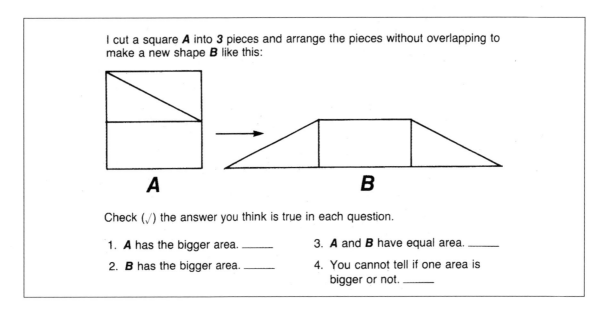

I cut a square **A** into **3** pieces and arrange the pieces without overlapping to make a new shape **B** like this:

A   **B**

Check (√) the answer you think is true in each question.

1. **A** has the bigger area. _____   3. **A** and **B** have equal area. _____

2. **B** has the bigger area. _____   4. You cannot tell if one area is
                                              bigger or not. _____

Fig. 4

During an interview, many children who were given a card cut as shown in **figure 4** could not believe that the perimeters were different although the areas were the same. They would say, "I'm not doing it accurately enough, they must be the same."

Volume

All the questions involving volume were considered with the volume of a cuboid or a triangular prism. On the written test, diagrams of three-dimensional figures were provided, but actual blocks were presented on the thirty follow-up interviews. Little difference in response to the two presentations was found.

Piaget distinguishes between *interior volume*, where the space is confined within boundaries, and *occupied volume*, where the volume in question is viewed in relation to other objects around it. The latter was tested on the written paper by presenting two different configurations of the same number of bricks, as in **figure 5**.

A number of children, when interviewed, visualized a layer of bricks and counted layers both to find the volume in **figure 5a** and also to use the total of 36 bricks in **figure 5b**. This counting method is very nearly impossible to perform on such items as shown in **figure 6**. The success rates for 12-, 13-, and 14-year-olds were 14.2, 18.7, and 27.9 percent, respectively.

The corresponding drop in facility seems partly due to the difficulty of counting the parts of cubes at the back, but it also occurred because the children who used the formula were now faced with the multiplication of fractions. This was the most difficult skill in the hierarchy.

Finding the volume of a triangular prism was one of the hardest items on the test (see **fig. 7**). The success rates for 12-, 13-, and 14-year-olds were 15.4, 21.2, and 32.2 percent, respectively. About 16 percent of the same gave the correct answer, 24. The formulas for volumes were not necessarily par of a child's repertoire. Children probably counted whenever they could.

Measurement Hierarchy

The resulting hierarchy is, of course, dependent on the particular items given to children. The methods used by the children have been provided for each level in the hierarchy (**table 1**).

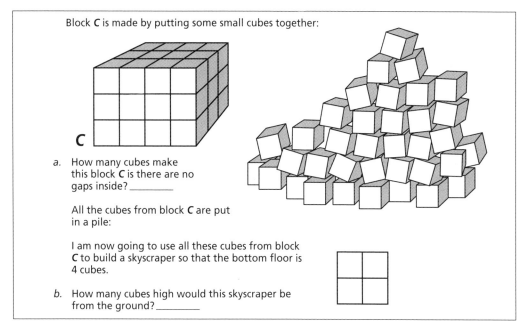

Block **C** is made by putting some small cubes together:

C

a. How many cubes make this block **C** is there no gaps inside? _____

All the cubes from block **C** are put in a pile:

I am now going to use all these cubes from block **C** to build a skyscraper so that the bottom floor is 4 cubes.

b. How many cubes high would this skyscraper be from the ground? _____

Fig. 5

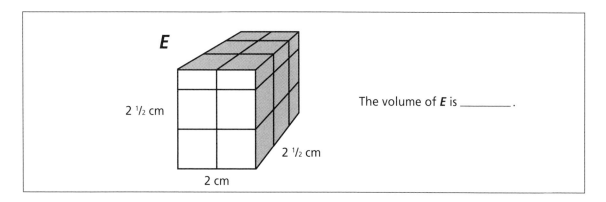

E

2 ½ cm

2 ½ cm

2 cm

The volume of **E** is _____.

Fig. 6

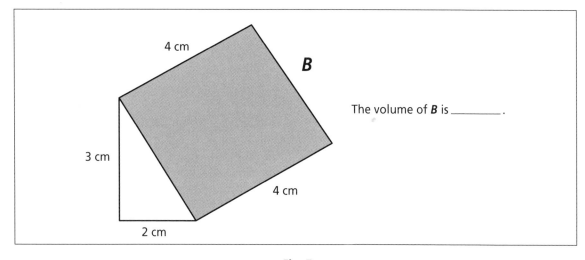

4 cm

B

3 cm

4 cm

2 cm

The volume of **B** is _____.

Fig. 7

Table 1

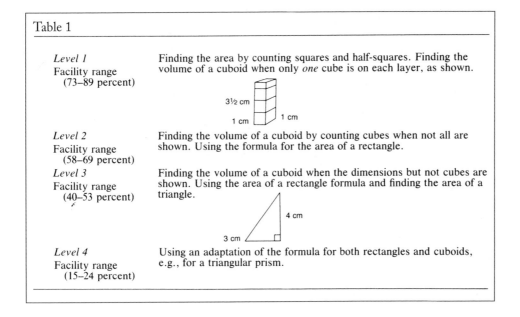

Level 1 Facility range (73–89 percent)	Finding the area by counting squares and half-squares. Finding the volume of a cuboid when only *one* cube is on each layer, as shown.
Level 2 Facility range (58–69 percent)	Finding the volume of a cuboid by counting cubes when not all are shown. Using the formula for the area of a rectangle.
Level 3 Facility range (40–53 percent)	Finding the volume of a cuboid when the dimensions but not cubes are shown. Using the area of a rectangle formula and finding the area of a triangle.
Level 4 Facility range (15–24 percent)	Using an adaptation of the formula for both rectangles and cuboids, e.g., for a triangular prism.

Piagetian Items

The items taken from Piaget did not correlate well with the other items on the measurement paper, so no attempt has made to label the measurement hierarchy according to Piagetian development terms. However, taking only those items that were adapted from *The Child's Conception of Geometry* and bearing in mind that they were all given in pencil-and-paper form, we offer some additional information on the development of the conservation of length, area, and volume.

Piaget suggests that the operational conservation of area appears at the same time as that of distance and length. He tested the idea of conservation of length by presenting the child with two sticks of equal length. If the child denies equality when one stick is pushed forward,

then the child has not recognized the conservation of length. This recognition is stated to be at level 3 (concrete operational). Just prior to this (level 2b–3), the child sees that a curve and a line with endpoints aligned are not equal in length, as in this example:

The conservation of area is tested by providing two congruent squares (fields) in each of which the owner builds the same number of houses. In one case they are built in a row, and in the other they are scattered all over the field. The question is whether the child recognizes that the same amount of grass remains in each field. In another question, the researcher cuts a rectangle and rearranges the pieces, then asks whether the area has changed.

In the context of the CSMS test, we define those children who appear to have grasped the idea of length as those who can successfully answer both questions 1a and 1c in **figure 8**. Seventy-three percent of the total population ($N = 986$) can correctly answer those questions. Those who have the correct ideas on the conservation of area are defined as those who can successfully deal with questions in **figure 9** and **figure 4**. Seventy-two percent of the total sample can successfully solve both questions. However, 70 percent of the children who cannot conserve length can solve the two area problems. Similarly, 70 percent of those who cannot conserve area can conserve length. Thus, it seems that one ability is not a prerequisite for the other.

The conservation of occupied volume tested by the question in **figure 5** is a difficult idea (level 4, or early formal in Piagetian terms). Of those children who can conserve length or area, 52 percent can success-

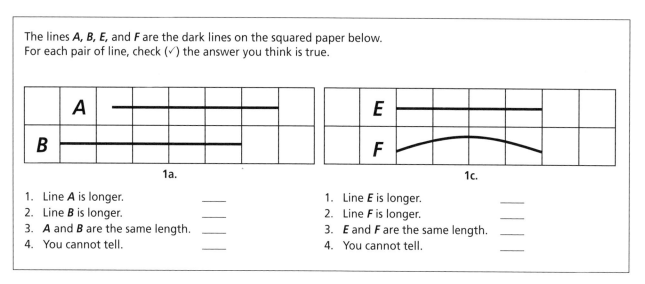

The lines *A, B, E,* and *F* are the dark lines on the squared paper below.
For each pair of line, check (✓) the answer you think is true.

1a.

1. Line *A* is longer. _____
2. Line *B* is longer. _____
3. *A* and *B* are the same length. _____
4. You cannot tell. _____

1c.

1. Line *E* is longer. _____
2. Line *F* is longer. _____
3. *E* and *F* are the same length. _____
4. You cannot tell. _____

Fig. 8

This picture shows two tin squares that are the same size.

A   B

A machine makes 8 equal holes in each tin square:

A   B

Check (✓) the answer you think is true.
1. Sheet *A* now has more tin. _____
2. Sheet *B* now has more tin. _____
3. *A* and *B* now have the same amount of tin. _____
4. You cannot tell if one now has more tin or not. _____
Give a reason for your answer: _____

Fig. 9

fully complete the tower question, whereas only 26 percent of nonconservers can do so. One might expect that those who can deal with the tower question have already succeeded on both the length and area sets of questions. This hunch is not correct. One hundred and twenty-nine children (445 succeeded in all) could solve the tower question but could not conserve length and area.

The progression through length, then area, then volume that appears in many texts is not as smooth as we might think. Just because a child appears to be able to cope with one topic does not mean we must expect the child to cope with other topics that we believe to be logical prerequisites. Careful analysis of the child's ideas on measurement is needed if teaching is to be effective.

References

Concepts in Secondary Mathematics (CSMS) Mathematics Team. *Children's Understanding of Mathematics, 11–16*. London: John Murray, 1980.

Hart, Kathleen. *Secondary School Children's Understanding of Mathematics*. Research Monograph, C.S.E. London, U.K.: Chelsea College, University of London, 1980.

Hughes, E. R. "Should We Check Children?' In *Cognitive Development Research in Science and Mathematics: Proceedings of an International Seminar*, edited by Wolfgang F. Archenhold. Leeds, U.K.: University of Leeds, 1979.

Kofsky, Ellin. "A Scalogram of Classificatory Development." *Child Development* 37, no. 1 (March 1966): 191–204.

Piaget, Jean, Bärbel Inhelder, and Alina Szeminska. *The Child's Conception of Geometry*. London, U.K.: Routledge & Kegan Paul, 1960.

Understanding Students' Thinking about Area and Volume Measurement

Michael T. Battista

Teaching area and volume measurement so that students learn the underlying ideas in personally meaningful ways requires a firm understanding of students' thinking about these ideas. This understanding is essential for choosing appropriate instructional tasks, guiding students' discussions, understanding students' learning difficulties, and monitoring as well as assessing students' learning progress. This article first examines the fascinating realm of students' thinking about area and volume, then it suggests instructional activities to help students develop genuine understanding of these important mathematical ideas.

Underlying Mental Processes

To measure area and volume in standard measurement systems, we determine the number of unit squares or cubes in the region we are measuring. Thus, the foundation for developing competence with measuring area and volume in standard measurement systems is understanding how to enumerate meaningfully arrays of squares and cubes such as those shown in **figures 1a** and **1b**. (Other shapes can be used as units, but squares and cubes are the standard units because usually they are easiest to reason with.)

Four mental processes are essential for meaningful enumeration of arrays of squares and cubes and will be used throughout this article to explain students' thinking: forming and using mental models, spatial structuring, units-locating, and organizing-by-composites. In the *forming and using mental models* process, individuals create and use imagistic or recall-of-experience-like mental representations to visualize, comprehend, and reason about situations. For instance, to give someone travel directions without the use of a map, you reflect on your mental model of the locality to visualize and describe a route to follow. In the *spatial structuring* process, individuals abstract an object's composition and form by identifying, interrelating, and organizing its components. For instance, to structure a rectangular array of squares spatially, you might see it as rows and columns. Fundamentally, students can meaningfully enumerate arrays of squares and cubes only if they have developed properly structured mental models that enable them to locate and organize the squares and cubes correctly.

To develop such properly structured mental models, two additional processes are required. The *units-locating* process locates squares and cubes, and composites of squares and cubes, by coordinating their locations along the dimensions of an array. For instance, to understand the location of square X in the array shown in **figure 1a**, an individual must see the square in a two-dimensional, coordinate-like system—for example, it is in the fourth column and the second row, or it is the fourth unit to the right and the second unit down.

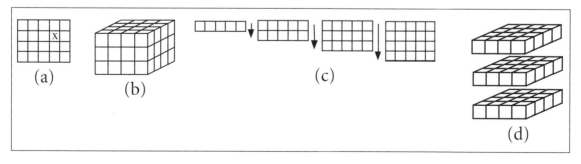

Fig. 1. Arrays of squares and cubes, (a) and (b); composite units, (c) and (d)

The *organizing-by-composites* process combines an array's basic units (squares or cubes) into more complicated, composite units that can be repeated or iterated to generate the whole array. (For brevity, the term *composite unit*—which is a unit consisting of more basic units—will be shortened to *composite*.) For instance, in a 2-D array, a student might mentally unite the squares in a row to form a composite unit that can be iterated in the direction of a column to generate the array (see **fig. 1c**). In a 3-D array, the cubes in a horizontal layer can be grouped into a layer-composite that can be iterated vertically to generate the array (see **fig. 1d**).

Levels of Sophistication in Students' Structuring and Enumeration of Arrays

The four mental processes described above will now be used to describe levels of sophistication in students' understanding of area and volume measurement. Students' thinking about area is illustrated with second graders' work; students' thinking about volume is illustrated with fifth graders' work.

Level 1: The absence of units-locating and organizing-by-composites processes

Students do not organize units into composites, and, because they do not properly coordinate spatial information, they are unable to locate all the units in arrays.

Area (Battista et al. 1998)

Katy was shown that a plastic inch square was the same size as one of the indicated squares on the 7-by-3-inch rectangle displayed in **figure 2a**. She was then asked to predict how many plastic squares it would take to completely cover the rectangle. Katy drew squares and counted 30 as shown in **figure 2b**.

On a similar problem, Katy was asked to predict how many squares would cover the rectangle shown in **figure 2c** (making her prediction without drawing). Katy pointed and counted as in **figure 2d**, predicting 30. When checking her answer, she pointed to and counted plastic squares as shown in **figure 2e**, getting 30. When she counted the squares again, first she got 24, then 27.

Although, as educated adults, we instantly "see" the squares covering these rectangles arranged by rows and columns, Katy had not yet mentally constructed a row-by-column structuring to organize and locate the squares properly. Instead, because Katy's mental model located squares along an almost random path, she got lost in her counting.

Volume (Battista and Clements 1996)

When asked how many cubes were needed to completely fill the box shown in **figure 3a**, Bob counted the 8 cubes shown in the box, then pointed to and counted 6 imagined cubes on the box's left side, 4 on the back, 4 on the bottom, and 5 on the top. Thus, Bob's units-locating process was insufficient to create an accurate mental model of the cube array.

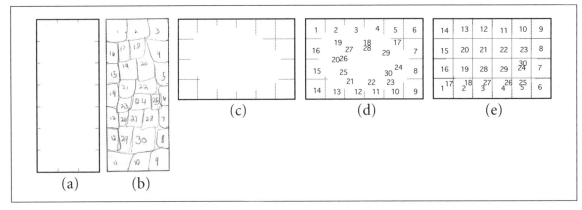

Fig. 2. Katy's work

Randa was shown a picture of a box with the length, width, and height labeled and was told, "This box contains three cubes along the bottom, three up from here to here, and four from here to here *[pointing appropriately at the box picture]*." When Randa said she could not find the number of cubes needed to fill the box, she was asked to "draw what the cubes look like on the outside." After about ten to fifteen minutes and many erasures, Randa's drawing looked like **figure 3b**, showing a clear lack of coordination of spatial information. (For instance, the right side shows four cubes in horizontal rows; the top shows only three.)

Further evidence that insufficient coordination causes major difficulty in the units-locating process is the ubiquitous "double counting" error. For instance, when Jeff tried to enumerate the cubes needed to make the building shown in **figure 1b**, he counted all cube faces that appeared on the six sides of the building, double-counting edge cubes and triple-counting corner cubes; he said there were two additional cubes in the interior. Because he did not properly coordinate what he saw on the different sides of the building, Jeff failed to see when adjacent cube faces were part of the same cube.

Level 2: Beginning use of the units-locating and the organizing-by-composites processes

Students not only start to form composite units, they use the units-locating process to see equivalent composites.

Area

> Bill: First I count the bottom and there's 6 *[moving his hands inward as shown in fig. 4.]* So the top and bottom would equal 12. And these 2 *[pointing to the middle squares on the right and left sides]* would be 14. *[Using fingers to estimate where individual squares were located]* I'd say maybe 12 in the middle; 12 + 12 = 24. So I'd say 24.

Bill was beginning to structure the array into composites (the top and bottom rows). Although he was unable to use the units-locating process to locate interior squares correctly, he did use it to see the numerical equivalence of his composites.

Volume

For the building shown in **figure 1b**, Fred counted 12 cubes on the front, then immediately said there must be 12 on the back; he counted 16 on the top and immediately said there must be 16 on the bottom; finally, he counted 12 cubes on the right side, then immediately said there must be 12 on the left side. In each instance, after counting the cubes visible on one side of the building, he inferred the number of cubes on the opposite side, clear evidence that he was organizing cubes into composites and that he was using the units-locating process to relate these composites spatially and numerically.

Level 3: The units-locating process becomes sufficiently coordinated to recognize and eliminate double-counting errors

A major breakthrough in thinking occurs when a student's units-locating process coordinates single-dimension views (e.g., top, side, front) into a mental model that is sufficient to recognize the same unit from different views. This refined mental model enables students to eliminate double-counting errors caused by insufficient coordination.

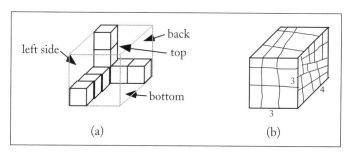

(a)   (b)

Fig. 3. Level 1, work of Bob (a) and Randa (b)

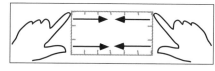

Fig. 4. Bill's work

Area

Bill was enumerating the squares in a 6-by-4 rectangle in which he had correctly drawn the array of squares. He counted the 6 squares in the left column, then immediately said there must be 6 in the right column. He counted 4 squares on the top, then said there must be 4 on the bottom. He counted 8 more squares in the middle, getting a total of 28. But when he explained his strategy to the teacher, Bill changed his mind. He then said there were 6 squares in each of the left and right columns and counted 2 on the top, 2 on the bottom, and 8 in the middle. Through an increase in coordination, Bill could simultaneously see a corner square as part of a row and as part of a column, enabling him to realize that he had initially double-counted such squares.

Volume

As shown in **figure 5**, Juan coordinated spatial information sufficiently to avoid double-counting edge cubes. However, his coordination was still insufficient to build a mental model that properly located interior cubes.

Level 4: The use of the organizing-by-composites process to see a whole array composed from maximal composites, but with improper iteration

Students see arrays as "maximal" composites (rows and columns for area, layers for volume) that can be iterated in a single direction to generate an array. But because of insufficient coordination, students cannot precisely locate these maximal composites, and they consequently make iteration errors.

Area

Joe was shown that 5 plastic squares fit across the top of a rectangle and that 7 fit down the middle (then the squares were removed). See **figure 12k**.

Joe: 5, 10, 15, …, 45 [*motioning along estimated row positions inside the rectangle*].

Teacher: How did you get that?

Joe: I was trying to guess where the bottoms of the squares were.

 Joe structured the array into row composites of five. However, his coordination of rows and columns was insufficient to enable him to properly imagine the locations of the rows.

Volume

Randa was shown a picture of a 5 × 3 × 4 cube array and was asked to build the bottom layer for the array. She built a 5 × 3 array of cubes and said that there were 15 cubes in the layer. When asked how many cubes were in the entire building, Randa counted from the bottom up on the picture, but continued to count on the top, getting seven layers (see **fig. 6**). She gave an answer of 105 cubes. When the interviewer asked Randa to make the building with cubes, she built and stacked four layers, and, was going to continue to build three more until the interviewer asked her to compare what she already built to the picture. Surprised, Randa concluded that the building was complete, then pointed to each layer saying, "15 here, 15 here, 15 here, 15 here; 15 × 4 = 60." Initially, Randa was unable to determine where the layers occurred. She could not coordinate the horizontal layers with the third dimension that was the prism's height.

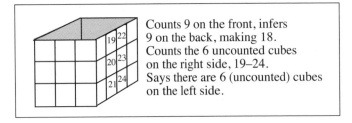

Fig. 5. Juan's work

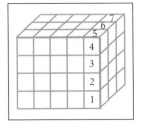

Fig. 6. Randa's work

Although both Joe and Randa took major steps by structuring arrays in maximal composite units, neither student had yet developed an accurate enough mental model in which these composites could, in imagination, be properly iterated to form the whole array.

Level 5: The use of the units-locating process sufficient to locate all units correctly, but with less-than-maximal composites employed

This is the first level in which the units-locating process is sufficient to create a mental model that correctly locates all squares or cubes in an array. However, although students sometimes obtain correct answers (as in the next two examples), because students inefficiently or inconsistently organize arrays into composites, they quite frequently lose their place in counting or adding and make enumeration errors. Furthermore, students' structuring and enumeration strategies are not generalizable and are inadequate for large arrays.

Area

Given rectangle (i) in **figure 12** and asked to predict how many unit squares would cover it, Billie correctly employed the units-locating process (see **fig. 7a**). However, although she organized the array as composites of two (which was sufficient for correct enumeration), these composites were not the maximal ones needed to give the array its row-by-column structure.

Volume

Mary counted the cubes visible on the front face (12), then counted those on the right side that had not already been counted (6). (See **fig. 7b**.) She then pointed to the remaining cubes on the top, and for each, counted cubes in columns of three: 1, 2, 3; 4, 5, 6; ...; 16, 17, 18. She then added 18, 12, and 6.

Level 6: Complete development and coordination of both the units-locating and the organizing-by-composites processes

Students' mental models fully incorporate row-by-column or layer structuring so that students can accurately reflect on and enumerate arrays without physical or perceptual material. An important point from a mathematical perspective is that such structuring is more general and powerful than using standard area and volume formulas. For example, layer structuring is extremely useful for thinking about the volumes of cylinders and many problems in calculus.

Area

Paul was shown that 5 plastic squares fit across the top of a rectangle and that 7 fit down the middle (then the squares were removed). See **figure 12k**.

Paul: *[Counting and pointing across the top row by ones]* 5 across; 7 down. *[Motioning across the top three rows]* 5, 10, 15. *[Counting on seven fingers]* 5, 10, 15, 20, 25, 30, 35; 35.

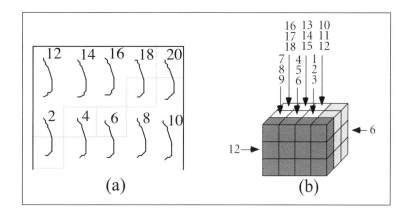

Fig. 7. Level 5, work of Billie (a) and Mary (b)

Teacher: How did you know to stop at 35?

Paul: There are only 7 down that way *[motioning vertically down the middle of the rectangle].*

Volume

For the cube array given in **figure 1b**, Julie counted cubes in the top layer, 1–12, pointed to the middle layer and said 24, then pointed to the bottom layer and said 36. Her partner, Juanita, pointed to the right side of the array and said 9. She then counted 4 columns of 3 on the top and said, "So it's 9 times 4 equals 36."

Further Discussion of Students' Structuring and Enumeration Difficulties

The root of the problem: lack of coordination

Properly coordinating spatial information is extremely difficult for many students. The first episode below illustrates how deep-seated this difficulty can be. The second episode shows the reasoning that students must use to resolve coordination difficulties.

A deep-seated problem

After Randa, a fifth-grader, built several rectangular buildings with interconnecting cubes, she was asked how many cubes it would take to make the building shown in **figure 8a**.

Randa: It has 4 × 3 and 4 × 4; 12 × 4 = 48, + 16 = 64. There's some you can't see in the picture. *[She multiplied 12, the number of cubes in each lateral face, by 4, the number of lateral faces. She then added 16 for the top (ignoring the bottom). Note that Randa's strategy double-counted cubes along most of the building's edges.]*

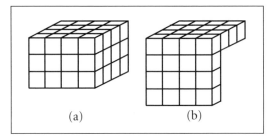

(a)   (b)

Fig. 8. Randa's cube configuration

Randa then spent about twenty minutes trying to construct the building with cubes. She built the configuration shown in **figure 8b** several times, making the 4-by-4 top and the 3-by-4 front, then joining them. Each time, however, she stopped and started over when she noted that the front or top of her configuration did not match the building pictured in **figure 8a**. Randa was then asked to find the number of cubes in the configuration shown in **figure 8b**.

Randa: Four rows of 4 on this side *[the top]* and 4 on this side *[the front].* So it's 16 + 16 = 32. *[Note that she still double-counted cubes along the top front edge.]*

Both in counting and in building, Randa showed a striking inability to coordinate different views of cube configurations. For the configuration shown in **figure 8b**, she constructed the top with cubes, then the front, but she could not figure out how these two parts fit together to make the configuration shown in **figure 8a**. To coordinate these views, Randa would have to decompose the top into individual cubes, do the same with the front, then establish a spatial relationship between the views that recognized that the four edge cubes were part of the front and top faces. Randa's difficulties are common among elementary and middle school students (Battista and Clements 1996).

Resolving coordination difficulties

Amanda, a second-grader, is predicting how many squares will cover a 4-by-3 rectangle, having been shown only that 4 plastic squares fit across the top and 3 fit down the left side (**fig. 12j**).

Amanda: *[Making her original prediction for an unmarked 4-by-3 rectangle; (see **fig. 9a**)]* There's 4 here *[top row]* and 4 here *[bottom row]* plus 2 here *[one on the left side, one on the right]*, and that equals 10. *[Pointing to what would be the two interior squares]* But I'm not sure if there's 2 in the middle or 1 in the middle. *[Amanda draws the picture shown in **figure 9b**.]*

Interviewer: Where are the 2 in the middle? *[Amanda draws the middle vertical segment in the second row and points to the 2 squares formed (see **fig. 9c**).]* So how many do you have in there now?

Amanda: So 12 or 11. I think there's 2 in the middle or 1 in the middle. *[Motioning across the second row]* I just changed my mind.... There's going to be 2 in the middle because if there's only 3 here *[motioning to the right column]* and 3 here *[motioning to the left column]*, then going across would be 4 *[motioning across the second row]*; 12.

Interviewer: Why do you now think 12?

Amanda: Because there's 4 on the top *[motioning to the top row]*, so going across down here *[motioning to the second row]* would be the same as going across up here *[motioning to the top row]*, so there's probably 2 in the middle.

Initially Amanda structured the array as a set of disjoint components—top, bottom, sides, and an amorphous interior. She was able to structure the rectangle's interior as two squares, and thus its middle row as four, only when she saw the two middle squares on the lateral sides, not as separate, but as part of the right and left columns. This coordinating action enabled her to infer the equivalence of the first and second rows because it vertically aligned their squares and set up a one-to-one correspondence between them. Such reasoning was crucial to Amanda's proper structuring of this array.

Difficulties with numerical procedures

Most students do not fully understand the spatial structuring that underlies traditionally learned numerical procedures for determining area and volume, and consequently they improperly apply these procedures to new problems.

Insufficient understanding

Bethany, a fifth grader, regularly determined the number of cubes in 3-D arrays using layers. She also had discovered that the number of cubes could be found by multiplying the length, width, and height. But as her class discussed this procedure, Bethany questioned its validity. She told her classmates that she was puzzled because "the corner cube gets counted once when you find the length, once for the width, and once for the height." Although almost every student in the class had discovered, and was routinely employing, a layer approach, not one of the students had an answer for Bethany's question. Even when the teacher posed Bethany's question in the context of area, the students had no answer.

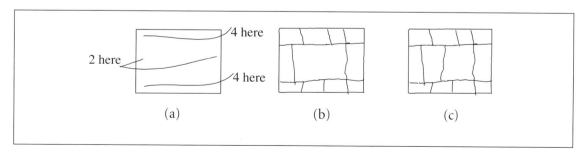

Fig. 9. Amanda's work

The teacher took advantage of this "teachable moment" by having students work on the problem in pairs. When I asked Bethany and her partner how they were thinking about the problem, they said that they were "stuck." So I posed questions that I thought might help them clarify their thinking.

Interviewer: [*Arranges the 3-by-3 set of cubes that the students had been working with into 3 rows of 3 and points successively to the cubes in one row*] 1, 2, 3. What am I counting here?

Partner: Cubes.

Bethany: Yeah.

Interviewer: [*Pointing to the three rows*] 1, 2, 3. What am I counting here?

Bethany: [*Excitedly*] Rows of cubes. You're not counting cubes this time. So, first, you count cubes, then you count rows.

Partner: So you're not really counting the cube twice. We got it!

Bethany's question posed a real conundrum for the students. They knew that multiplying the length times the width gave the number of cubes in a rectangular array. Almost all the students justified this procedure by saying that they were multiplying the number of cubes in a row times the number of rows, thus satisfying the traditional criterion that they had learned the procedure "meaningfully." But initially, their understanding of this enumeration strategy did not clearly identify exactly what was being counted. To overcome their difficulty, Bethany and her partner not only had to structure the array properly but also had to conceptualize that structuring properly. Whereas other students made, without aid, the same discovery as Bethany and her partner, still others gave explanations that lacked genuine appreciation of the difficulty. For instance, one pair of students argued that, since "a cube is in both the width and the length, it's okay to count it twice."

Misapplication

Pam, a bright eighth grader who was three weeks from completing a standard course in high school geometry, responded as follows on the problem shown in **figure 10**.

Pam: It's 45 packages. And the way I found it is I multiplied how many packages could fit in the height by the number in the width, which is 3 times 3 equals 9. Then I took that and multiplied it by the length, which is 5, and came up with 9 times 5, which is 45.

Observer: How do you know that is the right answer?

Pam: Because the equation for the volume of a box is length times width times height.

Observer: Do you know why that equation works?

Pam: Because you are covering all three dimensions, I think. I'm not really sure. I just know the equation.

Students in grades 3–5 made an identical structuring error on a simpler problem in which the box was only one layer high.

Student 1: We know 3 will fit across; we know 5 will fit downward; just multiply.

Student 2: I kept counting 5 along the side of the package until I counted 3 times because you can only fit 3 packages along the top of the box.

On both the one-layer and three-layer problems, students used numerical procedures without first mentally constructing appropriate spatial structurings of the situations. Apparently, the salience of the dimension-like information given in the problem automatically activated students' use of a familiar numeri-

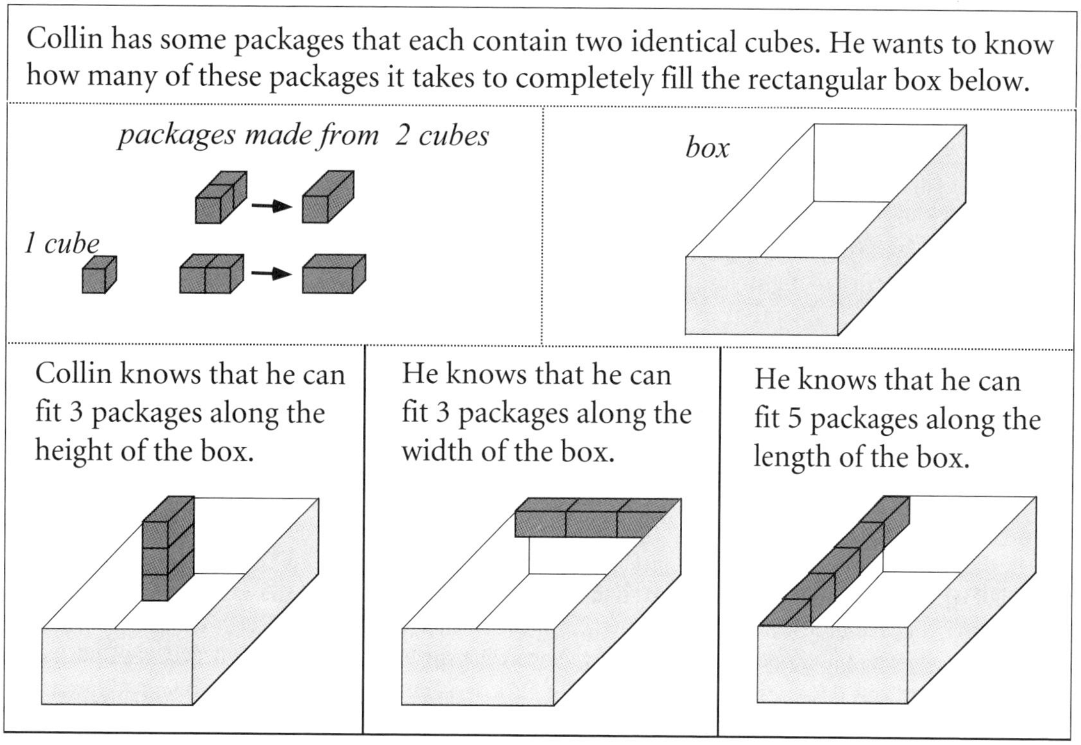

Collin has some packages that each contain two identical cubes. He wants to know how many of these packages it takes to completely fill the rectangular box below.

packages made from 2 cubes

1 cube

box

Collin knows that he can fit 3 packages along the height of the box.

He knows that he can fit 3 packages along the width of the box.

He knows that he can fit 5 packages along the length of the box.

Fig. 10. Two-cube problem

cal procedure, causing them to bypass careful spatial analyses of how the packages fill the box. A lack of depth in students' understanding of procedures caused them to misapply the procedures.

Even when using packages made from interlocking cubes and paper boxes, many students still have substantial difficulties with the problem in **figure 10**. For instance, Anita, a fifth-grader, asserted that 5 packages fit in the box across the length and 3 across the width. To test her assertion, she placed 3 packages along the width. But after placing 4 packages along the length, she was perplexed that the fifth package would not fit in the bottom of the box while the 3 packages along the width remained (see **fig. 11**). Eventually, Anita decided that she could place the packages into the box so that their longest sides were parallel to the longest side of the box. But she was unable to determine the number of packages that covered the bottom of the box until she completely covered it with packages.

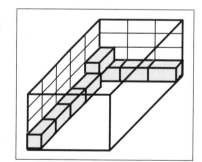

Fig. 11. Anita's work on the two-cube problem in figure 10

Instructional Activities

The ultimate goal of instruction on area and volume should be for students to develop properly structured mental models that enable them to reason powerfully about these concepts in a wide variety of situations. To cultivate students' creation of these mental models, instruction must nurture students' development of the four mental processes described at the beginning of this article. Instructional tasks must also encourage and support students' construction of personally meaningful enumeration strategies (i.e., those that are based on properly structured mental models). Students' construction of such strategies is facilitated, not by "giving" them formulas, but by encouraging students to invent, reflect on, test, and discuss enumeration strategies in a spirit of inquiry and problem solving. (Additional information on instruction can be found in Akers et. al 1997, Battista and Clements 1995, and Battista and Berle-Carman 1996.)

Teaching area measurement: Enumerating squares in rectangular arrays

To construct proper spatial structurings of two-dimensional arrays of squares, students need numerous opportunities to structure such arrays and to reflect on the appropriateness of their structurings. One good way of presenting such opportunities is to use, in inquiry-based instruction, problems similar to those already described. As you give students the rectangles shown in **figure 12** (which should have dimensions in inches), show students how a plastic inch square fits on one of the indicated squares. Students first predict how many squares it takes to cover the rectangle, then check their predictions with plastic squares.

Start with rectangles that give the most graphic information about the location of squares, then gradually move to rectangles that give less information (the rectangles in **fig. 12** are listed roughly in this order). Give students several problems of each type so that they have an opportunity to develop adequate structuring for that type before moving on to more difficult problems. As a variation, after students have made their first prediction, have them draw how they think squares will cover the rectangle, make another prediction, then check their predictions with plastic squares. Many students will be able to make a correct prediction after drawing squares on a rectangle, but their structuring will be inadequate for them to make a prediction without drawing. Students' explanations and drawings provide insights into the levels of sophistication of their thinking, information that can be invaluable in choosing appropriate instructional tasks, guiding discussions, and assessing students' progress.

Teaching volume measurement: Enumerating cubes in boxes

Once students can accurately determine the number of cubes in buildings using actual cubes (being allowed to take the buildings apart), they can move on to activities like that shown in **figure 13** (Battista and Berle-Carman 1996). The goal for this activity is for students to use the four basic mental processes previously described to develop correct strategies for enumerating the cubes. To illustrate how students' thinking progresses with appropriate instruction, one student-pair's work on this activity is summarized (Battista 1999). Especially important in this example is how students gradually overcome their spatial coordination difficulties as they refine their units-locating and organizing-by-composites processes.

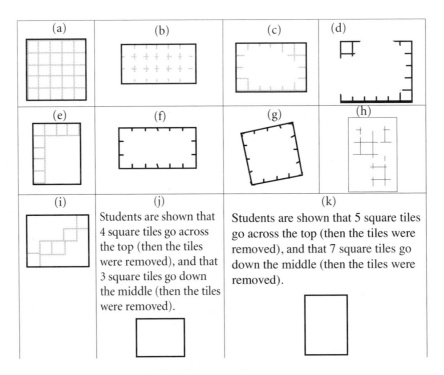

Fig. 12. Rectangle tasks

The teacher distributed the How Many Cubes? activity sheet (**figure 13**) to each student and explained that the students' goal was to find a way to predict correctly the number of cubes that would fill boxes described by pictures, patterns, or words. Students worked collaboratively in pairs, predicting how many cubes would fit in a box, then checking their answers by making the box out of grid paper and filling it with cubes. Students predicted and then checked their results for one problem before going on to the next.

Episode 1, day 1

For Box A, Nate counted the 12 outermost squares on the 4 side flaps of the pattern picture (see **fig. 14**), then multiplied by 2. Pablo counted the 12 visible cube faces on Box Picture A, then doubled that for the hidden lateral faces of the box. The boys agreed on 24 as their prediction.

Pablo: *[After putting 4 rows of 4 cubes into Box A]* We're wrong. It's 4 sets of 4 equals 16.

Nate: What are we doing wrong? *[Neither student has an answer, so they move on to Box B.]*

Pablo: *[Pointing at the 2 visible faces of the cube at the bottom right front corner of Box Picture B]* This is 1 box *[cube]*, those 2.

Nate: Oh, I know what we did wrong! We counted this *[pointing to the front face of the bottom right front cube]* and then the side over there *[pointing to the right face of that cube]*.

Pablo: So we'll have to take away 4 *[pointing to the 4 vertical edges of Box Picture A]*, no wait, we have to take away 8.

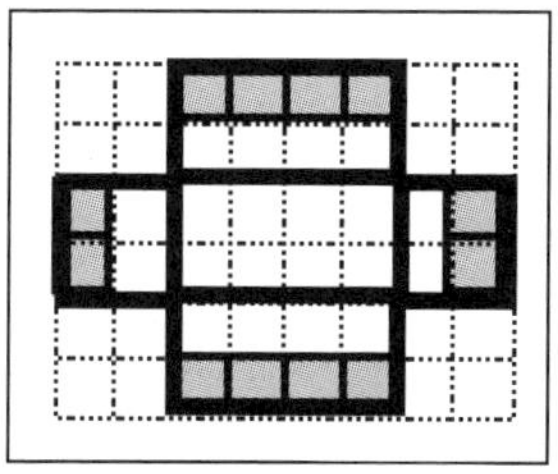

	Pattern Picture	**Box Picture**
Box A		
Box B		
Box C		
Box D		
Box E		
Box F	The bottom of the box is 4 units by 5 units. The box is three units high.	

How many cubes fit in each box? <u>Predict</u>, then build to check. Check your prediction for a box before going on to the next box.

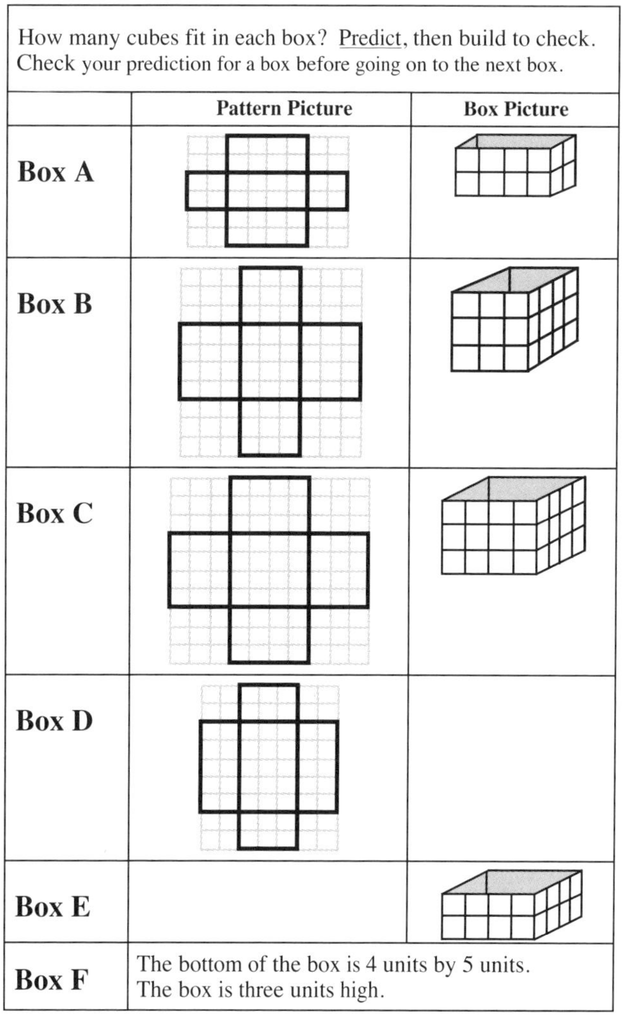

Fig. 13. How Many Cubes? activity (reduced in size)

Fig. 14. Work of Nate and Pablo

Although Nate and Pablo agreed on a prediction of 24 for Box A, the discrepancy between their predicted and actual answers caused them to reevaluate their reasoning. As the boys reflected on Pablo's strategy, they realized (through the type of mental coordination Randa had so much difficulty with) that he had mistakenly counted the front and right faces of the same cube. When they properly coordinated the positions of these faces in 3-D space, they realized that they were the front and right faces of the same cube. They had made progress in reconceptualizing the situation.

Episode 2

In their prediction for Box B, Pablo counted 21 visible cube faces on the box picture, doubled it for the box's hidden lateral faces, then subtracted 8 for double-counting (not taking into account that this box was 3 cubes high, not 2, like Box A), predicting 42 – 8 = 34. Nate added 12 and 12 for the right and left lateral sides of Box Picture B, then 3 and 3 for the middle column of both the front and back, explaining that the outer columns of 3 on the front and back were counted when he enumerated the right and left faces. He predicted 30. After Box B was constructed, the boys used cubes to determine that 36 cubes fill it. This puzzled the boys, leading them to reflect further on the situation. Nate thought that the error arose from missing interior cubes and tried to imagine the spatial organization of those cubes. Pablo thought the error arose from failing to account properly for the building height in his subtract-to-compensate-for-double-counted-cubes strategy; he attempted to adjust his strategy numerically.

In their predictions for Box B, Nate and Pablo dealt with the double-counting error in different ways. Pablo compensated for the error by subtracting the number of cubes he thought he had double-counted. He adjusted his original enumeration method by focusing on its numeric, rather than spatial, components. Nate attempted to imagine the cubes so he would not double-count them. He focused on obtaining a proper spatial structuring of the array. But neither boy had yet properly structured the array.

Episode 3

Nate and Pablo jointly counted 21 outside cube faces for Box Picture C, not double-counting cubes on the right front vertical edge. They then multiplied by 2 for the hidden lateral sides and added 2 for the interior cubes (which was how many cubes they concluded they had missed in the interior of Box B). Their prediction was 44. The boys made and filled the box and found that it contained 48 cubes. They were puzzled. As they reflected on their error, Pablo concluded that they failed to count some of the cubes in the four vertical edges. However, as in his previous adjustments, Pablo derived his correction by comparing the predicted and actual answers, not by finding an error in his spatial structuring. Nate dealt with the error by continuing his focus on spatial structuring; as a result, he made a conceptual breakthrough on the next prediction.

> *Nate:* I think I know Box D; I think it's going to be 30; 5 plus 5 plus 5 *[pointing to the columns in the pattern's middle]*, 15. And it's 2 high. Then you need to do 3 more rows of that because you need to do the top; 20, 25, 30 *[pointing to middle columns again]*.

Episode 4

On the next problem (Box Picture E), because neither boy was able to employ Nate's layering strategy in this different graphic context, both returned to variants of their old strategies, taking a step backward in their conceptualizing. However, after the boys completed the pattern for Box E and filled it with cubes, Nate commented that his layering strategy would have worked.

Episode 5

For Box F, once the boys drew the pattern, Nate silently pointed to and counted the squares in its 4-by-5 middle section, 1–20 for the first layer, 21–40 for the second, and 41–60 for the third. The boys built the box and filled it with cubes to verify their answer. But they were not at all surprised that they were correct; they were already sure of their answer.

After two-and-a-half one-hour sessions of small-group work, Nate and Pablo—along with the other students in their class—arrived at a layer-based enumeration strategy that they could apply in various situations (Battista 1999). They had moved from the second lowest level of reasoning about cube arrays to the highest level. Of course, this learning was not easy. Nate and Pablo struggled with these ideas. But because they were accustomed to inquiry-based instruction, they intensely and productively, and without getting frustrated, maintained their inquiry spirit to attain the instructional goals.

The predict-and-check approach was essential in students' development of appropriate mental models and enumeration strategies. Because students' predictions were based on their mental models, the cycle of making predictions, then checking them with cubes and boxes, encouraged them to reflect on and refine those mental models. Having students merely make boxes and determine how many cubes fill them would have been unlikely to have promoted nearly as much student reflection because (*a*) opportunities for reflection arising from discrepancies between predicted and actual answers would have been greatly reduced and (*b*) students' attention would have been focused on physical activity rather than thinking.

Ensuring proper spatial structuring

To ensure that students complete their attainment of Level 6, that they properly structure sets of volume units rather than use a numerical procedure that they do not fully understand, students should next move to the How Many Packages? activity shown in **figure 15**. Rotely applying a procedure such as $L \times W \times H$ will not work for these problems. Neither will applying division—reasoning, for example, that because 72 cubes fill the box and Package A is made up of 8 cubes, there are 72 divided by 8 Package A's. Although this strategy works for Packages B and C, it does not work for A because copies of this package do not completely fill the box (since we cannot break packages apart). This activity forces students to attend explicitly to how packages fit in a box, to structure the set of packages properly. Such structuring can also be encouraged by problems such as the two-cube problem shown in **figure 10**.

Extending students' conceptualizations

Meaningful use of linear measurements

Once students can properly structure and enumerate squares in 2-D arrays or cubes in 3-D arrays, they should explore what linear measurements reveal about these arrays. For instance, show students an unmarked rectangle, tell them it is 5 cm wide and 8 cm long, and ask, "What is the area of the rectangle in square centimeters? Exactly how and why can length measurements be used to find the number of square centimeters that cover a rectangle?" Be sure that students clearly distinguish length and area units. Similarly, for volume, students can be asked to find the number of cubic centimeters that fit in a closed, unmarked rectangular box.

Fractional and "deformable" area and volume units

When students are fluent in enumerating whole area and volume units, they need to expand their conceptions so that they can reason about fractional units and units that can be deformed to fit in or cover regions. For fractional units, students can be given problems in which the dimensions of boxes are not whole numbers. For instance, they can be asked, "How many one-inch clay cubes will completely fill a box that measures 6 inches by 4 inches by 3 1/2 inches? The cubes can be cut apart."

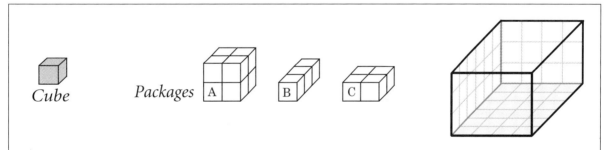

- How many of each package do you predict will fit in the box at the right? The bottom of the box is 6 cubes long and 4 cubes wide. The box is 3 cubes high.
- Use only one type of package at a time. You may not break packages apart.
- Predict, then make the box and fill it with cube packages to check your predictions.

Fig. 15. How Many Packages? activity

As students move to more abstract situations, they must expand their conceptualizations to "deformable" area and volume units, that is, units that maintain their areas or volumes but not their shapes. Students must progress from seeing area and volume as the number of rigid squares or cubes that cover or fit in a region to thinking about the actual amount of area or volume in these units. That is, they must move from covering and filling to quantitative comparison. For instance, students can be asked to determine the volume of a cone by filling it with rice, then dumping the rice into a box made from an overhead transparency in which individual cubic centimeters are indicated.

Conclusion

Designing and implementing instruction that supports students' meaningful learning of area and volume measurement must be based on firm understanding of the development of students' thinking about these concepts. Such understanding is essential to teaching in a way that is consistent with professional recommendations and modern research on students' mathematics learning. To enable students to achieve more than superficial understanding of area and volume concepts, instruction should focus on, guide, and support students' movement through the increasingly sophisticated levels of thinking described in this article.

References

Akers, Joan, Michael T. Battista, Anne Goodrow, Douglas H. Clements, and Julie Sarama. *Shapes, Halves, and Symmetry: Geometry and Fractions.* Palo Alto, Calif.: Dale Seymour Publications, 1997.

Battista, Michael T. "Fifth Graders' Enumeration of Cubes in 3D Arrays: Conceptual Progress in an Inquiry-Based Classroom." *Journal for Research in Mathematics Education* 30 (July 1999): 417–48.

Battista, Michael. T., and Douglas H. Clements. *Exploring Solids and Boxes.* Palo Alto, Calif.: Dale Seymour Publications, 1995.

———. "Students' Understanding of Three-Dimensional Rectangular Arrays of Cubes." *Journal for Research in Mathematics Education* 27 (May 1996): 258–92.

Battista, Michael T., and Mary Berle-Carman. *Containers and Cubes.* Palo Alto, Calif.: Dale Seymour Publications, 1996.

Battista, Michael T., Douglas H. Clements, Judy Arnoff, Kathryn Battista, and Caroline Van Auken Borrow. "Students' Spatial Structuring and Enumeration of 2D Arrays of Squares." *Journal for Research in Mathematics Education* 29 (November 1998): 503–32.

Assessment in Action: Mrs. Grant's Measurement Unit

Diana F. Steele

NCTM's *Professional Standards for Teaching Mathematics* (1991) describes teaching as a complex series of decisions that includes selecting, creating, and adapting appropriate instructional tasks; establishing and sustaining a positive learning environment; and analyzing the learning results of chosen tasks. For teachers to perform all these activities, they must continually integrate assessment into their instruction. This continual assessment serves as the means for monitoring students' understanding and making instructional decisions. Chambers (1993) noted, "Every instructional activity is an assessment opportunity for the teacher as well as a learning opportunity for the student" (p. 17).

Mrs. Grant, the teacher in this article, has a rich program for consistently integrating assessment and teaching throughout her lessons. Assessment is an ongoing process in her classroom. She uses assessment to discover what students know and to make instructional decisions. Mrs. Grant teaches a culturally diverse upper elementary school class with twenty-five students; English is the second language for five of them.

This article highlights a portion of a unit on linear measurement. Mrs. Grant chooses open-ended tasks, which give her students opportunities to develop measurement sense and provide her with a context to assess students' understanding of important measurement concepts, such as choice of units of measure, proportional reasoning, number sense, and computation.

How Do Students Develop Measurement Sense?

Students develop measurement sense by engaging in four general activities. First, students learn measuring skills by using measuring tools. When measuring, students must decide which tools to use, how to use the tools, and how to keep their places when moving the tools. In other words, students must understand that units of measure should be adapted to the object being measured, that all units must be identical when they are repeated in measuring an item, that the item must be subdivided along its length while it is being measured, and that the students themselves must keep track of the number of units as they measure.

Second, when measuring, students must understand how numbers are related (e.g., by comparing 1/2 and 1/4) and must keep in mind the relationship of parts to the whole. They must use proportional reasoning by relating different units and keeping ratios constant. They must choose correct units or convert from one measuring unit to another. They must also recognize the relationship between the units (e.g., how many centimeters are in a meter).

Next, students must make reasonable estimates according to the size of the numbers involved, and finally, students must compute the actual measurements.

Planning for Measurement Lessons

For the following measurement lessons, the students worked in cooperative groups because Mrs. Grant also wanted them to discuss estimation and to investigate together how to use the standard and nonstandard measuring units.

Mrs. Grant spent the month of February helping the students understand how to measure length, liquid capacity, and mass. The students used various manipulative materials to learn how to measure these attributes. Mrs. Grant chose familiar and unfamiliar measuring tools to help the students construct meaningful understanding of measurement. She explained her reasons for choosing particular measuring tools:

> For their first experiences, I deliberately chose things that were not real [not standard units], just experience-type things. My intent was to get them to estimate and then measure. I thought it would be more meaningful if they used different things. I wanted them to measure with [both appropriate and inappropriate] nonstandard units. I wanted to see [for instance] with the paper towel rolls, since they didn't have a real short

unit, if that made it hard to measure small distances. Whereas the groups that had the paper clips didn't have as much trouble measuring a shorter distance because it was a smaller unit. Also, some of the objects that I chose were more flexible and some were not. Some were harder to visualize what would be a half, a fourth. The egg carton would have been easily divided into sixths. The thing that I was trying to get them to understand was that there were ways in which their units were good to use, easy to use, or hard to use.

Day 1 of Linear Measurement

On the first day of the lesson on linear measurement, Mrs. Grant and the students talked about nonstandard tools that could be used to measure items. Some of the students' suggestions included hands and sticks. The class discussed the drawbacks of using these types of measuring tools. After about ten minutes, Mrs. Grant put the students into cooperative groups of five. Each group received an interactive box that contained one long (L) and one short (S) measuring tool and an index card on which was written the following:

Use long and short units, L or S, to measure:

1. Length of cardboard box

2. Width of cardboard box

3. Height of cardboard box

4. Circumference of lid top

5. Diameter of lid top

6. Radius of lid top

Group 1 used the length of an empty paper-towel roll for the long unit and the width (diameter) of the roll for the short unit. Group 2 used a long straw for the long unit and a coffee stirrer for the short unit. Group 3 used the length of one egg carton for the long unit and the width of one egg cup for the short unit. Group 4 used a paper-clip chain of ten paper clips for its long unit and one paper clip for the short unit. Group 5 used a long wooden stick for its long unit and a toothpick for the short unit. Mrs. Grant chose the measuring tools with the hope that the students would make associations between the long and the short units, such as that one paper clip is one-tenth of the paper-clip chain or that the long unit is equal to ten shorts. These experiences of comparing and using long and short units gave the students opportunities to think qualitatively about proportional reasoning.

Before the students began measuring items with their tools, Mrs. Grant asked them to estimate the measurements of their items and to write the estimates on worksheets that she had prepared. Mrs. Grant noted that the estimation task was intended to help her students develop benchmarks to compare their nonstandard units or to make comparisons among standard units, such as inches, feet, and yards compared with centimeters, decimeters, and meters. Such comparisons are additional aspects of proportional reasoning. Requiring the students to estimate before they measured forced them to reflect on the meaning of the measurement activities in addition to learning to use the tools. Mrs. Grant believed that this reflection helped the students develop conceptual knowledge of the procedures. Her students' estimation strategies also helped her assess what the students already knew about measurement, including both measurement skills and proportional reasoning. During the activity, the students talked animatedly with one another, arguing about the estimated measurements, and later, about the actual measurements. Some groups that finished measuring the items in their interactive boxes measured other items in the room, such as the chalkboard and door frame.

While the students worked in cooperative groups, Mrs. Grant observed whether all students were working and discussing the tasks and made informal assessments of students' understanding. As she moved from group to group, she listened to students' reasoning and for difficulties that they might be experiencing. She asked questions to ensure that all students contributed to the thinking and discussion of the group. Mrs. Grant explained later: "As I walk around, I look to see if a particular person is not doing as much of the thinking as others in the group. I question within the group and try to bring his or her thinking out."

The group using the paper-towel roll could not agree on the height of the box. One student said, "One-half," but another disagreed: "More like one-third." Mrs. Grant said, "One-third what?" A student said, "One-third paper-towel rolls." This group also had trouble deciding how to find the circumference of the round lid with the paper-towel roll. After observing other groups measuring with their nonstandard units, Mrs. Grant asked the class, "Are you getting more comfortable with your units? Some of you are saying 'feet' and 'inches,' but they are not feet and inches. Why are they not going to be the same?" A student answered, "Everyone has different things." The teacher asked, "What are 'things'?" Several students answered with names of the units that they had used.

Mrs. Grant also helped ensure that everyone participated in group work by including enough manipulative materials for the group members. Observing students' use of manipulatives, along with listening to their discussions, helped her make assessment decisions about students' understanding. She later explained,

> I circulate while they are working and make observations about how they are progressing. And I am very attentive to who is participating during discussions.... Based on these informal [assessments], I mark an E (excellent), S (satisfactory), or N (needs improvement). I also collect the math logs about every two to three weeks to evaluate. [They are] not evaluated according to right or wrong answers but based on completeness and amount of effort that is reflected.

Math logs, the name Mrs. Grant gave to the mathematics journals that all her students kept throughout the year, included students' answers and solution strategies to problems of the day, problems of the week, and problems that they needed to explain in words or diagrams. Mrs. Grant asked the students to write in their logs for the first fifteen minutes of each day of school. This writing period gave the students time to think about the questions that they thought she might ask when discussion began.

Mrs. Grant also used her informal assessments and the group products to evaluate students' work for grading purposes. She said,

> I try to set it up so that the group turns in one product with their names on it. Everyone will get the same grade. I try to monitor what is going on in each group. I want to see if there's a problem in any group and [whether] it looks like they are headed in a positive direction. If they are not, that's going to hurt their grade. If they are all working in the same direction, turn in a poor product, and they seem to be content with it, they all get the poor grade.

Occasionally, a student in a group was not satisfied with his or her group's product. When this situation occurred, Mrs. Grant allowed the student to turn in individual work. In addition, if a student disagreed with the group's answer for a problem but could not persuade the others to change their minds, even with a good argument, Mrs. Grant allowed the dissenting student to turn in a separate product.

On this day, after all the groups had completed the activities with the interactive boxes, Mrs. Grant guided a whole-class discussion in which the students talked about the following questions: What aspects of your L and S units made them easy to use? What aspects made them hard to use? Will your measurements be the same as those of the other groups? How did you feel about your estimates at the beginning? Is being incorrect in your estimations acceptable?

During the whole-class discussion, the group of students with the egg cartons decided that their units were difficult to use because they could not easily find halves and fourths of the small unit, the egg cup. The group of students with the sticks thought that their units were not flexible enough. The students with the straws did not like having to string their straws together to measure long items, such as the chalkboard. They found dropping the string down into the straws difficult. They also lost their place frequently because the string kept moving. These group members said that they had made a mark on the string when they got to the end of the item they were measuring. The students with the long chain of paper clips said that their chain kept moving also. They thought that the paper-clip chains were too flexible. The group members with the toothpicks said that picking the toothpicks up and moving them was difficult. Mrs. Grant assessed students informally during this whole-class discussion. She explained,

> I take into account and consideration [the students' contributions] during the interaction in class. That's important because that's part of what we are doing. That has to be evaluated. It is more subjective. I don't always make an immediate evaluation on a sheet of paper right after the math lesson, but I remember it.

Mrs. Grant ended the lesson by calling the students' attention again to how each group had recorded different lengths for their measured items. For example, one group had measured the length of the chalkboard as 10 paper-towel rolls; another had recorded it as 120 paper clips. The students agreed that the difference in naming the measured items with different nonstandard units caused misunderstanding in discussing measurement.

Day 2

The next day, the cooperative groups used standard measuring tools to measure objects that they would use in real life. In the interactive boxes, each group was given a tape measure, a 6-centimeter ruler, a 12-inch ruler with inch and centimeter marks, a string, and a calculator. One person from each group borrowed a yardstick and a meterstick from the supply area for her or his group's use. The activities again gave Mrs. Grant the opportunity to assess the students' proportional reasoning. Again, all groups estimated before measuring in both customary and metric units. The students had to decide which unit of measure would be appropriate for the objects. Mrs. Grant said, "Yesterday, some of you said you liked flexible, and some of you liked the stiff units, so today you are going to have both. You need to decide what to use." An index card in each interactive box had these directions:

Use customary and metric units to measure:

1. Two dog leashes [one thin and long, one thick and short]. Decide which leash would be for a big dog. Which for a small dog?

2. Circumference, diameter, and radius of two 8-mm movie projector reels—one large and one small. Will the movie in the canister fit on either reel?

3. Width of the bath towel. Decide how much trim would be needed to decorate the towel.

4. Length, height, and width of two baking pans.

5. Decide what size frame you need for the art print.

6. Make up your own word problem about measurement to ask other groups.

Mrs. Grant explained her choice of items this time:

I wanted them to know that we do need to measure real things. We do buy things according to the size, the length, and how much we need of those materials. If you needed an 8 × 10 frame, what did that mean? If you were putting stamps on an envelope, why would you put one or three or four? Was it because the mass of the envelope was greater? [They had measured the mass of objects with balance scales in cooperative groups previously.] As far as actual objects, I was also already thinking ahead to what word problems that I might want them to solve. I wanted these problems to be real-life problems.

As the students worked, Mrs. Grant again observed and asked questions of the groups. She asked one group of students why they did not use the string to measure the movie canisters. A student answered, "We had the tape measure that you gave us. It would bend, and it had measuring units marked on it. It wouldn't make sense to put string around it when you had a measure like a string." Mrs. Grant observed that the groups had found different answers for the length and width of the baking pans. When they came back to whole-class discussion, she asked the students how this difference could occur. After several groups explained how they had measured, the students discovered that some groups had measured across the top of the pan and that some had measured across the bottom. This contrast gave them different answers. Mrs. Grant closed the lesson by bringing the discussion back to the importance of using standard units of measure.

Day 3

The next day, Mrs. Grant asked the students to solve word problems in cooperative groups. The word problems were similar to tasks from the interactive box activities and based on situations that students would encounter in real life. The problems included the following:

1. Mrs. Grant wants to frame this Saint Augustine print. The frame that she has chosen is 2 inches wide. It costs $0.15 an inch. How many inches of framing does she need? How much will it cost?

2. Terry is going to put a decorative trim on four towels. The trim costs $0.89 a yard. How much trim is needed? How much will it cost?

3. Jordan is building a dog pen. Its dimensions are in the same ratio as those of your cardboard box. The scale is 1 inch = 1 foot. The fencing that he is using costs $5.50 a foot. What are the length and width of the dog pen? What is the perimeter of the pen? How much will the fencing cost?

After the students completed these word problems, a whole-class discussion about strategies occurred.

Day 4

On the last day of this unit, Mrs. Grant asked the students to work individually to solve measurement problems. This activity became her formal assessment of what the students had learned during the linear-measurement activities. In this formal assessment, Mrs. Grant asked the students to solve tasks that were similar to those in the previous activities. While she asked ten questions out loud, the students wrote their solutions in ten sections that they had blocked off on pieces of 11-by-14-inch newsprint. The students had to explain their thinking by drawing pictures and diagrams. Mrs. Grant repeated the questions several times and gave the students enough time to think about each problem before she went on to a new one. Five of the questions were similar to the word problems done in cooperative groups on day 3. For example, she said, "My mother-in-law sewed the trim on these towels. They did not come like this. She didn't want to buy fifty yards when she didn't need it. How much trim did she need to buy to decorate both towels?" To assess the students' estimating abilities, she also asked questions, including the following:

1. Which leash [holding up two leashes] is 6 feet long—the purple or the blue?

2. Which picture frame [holding up two frames] is 8 inches by 10 inches?

3. There are two speakers in this [holding up a stereo-speaker component]. If one needs to be replaced, I can't go up and say, "I need a speaker." I have got to tell them something about what size it is. Which speaker has a 4-inch diameter, top or bottom?

4. Which screw [holding up two screws] is 3 inches long, A or B?

5. I had a saleswoman come to my home. She was telling me I would get such-and-such-size pans. Which one [holding up two pans] is a 7-inch frying pan?

Implications for Assessment: Listening and Observing

Much of Mrs. Grant's assessment is informal, such as listening to students' responses during discussions or cooperative learning activities. According to Fennema and Carpenter (1992), children should regularly be asked to explain how they figured out answers. Because Mrs. Grant emphasizes conceptual knowledge in her teaching, her instructional activities include methods to assess her students' conceptual understanding. She plans activities that will be consistent with her assessments of the students' levels of thinking. She says, "You try to assess as close as you can to get to the child's understanding." To achieve this closeness, Mrs. Grant often asks the students to model their thinking with manipulative materials. Fennema and Carpenter (1992) suggest that manipulative materials are "of major use in helping teachers understand what the child is thinking" (p. 69). Mrs. Grant believes that these assessments often tell her more about what her students know than written ones but admits that these informal assessments can be a complex part of understanding students' reasoning. She elaborated as follows:

> I can't help them with a wrong answer if I don't know where they are coming from. . . . I am getting them to verbalize or explain so that when there is a problem, they are better at getting me or their next teacher to understand what it is they can't solve.

Lambdin (1993) notes that written tests often tell little about children's strategies. Because they lack information, teachers may jump to inaccurate conclusions about students' performance on tasks. Often, written tests make diagnosing students' mathematical misconceptions difficult. Researchers, such as Huinker (1993), suggest that listening to students allows teachers to "determine the level of understanding, to diagnose misconceptions and missing connections, and to assess verbal ability to communicate mathematics knowledge" (p. 80). With paper-and-pencil tasks, students' understanding is more likely to be hidden, and the teacher may be unable to determine whether a student's answer is incorrect because he or she lacked the necessary knowledge or simply made an error.

Assessment in Action

Chambers (1993) asserts that by thinking of instruction and assessment as simultaneous acts, teachers optimize both the quantity and the quality of their assessments and their instruction. In classrooms that are oriented toward problem solving, like Mrs. Grant's, teachers may demonstrate little difference between tasks that they use for instruction and those that they use for assessment. They assess in the ways that they teach. Tasks for both assessment and instruction should be interesting and challenging for students. The difference should be in not designating a task as either assessment or instruction, but in using the task for instruction and assessment. What serves as an instructional task for some students can be an assessment task for others. Teachers who simultaneously assess and teach place the focus of instruction on students' thinking, and when mathematical thinking is the focus of instruction, the teacher naturally has the information needed for assessment.

References

Chambers, Donald L. "Integrating Assessment and Instruction." In *Assessment in the Mathematics Classroom*, 1993 Yearbook of the National Council of Teachers of Mathematics (NCTM), edited by Norman L. Webb, pp. 17–25. Reston, Va.: NCTM, 1993.

Fennema, Elizabeth, and Thomas P. Carpenter. "Cognitively Guided Instruction." Madison: University of Wisconsin—Madison, 1992.

Huinker, DeAnn M. "Interviews: A Window to Students' Conceptual Knowledge of the Operations." In *Assessment in the Mathematics Classroom*, 1993 Yearbook of the National Council of Teachers of Mathematics (NCTM), edited by Norman L. Webb, pp. 80–86. Reston, Va.: NCTM, 1993.

Lambdin, Diana V. "The NCTM's 1989 Evaluation Standards: Recycled Ideas Whose Time Has Come?" In *Assessment in the Mathematics Classroom*, 1993 Yearbook of the National Council of Teachers of Mathematics (NCTM), edited by Norman L. Webb, pp. 7–16. Reston, Va.: NCTM, 1993.

National Council of Teachers of Mathematics (NCTM). *Curriculum and Evaluation Standards for School Mathematics*. Reston, Va.: NCTM, 1989.

———. *Professional Standards for Teaching Mathematics*. Reston, Va.: NCTM, 1991.

Packing the Packages

Did you ever notice that cereal comes in tall, thin boxes and that laundry soap comes in short, wide boxes? Is the way a product is packaged important? What box shape holds the most and uses the least amount of material to make? Let's explore the amount of packaging material needed to wrap a product.

1. Most cereal boxes are right rectangular prisms. That is, they have two parallel rectangular regions called *bases,* which are connected by four other rectangular regions called *lateral surfaces.* Suppose that your favorite cereal comes in a box that is 12 inches high, 10 inches long, and 3 inches wide. Sketch a picture of the box on a separate sheet of paper, and label it with the dimensions.

2. *a)* What are the dimensions of the bottom of the box? _____

   b) What are the dimensions of the front of the box?_____

   c) What are the dimensions of the side of the box? _____

3. What part of the cereal box has the same dimensions as the bottom panel?

4. Finding the amount of cardboard needed to make the cereal box is sometimes easier if you use a flat pattern of the box. This flat pattern is called a *net.* On a separate sheet of paper, draw a sketch showing the cereal box if you cut it apart and flattened it.

Take an empty cereal box, and cut along as many edges as necessary to lay the box completely flat and keep it in one piece. Did your sketch match the box?

To calculate the amount of material needed to make the box, you must find the surface area of the box.

5. How many rectangular regions make up the net? _____

6. On your sketch, label the front, back, top, bottom, and the right and left sides of the box. Also label the dimensions of the box.

7. *a)* Find the area of the front panel of the cereal box. _____

   b) Find the area of the top panel of the cereal box. _____

   c) Find the area of one of the side panels of the cereal box. _____

8. Find the total surface area of the box. _____

9. You can develop a formula for the surface area, *SA,* of all boxes that are rectangular prisms by representing the different edges of a box with variables. Assume that a box is sitting on its bottom surface with its front panel facing you, as pictured at right. Let b represent the bottom front edge of the box. Let s represent the top edge on the left side of the box. Finally, let h represent the left edge of the front panel of the box.
   Write an equation that represents the surface area (*SA*) of the box. _____

10. The amount of space inside the box is called its *volume.* You can find the volume of the box by calculating the number of one-unit cubes needed to fill the box.

    a) If you begin to fill the box with one-inch cubes, how many one-inch cubes would complete the first layer in the bottom of the cereal box? _____

    b) How many layers of one-inch cubes are needed to fill the whole box? _____

    c) Find the number of one-inch cubes needed to fill the box. _____

d) Write an equation that relates the dimensions of the box to the total number of one-inch cubes that would fill the cereal box. _____

11. Using the same variables that you used in problem 9, write an equation that represents the volume, V, of the cereal box. _____

12. Notice that the number of one-inch cubes in the bottom layer of the box is the same as the number of square inches in the area of the bottom panel. Will you always obtain this result? Explain your reasoning.

M.A.T.H. Corporation manufactures manipulatives for mathematics classrooms. One popular manipulative is a set of 100 blocks that are one-inch cubes. M.A.T.H. Corporation is trying to find ways to decrease its packaging costs. The company has decided to arrange each set of blocks in a box that is shaped like a rectangular prism.

13. Complete the chart to find all the possible box arrangements for 100 blocks. Turning a box or standing it upright does not constitute a new or different box shape. Find the surface area and the cost to manufacture the box if boxes can be made for 0.8¢, or $0.008, per square inch. Since the box must hold exactly 100 one-inch blocks, the volume of each box will be the same.

Base Front	Side	Height	Volume	Surface Area (sq. in.)	Cost ($0.008 per sq. in.)
100	1	1	100		
50			100	304	
			100		
			100		
			100		
	10	1	100		$1.92
			100		
			100		

14. *a)* What are the dimensions of the box that costs the most to manufacture? _____

    b) What does this box look like? _____

    c) Explain why this shape is the most expensive one for the box to have. _____

15. *a)* What are the dimensions of the box that costs the least to manufacture? _____

    b) How does its shape differ from that of the most expensive box? _____

    c) Why would you expect this box to cost less? _____

    d) If the box did not have to hold the cubes but still had a volume of 100 cubic inches, what would be the shape of the least expensive box? _____

16. An employee suggested that 125 one-inch blocks could be packaged for the same cost as 100 blocks.

    a) What are the dimensions of the box that would most economically hold 125 one-inch blocks? _____

    b) Find the surface area and the cost of this package. _____

c) Is the employee correct? Explain. _____

M.A.T.H. Corporation wants to ship the manipulatives in cartons that hold exactly 100 packages of the blocks. Using the 5-inch-by-5-inch-by-4-inch box from the chart in problem 13, design at least two cartons that hold 100 packages of the blocks.

17. *a)* On a separate sheet of paper, sketch your designs, and describe how the packages must be arranged to fill your cartons. _____

    b) The company wants the shipping cartons to be as compact as possible to keep costs to a minimum. The carton with the least amount of surface area would be the cheapest. Describe the shape that this carton must have. _____

    c) What are the dimensions of the carton with the minimum surface area that would hold 100 packages of the one-inch block manipulatives? _____

M.A.T.H. Corporation also sells balls as manipulatives. The balls come in sets of three and are 3 inches in diameter. The marketing team is trying to decide whether a rectangular prism is still the best design or whether a cylinder would require less packaging material.

18. *a)* On a separate sheet of paper, sketch possible configurations in which three balls could be packaged.

    b) On a separate sheet of paper, sketch possible packages to hold each of the arrangements of the balls. Label the dimensions of each package.

    c) Determine the surface area of each package. _____

    d) Which package would you recommend to M.A.T.H. Corporation? Justify your recommendation.

Can you . . .

- determine the surface area of these containers designed to hold three balls with 3-inch diameters?

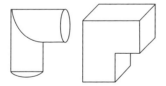

- find the surface area and volume of a sphere?
- determine the relationship of the volume of a cylinder, cone, and sphere when they

all have the same diameter and when the height of the cone and the cylinder equal the diameter of the sphere?

Did you know . . .

- that a sphere always has a smaller surface area than a cube with the same volume?

Mathematical content

Surface area, volume, optimization, spatial visualization

References

Lappan, Glenda, William Fitzgerald, Mary Jean Winter, and Elizabeth Phillips. *Middle Grades Mathematics Project: The Mouse and the Elephant*. Menlo Park, Calif.: Addison-Wesley Publishing Co., 1988.

Lappan, Glenda, James T. Fey, William M. Fitzgerald, Mary Jean Winter, and Elizabeth Difanis Phillips. *Filling and Wrapping: Three-Dimensional Measurement, Connected Mathematics Project*. Menlo Park, Calif.: Dale Seymour Publications, 1988.

Johnson, Christine V., and Nancy Cook. *Designing Environments: Real-World Mathematics through Science*. Orangeburg, N.Y.: Dale Seymour Publications, 1998.

Answers

1. Sample box

2. (*a*) 10 in. × 3 in.; (*b*) 10 in. × 12 in.; (*c*) 3 in. × 12 in.

3. The top panel

4. Sample nets

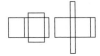

5. Six rectangular regions

6. Sample net

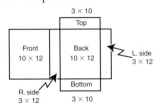

7. (*a*) 120 sq. in.; (*b*) 30 sq. in.; (*c*) 36 sq. in.

8. 372 sq. in.

9. $SA = 2bs + 2hs + 2bh$.

10. (*a*) 30 cubes; (*b*) 12 layers; (*c*) 360 cubes; (*d*) Total cubes = 3 × 10 × 12.

11. $V = bsh$.

12. Yes; the faces of the cubes that are touching the bottom of the box exactly cover the same area as the bottom panel.

13. Sample chart (see chart at bottom of page)

14. (*a*) 100 in. × 1 in. × 1 in.; (*b*) The box would be long and skinny; (*c*) It has the greatest surface area.

15. (*a*) 5 in. × 5 in. × 4 in.; (*b*) It is more compact, and its shape is closer to that of a cube; (*c*) It has less surface area; (*d*) A cube.

16. (*a*) 5 in. × 5 in. × 5 in.; (*b*) The box would require 150 square inches of material and would cost $1.20 to produce; (*c*) No; 100 cubes can be packaged for less, since the 5 in. × 5 in. × 4 in. box has a surface area of 130 square inches and costs $1.04.

17. (*a*) Sample cartons; (*b*) It must be close to a cube; (*c*) 25 in. × 20 in. × 20 in.

18. (*a*) Possible arrangements

(*b*) Sample containers

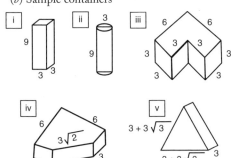

(*c*) The surface area of the rectangular prism (fig. *i*), cylinder (fig. *ii*), and triangular prism (fig. *v*) are 126 square inches, approximately 99 square inches, and approximately 132 square inches, respectively. Figure *iii* has a surface area of 126 square inches. Figure *iv* has a surface area of approximately 130 square inches.

(*d*) The cylinder should be recommended, because it has the least amount of surface area and would cost the least to produce.

13. Sample chart

Base Front	Side	Height	Volume	Surface Area (sq. in.)	Cost ($0.008 per sq. in.)
100	1	1	100	402	$3.22
50	2	1	100	304	$2.43
25	2	2	100	208	$1.66
25	4	1	100	258	$2.06
20	5	1	100	250	$2.00
10	10	1	100	240	$1.92
10	5	2	100	160	$1.28
5	5	4	100	130	$1.04

Spatial Visualization: What Happens When You Turn It?

Óscar Chávez, Robert Reys, and Dusty Jones

SPATIAL visualization is an important skill that deserves instructional attention. Strong evidence supports the claim that "measures of mathematical ability tend to be strongly correlated with spatial ability" (Anderson 2000). Thus, there is every reason to believe that time spent helping students develop their spatial visualization skills will have additional benefits for their mathematical growth, perhaps even going so far as to improve test performance.

Spatial visualization takes many different forms. In this article, we are going to share some research results, some ways of exploring spatial visualization, and some ideas that might help students engage in logical reasoning and mental computation.

First, take a look at the blocks in **figure 1**. The number of blocks in these prisms is the same but each arrangement has a different appearance.

Having students build prisms will help them confirm that the number of blocks is the same in each arrangement (see **fig. 2**). It will also help students recognize that the number of blocks in the rectangular prisms depends on the height, length, and width of the prism. This activity will also provide a natural application of multiplication involving three factors. It helps show students that although the arrangements in figures 1 and 2 are perceptually different, their respective volumes are the same.

Research has documented the difficulties that students have in determining the volume from pictures or drawings of prisms. This is not a new phenomenon. For example, over twenty years ago, the Second Mathematics Assessment reported the low score on the item shown in **figure 3**, which was completed by middle school students (Carpenter et al. 1981). Classroom teachers and researchers have observed these difficulties. For example, Battista documented some of the specific problems that middle-grades students have in developing this type of spatial structuring (1998) and offered some instructional ideas. These instructional suggestions were drawn from extensive research on one aspect of spatial visualization, namely, focusing on three-dimensional cubes (Battista and Clements 1996). Giving students hands-on experience building prisms with blocks is one of their suggestions.

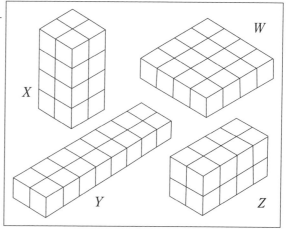

Fig. 1. Different prisms with the same number of cubes

Some Things Learned from One Open-ended Problem

In this study, we administrated the tasks in the *Balanced Assessment in Mathematics* (2002) to more than 2000 sixth graders. One of the items regarding spatial visualization is shown in **figure 4**. This item proved to be very difficult. The first question

Fig. 2. Different prisms with the same volume

was answered correctly by 9 percent of the sixth graders. Less than 3 percent of the students answered both parts of the problem correctly. Nearly 75 percent of the students either left the question blank or did not calculate any volume related to the question.

In the first part of the problem, every student who answered correctly multiplied the length, width, and height of the water in the tank. The most common incorrect answer given was to add all the numbers in the problem, so 24 + 12 + 10 + 16 = 62 was a frequent answer to the first part. When students encounter an unfamiliar problem, it is not uncommon for them to assume that they are expected to use the numbers in the problem (Schoenfeld 1992). This phenomenon was observed after those students who we were able to identify had incorrectly answered 62.

More creative and interesting strategies were used to find the height of the water in the second part of the problem. The majority of students who answered correctly used the strategy of dividing the volume of the water calculated in the first part by the dimensions of the base in the second part. A related strategy that was popular involved students answering the question, "Sixteen times 12 times what equals 3840?"

A powerful but less common appropriate strategy involved the use of proportional reasoning. Some students noted that the height dimension of the tank in part 2 was twice that of the tank in part 1, therefore, the water level in part 2 should be twice that of part 1. A student wrote, "It is filled 10 in. out of 12, then just multiply by two and get 20 out of 24."

Another interesting strategy involved calculating the volume of the entire tank and the space without water shown in the first part. When dividing this number by the dimensions of the base of the second tank, the student arrived at the height of the empty space in the second figure. The student then subtracted this value from the height of the tank to determine the height of the water (see **fig. 5**).

About half the students who calculated the volume of water correctly could not find a successful approach to the second part. The fact that the volume of water was the same but that the dimensions had changed was not readily apparent. These students tried to guess the depth of water in the rotated tank, in

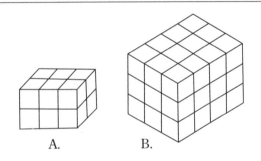

A.   B.

	RESPONSE	PERCENT OF THIRTEEN-YEAR-OLDS
A.	12*	58
	6	11
	16	12
	32	2
	I don't know	6
	Other	11
B.	36*	24
	33	26
	66	10
	I don't know	1
	Other	39

* Indicates correct response

Fig. 3. How many cubes are in these rectangular solids?

A closed tank is 24 inches long, 12 inches high, and 16 inches wide. **It is filled with water to a depth of 10 inches.**

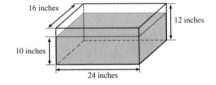

1. What volume of **water** is in the tank?
2. How deep will the water be if the tank is turned so that it stands on one end?

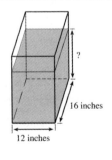

Fig. 4. The Tank Problem

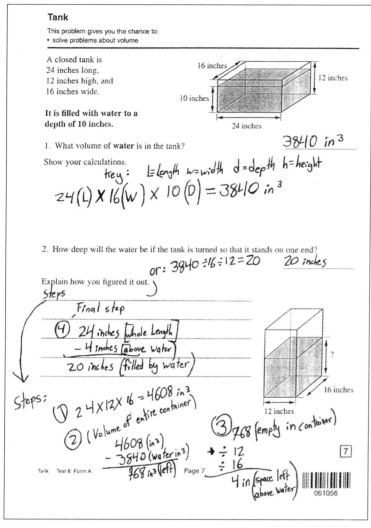

Fig. 5. A solution to the Tank Problem

some cases based on a literal interpretation of the diagram, assuming that the figure was drawn to scale and estimating the height. For example, a student whose answer was 16 inches explained, "The width is the same as the height of the water right now." Another popular incorrect strategy used information from the first diagram and assumed that the water level was 24 inches, even when the tank was turned.

The Tank Problem produced a variety of responses, and **figure 6** summarizes some solutions—both correct and incorrect—that students offered. The most common among the partially correct responses was to calculate the volume of the tank or the volume of the water, without answering the second part of the problem.

Helping Students Develop Spatial Visualization

The item in **figure 4** prompted us to develop some ways of getting students to think more carefully about this problem situation. First of all, if the rectangular container is completely filled (and has a lid so nothing spills), then any rotation of its position will still result in a completely filled container. This situation is analogous to the arrangements shown in

	CORRECT	INCORRECT
Part 1	Multiply 10 × 16 × 24.	Add 10 + 16 + 24 + 12.
		Add 10 +16 + 24.
Part 2	Find area of base (16 × 12) and divide volume of water by that number.	Assume that the drawing has been made to scale and visually estimate the height of the water.
	Find a number that, when multiplied by 16 × 12, equals 3840.	State that the height of the water is 24 inches, since that dimension of the tank is 24 inches.
	Using proportional reasoning, since the height of the tank in the second part is twice the height of the tank in the first part, the height of the water in the second part must also be double that in the first part.	
	Find volume of empty space, calculate height of empty space, and subtract that from the height of the tank.	

Fig. 6. Observed student strategies

figure 1. Moving arrangement *X* to arrangement *Z* might change the relative position of the height, length, and width from 2 − 2 − 4 to 2 − 4 − 2, but the dimensions have remained constant.

Now let's examine the container C_1 shown in **figure 7**. Notice that how the container is sitting influences the resulting height. To get started, fill a rectangular container half full. Before placing it on a different side, ask students to conjecture about its "new" height when the rectangular container is placed on a different side. How would the "new" height be related if the container were three-fourths full? One-third full? Making and verifying these conjectures provide some good readiness for cases when specific dimensions are encountered. This discussion allows an opportunity to make a direct connection to different but equivalent algebraic representations, for example,

$$V = \frac{l}{3}wh = l\frac{w}{3}h = \frac{1}{3}lwh.$$

A search for patterns will be aided if the container has some dimensions. Consider **figure 7** where the rectangular prism has dimensions of 20, 10, 10, but instead of being full of rice (which should behave like a liquid), it is only partially full. It is resting on a base that is 20 × 10, or

Fig. 7. A tank in two different positions

200, square units, and the rice height is 2 units. Ask students to predict what will happen when C_1 is moved to position C_2 (where the base is 10 × 10). Do you think the height will increase or decrease? Perhaps ask students to place a finger on the side to estimate about where the rice will level off. Reflecting on the area of the new base that will be 10 × 10 suggests that the smaller area will allow the grains of rice to spread out less, so the height will be greater. How much greater? A few of these experiences will help remind students that the volume remains unchanged. Therefore, the new height can be determined mentally—remembering that the volume of C_1 was 20 × 10 × 2, the volume of C_2 must be 10 × 10 × *h*, so the new height with the smaller area for the base must be

$$\frac{20 \times 10 \times 2}{10 \times 10} = 4.$$

Careful selection of the dimensions of prisms can provide valuable practice in spatial visualization as well as logical reasoning and mental computation. For example, the rectangular prisms shown in **figure 8** provide opportunities for conjecturing and then determining the volume of the material contained in the various positions.

Fig. 8. Other rectangular prisms

Figure 9 is a structured sequence of additional practice activities that illustrates some natural stages. In **figure 9a,** students make a prism with a fixed number of red and blue cubes and are asked questions such as those in 1a–1c. In question 2, students are given the dimensions for the base and are asked to make a conjecture about the height of the blue cubes if a new prism is built on the base using all the blue cubes first and then the red cubes.

Materials: Blue cubes and red cubes

1. Make a 6 × 2 × 3 prism with blue and red cubes. Begin by making a 6 × 2 rectangle with blue cubes. This is the first layer. Make a second layer with blue cubes. Make a third layer with red cubes.

   a. What is the volume of the prism?

   b. What fraction of it is made of blue cubes?

   c. What is the height of the prism? What is the height of the blue part?

Fig. 9a. A 6 × 2 × 3 prism

2. Predict what would be the height of the blue part if the same prism were standing on the 2 × 3 side and if all the blue cubes were at the bottom. Verify your conjectures.

Fig. 9b. The start of a prism with a 2 × 3 base

3. Make a 2 × 3 rectangle with blue cubes; this will be the first layer. Continue adding layers of blue cubes until all are used. Complete the prism with the red cubes.

   a. What is the volume of the prism?

   b. What fraction of it is made of blue cubes?

   c. What is the height of the prism? What is the height of the blue part?

Fig. 9c. A 3 × 2 × 6 prism

4. Answer similar questions for prisms with different dimensions, without constructing them with manipulatives.

   The dimensions of prism A are 8 cm, 24 cm, and 12 cm. Resting on a base of 8 cm × 24 cm, the height of the liquid is 9 cm.

   a. Turning the prism so that the base is 8 cm × 12 cm, what is the new height of the liquid?

   b. Turning the prism so that the base is 24 cm × 12 cm, what is the new height of the liquid?

Fig. 9. Some possible practice activities

Figure 9b shows the start of a prism with a 2 × 3 base that will produce the prism shown in **figure 9c**. Answering questions 3a–3c will reinforce some important relationships that are featured in the earlier Tank Problem.

Where Do We Go from Here?

Spatial visualization together with logical reasoning call on higher-level cognition and processing. Progress may not happen immediately, but the data reported here are a reminder that much needs to be done to improve student performance. These activities help students develop spatial visualization and realize how useful this skill is in the real world. Turning some things over physically may be impossible, but one beauty of mathematics thinking is that these objects can be turned over *mentally*. In this process of *turning it over* or *turning it on its side,* spatial visualization becomes a powerful tool that encourages and rewards thinking.

References

Anderson, John R. *Cognitive Psychology and Its Implications.* 5th ed. New York: Worth Publishers, 2000.

Balanced Assessment in Mathematics, Form A. Monterey, Calif.: CTB/McGraw-Hill, 2002.

Battista, Michael T. "How Many Blocks?" *Mathematics Teaching in the Middle School* 3 (March–April 1998): 404–11.

Battista, Michael T., and Douglas H. Clements. "Students' Understanding of Three-Dimensional Rectangular Arrays of Cubes." *Journal for Research in Mathematics Education* 27 (May 1996): 258–92.

Carpenter, Thomas P., Mary K. Corbitt, Henry S. Kepner, Mary Lindquist, and Robert E. Reys. *Results from the Second Mathematics Assessment of the National Assessment of Educational Progress.* Reston, Va.: National Council of Teachers of Mathematics, 1981.

Schoenfeld, Alan H. "Learning to Think Mathematically: Problem Solving, Metacognition, and Sense Making in Mathematics." In *Handbook of Research on Mathematics Teaching and Learning,* edited by Douglas A. Grouws, pp. 334–70. Reston, Va.: National Council of Teachers of Mathematics, 1992.

How Many Times Does a Radius Square Fit into the Circle?

Alfinio Flores and Troy P. Regis

This article presents alternative and interesting approaches to exploring π. The first part of the article describes an empirical method that allows students to estimate the area of a circle with surprising accuracy. This method can be used as an extension of the approach of using a grid to approximate the area of a circle. The use of a grid is conceptually illuminating; it emphasizes the idea that the area is measured in square units and that areas of shapes that do not have straight sides can nevertheless be measured with square units. An example of such an approach is described in "Covering a Circle" (Lappan et al. 1998); however, when students actually count squares, the values they find may not be exact. For example, in a sixth-grade classroom, when students counted the squares in a grid containing a circle with radius 7, their answers ranged from 142 to 178 square units for the approximate area of the circle. Dividing such numbers by the square of the radius, that is, 49, we obtain values ranging from 2.9 to 3.6. The area approximation was not exact enough to determine the value of π with two significant digits. In the first activity we describe, the goal is to help students understand that the area of the circle is about 3.1 times the area of the radius square (that is, a square with a side length that is equal to the radius).

Frequently, even after students conduct an empirical exploration of the area of the circle and its circumference, they are not helped to understand why the same number, π, appears in the formulas for both the area and the circumference of a circle. The second activity in this article is geared to help students see the connection. This second activity may be more appropriate for revisiting the topic in seventh or eighth grade. We assume that students have done an activity for finding the ratio of the circumference to the diameter, for example, by measuring around circular objects, measuring along the corresponding diameters, and computing the ratio. An example of such an activity is "Surrounding a Circle" (Lappan et al. 1998). Also, we assume that students know and understand the formulas for the areas of a triangle and a parallelogram.

Activity 1:
The Ratio of the Area of a Circle to the Radius Square

Students are given a circle and a square with a side length that is equal to the radius—the radius square (see **fig. 1**). They are asked to guess how many times the radius square fits into the circle. Students in sixth grade figured out fairly quickly that the answer had to be more than two but less than four. **Figure 2** shows a way to help students visualize that the radius square fits more than two times in the circle. The area of the square inscribed in the circle is equal to two radius squares because the area of the shaded part is one-half of the radius square, and four such halves fit in the circle. **Figure 3** shows that the radius square fits fewer than four times because four radius squares cover and extend beyond the circle.

Cutting and pasting radius squares

Copy the four radius squares and the circle from the materials section in **Appendix 1** on page 245 and distribute the copies to students. Note that **figure 4** shows one possible response; the pieces of the squares fit in other ways. Then, give students the following instructions:

> Color the four radius squares with different colors. Cut out the circle. Cut out the first square and fit it entirely inside the circle. Cut out the second square and fit it inside without overlapping the previous color. You will have to cut parts of the second square so that they fit inside the circle without extending beyond it. Use all of the second square before using the third square. Continue with the third and fourth squares in the same manner. Save the remainder of the fourth square and use the grid to estimate how much of the fourth square you were able to fit.

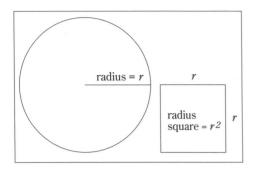

Fig. 1. The circle and the radius square

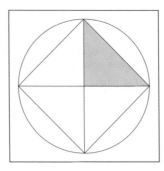

Fig. 2. The shaded triangle is one-half of the radius square.

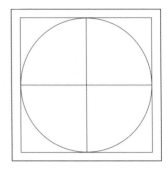

Fig. 3. The area of the circle is less than the area of four radius squares.

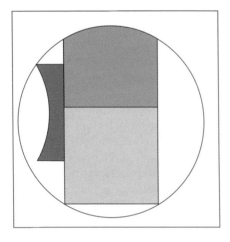

Fig. 4. Students fit two radius squares into the circle before using the third one.

Results of the activity

Students see that they can fit three squares completely and a little of the fourth one. That is, the radius square fits "three and a little more" times into the circle. Using a radius of ten units and the corresponding ten-by-ten grid to draw the fourth radius square is convenient for this activity. By counting the number of small unit squares of the fourth radius square that were actually used, students can see that the ratio of the area of the circle to the area of the radius square is about 3.1 to 1, or about 3.1.

This activity required about two 45-minute sessions to complete in a sixth-grade class. The teacher may want to have wax paper, patty paper, or other translucent paper available to allow students to trace areas that are not yet covered on the circle and use the tracing to cut the corresponding parts on the colored radius squares. Students have different strategies to fit parts of the fourth square, some of which lead to better estimates. However, in the sixth-grade class mentioned, students' estimates of the ratio of the area of the circle to the area of the radius square were all between 3.10 and 3.20.

By using circles of other sizes, students can also be convinced that the ratio between the area of the circle and the area of the radius square is the same for circles of any size. At this point, some students will notice that this value of 3.1 is the same as the ratio of the circumference to the diameter and may guess that this fact is not a coincidence. The next part of the activity helps students see why the same constant, π, appears in the formulas for both the circumference and the area of the circle.

Activity 2: The Relation to π in the Formula of the Circumference

Students need to recall that the ratio of circumference to diameter is approximately 3.1. The exact value of the ratio is called π, and its first digits are 3.14, which for most practical purposes gives enough accuracy. Many calculators have a key for π in the event that more digits are needed.

Approximating the circle by regular polygons (a thought experiment)

Imagine that you have a family of regular polygons inscribed in the same circle constructed in the following way: Starting with a regular hexagon (see **fig. 5a**), the next polygon will have twelve sides. Six of the vertexes will be common with the hexagon; the additional vertexes will be the midpoints of the arcs (see **fig. 5b**). In the same way, each successive term of the family of polygons has twice as many sides. The more sides contained in the regular polygon, the closer the perimeter of the polygon is to the circumference of the circle.

Furthermore, by using a polygon with a large enough number of sides, we can make the difference between the perimeter of the polygon and the circumference as small as we want. The areas of the regular polygons, then, offer an increasingly close approximation to the area of the circle. The difference between the area of the circle and the area of one of the polygons can also be made as small as we want by choosing a polygon with a sufficiently large number of sides.

The area of the regular polygon can be computed by multiplying the perimeter by the height of one of the triangles forming the regular polygon (see **fig. 6**) and dividing by 2. This formula can be proved in several ways. One is to imagine all the triangles laid out side by side (see **fig. 7**). The total area of the polygon is the sum of the areas of the triangles. One method to obtain the total area is to compute the area of each triangle by multiplying the base times the height, then dividing by 2, and adding the areas. Alternatively, we can add all the bases first, which gives us the perimeter; then multiply by the height; and divide by 2. As the number of sides on the polygon increases, the sum of the bases will be very close to the circumference of the circle ($2\pi r$), and the height of the triangle will be very close to the radius (r). Therefore, the area of the polygon will be close to

$$\frac{\text{circumference} \times \text{radius}}{2}.$$

Because the area of the circle and that of the polygon can be made as close to each other as we want, we can find the area of the circle by this calculation:

$$\frac{\text{circumference} \times \text{radius}}{2} = \frac{\text{diameter} \times \pi \times \text{radius}}{2} = \frac{2 \times \text{radius} \times \pi \times \text{radius}}{2} = \pi \times \text{radius}^2$$

We can also arrange the triangles that form the regular polygon into a parallelogram (see **fig. 8**). Its base will be close to half of the circumference, or $1/2 \times d \times \pi = 1/2 \times 2 \times r \times \pi$, that is, $r \times \pi$, and its height will be close to the radius of the circle. The area of the parallelogram will, therefore, be close to πr^2. As the number of sides of the regular polygon increases, the height of the corresponding parallelogram gets closer to the radius of the circle, and its base gets closer to πr. The area of the circle is given by $\pi r \times r = \pi r^2$.

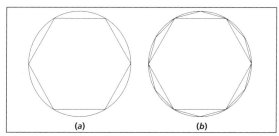

Fig. 5. Regular polygons that approximate a circle

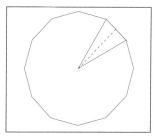

Fig. 6. A triangle with a base that is one side of the polygon

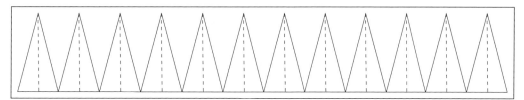

Fig. 7. The polygon is broken into triangles.

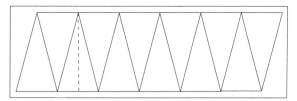

Fig. 8. The polygon rearranged into a parallelogram

Activity 3: Approximating the Area of the Circle Using Parallelograms

Figure 9 shows a circle of radius 5 units. Its circumference can be computed using the formula $2 \times r \times \pi$; in this example, the circumference of the circle is $2 \times 5 \times 3.14 = 31.4$ units. Imagine that you cut out the circle into sixteen sections and rearranged them to form a shape that resembles a parallelogram, as shown in **figure 10**. The area of the circle is the same as the area of this shape. To compute the area of this shape, we will use the fact that it resembles a parallelogram and refer to it as a parallelogram for our purposes, although its "base" is not quite a straight line. We will use the formula for the area of a parallelogram, area = base × height. The length of the base of this parallelogram is half the circumference of the original circle because half of the sections point down and the other half point up. Therefore, the length of the base is close to 5π. If you measure along the base on a straight line, you will find that the length is about 15.7 units. (Note: The original article used measurements in centimeters for this activity. We changed *centimeters* to *units* to avoid confusion in measuring **figures 9** and **10**, the radius and length of which, respectively, as they appear here, are much less than 5 cm and 15.7 cm, respectively.) The "height" of the parallelogram is close to the length of the radius of the original circle, that is, 5. The area of this parallelogram will be close to the length of the base times the height, that is, $5 \times 5\pi = 25\pi$. Notice that 25 is the value of the radius squared. Because the area of the parallelogram is equal to the area of the circle, we can compute the area of the circle by squaring the radius and multiplying by π. The ratio of the area of the circle to the area of the radius squared, then, is precisely π. The fact that in our first activity, we obtained 3.1 for the ratio of the area of the circle to the area of the radius square, the same value as the ratio of the circumference to the diameter, was not just a coincidence.

Instead of cutting the circle into sixteen parts, suppose that we cut it into more sections, say, thirty-six, and rearranged the sections as before; the new shape will resemble a parallelogram even more (see **fig. 11**). The length of the base of this new parallelogram is half the circumference, that is, $5 \times \pi$, and it is even closer to being a straight line, and the height of the parallelogram is even closer to the radius, that is, 5. We can conclude that the area of the circle is given by 25π, that is, $5^2\pi$.

We can imagine the same process with circles of different radii. If the radius of the circle is 4, the circumference would be $2 \times 4 \times \pi$; half the circumference would be $4 \times \pi$, which would be approximately the base of the parallelogram. The height of the parallelogram would be approximately 4; therefore, its area would be $4 \times 4 \times \pi$, or $4^2\pi$. In general, if the circle has a radius of length r, its circumference will be $2r\pi$. Half the circumference will be $r\pi$. If we cut the circle into thin slices and rearrange them to form a parallelogram, the length of its base will be $r\pi$ and its height will be close to r. Its area, therefore, will be close to $r^2\pi$. The ratio of the area of the circle to the radius squared, $\pi r^2/r^2$, is precisely π.

The two methods discussed in the second part of this article are closely related (see **fig. 12**). Some students may prefer working with real parallelograms that offer closer approximations to the area of the circle.

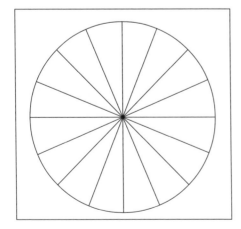

Fig. 9. A circle cut into sixteen slices

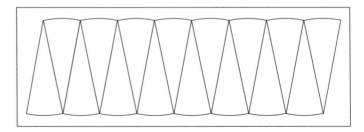

Fig. 10. The slices of the circle rearranged

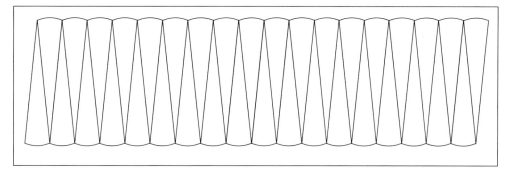

Fig. 11. A better approximation to a parallelogram of height *r*

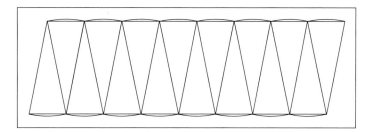

Fig. 12. A real parallelogram and the circle rearranged

Others may prefer working with families of shapes, all of which have the same area as the circle and more closely resemble a real parallelogram.

Concluding Remarks

According to van Hiele (1999), students progress through levels of geometric thinking. Learning opportunities and guidance from the teacher will help them make the transition from one level to the next. In the middle grades, a particularly important transition is from the level of development, in which students rely heavily on empirical verification, to a level at which deductive and more abstract thinking plays an increasingly important role. Our approach to mathematics, although still based on concrete and visual representations, should, therefore, gradually rely less on empirical measurement and more on thought experiments and convincing arguments. By allowing students to explore the topic of the area of the circle, first through an empirical approach and, later, through a more deductive one, we hope to help students in the middle grades make that important transition.

References

Lappan, Glenda, James T. Fey, William M. Fitzgerald, Susan N. Friel, and Elizabeth D. Phillips. *Covering and Surrounding*. Connected Mathematics—Geometry. Menlo Park, Calif.: Dale Seymour Publications, 1998.

van Hiele, Pierre M. "Developing Geometric Thinking through Activities That Begin with Play." *Teaching Children Mathematics* 5 (February 1999): 310–16.

Appendix 1

Activity 1: The Ratio of the Area of a Circle to the Radius Square

Materials

The squares on this page are radius squares of the given circle. Color each square with a different color. Cut out the squares and the circle. Follow the instructions for Activity 1.

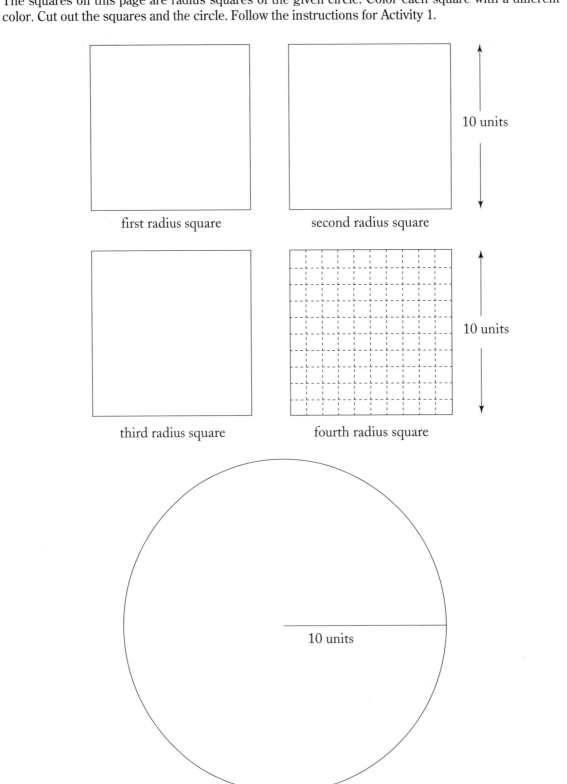

first radius square

second radius square

10 units

third radius square

fourth radius square

10 units

10 units

SECTION 8

Geometry

Introduction

Principles and Standards for School Mathematics (NCTM 2000, pp. 232–33) indicates that students should have experiences in investigating "relationships by drawing, measuring, visualizing, comparing, transforming, and classifying geometric objects." In particular, the geometry standard specifically calls for students to have opportunities to "analyze characteristics of two- and three-dimensional geometric shapes and develop mathematical arguments about geometric relationships" and "specify locations and describe spatial relationships using coordinate geometry and other representational systems," as well as using "visualization, spatial reasoning, and geometric modeling to solve problems."

An analysis of the geometry expectations for grades K–8 in 42 state, grade-level expectations documents (Smith 2010) reveals that the level of geometric reasoning expected in these state grade level expectations (GLEs) for grades K–8 falls far short of the expectations found in a sampling of states with high school geometry GLEs. This indicates that there is a gap between what students are learning in grades K–8 and what they are expected to do in high school geometry. The geometry tasks in the articles in this section give help in closing this gap and engaging students with rich tasks that help realize the kind of geometric learning called for in *Principles and Standards*. The kinds of tasks in the selected articles help students engage in mathematical thinking, reasoning, and argument in geometric contexts.

"Problem Solving with Five Easy Pieces" (Lindquist 1981) is a wonderful set of thinking tasks for students. Fundamental measurement concepts are embedded in activities with five basic shapes that are related to one another. Questions are asked that engage students in computing areas and costs, in reasoning about shapes, in creating patterns, and in logical thinking.

"Unexpected Riches from a Geoboard Quadrilateral Activity" (Britton and Stump 2001) is a good starting task to introduce students to geoboards and to explore an interesting class of geometric figures—quadrilaterals. The tasks also engage students in finding the area of the quadrilaterals they create on the geoboard. A subtheme in the activity is learning to communicate mathematical thinking and reasoning.

Similarity is an everyday word in English. However, its mathematical meaning is different and more precise than the everyday use of the word. This causes confusion for many students. "Similarity: Investigations at the Middle Grades Level" (Friedlander and Lappan 1987) includes several rich tasks that can help students both understand the mathematical meaning of similarity and connect these ideas to proportional reasoning.

"Euclidian Tools and the Creation of Euclidean Geometry" (Kastberg 2002) presents students with a hands-on opportunity to construct specified geometric figures using Euclidean tools. Even in this modern day with electronic, interactive geometry tools widely available, having a hands-on experience with Euclidean tools can enrich students' mathematical vocabulary and understanding, and their engagement with electronic tools.

References

Britton, Barbara J., and Sheryl Stump. "Unexpected Riches from a Geoboard Quadrilateral Activity." *Mathematics Teaching in the Middle School* 6 (April 2001): 490–493.

Friedlander, Alex, and Glenda Lappan. "Similarity: Investigations at the Middle Grades Level." In *Learning and Teaching Geometry, K–12*, 1987 Yearbook of the National Council of Teachers of Mathematics (NCTM), edited by Mary Montgomery Lindquist, pp. 136–43. Reston, Va.: NCTM, 1987.

Kastberg, Signe E. "Euclidean Tools and the Creation of Euclidean Geometry." *Mathematics Teaching in the Middle School* 7 (January 2002): 294–95.

Lindquist, Mary Montgomery. "Problem Solving with Five Easy Pieces." In *Activities for Junior High School and Middle School Mathematics*, edited by Kenneth E. Easterday, Loren E. Hamilton, and F. Morgan Simpson, pp. 198–201. Reston, Va.: National Council of Teachers of Mathematics, 1981.

National Council of Teachers of Mathematics (NCTM). *Principles and Standards for School Mathematics*. Reston, Va.: NCTM, 2000.

Smith, John P., ed. *Variability Is the Rule: A Companion Analysis of K–8 State Mathematics Standards*. Greenwich, Conn.: Information Age Publishing, 2010.

Problem Solving with Five Easy Pieces

Mary Montgomery Lindquist

MANY OF the best problem-solving situations in primary schools come from everyday situations: "How many more chairs will we need if we are having five visitors and two children are absent?" "How many cookies will we need if everyone has two?" However, these situations do not always arise at the appropriate time, nor do we always have time to take advantage of them when such situations do arise. There is a need for a set of problems that can be used at any time, and the problems selected for this article are of this type. They require a minimum amount of computation but, often, a maximum amount of thinking.

All the problems use a set of geometric pieces. The problems involve not only geometry, including area, but also logic, combinations, division, and money. None of these topics is dealt with formally; all are presented in the form of a puzzle or problem.

The pattern for the five easy pieces is shown in **figure 1**. There are four *A*s, four *E*s, one *I*, two *O*s, and one *U*, or twelve pieces altogether. The problems are written for yellow and blue pieces. If you are making classroom sets, make a duplicating master and run off copies on yellow and blue construction paper. If you want more durable sets, use heavy tagboard. You might also want to make and use only one complete yellow and one complete blue set with a class.

The problems can be put on four-by-six-inch index cards from which you can make up sets suitable for your children. Or you may wish to use the problems in other ways—oral directions to the children or a problem each week posted on the board. The pieces that are needed for each problem are indicated; "one complete set" refers to either one yellow or one blue set. The answers to the problems are included.

As you and the children work with these activities, you will see other problems or questions. For younger children, you may want to make more of the problems they find within reach (probably the simpler puzzles, patterns, and cost cards), and for older children you will want to extend the problems.

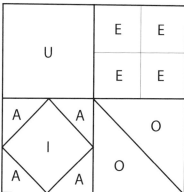

Fig. 1.

Basic Relationships

In these three sets of problems, the children are asked to investigate the area relationships among the pieces. Doing these problems, especially those in Basics 1, should help the children do the later logic and cost problems.

In Basics 1, most children will have no difficulty seeing that two *A*s cover an *E*; more children will have trouble seeing that four *A*s cover an *I* as well as an *O*. There are not enough *A*s to completely make a *U*, but with a little ingenuity, children should be able to see that it takes eight *A*s. Notice how the children solve the problems. Do any cover as much as they can with *A*s and see that half of *U* is covered? Do any of the children use *E*s to help solve the problem? Do any use *O* to help?

Basics 1

Take: One complete set

How many *A*s does it take to cover an *E*? *I*? *O*? *U*?

Answers: *E*, 2; *I*, 4; *O*, 4; *U*, 8

Since the *E*s will not completely cover *I* or *O*, the problems in Basic 2 are more difficult than those in Basics 1. The children will either have to imagine cutting up piece *E* or use the relationship they found in Basics 1—since two *A*s cover an *E*, and four *A*s cover an *I*, it would take two *E*s (if they were cut) to cover an *I*.

Basics 2

Take: One complete set

How many *E*s does it take to cover an *I*? *O*? *U*?

Hint: You may have to pretend to cut piece *E*. Use *A* to help you.

Answers: *I*, 2; *O*, 2; *U*, 4

The problems in Basics 3 reinforce the relationship that *I* and *O* are the same in area, and *U* is twice as large as *I* and twice as large as *O*.

Basics 3

Take: One complete set

1. If you could cut up piece *I*, would it cover piece *O*?
2. How many *O*s does it take to cover *U*?
3. How many *I*s (pretend that you can cut an *I*) does it take to cover *U*?

Answers: 1, yes; 2, 2; 3, 2

Puzzles

Do not expect all children to come up with all the variations on Puzzles 1. As the children find them, you may want to put the possible arrangements on the bulletin board.

Puzzles 1

Take: One complete set

How many different ways can you make a copy of the square *U*?

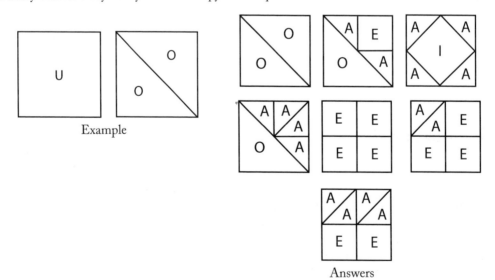

Example

Answers

Other arrangements of the pieces are possible in some of these squares.

Only one solution for Puzzles 2 is given here; other solutions are possible. You may vary this puzzle by asking the children to make one triangle, one rectangle, or one parallelogram.

Puzzles 2

Take: One complete set

    Take all the pieces. Can you make one large square?

       Answer:

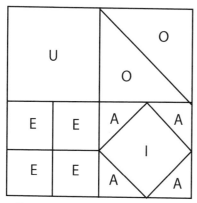

One solution. Others are possible.

    Let children experiment with Puzzles 3 through 6 and make up other puzzles. For young children, put only one question on a card. Be sure children understand that in all these puzzles, when two pieces are fit together, sides of equal length must be matched. For example:

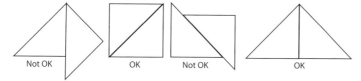

Puzzles 3

Take: Two *A*s

       1. Can you make a triangle?

       2. Can you make a square?

       3. Can you make a four-sided figure that is not a square?

       Answers:

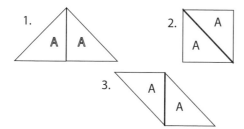

Puzzles 4

Take: Three *A*s

       1. Can you make a four-sided figure?

       2. Can you make a five-sided figure?

Answers:

1.

2.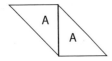

Puzzles 5

Take: Four *A*s

1. Can you make a triangle?

2. Can you make a square?

3. Can you make a rectangle that is not a square?

4. Can you make a four-sided figure that is not a rectangle?

5. Can you make a five-sided figure?

6. Can you make a six-sided figure?

Answers:

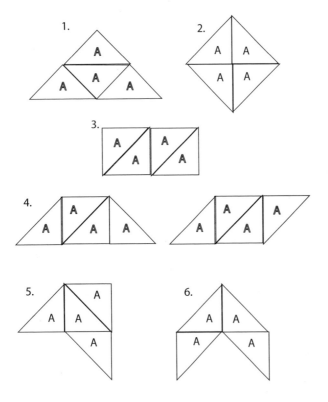

Puzzles 6

Take: Four *E*s

     1. Can you make a four-sided figure?

     2. Can you make a five-sided figure?

     3. Can you make a six-sided figure?

     4. Can you make an eight-sided figure?

     Answers:

1. 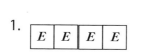   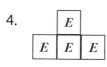   3.

2. not possible

4.

Patterns

In the pattern-making problems, children may come up with answers different from those given. Ask children to explain their patterns—their patterns, though different, may be legitimate. Also ask the children who come up with the given solutions to explain the patterns—they may be seeing a pattern in a different way.

Patterns 1

Take: Yellow and blue *A*s and *E*s

Put in a line:

     1. yellow *A*, yellow *A*, blue *A*, yellow *E*.

What would be the next two pieces?

     2. yellow *A*, blue *E*, blue *A*, blue *E*.

What would be the next two pieces?

     3. yellow *A*, yellow *A*, yellow *E*, blue *A*.

What would be the next two pieces?

     Possible solutions:

     1. yellow *E*, blue *E*; 2. *A*, *E* (either color); 3. blue *A*, blue *E*.

As with the puzzles, the rule of putting pieces together by matching sides of equal length must be followed. The restriction that one side of one piece must be placed on a given line limits the endless possibilities of "tipping." The further restrictions that the patterns must be above or, if problems are written on the cards, "on the card," is optional. Either eliminates the possibility of flipping the pieces over the line—getting a mirror image, in other words. Feel free to omit these restrictions, but if you do, you can expect many other possible results.

Patterns 2

Take: Two blue *A*s and two yellow *A*s

Using two pieces how many different figures can you make? (One triangle must be on the line, and the figure should be above the line.)

Example:

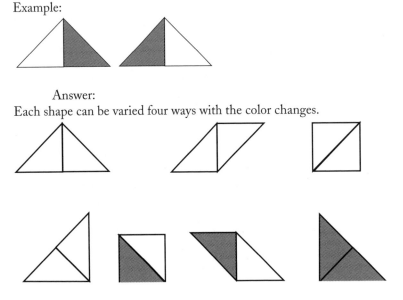

Answer:
Each shape can be varied four ways with the color changes.

Patterns 3

Take: Three yellow *E*s and three blue *E*s

Using three pieces, how many different patterns can you make? (One square must be on the line and the pattern should be above the line.)

Example:

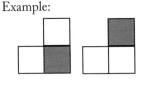

There are eight color variations of this shape.

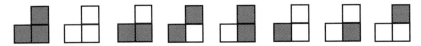

There are five other shapes. Each can be varied eight ways with color.

Patterns 4

Take: Four yellow *A*s and four blue *A*s

Take any four pieces and make a shape. How many variations of your shape can you make by changing colors?

Answer: Suppose the shape is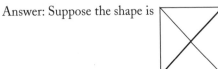

There are sixteen color variations.

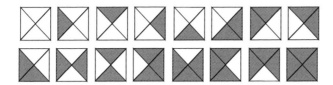

Some children may realize that once they specify a shape in Patterns 2, there are four ways to vary the color. Patterns 4 is a variation of the ideas begun in Patterns 2 and 3. If there are children who see that there are sixteen ways to vary the colors, you may want to look at Patterns 2, 3, and 4 with them. There are four ways to vary the colors with two pieces, eight ways with three pieces, and sixteen ways with four pieces. What would you expect with five pieces?

Do not expect many children at this level to see the numerical pattern. You can be satisfied if they begin by moving the pieces to see the variety of possibilities. You can help those children who are ready to organize their work by asking questions like the following: How many variations can you make if no triangles are blue? If only one triangle is blue? If two triangles are blue? If three triangles are blue? If four triangles are blue?

Logic

The logic cards progress in difficulty from 1 to 6. It may help some children to write the new names for the pieces on slips of paper so they can move the names around to match the clues.

Logic 1

Take: One *E*, one *I*, one *U*

These three squares renamed themselves—Ali, Bet, and Tim.

Ali said, "I'm bigger than Tim."

Bet said, "I'm bigger than Ali."

Who's who?

Answers: Tim is *E*, Ali is *I*, Bet is *U*.

Logic 2

Take: One *A*, one *E*, one *O*

These three pieces renamed themselves—Bill, Jill, and Lil.

Bill said, "I'm twice as large as Jill."

Jill said, "I'm the same shape as Lil."

Who's who?

Answers: Jill is *A*, Bill is *E*, Lil is *O*.

Logic 3

Take: One *A*, one *E*, one *O*, one *U*

The four pieces renamed themselves—Mary, Larry, Harry, and Cary.

Mary said, "I'm a fourth as large as Harry."

Larry said, "I'm bigger than Harry."

Who's who?

Answers: Mary is *A*, Cary is *E*, Harry is *O*, Larry is *U*.

Logic 4

Take: One *A*, one *I*, one *O*, one *U*

These four pieces renamed themselves—Floe, Joe, Moe, and Woe.

Joe said, "I'm twice as large as Moe."

Floe said, "I'm the same shape as Woe."

Woe said, "I'm smaller than Moe."

Who's who?

> Answers: Woe is *A*, Moe is *I*, Floe is *O*, and Joe is *U*.

Logic 5

Take: One *A*, one *E*, one *I*, one *O*, one *U*

These five pieces renamed themselves—Dan, Nan, Stan, Ann, and Fran.

Fran said, "I'm the same size as Dan, but larger than Stan."

Dan said, "I'm larger than Nan, but smaller than Ann."

Nan said, "I'm smaller than Fran, but larger than Stan."

Fran said, "I'm the same shape as Nan."

Who's who?

> Answers: *A* is Stan, *E* is Nan, *I* is Fran, *O* is Dan, *U* is Ann.

Logic 6

Take: One *A*, one *E*, one *I*, one *O*, one *U*

These five pieces renamed themselves—Al, Cal, Mal, Pal, and Sal.

Pal said, "I'm twice as large as Sal."

Mal said, "I'm four times as large as Al, and the same shape."

Pal said, "I'm larger than Mal."

Who's who?

> Answers: *A* is Al, *E* is Cal, *I* is Sal, *O* is Mal, *U* is Pal.

Areas

Instead of having the children cover the figures with other pieces to find the area of the figures, they are given the results of someone's covering. The children then have to determine what units were used. If the children enjoy this challenge, make up some larger shapes that permit more possibilities.

Areas 1

Take: One complete set

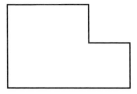

1. Bob covered this figure with pieces. He took 4 of one kind and 3 of another. What pieces did he use?
2. Karen covered this with pieces. She took 2 of one kind and 2 of another. What pieces did she use?

> Answers: 1. Four *A*s and three *E*s; 2. Two *O*s and two *A*s

Areas 2

Take: One complete set

1. Hal covered this rectangle with pieces. He took 4 of one kind, 1 of another, and 1 of another. What pieces did he use?
2. Sue covered this with pieces. She took 2 of one kind, 2 of another, and 1 of another. What pieces did she use?

Answers: 1. One *O*, one *I*, four *A*s; 2. Two *O*s, two *A*s, one *E*

Costs

Costs 1 depends on the children seeing the basic area relationships between the pieces. It may help younger children to work with pennies (or chips).

Costs 1

Take: One complete set

1.   If *U* costs 12¢, how much does *E* cost? *A* cost?

2.   If *I* costs 8¢, how much does *E* cost? *U* cost?

Answers: 1. 3¢, 1 1/2¢; 2. 4¢, 16¢

It may help in question 2 of Costs 2 to have children paper clip the price on each of the four pieces.

Costs 2

Take: One *A*, one *E*, one *O*, and one *U*

1. If *A* costs 1¢, how much would each of the other pieces cost?

2. Using just these 4 pieces, how would you pay a bill for each of the following?

1¢, 2¢, 3¢, 4¢, 5¢, 6¢, 7¢, 8¢, 9¢, 10¢, 11¢, 12¢, 13¢, 14¢, 15¢

Answers:

1. *E*, 2¢; *O*, 4¢; *U*, 8¢

2. 1¢, *A*; 2¢, *E*; 3¢, *A* and *E*; 4¢, *O*; 5¢, *O* and *A*; 6¢, *O* and *E*; 7¢, *O*, *A*, and *E*; 8¢, *U*; 9¢, *U* and *A*; 10¢, *U* and *E*; 11¢, *U*, *E*, and *A*; 12¢, *U* and *O*; 13¢, *U*, *O*, and *A*; 14¢, *U*, *O*, and *E*; 15¢, *U*, *O*, *E*, and *A*.

Costs 3 is similar to the puzzles, and the rule of fitting sides together applies. Again, for younger children you may want to separate the questions, one question to a card. For children who find these problems easy, change the price of *A* to 3¢, or make up cost variations for Puzzles 3 through 7.

Costs 3

Take: Four *A*s. Each *A* costs 1¢.

1. Can you make a four-sided figure that costs 3¢?

2. Can you make a three-sided figure that costs 4¢?

3. Can you make a five-sided figure that costs 3¢?

4. Can you make a five-sided figure that costs 4¢?

Answers:

On Costs 4, the children have to focus on both the total number of pieces and the total cost.

Costs 4

Take: One complete set

1. If *A* costs 1¢, what would each of the other pieces cost?

2. Can you sell the pieces to two people so that each person get the same number of pieces and each person would have to pay the same amount?

   Answers:

1. *E* costs 2¢, *I* costs 4¢, *O* costs 4¢, and *U* costs 8¢.

2. First person: one *U*, three *E*s, two *A*s

   Second person: two *O*s, one *I*, one *E*, two *A*s

   (Each person gets six pieces that cost 16¢.)

The ideas for many of the problems that have been described here come from Developing Mathematical Processes (DMP). Acknowledgement is due the many writers of DMP who inspired these problems and the many teachers and children who have tried similar problems.

Unexpected Riches from a Geoboard Quadrilateral Activity

Barbara J. Britton
Sheryl L. Stump

EXPLORING the simple quadrilaterals in a three-peg-by-three-peg section of a geoboard has proved to be a very stimulating activity in elementary mathematics content and methods classes. In the April 1998 issue of *Mathematics Teacher*, Kennedy and McDowell described a wonderful activity that focused on counting quadrilaterals on geoboards of various sizes. Our focus in this article is on the properties of quadrilaterals. The activity that we describe is often used as an introduction to a unit on geometry. Tom Lewis, who is with the Moline Public Schools in Illinois, also used these activities in his fifth-grade classroom and reports similar results.

Beginning the Activity

The classroom activity begins with students working in groups to find all the quadrilaterals that they can on the three-peg-by-three-peg geoboard section. They keep track of their figures on dot paper. The groups discuss the meaning of *different* quadrilaterals. Most groups understand that *different* means *noncongruent* and launch into the activity. Other groups are puzzled. Typically, these students ask the instructor whether two squares of different sizes are considered different, or whether they are the same because they are the same shape. The instructor asks whether the students would consider the squares to be the same. The group usually says no. Through discussion, the students decide that the shapes are different if they do not fit exactly on top of each other. The students begin to identify figures related by reflections, rotations, and translations as congruent, although they may not use that terminology.

When all groups think that they have found all the quadrilaterals, the class comes together to share results. The geoboards themselves can be propped up in the chalk tray for this discussion, or students can be asked to transfer their figures to large sheets of paper with three-by-three dot grids to allow the figures to be displayed and viewed easily. One by one, each group selects a figure and presents it to the class. The selected figure must be different from any other shapes that have already been presented. Occasionally, a congruent figure is presented, leading to a whole-class discussion of rotations, reflections, and translations. The names and properties of the various shapes are discussed as the shapes are presented.

When all the groups have presented their quadrilaterals, the instructor notes whether all sixteen have been found, usually stating how many are left, and the groups attack the problem of finding the missing shapes. One semester, none of the groups considered the possibility of outlining concave quadrilaterals. When one of the students discovered this possibility, the "Aha!" could be heard throughout the room. All the remaining concave quadrilaterals were quickly found.

One of the most interesting discussions stemming from this activity arose when a student claimed that the shape shown in **figure 1** was a quadrilateral. The instructor asked the class to decide whether the figure was, in fact, a quadrilateral. The class decided that it was not. The students realized that although the pegs had diameter, conceptually they were meant to be points and the rubber bands were meant to be lines. Hence, being on one side or the other of a peg did not mean that the rubber band was actually passing through a different point.

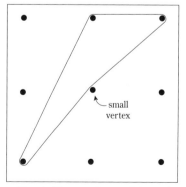

Fig. 1. The students debated whether this shape qualified as a quadrilateral.

Sorting the Quadrilaterals

After the students have found and discussed all the quadrilaterals, the instructor leads the class in a sorting activity. By moving the geoboards or large sheets of dot paper, the instructor sorts the sixteen quadrilaterals into two groups and tells the class that *all* the quadrilaterals in one group have a property that is shared by *none* of the quadrilaterals in the other group. The students then try to identify the property. Some examples of properties that have been used include having one pair of parallel sides, two pairs of parallel sides, a right

angle, four right angles, an obtuse angle, a convex or nonconvex shape, and line symmetry. The sorting activity gives students an opportunity to communicate their mathematical thinking out loud. Some students struggle to find the language to describe the geometric properties that they see. The instructor may help the students connect their ideas with formal mathematical terminology. If time permits, individual students may come to the chalkboard to demonstrate different methods of sorting. The notion of sorting itself is a challenge for some students.

For homework, the students receive a sheet containing the sixteen quadrilaterals drawn on three-by-three dot grids (see **fig. 2**). Students cut apart the set of sixteen quadrilaterals and sort the shapes by pasting them in two groups onto a sheet of paper. The students also write explanations of the properties used in their methods of sorting. Students must use a property that has not previously been discussed in the whole-class sorting activity.

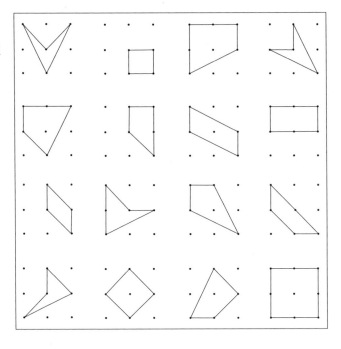

Fig. 2. Homework assignment for sorting quadrilaterals

Determining the Areas of the Quadrilaterals

As a further extension of the activity, students are asked to find the areas of the quadrilaterals. This activity can be done in groups in class or as a homework assignment. After the students have found the areas, they share their answers and methods with the class. The variety of methods is astonishing. Students discuss numerous geometry concepts as they make convincing arguments that their methods are sound. Many students use a cut-and-paste approach (see **fig. 3**). They see that one part of the figure fits into an uncovered part of another square and must convince the rest of the class that the pieces are congruent. Their arguments lead to a review of many geometric principles about congruent triangles because the cut pieces are usually triangular. Occasionally, a student will say that he or she actually cut the figures into pieces and thus the student knows that the pieces fit.

Another approach to finding the area of these quadrilaterals is illustrated in the statement "That part looked like one-fourth and that part looked like one-half" (see **fig. 4**). Such statements are usually correct, but the reasoning behind them is not intuitively obvious. Teachers can introduce a problem-solving opportunity by having students prove that the section of the shape believed to be one-fourth or one-half or one, in some instances, does in fact have that area measure.

Of course, some students use area formulas to determine areas. Other approaches that we have seen include determining the area outside the figures and subtracting that value from 4, thinking of triangles as half-rectangles on the geoboard, and using previously found areas to aid in finding new ones. No doubt, students can come up with other strategies, as well. Every now and then, students surprise us with new strategies.

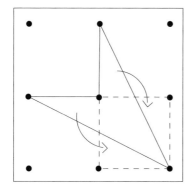

Fig. 3. Cut-and-paste method for finding the area of a quadrilateral

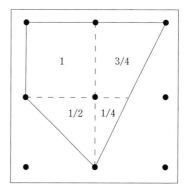

Fig. 4. Another student method for finding the area of a quadrilateral

Conclusion

What started out as an activity to introduce students to the geoboard turned out to be surprisingly rich. A recognition of shapes and their attributes; concepts of point and line, reflection, rotation, and translation; congruent figures; geometric proof; and area concepts are all represented in one problem. This activity also clearly shows the students that problems can be solved in a variety of ways.

Reference

Kennedy, Joe, and Eric McDowell. "Geoboard Quadrilaterals." *Mathematics Teacher* 91 (April 1998): 288–90.

Similarity: Investigations at the Middle Grades Level

Alex Friedlander and Glenda Lappan

The famous Dutch mathematician Hans Freudenthal describes geometry as experience with, and interpretation of, "the space in which the child lives, breathes, and moves" (1973, p. 403). From this perspective we can think of children beginning to learn geometry as soon as they are able to see, feel, and move in the space they occupy. As children grow, they begin to perceive characteristics of the objects in that space, such as shape, size, position, motion, order, and growth. Our task as teachers of geometry is to provide the kinds of experiences for students that will enhance their understanding of the space about them.

Teaching the concept of geometrical similarity will be used in this article as an example of teaching geometry through informal, exploratory activities that employ concrete materials. Most of the ideas described here are taken from an instructional unit developed by the NSF-funded Middle Grades Mathematics Project (Lappan et al. 1986).

Why Teach Similarity?

We chose this topic to illustrate some principles in teaching geometry at the middle grades level, since the acquisition of the concept of similarity is important to the development of children's geometrical understanding of their environment and of proportional reasoning. Phenomena that require familiarity with enlargement, scale factor, projection, area growth, indirect measurement, and other similarity-related concepts are frequently encountered by children in their immediate environment and in their studies of natural and social sciences. Fuson points out the need for instruction in similarity (1978, p. 259):

> Similarity ideas are included in many parts of the school curriculum. Some models for rational number concepts are based on similarity; thus, part of students' difficulty with rationals may stem from problems with similarity ideas. Ratio and proportion are part of the school curriculum from at least the seventh grade on, and they present many difficulties to the student. Standardized tests include many proportion word problems. Verbal analogies (*a:b::c:d*) form major parts of many intelligence tests. Similar geometric shapes would seem to provide a helpful mental image for other types of proportion analogy situations.

Identifying Similar Shapes

Two informal tests for similarity can be explored to build basic notions of similarity: (1) the overhead projection test and (2) the diagonal test.

Overhead projection test

Children will quickly recognize that the shadow of a shape placed on the overhead projector is similar to the original figure.

Therefore, whenever we have to consider whether two cut-out shapes are similar (i.e., one is the enlarged version of the other), we place the small figure on the projector and attach the larger one to the screen; by moving the projector back and forth, we attempt to match the larger figure with the projected shadow. Even though the projector can always be moved so that at least one edge of the figure image matches an edge of the figure attached to the screen, it is only when both entire figures can be made to match that they are similar. Several activities make use of this overhead projection strategy for determining similarity.

1. Have the children apply the overhead projection test to different pairs of rectangles.

2. Have them create a sequence of rectangles by folding a sheet of paper in half crosswise and cutting it on the fold line; repeat this step six to seven times, each time with one of the newly created rectangles (**fig. 1**). Then have them categorize the resulting rectangles into groups of similar rectangles using the overhead projector.

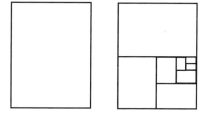

Fig. 1. Creating a sequence of rectangles

1. Use the projection test for other than rectangular shapes.

2. Use the projection test for different pairs of circles. Ask the students what they can conclude.

Diagonal Test

Children can be led to discover that the diagonals of similar rectangles fall in a straight line when the rectangles are nested. This gives a quick visual way of determining whether two rectangles are similar.

Have the children apply the diagonal test to the collection of rectangles from part 2 of the overhead projector activities:

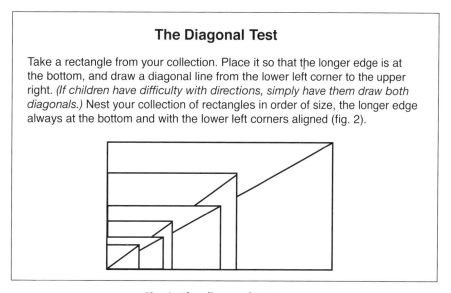

Fig. 2. The diagonal test

In part 2 of the overhead projector activities, the children will already have decided that the rectangles belong to two families of similar rectangles. Here they will see that the diagonals of each family align.

Creating similar shapes

Intuitive notions about similarity can be strengthened and expanded by introducing children to some techniques that enable them actually to *create* similar shapes. Two of these techniques are based on the principle of point projection: (1) the variable tension proportional divider (VTPD) and (2) the constant tension proportional divider (CTPD).

Variable tension proportional divider

This is an intriguing way to enlarge a figure that gives reasonable results in the hands of most children. The final figures are not perfectly accurate, but they do clear convey the intuitive "same shape" notion of similarity. The VTPD allows children to make enlargements of irregular figures, figures with curved edges, or simple pictures from magazines or cartoons.

1. Have them build a VTPD by knotting together two identical rubber bands (#18's work well). Use masking tape to attach a large sheet of paper to the desk. Choose an anchor point to the left of the figure to be enlarged so that the knot will be taut on all parts of the figure to be enlarged.

2. Have them put one end of the rubber band at the anchor point and the pencil at the other end. Holding the anchor end firmly, they move the pencil as the knot traces the figure. They must keep their eyes on the knot while the pencil hand does the drawing. See **figure 3**.

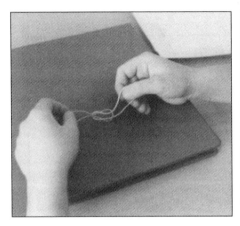

Fig. 3. Preparing and working with a VTPD

3. Ask what happens if you change the anchor point to another place.

4. Ask what happens if you knot three rubber bands in a row and let the first knot trace the figure.

Constant tension proportional divider

Using paper strips (which have a "constant tension"), children can very precisely enlarge simple geometric figures composed of straight edges. (The technique is cumbersome for figures that have curved edges.) We shall illustrate making an enlargement that has linear dimensions double those of an original triangle *ABC*. (For young children, you may need to present this activity in somewhat simpler terms than those used here.)

1. Cut out several stiff paper strips about a half-inch wide and eleven inches long. Mark an anchor point *P* for the enlargement (**fig. 4a**). Position the paper strip with one of its ends at vertex *A* and with its edge along the line from the anchor point to vertex *A*. Mark the strip at the anchor point (**fig. 4b**). Slide the strip along the line from *P* to *A* until the mark that was at *P* is at *A*. Mark your paper at *A′*, which is now at the end of the strip (**fig. 4c**). This is the position of the vertex of the new triangle. Notice that *A′* is twice as far from *P* as *A* is from *P*.

2. Repeat this process with *B* (i.e., find a point *B′* twice as far from *P* as *B* is from *P*) and then with *C* (**fig. 4d**).

3. What happens if you move the anchor point to another place?

4. What happens if you mark *A′*, *B′,* and *C′* three times as far from the anchor point?

5. What happens if you mark *A′*, *B′,* and *C′* only one-half as far away from *P* as *A*, *B*, and *C* are? (Fold the paper strip to find half distances.)

Area Growth

The principle of area growth presents many cognitive difficulties to children of this age and even to high school students and adults. The area growth of similar shapes requires the recognition of the (somewhat

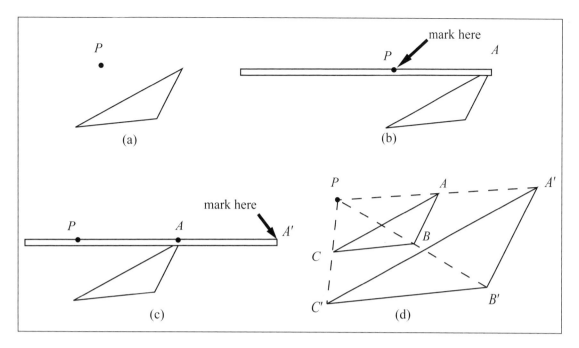

Fig. 4. Projecting with a CTPD

counterintuitive) fact that enlargement of a figure by a linear scale factor of n will increase its area by a factor of n^2. For example, if a rectangle 3 cm by 4 cm is enlarged into a rectangle 9 cm by 12 cm, the linear scale factor is 3 but the new area is 9 times as large as the original area.

Two activities have been designed to present the area relationship in a visual manner: "rep-tiles" and everyday applications.

Rep-tiles

Exploring figures that replicate in specific ways gives an informal setting for beginning notions about how area grows. The following activity is based on an idea from Martin Gardner's book *The Unexpected Hanging* (1969; chap. 19, "Rep-tiles: Replicating Figures on the Plane").

Through this exploration, children see examples of an area growth factor of 4 (or 9) in a figure that has dimensions twice (or three times) the original.

Everyday applications

The principle of area growth is frequently encountered in everyday situations, such as predicting the cost of painting a given area or the amount of material needed to build a reduced or enlarged version of a given shape. The following two problems are examples of such situations:

1. It costs $30 for paint to cover a blackboard at a school. How much would it cost for paint to cover a board half that long and half that wide?

2. A package of rectangular paper sheets weighs 3 lb. What will be the weight of a package (same number of sheets and same quality of paper) with sheets twice as long and twice as wide?

The quantities involved in these situations depend on area. However, the questions require an understanding of area growth relationships and not just area measurements.

We suggest that initially the problems be posed in the same direct and abstract way as presented here. Usually the children will make the mistake of using the slide scale factor in their answer (e.g., $15 for paint for the smaller blackboard).

Next, children are asked to present the corresponding reduction or enlargement in a concrete way by actually cutting out paper rectangles. For example, by cutting out rectangles they should be able to show the smaller board and see that it is one-fourth, not one-half, of the larger board in area.

At this point, students should become aware of a discrepancy between the answer they have given and their own concrete representation of the problem. If this does not occur, the teacher must ask more leading questions to make it happen.

---

1. Cut out four exact copies of each of these shapes (**fig. 5**).

Fig. 5. Rep-tiles

Try to put four figures of a kind together to form a figure that is *similar* to the original. This is called "rep-tiling" (**fig. 6**).

Fig. 6. Rep-tiling: Constructing similar figures

2. Draw a triangle and cut it out. Cut out three more copies of your triangle. Can you rep-tile with your four triangles? Can a rep-tile be formed from any triangle?

3. What about rectangles? Do they always rep-tile?

4. In a rep-tile made of four small figures, how does an edge of the rep-tile compare to an edge of the small figure?

5. Cut out nine copies of a triangle. Put all nine together to form a rep-tile. Remember that the big triangle must be similar to the original small triangle. Measure the edges of the small and large triangle. How do they compare?

Conclusion

The activities described here provide the child a first encounter with the concept of similarity and are presented at the first two van Hiele levels of geometric understanding. In a spiral curriculum, a more systematic approach may be employed the second time around: measurements, ratios, and proportions should emphasize the numerical aspects and the general principles involved in similarity.

We believe that only with such a background does the average student have any chance to understand the Euclidean approach to similarity at the high school level or to cope with real-life situations that involve the concept of geometrical similarity.

References

Freudenthal, Hans. *Mathematics as an Educational Task.* Dordrecht, Netherlands: D. Reidel Publishing Co., 1973.

Fuson, Karen C. "Analysis of Research Needs in Projective, Affine, and Similarity Geometries, Including an Evaluation of Piaget's Results in This Area." In *Recent Research Concerning the Development of Spatial and Geometric Concepts,* edited by Richard Lesh, pp. 243–60. Columbus, Ohio: ERIC/SMEAC, 1978.

Gardner, Martin. *The Unexpected Hanging and Other Mathematical Diversions.* New York: Simon & Schuster, 1969.

Lappan, Glenda, William Fitzgerald, Elizabeth Phillips, and Mary Jean Winter. *Similarity and Equivalent Fractions.* The Middle Grades Mathematics Project Series. Menlo Park, Calif.: Addison-Wesley Publishing Co., 1986.

Euclidean Tools and the Creation of Euclidean Geometry

Signe E. Kastberg

Used by mathematicians over two thousand years ago, the compass and straightedge are still used by mathematics students today. The straightedge is similar to the ruler in that the user can draw a straight line with it, but the straightedge is not marked and cannot be used to measure things. Although many different types of compasses exist, your students probably use the modern compass. The characteristic that makes the modern compass special is tension, which allows the opening between the lead and the pointer to be fixed. By fixing the opening, the user can draw a circle of a given radius and copy a line segment.

The compass used in 300 B.C. was different from the one that we use today. It did not have the special property that the width could be fixed. Instead, between each use, the compass collapsed. This drawback made copying a line segment difficult, but the collapsible compass was still useful for drawing circles of a given radius.

Today, we call the straightedge and collapsible compass used in 300 B.C. *Euclidean tools*. This name celebrates the special role that this pair of mathematical tools played in the development of one branch of mathematics and mathematical thought, which can be traced to a Greek mathematician and mathematics teacher named Euclid.

Very little is known about Euclid. We do not even know where he was born (Boyer 1991). We do know that he was a teacher in Alexandria at a school established by Ptolemy I, a Roman ruler whose empire included what is now Alexandria, Egypt. The teachers at the school were the most learned scholars in the region, and Euclid was one of those teachers. He contributed to both culture and mathematics as a teacher and a writer. Euclid and his students compiled what they believed was the essential mathematical knowledge of the day in thirteen books titled the *Elements*.

Developed as a geometry textbook, Euclid's *Elements* is the most popular book of its type ever written. More than 1000 editions of Euclid's *Elements* are known to have existed (Bunt, Jones, and Bedient 1976). Even Abraham Lincoln studied from a copy of *Elements* as late as 1849 (Rogers 1966).

Euclid built the mathematical system that he used in the *Elements* on definitions, postulates, and common notions (Kline 1972). Euclid's *definitions* were meant to clarify and explain the terms that he used. For example, Euclid defined a line to be a "breadthless length" (Katz 1993, p. 57). This explanation helps people understand what Euclid meant when he used the term *line*.

Postulates are truths that apply only to geometry. These postulates are the bases for the *Elements* and explain the central role that the straightedge and compass played in the development of Euclid's mathematical system. Book I of Euclid's *Elements* tells the reader that only three constructions are allowed. These three constructions on which Euclid based the rest of his work were the following: (1) a straight line through two given points; (2) a line segment as part of a straight line; and (3) a circle, given a center and any distance (Retz and Keihn 1969).

The *common notions* in the *Elements* are the truths that apply to all the sciences (Kline 1972). According to Kline, one of Euclid's common notions was "If equals are added to equals, the wholes are equal" (p. 59). Definitions, postulates, and common notions need no proof; they stand as fundamental truths and serve as a common language for those studying Euclid's *Elements*. From this common language and the constructions allowed in the first three postulates, Euclid made certain claims. Once proved using the definitions, common notations, and postulates, these claims became propositions and were considered truths that could be used to support proofs of subsequent propositions.

Accordingly, Euclid claimed that he could use a straightedge and compass to construct a geometric object. Then, to prove his claim, Euclid showed how he could do so. Euclid's first claim was that he could construct an equilateral triangle on a given line segment using only a straightedge and collapsible compass. See **figure 1** for the claim and how Euclid proved it.

Euclidean tools were used to generate the geometry in Euclid's *Elements*. The postulates explain how the tools are to be used, and each of the proofs of the claims is based on a construction done with those tools. The precise drawings that could be made using Euclidean tools probably motivated many of the claims made by Euclid. For example, if you draw a circle with a compass, you might wonder what else you could draw with the compass? Could you draw a triangle? What kinds of triangles could you draw? Euclid and those mathematicians who preceded him thought about what kinds of geometric objects they could construct with the compass and straightedge. The tools themselves helped Euclid investigate and prove his claims through deductive reasoning. Without the compass and straightedge and the ideas of Euclid, the branch of mathematics that we now call Euclidean geometry might never have been created.

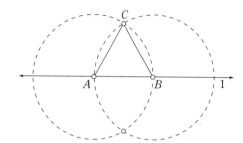

CLAIM. "On a given straight line to construct an equilateral triangle" (Kline 1972, p. 60)

PROOF. Construct two points *A* and *B* on line l. Construct a circle whose center is *A* and whose radius is *AB*. Similarly, construct a circle whose center is *B* and whose radius is *BA*. Point *C* is the point of intersection, and triangle *ABC* is equilateral. Why?

Fig. 1. Construction of an equilateral triangle

Teaching Notes

In the activities that follow, students will use Euclid's three basic constructions: (1) a straight line through two points; (2) a line segment as part of a straight line; and (3) a circle, given a center and any distance. They will need straightedges and compasses.

In the first activity, students will construct a circle with a radius of length *AB*. In the second part, they will bisect *AB*. Angle *CEB* can be proven to be a right angle using deduction, but most students can verify their guesses using protractors. However, the protractor is not a Euclidean tool, since it is a relatively modern instrument compared with the compass and straightedge. The third activity has students bisect the sides of an equilateral triangle using the construction for a perpendicular bisector. In the case of the equilateral triangle, these perpendicular bisectors are also the medians, the angle bisectors, and the altitudes of the triangle. Their intersection point *E* is four different points of concurrency (where the special lines of the triangle intersect) in one, since it is simultaneously the incenter formed by the angle bisectors, the circumcenter formed by the perpendicular bisectors, the orthocenter formed by the altitudes, and the centroid for the median.

References

Boyer, Carol B. *A History of Mathematics*. Rev. ed. New York: John Wiley & Sons, 1991.

Bunt, Lucas N. H., Phillip S. Jones, and Jack D. Bedient. *The Historical Roots of Elementary Mathematics*. New York: Dover Publications, 1976, 1988.

Katz, Victor J. *A History of Mathematics: An Introduction*. New York: HarperCollins, 1993.

Kline, Morris. *Mathematical Thought from Ancient to Modern Times*. Vol. 1. New York: Oxford University Press, 1972.

Retz, Merlyn, and Meta Darlene Keihn. "Compass and Straight Edge Constructions." In *Historical Topics for the Mathematics Classroom*, 1969 Yearbook of the National Council of Teachers of Mathematics (NCTM), pp. 192–96. Washington, D.C.: NCTM, 1969.

Roger, James T. *The Pantheon Story of Mathematics for Young People*. New York: Pantheon Books, 1966.

Student Activity Sheet   NAME_____

Use your straightedge and modern compass to construct the following objects, which were also constructed by Euclid.

1. Construct a circle with a center and a given radius.

   a) Use segment *AB* below as the given radius.

   b) To construct a circle with center *A*, put the pointer on point *A* and the lead of your pencil on point *B*. To draw a circle, apply gentle, steady pressure to the compass as you turn it.

2. Bisect segment *AB*.

   a) Bisecting a segment means to cut the segment into two equal parts. Use the circle with center *A* and radius $\overline{AB}$, and construct another circle with center *B* and radius $\overline{AB}$.

   b) Label the points where the circles cross, or intersect, as points *C* and *D*.

   c) Use the straightedge to draw a line through points *C* and *D*. This line should intersect segment *AB*. Label this point of intersection *E*.

   d) Point *E* is called the *midpoint* of $\overline{AB}$. Why?

   e) Line *CD* is *perpendicular* to $\overline{AB}$. Look at angle *CEB*. Estimate the angle measurement. How could you determine this measurement?

3. Using your knowledge gained from making the other constructions, bisect each side of equilateral triangle *ABC* below.

   a) What do you notice about the intersection of these bisectors? Call this intersection point *E*.

   b) Construct a circle with center *E* and radius $\overline{EC}$.

   c) What do you observe about this circle?

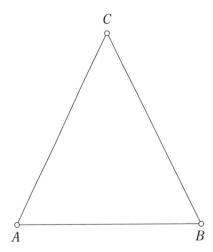

SECTION 9

Data Analysis and Probability

Introduction

Data analysis and probability have become important components of the middle school curriculum over the last two decades. This is evidenced by the inclusion of data analysis and probability in the published curriculum frameworks for mathematics from 44 states (Smith 2010), in most curricular materials targeting elementary and middle grades students, and by the composition of the National Assessment of Educational Progress (NAEP) for mathematics. Approximately 15 percent of the items on the NAEP at grade 8 between 1996 and 2003 focused on data analysis, statistics, and probability (Tarr and Shaughnessy 2007). (This is nearly double the percent of items that focus on these topics on the 1986 NAEP.)

This increased attention is due, in large measure, to recommendations by the National Council of Teachers of Mathematics (NCTM 1989, 2000) for the inclusion of data analysis and probability at all grade levels in order to help students become "informed citizens and intelligent consumers" (NCTM 2000, p. 48). More recently, the *Curriculum Focal Points* (NCTM 2006) explicitly identified data analysis as a focus of attention in grade 8, and the recent GAISE Report (Franklin et al. 2007) provided a set of recommendations regarding the teaching and learning of statistics in the pre-K–grade 12 curriculum that is intended to develop students' capacity "to make reasoned judgments, evaluate quantitative information, and value the role of statistics in everyday life" (Franklin and Garfield 2007, p. 373).

Despite the increased attention to data analysis and probability, and the steady improvement of performance on NAEP items in these content domains, students had "profound difficulties" on constructed-response items that required justification of statistical or probabilistic reasoning (Tarr and Shaughnessy 2007, p. 165). This suggests that students need more opportunities to engage in challenging mathematical tasks that go beyond the application of procedures.

The articles in this section are intended to provide teachers with tasks that are both challenging and engaging and that will enable them to:

- formulate questions that can be addressed with data and collect, organize, and display relevant data to answer them,

- select and use appropriate statistical methods to analyze data,

- develop and evaluate inferences and predictions that are based on data, and

- understand and apply basic concepts of probability (NCTM 2000, p. 48).

"Exploring Probability through an Evens-Odds Dice Game" (Wiest and Quinn 1999) is a good starting task that encourages students to make conjectures and allows students to discuss their findings and make predictions based on data. The article has suggestions for task extensions that include ties into number theory.

The tasks in "Determining Probabilities by Examining Underlying Structure" (Norton 2001) encourage students to determine whether a game is *fair* or not and, as an extension, to determine a way to make unfair games fair. The tasks also require students to assign and justify theoretical probabilities of outcomes and events. In order to complete the tasks included in this article, students need to be familiar with histograms.

The Norton (2001) article segues nicely to "Rethinking Fair Games" (Coffey and Richardson 2005), where students formulate the mathematical notion of *fairness* in games; students may find the computation of the theoretical probabilities challenging.

The simulation task mentioned in the article requires a graphing calculator with programming capabilities. Extensions of the task are also provided.

References

Coffey, David C., and Mary G. Richardson. "Rethinking Fair Games." *Mathematics Teaching in the Middle School* 10 (February 2005): 298–303.

Franklin, Christine A., and Joan B. Garfield. "The GAISE Project: Developing Statistics Education Guidelines for Grades Pre-K–12 and College Courses." In *Thinking and Reasoning with Data and Chance*, Sixty-eighth Yearbook of the National Council of Teachers of Mathematics (NCTM), edited by Gail F. Burrill, pp. 345–75. Reston, Va.: NCTM, 2006.

Franklin, Christine, Gary Kader, Denise Mewborn, Jerry Moreno, Roxy Peck, Mike Perry, and Richard Scheaffer. *Guidelines for Assessment and Instruction in Statistics Education (GAISE) Report: A Pre-K–12 Curriculum Framework.* Alexandria, Va.: American Statistical Association, 2007.

National Council of Teachers of Mathematics (NCTM). *Curriculum and Evaluation Standards for School Mathematics.* Reston, Va.: NCTM, 1989.

———. *Principles and Standards for School Mathematics.* Reston, Va.: NCTM, 2000.

———. *Curriculum Focal Points for Prekindergarten through Grade 8 Mathematics: A Quest for Coherence.* Reston, Va.: NCTM, 2006.

Norton, Robert M. "Determining Probabilities by Examining Underlying Structure." *Mathematics Teaching in the Middle School* 7 (October 2001): 78–82.

Smith, John P., ed. *Variability Is the Rule: A Companion Analysis of K–8 State Mathematics Standards.* Greenwich, Conn.: Information Age Publishing, 2010.

Tarr, James, and J. Michael Shaughnessy. "Student Performance in Data Analysis, Statistics, and Probability." In *Results and Interpretations of the 2003 Mathematics Assessment of the National Assessment of Educational Progress*, edited by Peter Kloosterman and Frank K. Lester, Jr., pp. 139–68. Reston, Va.: National Council of Teachers of Mathematics, 2007.

Wiest, Lynda R., and Robert J. Quinn. "Exploring Probability through an Evens-Odds Dice Game." *Mathematics Teaching in the Middle School* 4 (March 1999): 358–62.

Exploring Probability through an Evens-Odds Dice Game

Lynda R. Wiest and Robert J. Quinn

Middle-grades students should have opportunities to experiment actively with situations that model probability, including "making hypotheses, testing conjectures, and refining their theories on the basis of new information" (NCTM 1989, 111). These experiences should include a discussion of theoretical probabilities, where appropriate, and the use of correct mathematical terminology and expressions.

Exploring probabilistic thinking not only exercises students' general reasoning abilities but also helps build a foundation for more informed decision making in everyday life. Students, like adults, regularly use their knowledge of probabilities to make choices about important issues, such as health and safety, and to determine strategies in some recreational pastimes, such as sports and games. In this article, we describe a dice game that can be used by students as a basis for exploring mathematical probabilities and making decisions while they also exercise skills in multiplication, pattern identification, proportional thinking, and communication. As we observed and listened to the sixth graders participating in the activity, we gained some interesting insights into student thinking at this age level.

Game Overview

Students play the game in pairs, although groups of three or four would also work. On her or his own game board (see **fig. 1**), each student divides a given number of chips between the two categories of "even" and "odd." Students take turns rolling two dice, finding the product of the values on the faces, and removing—only for their own roll—an "even" chip for an even product and an "odd" chip for an odd product. The first to remove all chips for both categories wins. Rolls that come up for a category for which all chips have already been cleared result in a lost turn. Students get an equal number of turns, so whoever rolls the dice second at the start of a two-player game may roll last.

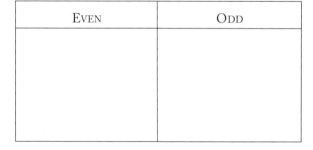

Fig. 1. An "evens-odds" game board

Playing with Tetrahedral Dice

To begin playing the game, students were given a pair of tetrahedral, or four-faced, dice; a game board; and sixteen chips. Dice with a greater number of faces could be used. Students were divided into four-member discussion groups. Each student had a game board, and each pair of students had two four-faced dice. Students were instructed how to read these dice. After playing instructions were given, students were asked to take a few minutes to discuss in their groups the strategies that they might consider for dividing their chips into the "even" or "odd" categories on their game boards. The group then split into two pairs to play the game. Each student decided how to place her or his chips on the game board.

Unsurprisingly, most sixth graders who participated in this lesson evenly split their chips into two groups of eight for the first game. Students played the game once then returned to their groups of four to discuss the effectiveness of their strategies and ways to revise them for replaying the game. Most noticed that more even than odd products had appeared. However, they could not seem to determine why. They decided, though, to place more chips on "even" for the next game. In the next game, the students' strategies were more varied; most students placed from eleven to fifteen of their sixteen chips on "even," with the majority choosing fourteen and fifteen.

After this second game, students again discussed with their group the success of their strategies and possible revisions, and they were encouraged to search for systematic or organized ways to determine how they might place the chips to increase their chances of winning. Still, they knew only that more evens than odds had appeared without seeing a mathematical justification. We were pleased, however, that one girl described using proportional reasoning. She noticed, "One out of every five times I get an odd. That's why I put three chips on odd because that would be out of fifteen." Although the expected proportion is really one out of four, her thought process was correct. Asked how many chips they would place in each category if they were to play the game again, more than half the class said that they would place from twelve to fourteen chips on "even."

We asked students to return to their pairs to play the game a third time by using twelve chips but without discussing strategies with their group. Two-thirds of the students chose an 8-4, 9-3, or 10-2 even-odd split, with half of these students opting for 9-3. For this game, we asked students to record their rolls, including missed turns, by placing pairs of factors in an even- or odd-products column. **Figure 2** shows one student's sheet for recording her rolls.

OUTCOMES OF DICE ROLLS						
EVEN PRODUCTS				ODD PRODUCTS		
FACTOR	FACTOR	PRODUCT		FACTOR	FACTOR	PRODUCT

Fig. 2. A student's recording sheet for dice-roll products

Using their game data, students discussed their results for this game in small groups. We then discussed their findings as a class. Students said that the chances of getting odd products were fewer because only 1's and 3's appeared in that column on their recordkeeping sheets. This conclusion was the extent of any rule or pattern they detected. We listed on the chalkboard possible pairs of factors that would yield even or odd products (see **fig. 3**). We then generated these possible outcomes—the sample space—systematically, as the organized list in **figure 4** shows. Students might also make a tree diagram to illustrate possible pairs.

Students discovered that even products should, theoretically, appear three-fourths of the time and odd products, one-fourth of the time. The lists helped make apparent that even-even, even-odd, and odd-even combinations result in even products and account for three-fourths of all possible products, whereas only odd-odd combinations result in odd products, or one-fourth of all possible products. The best strategy for placing sixteen chips, then, would be to put twelve, or three-fourths, in the "even" category and four, or one-fourth, in the "odd." For twelve chips, nine chips would be put in "even" and three in "odd."

EVEN PRODUCTS			ODD PRODUCTS
3, 4	4, 4	2, 3	1, 1
1, 4	2, 2	4, 3	3, 1
2, 4	3, 2	4, 2	3, 3
4, 1	2, 1	1, 2	1, 3

Fig. 3. Randomly generated list of pairs of factors that yield odd or even products for rolled "factors" on two tetrahedral dice

(1) 1, 1	(2) 2, 1	(3) 3, 1	(4) 4, 1
(2) 1, 2	(4) 2, 2	(6) 3, 2	(8) 4, 2
(3) 1, 3	(6) 2, 3	(9) 3, 3	(12) 4, 3
(4) 1, 4	(8) 2, 4	(12) 3, 4	(16) 4, 4

Fig. 4. Possible outcomes, or sample space, for two tetrahedral dice; products in parentheses

For any one roll of the dice, an event, the probability then is 3/4 for getting an even product and 1/4 for getting an odd product, which represents in each example the ratio of favorable outcomes to total outcomes. As an extension, the class can also examine other probabilities related to the game, such as the probability that a particular student who has only two "even" chips remaining will finish the game in her or his next two rolls of the dice. The probability of getting even products for two consecutive rolls is

$$\frac{3}{4} \times \frac{3}{4} = \frac{9}{16};$$

for two consecutive odd products, the probability is

$$\frac{1}{4} \times \frac{1}{4} = \frac{1}{16}.$$

These ideas should be discussed and worked through carefully with students, and students should understand that ratios obtained by experimentation, as in the evens-odds game, are approximations to theoretical probabilities. Experience in playing the game can help students improve their strategies, but a mathematical analysis of probabilities, when possible, is the best foundation for decision making. Another important concept is that estimates of probabilities made from ratios obtained by experiment should improve as the number of trials increases. In this example, probability estimates for even and odd products tend to approach 3/4 and 1/4, respectively, as the number of rolls increases.

After students had played the game with tetrahedral dice, we had them play it with standard dice. Different groups of students started with different numbers of chips—fourteen, sixteen, twenty-four, or thirty-six—only the last three of which can be divided evenly into three-fourths and one-fourths proportions. We made this distribution not only to save time from having all students experiment with these initial numbers but also to enrich our understanding of students' thinking and to foster better class discussion. Interestingly, more than one-third of the students reverted to using the same number of chips, such as twelve and twelve, in both categories. This lack of generalization of the pattern we had discussed after the earlier games with the tetrahedral dice shows that students continue to need much practice thinking about what they are doing and applying it to new situations by identifying like and unlike features of source (old) and target (new) situations and what effects, if any, the differences might have.

At various points in these games, we asked students who of their pair they believed was currently winning. We wanted to see whether students would reason on the basis of whose chips more nearly approximated the three-fourths (even)-to-one-fourth (odd) proportion that represents the theoretical probability for this activity. Students did not offer such an explanation. They were apt to respond, "Me, because I have fewer chips" or "Me, because I still have one on odd and she doesn't," meaning, in the latter statement, a reduced chance of having to skip a turn. Teachers can ask this question informally of pairs while moving about the room or pose the question to the entire class during a time-out for all pairs to discuss the question briefly.

Students' Response to the Game

Our students loved playing the game. They said that they enjoyed the hands-on aspect and the challenge posed by thinking about better strategies and expressing opinions about their ideas. Asked what they gained or learned, students highlighted three things:

- Practice with multiplication skills

- Finding that more even than odd products of possible number-pair combinations exist

- The pattern (E = even, O = odd): E × E = E; E × O = E; O × E = E; O × O = O

Game Extensions and Variations

Students can also play the game with dice of eight, ten, twelve, or twenty faces, which are common in many sets of polyhedral dice. Since ten-faced dice are usually numbered 0–9, 0 can represent 10. These dice can be mixed and matched. Note that the pattern found in the original version of the game still holds here: An equal number of even and odd numbers on each die, that is, an even number of numbers, yields possible products that are three-fourths even and one-fourth odd. Students could also play the game with three dice, or at least hypothesize the results. In this situation, only one of eight possible combinations—odd on all three dice—yields an odd product. Students can look for patterns as the number of dice increases. A geometric progression results in which, for example, the probability of getting an odd product can be shown as $1/2^n$ where n = number of dice; the probability of attaining an odd product decreases as the number of dice increases. Calculators might be appropriate for some of these game variations.

One hypothetical question to pose to students is whether using a die with an odd number of faces would change the three-fourths-to-one-fourth proportion of the "evens-odds" game. It would. For example, with a four-faced and a five-faced die, assuming that both are numbered consecutively beginning with 1, the proportion would change to seven-tenths-even (fourteen of twenty products)–to–three-tenths-odd (six of twenty products).

A game variation could be to play the game using the two categories of "doubles" and "nondoubles." For two tetrahedral dice, doubles would occur one-fourth of the time and nondoubles, three-fourths of the time; for two standard dice, doubles would occur one-sixth of the time and nondoubles, five-sixths of the time; and so on. This pattern holds for two identical dice that have an even number of faces; a spin-off could be to use two dice with different numbers of faces.

Closing Thoughts

Mathematical experiences that encourage students' reasoning are most valuable. They are even more so when they require probabilistic thinking that leads to decision making. In this article, we described one such experience in which students used a hands-on game format to exercise these and several other mathematical abilities.

Reference

National Council of Teachers of Mathematics (NCTM). *Curriculum and Evaluation Standards for School Mathematics.* Reston, Va.: NCTM, 1989.

The authors would like to thank Lou Loftin and Linda Simonton for allowing this lesson to be conducted in their classrooms.

Determining Probabilities by Examining Underlying Structure

Robert M. Norton

One way of grabbing students' interest in probability is to present the rules of a game of chance, ask them whether the game is fair, and have them use their intuition to give a ballpark estimate of the probability of winning. The issue of fairness can be counted on to arouse the interest of many students, and fairness of games is a topic that has found its way into textbooks (see, e.g., Chapin et al. [1994]). Having students commit to an answer helps to arouse and sustain their interest because they want to see whether their intuition is correct. Students also learn that giving an impulsive, intuitive, and incorrect answer to a probability question is easy, but a good approach to finding the correct answer is to examine how each possible outcome is produced under the rules of the game. Giving students experiences in looking at the underlying structures of a number of games offers them opportunities to enhance their probability intuition.

We examine three games involving dice, the first of which is discussed by Freda (1998). The structure is examined in a way that leads directly to the distribution of theoretical probabilities for all possible outcomes.

Game 1: The Difference in Faces

Tell students these rules of the game: Players 1 and 2 each toss a six-sided die. Player 1 wins if the faces differ by 0, 1, or 2. Player 2 wins if the faces differ by 3, 4, or 5. Many students think that this game is fair because each player has three ways to win. As they collect data from which to calculate experimental probabilities, however, these probabilities surprise those who think that the game is fair. Theoretical probabilities can be calculated and compared with experimental probabilities. Theoretical probabilities show that the game is not fair.

The students are divided into pairs, and each pair plays the game many times. Each pair records the number of times that the difference is 0, the number of times that it is 1, and so on, as well as the number of times that each player wins. When the data from all pairs are combined and examined, patterns should emerge. From the combined data, each student makes a histogram and uses it to determine which differences occurred most often and which differences occurred least often. They find the experimental probabilities that the difference is 0, that the difference is 1, and so on. The students are also asked to describe the "shape" of the histogram and think about whether the shape suggests that the game is fair.

Next, the students examine the theoretical probabilities. **Table 1** shows the difference in die faces that goes with each of the thirty-six possible outcomes resulting when two players each toss a die. We see, for example, that the chance that the faces differ by 5 is only 2 out of 36, but the chance that the difference is 1 is 10 out of 36. The students determine the theoretical probabilities and enter them in **table 2**, which shows the probability distribution for the difference in die faces.

According to the law of large numbers (for a more thorough explanation, see Moore and McCabe [1993]), when a game is repeated many times under identical conditions, the fraction of games that result in any particular outcome tends to approach that outcome's theoretical

Table 1
Difference in Faces When Two Dice Are Tossed

			Die 2				
		1	2	3	4	5	6
	1	0	1	2	3	4	5
	2	1	0	1	2	3	4
	3	2	1	0	1	2	3
Die 1	4	3	2	1	0	1	2
	5	4	3	2	1	0	1
	6	5	4	3	2	1	0

Table 2
Distribution of Theoretical Probabilities for the Absolute Difference of Two Dice

Difference	0	1	2	3	4	5
Probability	6/36	10/36	8/36	6/36	4/36	2/36

probability of occurrence. Therefore, roughly one-sixth of all games should produce a difference of 0, roughly 5/18 of the games should produce a difference of 1, and so on. Additionally, player 1 should win roughly 2/3 of the games, a fraction that is derived from the calculation of the theoretical probability:

$$p(0) + p(1) + p(2) = \frac{6}{36} + \frac{10}{36} + \frac{8}{36} = \frac{2}{3}.$$

At this point, students compare the theoretical probabilities in **table 2** with the experimental probabilities obtained previously. The experimental probabilities should be reasonably close to the theoretical probabilities.

Under the existing rules, player 1 wins when the difference is 0, 1, or 2 and should win roughly two-thirds of the games played. A good puzzle to give students is to find ways to change the rules to make the game fair. Multiple answers are possible:

Player 1	Player 2
0, 1, 5	2, 3, 4
1, 2	0, 3, 4, 5
1, 3, 5	2, 4, 6

Game 2: The Maximum of Two Faces

Again, the students are divided into pairs. Each player tosses a six-sided die. Player 1 wins if the maximum result of the two tosses is a 1, 2, 3, or 5. Player 2 wins if the maximum face is a 4 or 6. Does the game favor either player? Encourage the students to commit to an answer by using their intuition. Again, pairs collect and pool their data. The structure needed to find the theoretical probabilities for the maximum face is shown in **table 3**. **Table 4** shows the distribution of theoretical probabilities for this game.

Player 2 wins only if the maximum is a 4 or 6. From **table 4**, however, we see that the game is fair because each player has probability 1/2 of winning, as shown here:

$$p(4) + p(6) = p(1) + p(2) + p(3) + p(5), \quad \text{and} \quad \frac{7}{36} + \frac{11}{36} = \frac{1}{36} + \frac{3}{36} + \frac{5}{36} + \frac{9}{36} = \frac{1}{2}.$$

Game 3: My Favorite Horse

This game involves a race between two plastic horses across a hardwood floor and is based on an activity with which the author entertained himself as a boy. The students are divided into pairs, and each player is given a horse. Each student throws a die simultaneously, and each horse moves forward the number of boards shown on the appropriate die face. If both horses cross the finish line on the same turn, the result is a tie. Otherwise, the first horse to cross the finish line wins. In a classroom, markers may be substituted for horses and oval racetracks drawn on sheets of paper may be substituted for the hardwood floor.

TABLE 3
Maximum Outcome from Two Tosses of a Die

		Die 2					
		1	2	3	4	5	6
	1	1	2	3	4	5	6
	2	2	2	3	4	5	6
	3	3	3	3	4	5	6
Die 1	4	4	4	4	4	5	6
	5	5	5	5	5	5	6
	6	6	6	6	6	6	6

TABLE 4
Distribution of Theoretical Probabilities for the Maximum Outcome from Two Tosses of a Die

Maximum	1	2	3	4	5	6
Probability	1/36	3/36	5/36	7/36	9/36	11/36

The author had a favorite horse, which was given a slight edge. When the die toss for the favorite horse resulted in a 1, this result was ignored, the die was tossed again, and the horse moved forward as many boards as were indicated on the second toss—even if the second toss resulted in a 1. After all, some element of fairness had to be incorporated in the game.

How much of an advantage would these rules give the favorite horse? For each horse, have the students find the distribution of theoretical probabilities for the number of boards moved forward on one turn. The one for the ordinary horse is the easier of the two; see **table 5**.

The distribution of theoretical probability for the favorite horse is easy to obtain if students understand that each turn for this horse always involves a first toss and a second toss but that the second toss is never used unless the first toss is a 1. From **table 6**, we see that the favored horse has only 1 chance in 36 of moving just one board forward. The other probabilities needed are also easily deduced (see **table 7**).

In a short race, the slight edge would not be expected to make much of a difference. In a long race, however, in which each horse gets several turns, the law of large numbers says that the favored horse will tend to receive a smaller percent of die rolls of 1 than the ordinary horse, a slightly larger percent of 2's, and so on. The more turns that take place in the game, the greater the chance that the favored horse will win.

As a concrete illustration, students can conduct a race in which each horse gets 36 turns and the horse that is ahead after the last turn wins. The ordinary horse would be expected to roll roughly six of each number 1–6 on its 36 turns. This prediction is obtained by multiplying the theoretical probability of rolling each number by the total number of turns. We would expect, therefore, that the ordinary horse would have moved a total of 6 + 12 + 18 + 24 + 30 + 36, or 126, boards forward, give or take a few boards. The favorite horse, however, would be expected to roll roughly one 1, seven 2s, seven 3s, and so on. We would expect this horse to move, then, 1 + 14 + 21 + 28 + 35 + 42, or 141, boards forward, give or take a few.

Naturally, at times the ordinary horse will have good luck and the favorite horse, bad luck, and the ordinary horse will win. The probability is, however, that the favorite horse should win roughly 86 percent of the time. For this activity, the students can again be divided into pairs, with one student rolling a die for the ordinary horse and the other student rolling a die for the favorite horse. Students can pool their data on the total number of boards that each horse advanced in the game and which horse won. A histogram for total boards advanced can be compared with the theoretical probability of 126 boards for the ordinary horse and 141 boards for the favorite horse. The percent of races won by the favorite horse should be close to 86 percent.

A reasonable question to ask is whether the game can be made fair. A natural way to have students work on this problem is to present it to them as a problem of distance = rate × time. As noted, the favorite horse is expected to cover 141 boards in 36 turns, yielding an expected speed of 141/36, or about 3.92, boards per turn. The ordinary horse has an expected speed of 126/36, or 3.5, boards per turn. The only way that the ordinary horse could be expected to cover the same distance as the faster horse is with more time, that is, turns. Students should be able to discover that the ordinary horse needs 141 turns to the favorite horse's 126, or a ratio of 47 to 42.

Table 5

Theoretical Probabilities for Boards Advanced by the Ordinary Horse on One Turn

Boards Advanced	1	2	3	4	5	6
Probability	1/6	1/6	1/6	1/6	1/6	1/6

Table 6

Number of Boards That the Favorite Horse Advances on One Turn

		Toss 2					
		1	2	3	4	5	6
	1	1	2	3	4	5	6
	2	2	2	2	2	2	2
	3	3	3	3	3	3	3
Toss 1	4	4	4	4	4	4	4
	5	5	5	5	5	5	5
	6	6	6	6	6	6	6

Table 7

Theoretical Probabilities for Boards Advanced by the Favorite Horse on One Turn

Boards Advanced	1	2	3	4	5	6
Probability	1/36	7/36	7/36	7/36	7/36	7/36

Conclusion

Other games are possible. Suppose that player 1 wins if the product of die faces is a number from 1 to 10 and that player 2 wins when the product is a number from 12 to 36. Theoretical probabilities show that player 1 has the greater probability of winning. In a game that focuses on the sum of the faces of two dice, theoretical probabilities show that a sum of 7 is more likely than any other sum, yet the sum is equally likely to be odd or even. Dice games naturally pose fairness issues that appeal to students. Further, dice games have a structure that readily leads to the distribution of theoretical probabilities of the outcomes in the game and, therefore, to a determination of whether the game is fair.

References

Chapin, Suzanne, Mark Illingworth, Marsha Landau, Joanna Masingila, and Leah McCracken. "Fair Games, Permutations, Combinations." In *Middle Grades Mathematics: An Interactive Approach*. Needham, Mass.: Prentice Hall, 1994.

Freda, Andrew. "Roll the Dice—an Introduction to Probability." *Mathematics Teaching in the Middle School* 4 (October 1998): 85–89.

Moore, David, and George McCabe. *Introduction to the Practice of Statistics*. New York: W. H. Freeman & Co., 1993.

Rethinking Fair Games

David C. Coffey and Mary G. Richardson

Take a moment to think about how you would answer this question: What does it mean for a game to be fair? When asked this question, many people focus on *playing* fair or the fact that neither player cheats. This response seems reasonable, since most people are accustomed to playing commercially produced games that are fair to each player. Because they have not had much experience with games that have rules that make them unfair, they may be unaware of the mathematical concepts related to fair and unfair games. Consequently, our goal was to develop an activity that would give students an opportunity to explore the mathematics associated with fair games and the procedures used to make unfair games fair.

As we were developing this activity, we discovered that a well-established guideline for modifying an unfair game to make it fair works theoretically, if the game were to go on forever. However, it is not sufficient for games that have a finite number of turns. This article chronicles the steps we took that led to this discovery and explains why it is important for teachers of mathematics to be reflective practitioners.

The "Matching Game"

In the "matching game," a single round consists of player A and player B counting to three and then each displaying a single index finger; an index and a middle finger; or an index, middle, and ring finger. If the number of fingers displayed by both are the same, then player A scores 1 point. If the number of fingers displayed does not match, player B scores 1 point. The player with the most points after three rounds wins the game.

Try It for Yourself

In *Principles and Standards for School Mathematics* (2000), NCTM suggests that students should make predictions before engaging in an experiment, then compare those predictions with the actual results. This will motivate students to determine why predictions and outcomes may differ. Before you read any further, answer the following question: Is the "matching game" fair? Your answer to this question may depend on the definition of a fair game that you developed in the opening paragraph. Most people who focus on the mathematics rather than ethical play define a fair game as involving equally likely outcomes, either in terms of wins and losses or total points.

Play ten rounds of the game and keep track of the results. Do your results suggest that the game is fair using either definition? We simulated 100 three-round games and obtained the following results: player A won 27 games and lost 73. Player A averaged 1.05 points per game compared with 1.95 points per game for player B. How do these results compare with your findings? Playing the "matching game" and collecting the relevant data introduce people, through experimentation, to a game that is inherently unfair.

The Theoretical Probability of Winning the "Matching Game"

The calculations associated with determining theoretical winning probabilities for each player are complicated, but they are accessible through the use of a tree diagram. On a single round of the game, nine equally likely outcomes are possible. If we let 1, 2, 3 represent one, two, or three fingers displayed, respectively, then we can list the nine possible outcomes for a single round: {11, 22, 33, 12, 13, 23, 21, 31, 32}. Here, the outcome "12" represents player A showing 1 finger and player B showing 2 fingers; the outcome "21" represents player A showing 2 fingers and player B showing 1 finger. In a single round of the game, three outcomes are favorable to player A (11, 22, and 33), and six outcomes are favorable to player B (12, 13, 23, 21, 31, and 32), which means that the P(player A winning 1 point) = 3/9, or 1/3, and P (player B winning 1 point) = 6/9, or 2/3.

We can use these probabilities to create a tree diagram that represents all three rounds of the "matching game" (see **fig. 1**). As you can see, twenty-seven outcomes are possible for a three-round game, and only seven of them result in a win for player A. At approximately 26 percent, this number is very close to the percentage of wins we found when we simulated 100 games, which was 27 percent.

The theoretical probability of player A winning is also computationally accessible. For example, there are three ways for player A to win a game of three rounds with a score of 2 to 1, namely (AAB, ABA, or BAA), where an A indicates a win by player A and a B refers to a win by player B. Thus,

P(player A winning two rounds)
    $= P(\text{AAB}) + P(\text{ABA}) + P(\text{BAA})$
    $= (1/3 \cdot 1/3 \cdot 2/3) + (1/3 \cdot 2/3 \cdot 1/3) + (2/3 \cdot 1/3 \cdot 1/3).$

Using the commutative property of multiplication, we have

$(1/3 \cdot 1/3 \cdot 2/3) + (1/3 \cdot 1/3 \cdot 2/3) + (1/3 \cdot 1/3 \cdot 2/3),$
or
$3(1/3 \cdot 1/3 \cdot 2/3).$

Player A can also win by a score of 3 to 0, namely, AAA. $P(\text{AAA}) = 1/3 \cdot 1/3 \cdot 1/3$; so the probability of A winning two or more games is P(player A winning two rounds) + P(player A winning 3 rounds), or

$(1/3 \cdot 1/3 \cdot 2/3) + (1/3 \cdot 1/3 \cdot 1/3).$

We confirm that the probability of player A winning the game is 7/27, or about 26 percent.

Using these theoretical results, the calculations required to find the expected number of points for each player are straightforward. Player A would be expected to score 3 points once, 2 points six times, 1 point twelve times, and 0 points eight times. This results in a total of 27 points over the twenty-seven possibilities, or an average of 1 point per game. Player B's points can be calculated using the same method or by using a strategy that recognizes the complement—player A and player B will score a combination of 3 points each game. Because 81 points are possible in the twenty-seven possible outcomes, player B would be expected to score 81 – 27, or 54, points total for an average of 2 points per game. Thus, in a three-round game, we expect player A to receive only 1 point compared with 2 points for player B (again, these numbers are very close to our experimental averages of 1.05 and 1.95, respectively).

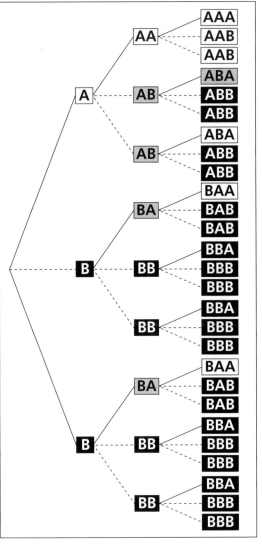

Fig. 1. The tree diagram for the original "matching game." A white box shows player A wins, a black box shows player B wins, and a gray box shows a tie.

What Is Fair?

Having shown that the original game is not fair using both experimental and theoretical methods, a typical extension would be to ask participants to alter the rules to make the game fair. The premise is that making the game fair requires participants to apply what they know about probability in a slightly different context. Take a few minutes before reading on to think about various ways that you might try to make the "matching game" fair.

In our experience, participants in classes and seminars suggest two different methods for making unfair games fair. (These participants include middle-grades students, college students, in-service teachers, mathematicians with doctorates, mathematics educators, and statisticians.) One method is to rewrite the rules so that each player has an equally likely chance of winning a round. Because of the odd number of outcomes that may occur on any round, this result cannot be accomplished without eliminating some combination or combinations. For example, assign player A the matches (11, 22, and 33) and player B the times when his or her number is larger than player A (12, 13, and 23). If player A's number is higher (21, 31, or 32), then repeat the round.

Although this activity gives each player an equally likely chance of winning a round, approximately one-third of the time the round will need to be replayed. Since this is not an acceptable solution to many participants, they often suggest a different method for making the game fair—adjust the points so that each player's expected points for the game are equal. To accomplish this, they suggest that player A earns 2 points for each match, whereas player B continues to earn 1 point per mismatch. The idea is that since player B is twice as likely to win a round as player A, giving player A twice as many points per round will balance out the game. Although this point-adjusting procedure is widely used and sounds reasonable, we have found that it may be problematic depending on your definition of fairness and the length of the game.

Evaluating the Fairness of the "Modified Matching Game" Using a Simulation

One way to determine if the "modified matching game" is fair with the new point system—player A earns 2 points for a match and player B scores 1 point for a mismatch—is to play the game and collect data. Before going further, we would encourage you to play 100 games (remember, a game is three rounds) using the adjusted scoring. One easy method we have found involves using two dice with sides four, five, and six replaced with the numbers 1, 2, and 3. Keep track of the total points for each player for each game and the number of wins and losses.

Based on suggestions made by NCTM (2000) for addressing misconceptions in probabilistic thinking, we wrote a TI-73 graphing calculator program to simulate the "modified matching game" (see **fig. 2**). Each run of the program simulates 100 three-round games and allows the user to specify the points awarded to each player for a successful round. After simulating 1000 games, we found that the point-adjusting procedure had mixed results.

As expected, the average number of points scored by each player over the 1000 games was nearly equal. Player A averaged 2.002 points per game, and player B averaged 1.999 points per game. Based on these averages, the modified game certainly seems fair if the players are keeping a running total of points scored over many games. On the other hand, many people consider a game fair only if each person has an equal chance of winning (Aspinwall and Shaw 2000). They might not keep a running total of accumulated points but they would keep track of wins and losses to determine fairness.

Would these people consider the "matching game" with the adjusted scoring to be fair? What were the results of your 100 games? Did each player win about the same number of times? In our 1000 games, there were 436 ties, 261 wins for player A, and 303 wins for player B (see **table 1**). Although these numbers were an improvement over the original game and although the average scores are almost equal, the simulation suggests that the game remains unfair from a probability standpoint. To understand why, we turn our attention to the theoretical results.

Evaluating the Fairness of the "Modified Matching Game" Theoretically

Recall that the modified game gives player A 2 points every time the number of fingers displayed is the same and player B 1 point for any other outcome. Therefore, any game containing two wins for player B and one win for player A in three rounds would be a tie—2 points to 2 points. (See **fig. 3** for a modified tree diagram.) In **table 2**, we have separated the outcomes into player A wins, player B wins, and the ties. As you can see,

TABLE 1
Results from 1000 Trials from the "Modified Matching Game" Simulation

	AVERAGE POINTS	WINS
A wins	2.002	0.261
B wins	1.999	0.303
Ties		0.436

```
ClrList L1 , L2 , L3 , L4                    Clears lists for player totals, games, and percents.
Disp "WELCOME  TO THE"
Disp "MATCHING GAME"
Pause
Input "ROUNDS PER GAME?" , R                 Allows the user to set the number of rounds in a game.
Disp "POINTS FOR A"
Input "MATCH?" , M                           Sets the score for player A for a (M)atch.
Disp "POINTS FOR A"
Input "MISMATCH?" , N                        Sets the score for player B for (N)o match.
0→G                                          Initializes the number of games that player A wins.
0→T                                          Initializes the number of nontie games.
0→Xmin                                       Begins initialization of graphing window.
0→Ymin
1→Ymax
.1→Yscl
100→Xmax
100→Xscl                                     Ends initialization of graphing window.
100→dim(L1)                                  Begins initialization of list dimensions.
100→dim(L2)
100→dim(L3)
100→dim(L4)                                  Begins initialization of list dimensions.
For(I, 1, 100)                               Conducts 100 trials of the game.
I→L3(I)                                      Stores trial number in the list for later graphing.
For(J,1,R)                                   Conducts R rounds per game.
randInt(1,3)→A                               Randomly assigns player A's number.
randInt(1,3)→B                               Randomly assigns player B's number.
If A=B                                       Do the players' numbers match this round?
Then
M+L1(I) →L1(I)                               If yes, add M points to player A's round total.
Else
N+L2(I) →L2(I)                               If no, add N points to player B's round total.
End
End                                          End of round loop.
If L1(I)>L2 (I)                              Did player A score more points in the round?
1+G→G                                        If yes, add 1 to player A's win total.
If L1 (I) ↑L2(I)                             Was the game a nontie?
1+T→T                                        If yes, add 1 to the nontie total.
If T=0                                       Have all the games so far resulted in a tie?
Then
0→L4(I)                                      If yes, assign 0 to the percent of A wins after I trials.
Else
G/T→L4(I)                                    If no, assign G/T to the percent of A wins after I trials.
End
End                                          End of game trials loop.
Disp "MATCH AVERAGE" ,mean(L1)
Disp "MISMATCH AVERAGE" ,mean(L2)
Disp "HIT ENTER TO"
Disp "CONTINUE"
Pause
PlotsOn (1)
Plot1(xyLine, L3, L4, .)                     Plot percentage of A wins over the number of trials.
".5"→Y1                                      Plot $y = .5$ as a referent (each player equally likely).
DispGraph
```

Fig. 2. A TI-73 graphing calculator program to simulate the "modified matching game"

theoretically the game is not fair from a probability standpoint because each player does not have an equal chance of winning.

Is the "modified matching game" fair in terms of expected points? By examining **table 2**, we see that player A would be expected to score 6 points one time, 4 points six times, 2 points twelve times, and 0 points eight times. Thus, we expect player A to score a total of 54 points (6 × 1 + 4 × 6 + 2 × 12 + 0 × 8 = 54) over the twenty-seven possibilities, or an average of 2 points per game. Player B would be expected to score 3 points eight times, 2 points twelve times, 1 point six times, and 0 points one time, or 54 points total, for an average of 2 points per game. Thus, in a three-round game, we expect players A and B to receive the same number of points. If we define a fair game as one with equal point expectations, the "modified matching game" is fair according to this definition.

A Rich Problem

Adjusting the scoring system so that each player's expected points would be equal did not create a fair game when considering probability. After discovering this, we believed that the process was flawed and suggested that mathematics teachers refrain from using it in their classes. Our perspective changed, however, as we prepared this article and presented our results. The reactions to our findings suggest that a great deal of confusion surrounds the use of the terms *fair* and *unfair* as they relate to games played in a realistic context. We also discovered, however, that experimenting with the point-adjustment process from both expected value and probabilistic contexts provides an opportunity to engage in discussions that help participants realize the importance of context and mathematical language in applying preexisting procedures.

Furthermore, we were reminded of the power of using a large number of simulations to investigate the long-term behavior of mathematical phenomena. Had we not simulated several thousand games, we would have continued to believe in the probabilistic fairness of the "modified matching game." Only after conducting an initial simulation that produced counterintuitive results did we begin to explore the possibility that the point-adjustment process does not result in a fair game for a finite number of rounds.

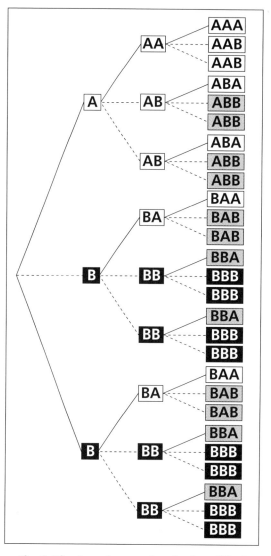

Fig. 3. The tree diagram for the "modified matching game." A white box shows player A wins, a black box shows player B wins, and a gray box shows a tie.

Through simulating the "modified matching game," we discovered that adjusting the points awarded to players of unfair games does result in final scores that are more equitable (a fair game based on expected value). However, further analysis demonstrated that the likelihood of either player winning continues to favor player B (an unfair game from a probability standpoint). On the other hand, revising the rules so that each player is equally likely to win any round creates a game that is fair in both expected value and probability. Consequently, as is true in most mathematics, it is important to communicate clearly the meaning of the words being used to describe a situation and to keep in mind the context of the problem. The procedure for making an unfair game fair creates an excellent opportunity for groups to engage in simulation, problem solving, mathematical discussion, and reasoning.

Instead of focusing on the flaw in the process found in the situation of a finite number of rounds, we became aware of the richness of the problem as demonstrated by the activity described in this article. This task

Table 2
Probabilities Associated with the "Matching Game"

EVENT	OUTCOMES	OCCURRENCES OUT OF 27	PROBABILITY
A wins	AAA	7	7/27 = 25.93%
	ABA		
	AAB		
	BAA		
B wins	BBB	8	8/27 – 29..63%
Ties	BBA	12	12/27 = 44.44%
	BAB		
	ABB		

also includes opportunities for extending the exploration. One direction that we researched involved determining what happens when you change the number of rounds per game. We discovered some interesting patterns and began thinking about probabilistic fairness for games that go on forever. Although this scenario is not realistic, it does demonstrate that the mathematical reasoning behind the point-adjustment procedure is sound in the infinite case. We also explored fair and unfair games that contain a finish-line element, for example, playing the "matching game" until someone scores 4 points. This play, too, can be used to foster mathematical discourse, since the results are counterintuitive.

Conclusion

Students in mathematics continue to encounter procedures that they apply without understanding. They blindly trust that the procedure will accomplish exactly what it promises. The same can be said about teachers, as the point-adjusting procedure proves. Exploring activities like adjusting points to make an unfair game fair introduces students and teachers to a process that offers conflicting results depending on the definition of fairness being used and the context of the problem (an infinite versus a finite game). The discourse that results from determining whether or not the modified game is fair provides a context for exploring other mathematical processes and their related conceptual principles. We hope that the question that students and teachers will begin to ask themselves is this, "Under what circumstances does this really work?"

References

Aspinwall, Leslie, and Kenneth L. Shaw. "Enriching Students' Mathematical Intuitions with Probability Games and Tree Diagrams." *Mathematics Teaching in the Middle School* 6 (December 2000): 214–20.

National Council of Teachers of Mathematics (NCTM). *Principles and Standards for School Mathematics*. Reston, Va.: NCTM, 2000.

SECTION 10

Statistics

Introduction

The previous seven articles focus on providing experiences with probability and probabilistic thinking. The American Statistical Association published the Guidelines for Assessment and Instruction in Statistics Education (GAISE) Report (Franklin et al. 2007). This report makes clear the grades K–12 relationship between probability and statistics—in particular data analysis. GAISE says, "Statistics uses probability, much as physics uses calculus, but only certain aspects of probability make their way into statistics" (p. 84). The report gives the following guidelines for the important basic understandings of probability that students need in order to make sense of statistical reasoning. Their recommendations for what students should know and understand are (p. 85):

- probability as long-run relative frequency;
- the concept of independence; and
- how probability can be used in making decisions and drawing conclusions.

The report goes on to say that students should also be able to evaluate probabilities using the normal distribution with technology as an aid.

GAISE views "probability as an attempt to quantify uncertainty" and says "the concepts of probability play a critical role in developing statistical methods that make it possible to make inferences based on sample data and to assess our confidence in such conclusions" (Franklin et al. 2007, p. 85).

In this section, we turn to the articles on statistics, in particular, data analysis experiences that use and build on the probabilistic reasoning developed earlier. In these articles you will encounter major components of the GAISE Framework: Formulate the Question; Collect Data; Analyze Data; and Interpret Results. Two other important data analysis concepts are explored: the nature of and sources of variability—measurement variability, natural variability, and induced variability (Franklin et al. 2007, pp. 14–15).

The basic nature of the task in the opening article, "Lollipop Statistics" (Goldsby 2003), is a good starting point for students to become familiar with *bar graphs*, counting, and the notion of *frequency*.

In "Capture and Recapture Your Students' Interest in Statistics" (Morita 1999), students use goldfish crackers to model the capture-recapture technique biologists use to estimate fish populations in lakes. The tasks require two class meetings, and students need to be able to solve *proportions*. In addition, task extensions are suggested.

In "Developing a Meaningful Understanding of the Mean" (Bremigan 2003), a research-inspired article, students use data to determine which of five groups was most successful during a fundraising candy sale. Before being able to solve the task, students should be able to find the mean, median, mode, and range of a given set of values.

References

Bremigan, Elizabeth George. "Developing a Meaningful Understanding of the Mean." *Mathematics Teaching in the Middle School* 9 (September 2003): 22–26.

Franklin, Christine, Gary Kader, Denise Mewborn, Jerry Moreno, Roxy Peck, Mike Perry, and Richard Scheaffer. *Guidelines for Assessment and Instruction in Statistics Education (GAISE) Report: A Pre-K–12 Curriculum Framework*. Alexandria, Va.: American Statistical Association, 2007.

Goldsby, Dianne S. "Lollipop Statistics." *Mathematics Teaching in the Middle School* 9 (September 2003): 12–15.

Morita, June G. "Capture and Recapture Your Students' Interest in Statistics." *Mathematics Teaching in the Middle School* 4 (March 1999): 412–18.

Statistics

Lollipop Statistics

Dianne S. Goldsby

As NCTM's *Principles and Standards for School Mathematics* (2000) points out, students should work directly with data to understand the fundamentals of statistical ideas. Teachers should also introduce statistics in a way that will capture the attention of students of varying abilities and interests. The constructivist approach to teaching emphasizes the idea that students work better when presented with tasks that are meaningful and relevant; in other words, they expend energy on topics that interest them (Brahier 2000). One way to harness that energy in the classroom is to teach with music, an area of interest for most middle school and high school students. This article describes the use of the 1950s hit "Lollipop" (Ross and Dixon 1986), heard in the movie *Stand by Me*, as a launching point to introduce ideas of counting, working with frequency tables, and graphing data.

Introducing the Activity

During Math Week activities at Rye Neck Middle and High School, several sixth-grade classes explored the data represented in the lyrics of "Lollipop." To introduce the lesson, students were asked to share the first mathematics activity that they could remember doing. They immediately responded, "counting." They were then asked why counting was important, to which they typically responded, "We need to know how many there are" or "So we can get the total." When asked for examples of counting activities in real life, students listed taking inventories in stores, determining the number of students in the classroom, preparing the U.S. Census, planning for a dinner party, making reservations for a play, and so on. Students were asked how they keep track of the number of items they are counting. Several students used the term *tally* and illustrated the use of the tally mark to keep count. Thus, the ideas of counting were grounded in students' real-life experiences.

Listening to "Lollipop"

The song "Lollipop" was played through one time for the students. They were then asked if they noticed any words or phrases that occurred more than once in the song, which led to the introduction of the term *frequency*. Words and phrases students identified, namely, "lollipop" and "o lolly lolly," were listed on the overhead projector. Some students pointed out that "pop" also occurred several times. When asked if they noticed any other repetitions, students expanded the list to include the "ba boom ba" musical phrase and the hand claps.

At this point, students counted off and were assigned one of the words, phrases, or musical elements to count. Students in group 1 counted "lollipop," students in group 2 counted "o lolly lolly," and so on. The song was played through and the students recorded their counts on the tally sheet (see **fig. 1**) using various techniques. For example, James used 46 vertical marks to record his count of the repetitions of "lollipop" while Brian grouped his marks in sets of five.

SOUND/PHRASE	TALLY	FREQUENCY
Lollipop		
Pop		
O lolly lolly		
Ba boom		
Claps		

Fig. 1. Tally sheet used by students

Next, students were grouped by number and asked to compare their tallies. Some discrepancies in counts were discovered, and students were asked how this situation should be handled. Several said that the "average" should be used. When asked if the average would give an exact count, the students considered the meaning of the term and decided that the average would not be exact. After some discussion, the students decided that the song should be replayed and another careful count taken. Students decided how to do the recount in their groups and proceeded. The counts for the various elements were then recorded on the overhead projector.

This point in the lesson is a good opportunity to discuss when to use actual counting and when to use representative samples. The issue of counting difficult elements, such as the hand claps, was raised to examine the importance of specifically defining what constitutes an element to be counted. In this classroom, an approximate count was used because of time constraints.

When asked how the data could be displayed, students suggested various kinds of graphs. Jennifer came up with the overall idea of using a graph while Alyssa declared that a bar graph would be appropriate and another student suggested a line graph. Students discussed the purpose of each type of graph and decided that a bar graph would best display the data. The elements of a graph, including the title, legend, scale, and so on, were reviewed. The appropriate size for the scale was also discussed, and students suggested using 5 or 10 for the scale. Because the counts ranged from 5 to more than 45, the students thought that 10 would be a difficult scale to use to record the counts. They decided that 5 would be the best unit to use to make the graph easy to read. This discussion presented a chance to examine the necessity of selecting a scale that will fit on the given graph and show all data but still be large enough to allow viewers to distinguish between quantities.

The students then graphed their data on graph sheets (see **fig. 2**). Joanna decorated her bars to designate the different quantities (see **fig. 3**). Michael included the title for the scale on the y-axis (see **fig. 4**). The graphs could have been improved if graph paper and rulers had been used, but the activity did not take place in a typical classroom where these materials are readily available.

The assignment for the students at the completion of the activity was to find another song and do the same activity for the next day's mathematics class. Students were told that their chosen songs could not contain inappropriate lyrics. Teachers should make sure to follow the policies of their school districts and divisions in this regard. The students did not view this assignment as "homework" in the traditional sense.

Student Engagement

One of the bright points of the activity was the engagement of the students. In one of the sessions, a special education teacher commented, "Our students were so involved in the activity. They could participate and did. It caught their attention immediately. You have to get them involved and keep their attention. This did." Another teacher pointed out that even those who had difficulty concentrating in mathematics class were absorbed by this activity.

Because music can be viewed as a universal language, its use in the classroom taps into the interests of more students than just those who are mathematically inclined. This activity can be tailored to the ages and interests of any

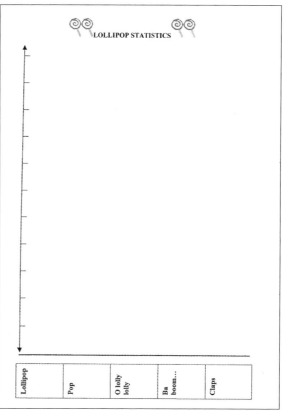

Fig. 2. Student graph sheet

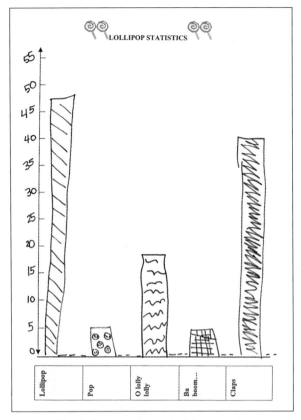

Fig. 3. Joanna decorated her graph.

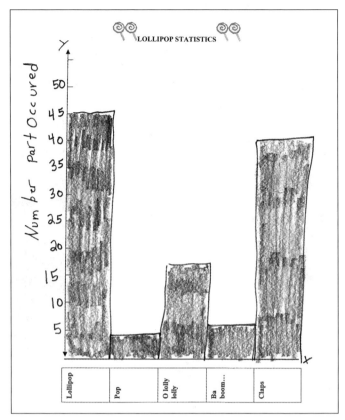

Fig. 4. Michael included the title for the scale.

students and is not restricted to one type of music. The song "Lollipop" was chosen because of its catchy beat and its familiarity to many students who have seen *Stand by Me.* Even students who have a natural affinity for mathematics need to have their interest stimulated through appropriate teaching techniques and procedures (Sobel and Maletsky 1999), and this activity gets their attention. The students' curiosity is awakened and becomes a means of motivation (Posamentier and Stepelman 1995). As the interaction in the activity demonstrated, "students work most effectively if they are truly interested in the subject at hand" (Sobel and Maletsky 1999, p. 33).

Extensions

As an extension, teachers might ask students to count elements in different portions of a song or for certain time frames, such as 60 seconds, then try to estimate the total count from their sample. Students could then do a total count and compare the results.

The activity can also be extended to creating survey instruments involving music. Students might conduct surveys to find out—

- types of music preferred by parents, teachers, or students in each grade in the school;

- number of CDs or tapes owned by students;

- number of new songs released in a month in various categories; or

- number of different types of albums and CDs sold in record stores.

This information can then be compared and used to discuss the concepts of mean and median. Further, students can analyze data collected on various types of music to determine which types have more repetitions of words or musical elements. In this way, students can connect mathematical ideas with experiences in their lives (NCTM 2000) and use new tools to compare sets of data.

Conclusion

Statistics is an essential part of the mathematics curriculum and an ever-present part of life. The presentation of statistical concepts can be done in ways that intrigue and motivate students. Such activities as "Lollipop" Statistics can be used to meet the recommendations of the Standards (NCTM 2000) for engaging students in formulating questions and designing experiments to collect relevant data.

References

Brahier, Daniel J. *Teaching Secondary and Middle School Mathematics*. Boston: Allyn and Bacon, 2000.

National Council of Teachers of Mathematics (NCTM). *Principles and Standards for School Mathematics*. Reston, Va.: NCTM, 2000.

Posamentier, Alfred S., and Jay Stepelman. *Teaching Secondary School Mathematics: Techniques and Enrichment Units*. 4th ed. Englewood Cliffs, N.J.: Merrill, 1995.

Ross, Beverly, and Julius Dixon. "Lollipop." Performed by the Chordettes. Courtesy of Edward B. Marks Music Co., *Stand by Me* Original Motion Picture Soundtrack. New York: Atlantic Recording Corp. and Columbia Pictures Industries, 1986.

Sobel, Max A., and Evan M. Maletsky. *Teaching Mathematics: A Sourcebook of Aids, Activities, and Strategies*. 3rd ed. Boston: Allyn and Bacon, 1991.

Capture and Recapture Your Students' Interest in Statistics

June G. Morita

Take your class fishing without getting wet! Linking our mathematics lessons with the real work of real scientists provides lasting motivation for our students. In this hands-on activity, students gain the feeling of power and ownership of a statistical method that they themselves derive—and they have fun!

Middle school students have the tools to derive the basic procedure used by wildlife biologists worldwide for estimating the sizes of wildlife populations. It is called *mark-recapture* or *capture-recapture* estimation. Its applications include estimating the number of bowhead whales in the world, sea lions in a region, fish in a lake, moose in a region, people in the United States, and fish in our local school's fish pond.

Lake Amanda

Picture a classroom of sixth-grade students as they embark on their study of this topic. Listen in as I set the stage for their first activity, titled "Lake Amanda":

> Today we will run through an actual investigation, much the way fisheries biologists do in attempting to estimate the number of fish in a lake. As we do so, I hope you will be thinking about how we can use the data we gather to get an appropriate estimate. It is going to be up to you to come up with a way to estimate our fish population size.

Twenty-three students are present. The activities described here span two class meetings.

"Here is Lake Amanda." I hold up an empty, rectangular, see-through storage bin, approximately 10" × 14" × 5". Naming my lake after a student in the class encourages that student to be more engaged in this activity. "Lake Amanda is filled with fish." Next I open a large, 38-ounce carton of cheddar-cheese goldfish-shaped crackers and pour the fish into the bin. Students are chuckling already, and all eyes are riveted on the bin of goldfish crackers.

"How many fish are in Lake Amanda?" I elicit estimates to stimulate using number sense. These students have been exposed to estimation problems since early elementary grades, so they are impressively good at them. If any student is astute enough to remark that we could get a good estimate by reading the product information label or by dividing the chore up and counting the fish, I acknowledge that student's cleverness and mention that these methods will come up later.

"Well, actually I caught 450 of the fish yesterday and sent them to the fish-tagging station down the road. The fish were tagged there and are now being trucked back to us for release back into Lake Amanda." I open two 5 1/2-ounce bags of pretzel-flavored fish crackers, with approximately 225 pieces in each bag, and pour the pretzel fish into Lake Amanda. "Notice how easy it is to see which fish are tagged"—I hold up a pretzel fish cracker—"and which are untagged"—I hold up a cheese fish cracker. "This bunch of tagged fish is called our 'initial sample' or 'tagging sample.' Now the fish from our initial sample must mix and mingle with the rest of the fish in the lake." I stir the fish mixture well. "In practice with real live fish, we wait for some time to elapse to allow the fish to mix."

Gathering the Data

"Class, each of you is a fisheries biologist working on this project. We now are going to sample fish from the lake. Josina will take this 'net' and scoop a sample of fish." I hand her a 3-ounce, fish-decorated paper cup and a small plastic bag. Using the bag as a "glove" keeps the fish clean enough for the students to munch on after the sampling has been completed. Josina scoops, then on request, counts the number of fish she has sampled and the number of tagged fish in the sample. "Josina has just taken a 'recapture sample.' That is, in this sample she has recaptured some of the fish from our initial sample." Josina counted 6 tagged fish in her sample of 36 fish. I write the following on the chalkboard:

recapture sample number tagged = 6
total number in recapture sample = 36

"What proportion of Josina's sample is tagged?" Students suggest answers to that question, and we end up writing the following:

$$\frac{\text{sample number tagged}}{\text{total number in sample}} = \frac{6}{36} = \text{sample proportion tagged}$$

"To simplify, I am going to call the recapture samples just samples. If this wording gets confusing, we can switch back to recapture versus initial samples."

After counting her fish, Josina returns them to the lake, which we then pass on to the next student in class, along with a paper cup and plastic bag. In turn, each student mixes the population, takes a sample, counts the number of fish in the sample and the number of tagged fish in the sample, returns the fish to the lake, then passes the lake to the next student. The students participate eagerly.

Estimating the Population Size

"One idea that statisticians rely on a lot is that we hope our sample mimics, or represents, the population from which it was drawn. We hope that the proportion of tagged fish in Josina's sample is somewhat close to the proportion of tagged fish in Lake Amanda. We will make precisely that assumption. Then we can write the approximation

sample proportion tagged ≈ population proportion tagged."

Students can help translate this approximation into

$$\frac{\text{sample number tagged}}{\text{total number in sample}} \approx \frac{\text{population number tagged}}{\text{total number in population}}$$

After writing this equation on the chalkboard, I ask, "What values do we know for the different elements of this equation?" Substituting 6 for the sample number tagged, 36 for the total sample, and 450 for the tagged population into the equation, we write the following:

$$\frac{6}{36} \approx \frac{450}{\text{total number in population}}$$

"We want to estimate the total number of fish in the population. This total is the 'unknown.' We can solve for it. How?"

Eric solves the problem in his head and spouts out, "2700," and explains his solution to the class. Discussing the solution, we find that some students work better with writing

$$\frac{6}{36} \approx \frac{\text{total number in population}}{450}$$

In this way, they see that the total number of fish in the sample is six times the number of tagged fish in the sample. That is, the numerator, 36, is six times its denominator, 6. So the numerator on the right-hand side, total number in population, should be 6 times 450, or 6 × 450 = 2700. This latter approach builds on the students' understanding of the actual problem we are trying to solve. Either way, using Josina's sample data, we can estimate the population size:

$$\text{Estimated total number in the population} = 450 \times \frac{36}{6} = 450 \times 6 = 2700$$

"Wow. You have just discovered a statistical estimation method—the one used most often by researchers estimating the size of a wildlife population. It is called the 'mark-recapture' or 'capture-recapture' method because first you capture and mark a sample of fish, then you later recapture some in another sample.

Researchers use this statistical procedure for fish, whales, moose, sea lions, . . . , and even people! If only you had been born fifty years earlier, you could have been the first to invent this method, and it might be named after you! . . . Eric's Estimation Method, or the Room 13 Estimation Method."

Our big assumption is that the sample proportion is at least somewhat close to the proportion of tagged fish in Lake Amanda. We next look at what Paloma found in her sample.

Paloma got 7 tagged fish in her sample of 25. Her estimated population size to the nearest whole fish is

$$450 \times \frac{25}{7} \approx 1607 \text{ fish.}$$

Working more intuitively, and approximately, some students reason that 25/7 is about 3 1/2, so the total number of fish in the lake should be about 3 1/2 times 450, which they calculate to be 1575.

Kenji, the third student, got 6 tagged fish in his sample scoop of 32 fish. His data lead to the estimated value of population size of

$$450 \times \frac{32}{6} = 2400 \text{ fish.}$$

Again, some students reason that 32/6 is 5 1/3. So the total number of fish in the lake should be about 5 1/3 times 450, which is 2400.

After each student has taken a sample, we pass Lake Amanda around the room together with a stack of paper-cup "nets" so that each student can take a sample to eat. As they munch on this snack, I point out that in practice, with real fish, a researcher should consider the effect of predators on this data-collection-and-estimation procedure. We also discussed other situations: "What about the partial fish? Do we count them?" Seiji actually got three fish that were stuck together.

Group Work, Writing, and Some Assessment

At this point in the lesson, the students work in their groups. Each student uses her or his own data to compute an estimate of the number of fish in Lake Amanda. They generally follow one of the computational procedures used here. Then, in their groups, I have them discuss how they could combine their data and estimates to get a single group estimate.

The student-to-student teaching and learning that go on in the small-group discussions are tremendous. Their conversations about how to combine each individual's data into group estimates are fascinating.

Their writing assignment is to explain their individual and group estimates and estimation procedures, including a discussion of how and why they chose those particular procedures. These explanations reveal quickly which students have attained a mastery of the lesson. Generally the small-group discussion that precedes the writing assignment helps the struggling students.

Classroom Discussion

It is interesting to see the students' different ideas for ways to combine the information from their samples. The most commonly proposed ways are to look at the different estimates of population size and (*a*) to choose one of the ones near the middle; (*b*) to take the one that seems somehow to be the most intuitively appealing; (*c*) to compute an average value, if they know about computing averages; or (*d*) to take Kenji's value because he is "good at math." Some students will propose combining the sample data into one single ratio—number tagged in the combined sample/combined sample size—then using this ratio in the computations done in the section called "Estimating the Population Size."

To illustrate these methods, consider the data shown in **table 1**, taken from one of our class sessions. To find the middle value for method (*a*), students ordered the estimated values as follows: 1607, 2250, 2400, 2520, 2700, 2850, 3150, 7425. A "middle" value, or median, would be midway between 2520 and 2700, or 2610. For method (*c*), computing the average or mean, they estimated the value at 3113. In using the last method, students combined the sample data into one single ratio,

$$\frac{\text{total sample number tagged}}{\text{combined sample size}} = \frac{43}{253}.$$

TABLE 1
Students' Data

STUDENT	NUMBER TAGGED	NUMBER IN SAMPLE	SAMPLE RATIO	ESTIMATE OF POPULATION SIZE
Josina	6	36	6/36	2700
Paloma	7	25	7/25	1607
Kenji	6	32	6/32	2400
Eric	6	38	6/38	2850
Amanda	5	28	5/28	2520
Carl	3	21	3/21	3150
Miya	2	33	2/33	7425
Seiji	8	40	8/40	2250
	Total = 43	Total = 253	Mean = 0.1718	Mean = 3113

Then they computed their estimate of the population size. Some computed it as

$$450 \times \frac{253}{43} \approx 2648,$$

whereas others reasoned that 253/43 was almost 6. So the total number of fish in the population should be about 6 × 450, or 2700.

One other method that students tried was to take the mean of the sample ratios, 0.1718, and use it by computing 450/0.1718 ≈ 2619 as an estimate.

Assumptions

Some central assumptions must be made for the mark-recapture estimation method to yield reasonably accurate estimates. In real life, these assumptions can be met only approximately. In discussion, the students are able to come up with some of these assumptions. I start by reviewing the overall procedure so that we get our jargon straight. First, a sample of fish is taken, tagged, and returned to the lake. In our activity, we tag 450 fish, which constitute the "marking sample." Then we observe one or more "recapture samples." In our activity, each student takes a recapture sample. The assumptions generally made in mark-recapture estimation relate to the requirement that for each sampling occasion—marking sample and recapture sample—each fish is equally likely to be caught. The major assumptions include the following:

• No animals are trap-happy or trap-shy. Thus, each animal or fish in our activity is equally likely to be caught during the initial capture for tagging, and each animal is equally likely to be caught during the recapture sampling.

• The population does not change between initial capture and recapture samplings. That is, no in- or out-migration, births, or deaths (including predation) occurred between the initial capture and the recapture samplings.

• Neither the tagging operation nor the presence of tags on the animal caused increased mortality.

A Sticky-Note Histogram

"Let's return to our estimates of the number of fish in Lake Amanda. Paloma, what was your estimate?"

"Mine was 1607."

"How about you, Miya?"

"I got 7425, but my group got a different number." Students eagerly shout their own estimated values and wave their arms.

"It seems that different people and different groups got different estimated values. Well, who is right? How would we know?" Some confident voices say, "I'm right, of course."

This discrepancy among answers brings up two important concepts about estimation based on sample data. First, for real statistical estimation problems such as this one, we might never know what the "right answer" really is. Second is the presence of sampling variability. Different samples lead to different estimates.

The best way to give students a feel for what sampling variability is like is to have them see the sampling variability from their own data. We make a graph of the different estimates of population size using a marvelous quick method—a sticky-note histogram.

I put up on the wall a long strip of masking tape to use as the base for our graph. Then I ask the class what range of values they got: "Who got the largest and who got the smallest estimates? And what were those estimated values?" On the basis of that information, I mark off the "bins" for our histogram. I made tick marks labeled 1000, 1500, 2000, . . . , 8000, with the markings about one sticky-note width apart. All students get one blue sticky note each, on which they write their initials and their estimate of the number of fish in Lake Amanda. Each student puts his or her note on the graph above the appropriate bin, which builds a histogram before their eyes.

Next, each group gets one yellow sticky note to show its combined estimated value. The group sticks this note on the graph below the appropriate bin.

More Data, Less Sampling Variability

This back-to-back histogram allows us easily to compare our two sets of estimates. Once the graph is made, I ask students what they see in the graph—what is the message? Immediately students point out that the notes below the line are clustered tightly, whereas the ones above the line are more spread out. "Excellent," I respond. I ask whether one distribution is shifted over from the other. Some squinting, head tilting . . . no, they are about the same. Through their own discussions, the students come up with the idea that the group estimates, which are based on larger samples, are less variable than are the individual estimates, which are based on smaller samples.

It is very uplifting to have my students discover these important ideas. They have formulated on their own this fundamental idea in statistical inference: larger sample sizes tend to yield less sampling variability and therefore more accuracy.

"Why are the yellow sticky notes less spread out than the blue ones?" I ask.

Eric suggests that the combined information was more accurate because we used information from more observations. The more observations we take, the more information we have, so we should get more-accurate estimates. "Yes. But how does Eric's notion of accuracy relate to the variability we see in our graph?" This question is very difficult. Eventually we come around to this conclusion: "If the group estimates are more accurate, then they should be closer to the actual population value. If they are closer to the actual population value, then they won't be so spread out."

Steve's Fish Pond

If students have access to an appropriate population of some sort of wildlife, actually marking and recapturing individuals is a natural extension. We did precisely that at Decatur Elementary School in Seattle, Washington.

Steve Chavez, a teacher at Decatur School, built a small fish pond in the school's courtyard, just outside his classroom. The pond is approximately 8 feet by 8 feet by 2 1/2 feet and was initially populated by about eleven goldfish. Over time, a few more fish were added as families donated their pet goldfish. The fish thrive in this pond. Each fall, when Steve returns to school, he has found some very small additions to the population. Apparently, the fish in the pond are multiplying! This situation gave us the perfect population for a mark-recapture experiment. We had a fixed population, whose size truly was not known.

The fish range in size from about the length of a standard paper clip to about 4 inches long. One problem we encountered was how to tag such small fish. A University of Washington researcher generously donated some tiny fluorescent polymer tags that could be injected under the skin of these fish. The tags are small enough not to weigh down the fish, and the tags fluoresce under ultraviolet light. Thus, when we capture a tagged, sedated fish and shine an ultraviolet flashlight on it, we see the tag as a glowing pink spot.

After completing the goldfish-cracker activity, we did the experiment on the real fish. What excitement!

Before we tagged the fish, the class was concerned about, and discussed the ethics of, conducting the experiment. We knew that tagging the fish could injure or kill some of them. Would it be OK to proceed anyway with the experiment? This quandry produced a great discussion. Would the tags fall out of, or possibly kill, the fish? We set aside ten tagged fish in a large jar of pond water and monitored them for the three weeks between the tagging operation and the recapture sampling. None rejected the tags, and none died. Whew!

Groups of students took recapture samples of size 10 and used the ultra-violet flashlights to determine the number of tagged fish in each sample. Our final estimate of population size was 117.

Tagging Friends and Family

As a follow-up activity for Family Math Night, we use a mark-recapture activity featuring students and their families. The question of interest is, How many people attended Family Math Night? This question is written at the top of a poster, which is prominently displayed.

First, people need to be selected randomly for tagging. As they arrive, each person rolls a die. People who roll 6 dots get a red fish-shaped name tag. They are our marked fish. Otherwise they get a blue fish-shaped name tag and are our unmarked fish. This way, each person has the same chance of being marked. Each person also is given a numbered raffle ticket. By keeping track of how many red tags are given out, we will know the number of marked fish in our population.

Partway through the event, twenty raffle numbers are selected randomly. These number holders will make up our recapture sample. For each selected raffle number, we ascertain whether its owner is a marked (red) or an unmarked (blue) "fish." Recall that we know the number of marked fish in our recapture sample. We already know the number of marked fish in the population and the number in the recapture sample, twenty. So we have all the data we need.

Parents ask, "Why go to all this trouble, rolling dice, tagging, and calculating, when you easily could have counted us as we came through the door?" This question presents a wonderful opportunity for the students to explain to the adults not only how to use the sample information to estimate the number of people at Family Math Night (population size) but also how to use this method to estimate the sizes of populations that cannot easily be counted, such as fish in a lake or wolves in a national forest. The students show how the mathematics they have learned at school is applicable in the real world. Parents are impressed.

For most middle school students, the mathematical tools used here are fairly easy to master. What makes this activity worth its weight in gold(fish) is not only that it gives an example of some mathematics used by real scientists but also that students get a confidence boost by seeing that they have already mastered the mathematical tools to derive this widely accepted estimation method. This activity can be used with various grade levels. The compelling example, the hands-on activity, and the element of food help it to be widely successful.

Now, what or who else can we tag? The possibilities are endless.

Bibliography

Bisbee, Gregory D., and David M. Conway. "Sharing Teaching Ideas: Studying Proportions Using the Capture-Recapture Method." *Mathematics Teacher* 92 (March 1999): 215–18.

Chapman, Douglas G. "The Plight of the Whale." In *Statistics: A Guide to the Unknown*, 3rd ed., edited by Judith M. Tanur, et al. Monterey, Calif.: Wadsworth & Brooks/Cole Advanced Books and Software, 1989.

Seber, George A. F. *The Estimation of Animal Abundance and Related Parameters*. 2nd ed. New York: Macmillan, 1982.

Developing a Meaningful Understanding of the Mean

Elizabeth George Bremigan

One of the first statistical measures that students encounter in their study of mathematics is the arithmetic mean. The procedure for determining the arithmetic mean of a given set of numbers is relatively simple, because it requires only two computational skills: addition and division. Thus, students are often introduced to the arithmetic mean in grades 4 or 5. At this level, computation of the arithmetic mean is frequently presented as an application of division rather than as a statistical concept. Initially, the arithmetic mean is often called the *average*; in this article, the arithmetic mean will be referred to simply as the *mean*.

Traditionally, many elementary school and middle school mathematics textbooks have defined the mean as the outcome of computations. For example, one glossary in a sixth-grade textbook defines the mean as a number obtained by dividing the sum of two or more addends by the number of addends (Bolster et al. 1994), and another explains the term as "the sum of a collection of data divided by the number of data" (Hoffer et al. 1994). In the classroom setting, students and teachers might easily assume that one's ability to successfully compute the mean of a given data set is synonymous with achieving an understanding of the concept of the mean. However, the possibility exists for students to successfully compute the mean without developing an understanding of what the mean actually represents, how it is related to the numbers in the data set, or how it is related to other measures of the center or spread of a data set (Zawojewski and Shaughnessy 2000).

For many years, I taught students the procedure for finding the mean without paying much attention to their conceptual understanding of this important statistical idea. My instructional decisions emphasized the development and application of a numerical procedure. The assessments I used measured students' abilities to successfully execute this procedure. The focus of the problem situations I presented and the questions I posed to students were limited. Although I knew that understanding the mean involved more than simply performing a procedure, it was not clear to me what a conceptual understanding of the mean was. I found myself asking the question, "What does it mean to understand the mean?"

An answer to my question came when the results of some mathematics education research caught my attention. In particular, Strauss and Bichler (1988) analyzed the concept of the arithmetic mean into its properties and investigated the development of children's understanding of these properties. The results of this research helped me to define conceptual understanding of the mean for students. In turn, my definition significantly changed how I taught this concept to middle school students and is clearly reflected in my current teaching of preservice elementary and middle school teachers.

Strauss and Bichler (1988) identified seven properties of the arithmetic mean that students must comprehend (see **fig. 1**). These properties serve as a useful guide for my instructional decisions as I seek to help students develop a rich conceptual understanding of the mean. My awareness of these properties has influenced my selection and construction of tasks that have the potential to lead students to encounter and pay specific attention to various aspects of the mean. The types of questions that I ask students during class discussions and the ways I respond to students' comments and questions have been affected by the properties that Strauss and Bichler defined. The results of their research have provided me with a framework to evaluate and improve my teaching of this mathematical topic in both significant and practical ways.

Principles and Standards for School Mathematics (NCTM 2000, p. 248) offers additional insight into the teaching and learning of this important statistical concept. The Data Analysis and Probability Standard advocates that teachers at all grade levels make instructional decisions that enable students to "select and use appropriate statistical methods to analyze data." In the middle school grades, students should learn to "find, use, and interpret measures of center and spread." This Standard draws our attention to additional aspects of the conceptual understanding of the mean, specifically, the idea that students must understand the mean's relationship to other measures of center (e.g., median and mode) and to measures of spread (e.g., range and standard deviation).

> A. The mean is located between the extreme values.
>
> B. The sum of the deviations from the mean is zero.
>
> C. The mean is influenced by values other than the mean.
>
> D. The mean does not necessarily equal one of the values that was summed.
>
> E. The mean can be a fraction that has no counterpart in physical reality.
>
> F. When one calculates the mean, a value of zero, if it appears, must be taken into account.
>
> G. The mean value is representative of the values that were averaged.

Fig. 1. Properties of the mean (Strauss and Bichler 1988)

As teachers, we are faced with the challenge of finding or creating problem situations and leading classroom discussions in which our students can explore the properties of the mean and the relationship of the mean to other measures of center and to measures of spread of the numbers in a data set. The following sections present two problem situations that I designed and used to meet these goals. References to Strauss and Bichler's properties of the mean are included in the discussions of the tasks.

The Fund-Raising Contest

The first problem, the Fund-Raising Contest, shown in **figure 2**, was inspired by a debate that occurred in the middle school where I was teaching. Students were struggling with the question of how to fairly determine which group had the best performance during a fund-raising contest when the groups were of different sizes. In designing this open-ended task for my seventh-grade class, I used the same context but adjusted the numbers to serve my instructional purposes.

I have found that this open-ended task generally works well when presented to small groups of students first, then discussed in a whole-class setting. Before performing any computations, many students suggest that the fund-raising group that collected the most money simply should be declared the winner. Students are surprised to find that each of the five groups collected the same amount of money. This finding leads students to consider other ways to compare the groups. Frequently, students then decide that finding the mean of each of the five groups could be useful and important. I usually present this task after students have

> During a fund-raising candy sale, the twenty-nine students in one seventh-grade class are divided into five groups. A prize is offered to the group that is the most successful. The amounts of money collected by the five groups of students are given below. Your goal is to determine which group is the most successful and should win the prize. Describe several different ways that you could reach a decision about which group is the most successful.
>
> | Group 1 | Group 2 | Group 3 | Group 4 | Group 5 |
> |---------|---------|---------|---------|---------|
> | 50 | 50 | 100 | 70 | 70 |
> | 40 | 50 | 45 | 60 | 60 |
> | 35 | 35 | 20 | 50 | 50 |
> | 30 | 25 | 20 | 20 | 20 |
> | 30 | 25 | 15 | 10 | 10 |
> | 25 | 25 | 10 | 0 | |

Fig. 2. The Fund-Raising Contest problem

learned how to identify the mean, median, mode, and range of a given data set. Solving the fund-raising task gives students an opportunity to apply their mathematical knowledge and skills in a real-world context.

Students' attention begins to focus on differences among, and within, the five groups. One difference among groups that quickly becomes apparent is that group 5 has one fewer person than the other four groups. Although the total amount of money collected for each group is the same, the mean for group 5 is greater than the mean of the other four groups because the number of students in group 5 is smaller. In examining the data sets and means of groups 4 and 5, students directly encounter property F as they compare the impact of a student's contribution of $0 in one group with the impact of being one member short in another group.

Differences in the spread, or distribution of the data in each group, also emerge as an interesting aspect of this problem situation. Determining the range of amounts collected by each fund-raising group is a common decision that small groups make in the classroom. Students attempt to find a way to measure the contributions of individual members of each fund-raising group in terms of how "equal" they are. Some students argue that a smaller range means that each member of the group has contributed "more equally" to the fund-raising effort. This observation can lead easily into a discussion of the location of the mean between the extreme values of the data set, as noted in property A, and recognition that the mean does not necessarily equal one of the values that was summed, as noted in property D.

Another way students attempt to measure the equality of contribution is to compare the money raised by individual group members with the group mean. Students are often surprised to discover that in all five groups, the sum of the differences of the mean and the numbers below the mean is the same as the sum of the differences of the mean and the numbers above the mean. If the differences between the mean and the numbers below the mean are assigned negative values and the differences between the mean and the numbers above the mean are assigned positive values, then we can say that the sum of the differences, or deviations from the mean, is 0. **Figure 3** shows that the sum of the deviations from the mean is 0 for both groups 1 and 3, even though the pattern of individual differences from the mean is quite different within, and between, the two groups. Guiding students to explore and discuss this aspect of the problem situation not only leads them to encounter property B but also lays the foundation for their future study of the standard deviation of a data set.

Money Raised by Students in Group 1	Difference between Money Raised by Students in Group 1 and the Mean
50	50 − 35 = 15
40	40 − 35 = 5
35	35 − 35 = 0
30	30 − 35 = −5
30	30 − 35 = −5
25	25 − 35 = −10
Mean = 35	Sum of deviations from the mean = 0

Money Raised by Students in Group 3	Difference between Money Raised by Students in Group 3 and the Mean
100	100 − 35 = 65
45	45 − 35 = 10
20	20 − 35 = −15
20	20 − 35 = −15
15	15 − 35 = −20
10	10 − 35 = −25
Mean = 35	Sum of deviations from the mean = 0

Fig. 3. Deviations from the mean for groups 1 and 3

What Happens If . . .?

Another task I created that was directly inspired by the properties identified by Strauss and Bichler (1988) is shown in **figure 4**. Note that each of the numbers presented in the given data set is a positive integer and that the data set is presented without a context. I deliberately constructed this data set so that the mean would not be an integer to give students a situation in which the mean can be a fraction, which is noted in property E.

One of the challenges presented to students in this task is to construct a realistic context that this data set could represent. In my experience, many students construct a context for this data set in which only whole numbers "make sense," such as the number of televisions in a household or the number of pets owned by students in the class. In these contexts, the numbers in the data set represent discrete quantities, but the mean, as property E states, "can be a fraction that has no counterpart in physical reality." For example, if the data set represents number of pets owned by students in the class, students have the opportunity to consider how 2.5 can be the mean number of pets while recognizing that having 2.5 pets is physically impossible. Other students may construct contexts in which the numbers in the data set represent continuous quantities that can be divided into fractional parts, such as money or time. In these contexts, the mean does have a counterpart in physical reality. The discussion that emerges surrounding property E of the mean is surprisingly rich and was never a part of my classroom before I used these properties to guide my instructional decisions.

Focusing students' attention on property C, that the mean is influenced by values other than the mean, was my primary motivation for constructing parts c–f of this task. Students should develop understanding of how the mean of the ten numbers given in the data set is affected when various new numbers are added to the data set. The questions posed in this task can be approached from several directions. Students may actually compute the new means, then be encouraged to explore why the resulting changes in the means occurred. These questions also can be answered without direct computation of the new mean by using the power of property B. Adding a new number to the data set creates a new deviation from the mean that must be taken into account. The direction of change in the mean can be determined by identifying if the new deviation from the mean is positive, negative, or 0.

For instance, suppose that 8 is the new number added to the data set (see part d of **fig. 4**). The mean of the original ten numbers was 2.5. The difference between the new number being added to the set and the mean is found to be a positive number, 8 – 2.5 = 5.5; thus, the sum of the deviations from the original mean in the new set is no longer 0. We can conclude, therefore, that the mean has changed when 8 is added to the set and that the mean must have increased to accommodate the new positive deviation. Students can easily confirm this conclusion by adding the eleven numbers in the new data set, dividing by 11, and determining that the mean of the new data set is 3. They can then verify that the sum of the deviations for the new set is 0 for the new mean of 3.

Similar reasoning can be used in parts (e) and (f) of this task. When 0 is added to the original data set, the difference between the new number, 0, and the mean is negative, 0 – 2.5 = –2.5, and the mean decreases. Property B also explains why the mean does not change when the two new numbers, 2 and 3, are added to the original data set with mean 2.5. The mean does not change because the effects of the new positive deviation, 3 – 2.5 = 0.5, and the new negative deviation, 2 – 2.5 = –0.5, have a sum of 0, which means that they offset each other.

Parts (g) and (h) of the problem situation are open-ended and give students the chance to find numbers that can be added to the data set but do not change the mean. This task offers another opportunity for students to encounter property B because the sum of the deviations from the mean must be 0 if numbers are added to the set but the mean is unchanged. Thus, solutions to part (g) include pairs of numbers that are equally distant from the mean, with one number larger than the mean and the other number smaller than the mean. Note that students can find both integer and fraction solutions to part (g).

Finding three numbers that can be added to the data set and not change the mean is more challenging. As students experiment with various combinations of numbers, they will discover that one solution to part (h) is to add one number that is the mean itself, 2.5 in this problem, and two other numbers that are equally distant from the mean, such as 1 and 4. Another solution to part (h) consists of using two numbers above the mean and one number below the mean or vice versa. Using property B once again, we can determine

---

Suppose that you are given the following data set:

1, 1, 2, 2, 2, 2, 3, 3, 4, 5

(a) Determine the mean and the median of the given set of numbers.

(b) Identify a real-life situation that this set of numbers could realistically represent.

(c) What happens to the mean if a new number, 2, is added to the given data set? Explain why this result occurs.

(d) What happens to the mean if a new number, 8, is added to the given data set? Explain why this result occurs.

(e) What happens to the mean if a new number, 0, is added to the given data set? Explain why this result occurs.

(f) What happens to the mean if two new numbers, 2 and 3, are added to the given data set? Explain why this result occurs.

(g) Find two numbers that can be added to the given data set and not change the mean. Explain how you chose these two numbers.

(h) Find three numbers that can be added to the given data set and not change the mean. Explain how you chose these three numbers.

(i) What happens to the mean if a new number, 30, is added to the given data set? How well does the mean represent the new data set? Can you find another statistical measure that better represents the data set?

(j) Find two numbers that can be added to the given data set that change the mean but not the median. Explain how you chose these two numbers.

(k) Find two numbers that can be added to the given data set that change the median but not the mean. Explain how you chose these two numbers.

Fig. 4. The What Happens If . . .? task

that although multiple solutions to this problem are possible, finding a solution in which all three new numbers are integers is impossible.

In part (i), students are asked to consider the effect on the mean of adding an extreme value, or an outlier, to the data set. The mean of this new data set changes significantly and helps to draw students' attention to the conditions under which the mean is a "good" representative of the data set. Understanding that the mean value is representative of the data set is stated as property G, but discussion about property G must also include situations such as this one, in which the mean may not be the best representative measure. One way to prompt such a discussion is to compare the mean to other measures of center. For the given data set, the addition of an outlier does not affect the median; thus, the median may be considered a more representative measure for this data set. In solving parts (j) and (k) of this task, students are challenged to consider not only the relationship of the mean and the median to the numbers in the data set but also the relationship of these two statistical measures of center to each other.

In Your Classroom

The results of Strauss and Bichler's research (1988) serve as a useful framework to guide instruction in the concept of the arithmetic mean. I encourage you to examine the problems in the curriculum materials you use and the discussions held in your classroom with respect to both the seven properties defined by Strauss and Bichler and the Data Analysis and Probability Standard (NCTM 2000). In addition, you may encourage your students to use various technological tools as they explore and discuss these properties of the mean. For instance, performing computations and examining the mean and the sum of deviations from the mean can easily be done using a basic spreadsheet. This tool can be used for the tasks presented in this article and is particularly helpful when working with large data sets. These seven properties of the mean have been a valuable resource in helping me (and, in turn, helping my students) to understand what it means to not just find, but to meaningfully understand the mean.

References

Bolster, L. Carey, Thomas Butts, Mary M. Lindquist, Jan Fair, Miriam Leiva, Mary Cavanagh, Clem Boyer, Marea W. Channel, and Warren D. Crown. *Exploring Mathematics*. Glenview, Ill.: Scott Foresman and Co., 1994.

Hoffer, Alan R., Martin L. Johnson, Steven J. Leinwand, Richard D. Lodholz, Gary L. Musser, and Tina Thoburn. *Mathematics in Action*. New York: Macmillan/McGraw Hill School Publishing Co., 1994.

National Council of Teachers of Mathematics (NCTM). *Principles and Standards for School Mathematics*. Reston, Va.: NCTM, 2000.

Strauss, Sidney, and Efraim Bichler. "The Development of Children's Concepts of the Arithmetic Average." *Journal for Research in Mathematics Education* 19 (January 1988): 64–80.

Zawojewski, Judith, and J. Michael Shaughnessy. "Data and Chance." In *Results from the Seventh Mathematics Assessment of the National Assessment of Educational Progress*, edited by Edward A. Silver and Patricia Ann Kenney, pp. 235–68. Reston, Va.: National Council of Teachers of Mathematics, 2000.